Archana Upadhyay is an Associate Professor in the School of International Studies, Jawaharlal Nehru University, New Delhi (India). Previously she taught International Relations and Foreign Policy in Dibrugarh University, Assam (India). She has been a Commonwealth Visiting Fellow at the International Policy Institute of King's College, London. Her research interest include International Relations with special focus on South Asian, Central Asian and Russian issues, Political Violence, Insurgency and Terrorism, Conflict and Conflict Management. Her previous publications are *Multiparty System in the Russian Federation: Problems and Prospects* and a co-authored monograph on Human Rights.

BLOOMSBURY INDIA
Bloomsbury Publishing India Pvt. Ltd
Second Floor, LSC Building No. 4, DDA Complex, Pocket C–6&7,
Vasant Kunj, New Delhi 110070

BLOOMSBURY, Bloomsbury Academic India and the Diana
logo are trademarks of Bloomsbury Publishing Plc

First published in India 2022
Published in 2009 by I.B.Tauris & Co Ltd
Distributed in the United States and Canada Exclusively by Palgrave Macmillan
175 Fifth Avenue, New York NY 10010

A catalog record for this book is available from the Library of Congress.
A catalogue record for this book is available from the British Library.

ISBN: 978-93-56400-98-6
For sale in the Indian subcontinent only

Exclusively distributed in the Indian subcontinent by
Manohar Publishers & Distributors
4753/23, Ansari Road
Darya Ganj, New Delhi 110002
Tel.: 23284848, 23289100
Email: sales@manoharbooks.com, manoharbooks@gmail.com

Printed and bound in India by Replika Press Pvt. Ltd.

To my parents

CONTENTS

TABLES

ABBREVIATIONS

AAGSP	All Assam Gana Sangram Parishad
AAPSU	All Arunachal Pradesh Students' Union
ABSU	All Bodo Students' Union
ACF	Adivasi Cobra Force
ADF	Arunachal Dragon Force
AFSPA	Armed Forces Special Powers Act
AGP	Asom Gana Parishad
AIDS	Acquired Immune Deficiency Syndrome
AK	Automatic Kalashnikov
ALMA	A'chik Liberation Matgrik Army
ALP	Arakan Liberation Party
AMCTA	All Manipur College Teachers Association
ANVC	Achik National Volunteer Council
APEC	Asia Pacific Economic Cooperation
ARNO	Arakan Rohingya National Organization
ASEAN	Association of South East Asian Nations
AASU	All Assam Students' Union
ATPLO	All Tripura People's Liberation Organization
ATS	Amphetamine Type Stimulants
ATTF	All Tripura Tiger Force
BAC	Bodo Autonomous Council
BCIM	Bangladesh-China-India-Myanmar Regional Economic Forum
BCP	Burmese Communist Party
BDR	Bangladesh Rifles
BIMST-EC	Bangladesh-India-Myanmar-Sri Lanka-Thailand Economic Cooperation
BLTF	Bodo Liberation Tiger Force
BLTF	Bodoland Liberation Tigers Front
BNCT	Borok National Council of Tripura
BNLF	Bru National Liberation Front
BPAC	Bodo People's Action Committee

BRPL	Bongaigoan Refineries and Petrochemical Limited
BSF	Border Security Force
BSMC	Bodo State Movement Council
CBM	Confidence Building Measures
CHT	Chittagong Hill Tracts
CNF	Chin National Front
CRPF	Central Reserve Police Force
DGFI	Directorate General of Forces Intelligence
DHD	Dima Halim Daogah
ENRC	Eastern Naga Regional Council
EU	European Union
FKJGP	Federation of Khasi, Jantia and Garo People
GOI	Government of India
GoM	Group of Ministers
HNLC	Hynniewtrep National Liberation Council
HNSRA	Hynniewtrep National Special Red Army
HPC-D	Hmar People's Convention-Democracy
HUJI	Harkat-ul-Jihad-al-Islami
HUJIB	Harkat-ul-Jihad-al-Islami Bangladesh
HuM	Harkat-ul-Mujahideen
IBRF	Indo-Burma Revolutionary Front
ICMR	Indian Council of Medical Research
ICS	Islamic Chhatra Shibir
IDU	Intravenous Drug Users
IED	Improvised Explosive Device
ILA	Islamic Liberation Army
ILAA	Independent Liberation Army of Assam
IMDT	Illegal Migrants (Determination by Tribunals) Act
INCB	International Narcotics Control Board
IOJ	Islami Oikya Jote
IR	Indian Rupees
IRF	Islamic Revolutionary Front
ISFI	Islamic Security Force of India
ISI	Pakistan's Inter Services Intelligence
JeM	Jaish-e-Mohammed
JIJ	Jamaat-I- Islami
JMB	Jama'atul Mujahideen Bangladesh
JMJB	Jagrata Muslim Janata Bangladesh
KCP	Kangleipak Communist Party
KIA	Kachin Independence Army
KLO	Kamptapur Liberation Organization
KNA	Kuki Liberation Army
KNF	Kuki National Front

KNO	Kuki National Organization
KRA	Kuki Revolutionary Army
KSU	Khasi Students' Union
KYKL	Kanglei Yawol Kunna Lup
LeT	Lashkar-e-Toiba
LIC	Low Intensity Conflict
LITF	Liberation Islamic Tiger Force
LTTE	Liberation Tigers of Tamil Eelam
MGC	Mekong-Ganga-Cooperation
MLAT	Mutual Legal Assistance Treaty
MNF	Mizo National Front
MPLF	Manipur Peoples Liberation Front
MULFA	Muslim United Liberation Front of Assam
MULTA	The Muslim United Liberation Tigers of Assam
MVF	Muslim Volunteer Force
NATO	North Atlantic Treaty Organization
NDFB	National Democratic Front of Bodoland
NEEPCO	North Eastern Electric Power Corporation
NEFA	North East Frontier Agency
NESO	North East Students' Organization
NFG	Naga Federal Government
NIA	National Investigation Agency
NLFSS	National Liberation Front of the Seven Sisters
NLFT	National Liberation Front of Tripura
NNC	Naga National Council
NPMHR	Naga People's Movement for Human Rights
NSCN (IM)	National Socialist Council of Nagaland (Issac-Muivah)
NSCN (K)	Socialist Council of Nagaland (Khaplang)
NSCN (U)	National Socialist Council of Nagaland (Unification)
NSF	Naga Students' Federation
OIL	Oil India Limited
ONGC	Oil and Natural Gas Commission
OSCE	Organization for Security and Cooperation in Europe
PCG	People's Consultative Group
PCPIA	People's Committee for Peace Initiatives in Assam
PDS	Public Distribution System
PIL	Public Interest Litigation
PLA	People's Liberation Army
PLFM	People's Liberation Front of Meghalaya
PREPAK	People's Revolutionary Party of Kangleipak
PTCA	Plains Tribal Council of Assam
PULF	People's United Liberation Front
RAW	Research and Analysis Wing

RDX	Research Developed High Explosives
RIHS	Revival of Islamic Heritage Society
RSO	Rohingya Solidarity Organization
RUF	Revolutionary United Front
SAARC	South Asian Association of Regional Cooperation
SAGQ	South Asia Growth Quadrangle
SASEC	South Asia Sub-regional Economic Cooperation Programme
SDUFSHR	Self-Defence United Front of the South East Himalayan Region
SIMI	Students' Islamic Movement of India
SIO	Students' Islamic Organization
ST	Schedule Tribe
SULFA	Surrendered ULFA
TADA	Terrorism and Disruptive Activities Prevention Act of 1985
Tk	Taka
TNT	Trinitrotoluene Explosives
TNVF	Tripura National Volunteer Force
TUJS	Tripura Upajati Juba Samity
UKLF	United Kuki Liberation Front
ULFA	United Liberation Front of Assam
UN	United Nations
UNDCP	United Nations Drug Control Programme
UNLF	United National Liberation Front
UNLFM	United National Liberation Front of Manipur
UNODC	United Nations Office on Drug and Crime
UPDS	United People's Democratic Solidarity
UWSA	United Wa State Army
WMD	Weapons of Mass Destruction
ZRA	Zomi Revolutionary Army

LOCATION MAP NORTH EAST INDIA

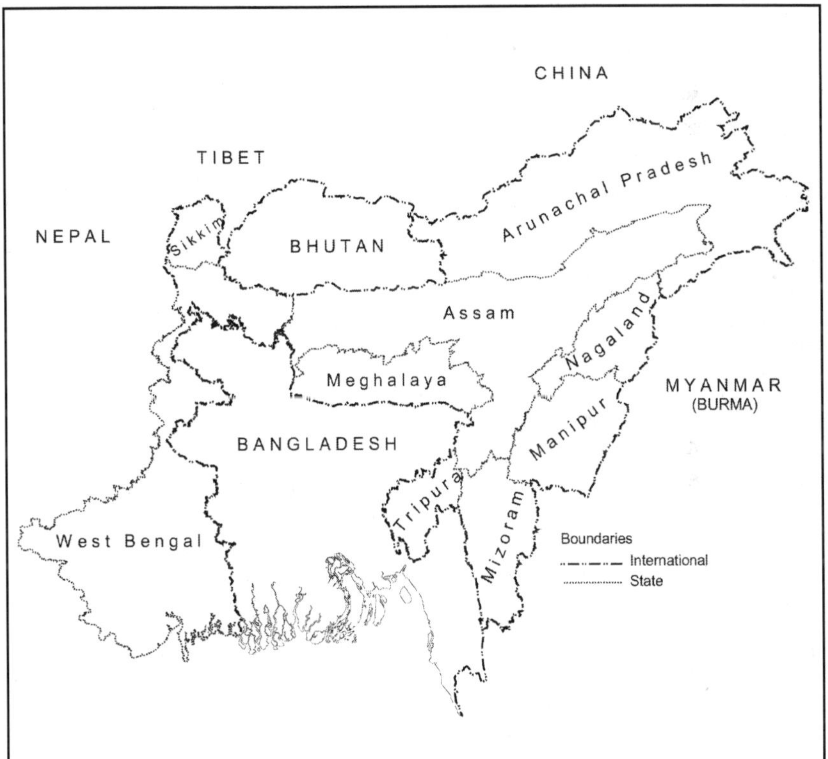

PREFACE AND ACKNOWLEDGEMENTS

Terrorism is an ambiguous variable not easily measured or quantified, in part because of its multiple manifestations. However, as a complex phenomenon of human interaction, it deserves serious and systematic examination. More often than not, terror acts are the handiwork of insurgent groups seeking to achieve a variety of objectives through multiple means including terrorism. Consequently, to comprehend terrorism, the understanding of insurgency becomes crucial. Central to the understanding of terrorism is its political, social and economic contexts. The likely impact of terrorism on this setting is a critical factor that often generates unanticipated consequences, some of which profoundly impact the functioning of the society. Even political institutions, values, and behaviour do not remain untouched. Therefore, it is critically important to assess the fallouts of terrorism on society and on the political processes as well as the responses to terrorism by both society and the political system. The present study does not focus exclusively on the causes of violence to the neglect of outcomes. The case studies in the volume relate terrorism to the management of social and political change and considers its effects on the political system both in terms of stability and democracy.

The focus of this study is North East India, a region of great differences that accounts for 7.9 per cent of the total land space of India. The region, comprising the states of Arunachal Pradesh, Assam, Manipur, Meghalaya, Mizoram, Nagaland, Tripura and Sikkim is undoubtedly one of the most diverse regions of Asia. Although the term 'North East' clearly falls short of encompassing the diversity the region represents, in the context of understanding terrorism, there are sufficient similarities and linkages among the constituent states of the region to warrant such an association. Through a holistic approach, the book intends to give the readers' fresh perspectives and useful insights into the complexities of the terrorist phenomenon in North East India, by examining and assessing the roots of the turmoil and the implications of the same in an increasingly globalized world. The framework used in this book is the product of an evolutionary process, involving changes suggested by the case studies. Terms like insurgents, guerrillas, militants, extremists, ultras, rebels, separatists and terrorists have been used interchangeably although efforts have been made to use the terms consciously and consistently. The framework is designed to bring together factors that can have crucial bearing on the progress and outcome of insurgent conflicts with terrorism as a defining feature. This particularly assumes significance in the context of the post 9/11 global security environment. These factors, as set forth in the succeeding sections of the book, focus attention on key questions that ought to be asked about all such conflicts, regardless of time and place.

The book is organized into four thematic parts, each dealing with comparative aspects of the phenomenon of terrorism. **Part I** deals with the conceptual and definitional issues that have come to surround the discourse on terrorism. It explores the causes of terrorism and discusses perspectives on motivations as well as the morality of terrorist violence. The following contentions emerge from the discussion. First, both state and non-state actors are culpable of reproducing terrorism. Second, the advent of globalization has profoundly impacted the understanding of terrorism both nationally and internationally. Third, crisis in governance, marginality of communities, national deprivation and existence of porous international borders are important factors that directly encourage non-state terrorism, particularly in peripheral societies.

Part II probes into the nature of terrorism in North East India and uses regional case studies to investigate different manifestations of terrorist violence. The everchanging dynamics of insurgencies that plague almost every state in the region, is analyzed within the broader conceptual context of terrorism along with the history, formation, capacity and threat posed by ultra outfits in their respective areas of influence. Terrorist objectives, methods, targets, external linkages are analyzed at length, as is the question of the 'effectiveness' of terrorism.

Part III explores counter-terrorist options and measures evolved by the Indian State in responding to the challenge of terrorism. These options include, the use of force, conciliatory operations and legalistic responses. Trends and other factors that can be used to project the future of terrorism in the region have also been touched upon. The line of argument revolves around a pertinent fact that in the absence of political initiatives, forceful means have limited utility. What is required is specific political and economic steps that would reduce friction, strengthen democracy and give governance a chance. And, considering the fact that the region is more open and linked to the 'outside world' than commonly admitted in political circles, there is a pressing need for reorientation of India's foreign policy. It is in this context that the prospect of India's 'Look East' policy has been discussed.

Part IV is a compilation of the agreements, accords, acts and protocol that have a direct bearing on the central theme of the book.

Work on this study started when I was a Visiting Fellow at the International Policy Institute (IPI), King's College, London (January-July 2004). IPI provided the material conditions and the intellectual space to go ahead with this venture. I am grateful to many, whose knowledge and experience I have had the good fortune to freely utilize. My debts are many and most of them are to my Advisor Dr Chris Smith. I take this opportunity to express my deep gratitude to Dr. Smith for his consistent guidance and support. His vision and unwavering commitment to South Asian security issues has been a great source of inspiration for this research.

I wish to place on record my sincere thanks to all those who have generously shared their time and expertise with me. I am much grateful to Dr Deepak Mishra of Jawaharlal Nehru University, for his unstinted intellectual support all through this academic venture. As the first reader and critic of this work, his perspective greatly contributed towards the enrichment of this publication. Special thanks are due to Dr Rahul Roy Choudhury of the International Institute of Strategic Studies (IISS), London and Prof. Robert G.Wirsing of the Asia Pacific Centre for Security Studies, for providing useful insights about various issues discussed in this work. I owe a special debt of gratitude to scores of people – government officials, security personnels, ex-militants, journalists, activists, migrants, businessmen and common citizens – who on condition of anonymity shared their experiences and provided valuable insights into the hidden dimensions of the issues discussed in the book. I also acknowledge with deep appreciation, the contributions of professors and colleagues whose writings have informed this study

Particular thanks are extended to my mentor Prof. Devendra Kaushik, Prof. A.N.S. Ahmed, Prof. Adil Ul Yasin, Prof. Mahavir Singh, Prof. K.K. Dwivedi, Prof. Tulsi Ram, Prof. Partha. S. Ghosh, Dr R. Thapa and Rubul Patgiri for their support and guidance at different stages of my career.

This work would not have seen the light of day without the continuous moral support and understanding from my family and friends, particularly – Meghali, Anand and Vandana. But for their encouragement, it would not have been possible for me to move forward in this academic venture.

I take this opportunity to thank the library staff of British Library, King's College, London School of Economics, International Institute of Strategic Studies, School of African and Oriental Studies, Jawaharlal Nehru University, Institute for Defence Studies and Analyses, New Delhi, Dibrugarh University and O.K.D Institute of Social Change and Development, Guwahati, for their cooperation and assistance in making available the required material and documents for the study.

This work is a modest attempt to understand the complexities of the conflict situation in North East India. However, I alone stand responsible for all errors and laxities, if any in this work.

Archana Upadhyay

AUTHOR'S NOTE, NOVEMBER 2008

The terror attacks in Mumbai on 26-28 November 2008 once again brought the discourse on terrorism to the centre-stage of Indian politics. Widely described as 'India's 9/11' these attacks took place within a month of the deadly high intensity blasts in four urban centres in Assam (Guwahati, Kokrajhar, Barpeta and Bongaigaon) on 30 October 2008, that left 80 people dead and hundreds injured. These blasts came close on the heels of the communal conflagrations in the Udalgiri-Darrang districts of Assam, which saw violent confrontations between the immigrant Muslims and the Bodo and Assamese peasants. These confrontations left over 50 dead, scores injured and almost 100,000 displaced. While the October blasts, given their nature and intensity, were a clear pointer to the active involvement of the Jihadi elements from across the borders, the violence in Udalgiri-Darrang brought the issue of cross-border migration and the resultant demographic change into sharp focus. These incidents are not isolated, nor region specific. They clearly reveal a trend and, perhaps, explain to some extent the hasty passage of the two key anti-terror bills in the parliament on 17 December 2008. The bills – The National Investigation Agency (NIA) Bill, 2008, and The Unlawful Activities (Prevention) Amendment Bill, 2008 – can at best be seen as initiatives on the internal security front. The NIA Bill creates a federal investigating agency to supersede the state police in the case of the investigation and trial of offences under certain Acts specified in its schedule. The Act provides for the constitution of a special court to try offences investigated by the NIA. The Chief Justice of the High Court would nominate the special judge and the case would be tried on a day-to-day basis. The Unlawful Activities (Prevention) Amendment Bill, 2008, has now a new section – 43D – that has increased the maximum period of custodial interrogation of a terror suspect to 180 days. Unlike previous terror acts, like the POTA and TADA, the Act does not have sunset clauses and is more in the nature of a permanent anti-terror legislation. It is noteworthy that in the discussions and debate, both inside and outside the parliament, the need for reform in the security establishment and the police machinery was particularly emphasized. However, the core issue of cross-border terrorism remains largely unaddressed, mainly due to the climate of suspicion, mistrust and hostility prevailing in South Asia.

Part I

THEORIZING TERRORISM: ATTEMPTS AND PITFALLS

Introduction

Terrorism in its multiple manifestations, has come to be accepted as a reality of political life in many parts of the world. Although in its modern guise, the phenomenon goes back to the French revolution, there clearly are many historical precursors. The urgency for the need to provide an analytical scheme by which to comprehend and come to grips with the complexities of the phenomenon, has thus been described by Paul Wilkinson: 'We live in a terroristic age. Few, even among the most favoured and secure, can fail to be haunted by the sights and ghastly dreams of terrorist murder, massacre and torture and the suffering of the innocent'.[1] The fact of the matter is that, terrorism today has not only increased in incidence and intensity, but has also impacted the framework of both national and international politics.

It goes without saying, that the task of defining contemporary variety of political terrorism is not without challenges. There is no unanimity among scholars on what kind of violence constitutes an act of terrorism. Over the years, hundreds of definitions have been developed and adopted by governments and private agencies. Academic experts have also proposed and analysed scores of definitional constructs. Commenting on the ongoing definitional debate, Laqueur says: 'Any definition of political terrorism venturing beyond noting the systematic use of murder, injury, and destruction or the threats of such acts towards achieving political ends is bound to lead to endless controversies'.[2] Scholars like Franck and Lockwood have suggested, that the concept itself is historically misleading. Referring to terrorism as a politically 'loaded' word, they point to the conceptual and ideological dissonance of the term.[3] There are other authors, who have argued that no commonly accepted definition is possible, as very often, states for a variety of reasons, rationalize even the killing of innocent people.[4] Attempts at building a 'transcendental' moral base to judge terrorism, has not been without risks of being open to charges of double standards. In this regard, clearly much depends upon 'who is in the saddle'.[5] Pointing at the inherent danger of using this word loosely, Whitbeck says:

> It is no accident that there is no agreed definition of 'terrorism', since the word is so subjective as to be devoid of any inherent meaning. At the same time, the word is extremely dangerous, because people tend to believe that it does have meaning and to use and abuse the word by applying it to whatever they hate as a way of avoiding rational thought and discussion, and, frequently, excusing their own illegal and immoral behavior.[6]

Concluding that the word 'terrorism' is 'fundamentally an epithet and a term of abuse, with no intrinsic meaning', Whitbeck adds, 'perhaps the only honest and globally workable definition of "terrorism" is an explicitly subjective one – violence which I don't support'.[7]

It is noteworthy that within the larger discourse on violence and terrorism, there is a tendency to treat conflictual interactions in social and political life as 'abnormal'.[8] Normality, in this context acquires a physiological quality that denotes the 'health' of the polity. However, this kind of statistical and 'functional' normality does not correspond to reality, as in several parts of the world, particularly the developing world, violence and conflict clearly are the norm. Such an ideological bias, that ignores the role of violence in political processes, create an analytical discontinuity and consequently the analysis of the phenomenon of terrorism gets thoroughly hampered.

Definitional Debate

Scholars have argued that the historical context – political, social and economic – profoundly impacts both the phenomenon of terrorism and conceptions of it.[9] However, no less important is an understanding of the subjective conditions. Considering the fact that there are rarely neutral terms in politics, it becomes necessary to recognize that an important aspect of terrorism is its social construction, which is relative to both time and place. According to Martha Crenshaw, within the discourse on terrorism, the political language adopted is significant, as it not only powerfully affects the perceptions of both the protagonists and audiences, it also impacts their expectations about the treatment that ought to be meted out to the problem.[10] Consequently, terrorism becomes both an organizing concept and a flexible label that depicts the phenomenon as it exists and offers a moral judgment.[11]

Defining terrorism and conceptualizations of the phenomenon is mainly an exercise driven by the researcher's perspective and world view. Definitional constructs, have thus ranged from those developed by governments, agencies within governments, private agencies and academics. Consequently, most perceptions on the dynamics of this complex phenomenon are the subject of personal opinion and academic debate.

Official definitions, have mainly emanated from those European countries that have endured terrorist campaigns. The *British* describe terrorism as 'the use of threat, for the purpose of advancing a political, religious or ideological cause, of action which involves serious violence against a person or property'.[12] In the *Federal Republic of Germany*, terrorism has been defined as 'enduringly conducted struggle for political goals, which are intended to be achieved by means of assaults on the life and property of other persons, especially by means of severe crimes'.[13] The definition of the *European Interior Ministers* notes that, 'terrorism is ... the use, or the threatened use by a cohesive group of persons of violence short of warfare to effect political aims'.[14]

Government agencies of the United States, have opted for the legalistic approach to terrorism that clearly distinguishes the phenomenon from more common criminal behaviour. The *Federal Bureau of Investigation* defines terrorism as 'unlawful use of force or violence against persons or property to intimidate or coerce a government, the civilian population, or any segment thereof, in furtherance of political and social objectives'.[15] The *Department of Defense* defines terrorism as 'the unlawful use of, or threatened use, of force or violence against individuals or property to coerce and intimidate governments or societies, often to achieve political, religious or ideological objectives'.[16] According to the *State Department*, terrorism is 'premeditated, politically motivated violence perpetrated against noncombatant targets by sub-national groups or clandestine agents, usually intended to influence an audience'.[17]

A study of the above definitions of terrorism, makes it evident, that the debate over an acceptable definition of terrorism is clearly 'the most confounding problem in the study of terrorism'.[18] However, despite the difficulties involved, the search for an acceptable definition of terrorism continues unabated. In this regard, Bruce Hoffman writes:

> We come to appreciate that terrorism is ineluctably political in aims and motives; violent-or, equally important, threatens violence; designed to have far-reaching psychological repercussions beyond the immediate victim or target; conducted by an organization with an identifiable chain of command or conspiratorial structure (whose members wear no uniform or identifying insignia); and perpetrated by a sub-national group or non-state entity. We may therefore now attempt to define terrorism as the deliberate creation and exploitation of fear through violence or the threat of violence in the pursuit of change.[19]

Ted Gurr describes terrorism as 'the use of unexpected violence to intimidate or coerce people in the pursuit of political and social objectives'.[20] Gibbs describes the phenomenon as 'illegal threatened violence against human or nonhuman objects, so long as that violence meets additional criteria such as secretive features and unconventional warfare'.[21] Walter Reich defines terrorism as 'a strategy of violence designed to promote desired outcomes by instilling fear in the public at large'.[22] Charles Tilly's description portrays terrorism as 'asymmetrical deployment of threats and violence against enemies using means that fall outside the forms of political struggle routinely operating within some current regime'.[23] Austin T. Turk's definition describes the phenomenon as 'organized political violence, lethal or non-lethal, designed to deter opposition by maximizing fear, specifically by random targeting of people or sites'.[24] Commenting on the political dimension of terrorism, Harold Lasswell described terrorists as 'participants in the political process who strive for political results by amusing acute anxieties'.[25] Cindy C. Combs defines terrorism as 'a dramatization of the most proscribed kind of violence – that which is perpetrated on innocent victims'.[26]

Accounts of terrorism mainly fall into two categories: those that understand the phenomenon as a form of warfare, and those that do not. Robert Taber describes terrorism as 'urban guerrillaism' – a form of warfare that is more humane than most other types of warfare.[27] In his words: 'terrorism, conventionally viewed with pious horror as political murder is far more humane being more selective, than most other types of warfare'.[28] Richard Clutterbuck interchangeably uses the term 'urban guerrilla warfare' and 'urban terrorism' and likewise 'rural guerrilla warfare' and 'rural terrorism'.[29]

These views vary from the traditional view of terrorism which is widely seen as an immoral way of waging war and hence a subject of revulsion. In contrast, guerrilla warfare is generally regarded as a legitimate form of conflict and guerrilla fighters, as described by Whittaker are: 'A numerically larger group of armed individuals who operate as a military unit, attack enemy military forces, and seize and hold territory, while also exercising some form of sovereignty or control over a defined geographical area and its population'.[30]

It is noteworthy, that despite the less indiscriminate and less destructive nature of terrorism than most other forms of warfare, there is a strong reluctance among many scholars to view it as a form of warfare. This clearly has much to do with the abhorrence that terrorist acts generate. In the words of Paul Wilkinson, 'terrorism is coercive intimidation. It is the systematic use of murder and destruction, and the threat of murder and destruction in order to terrorize individuals, groups, communities or governments into conceding to the terrorists' political demands'.[31] Highlighting the differences between terrorism and other forms of warfare, Ruth Linn observes:

> When compared to terrorism, conventional war has clear norms: there is a neutral territory which is recognized by the fighting forces, the armed forces are identified, there is a restriction to certain arms in the battlefield and there is an awareness that the use of armed forces against civilians is exceptional or aberration. In contrast, terrorism is aimed at the destruction of established norms. Unlike guerrilla fighters who are not breaking the laws of war, who know who is their enemy and attack only the superior combatants, terrorists blur the combatant-non-combatant distinction by saying that 'WAR IS WAR and that any attempt to define ethical limits to war is futile'.[32]

Linn, further opines: 'When no distinction is made between combatant and non-combatant, nor in regard to the proportion of damage done, terrorism takes the entire free society as its field of combat, though, paradoxically, very often demands a treatment with respect given to legitimate warfare'.[33]

Linn's observation however, has been subjected to criticism. Terrorists, it is argued, are ill equipped to fight conventional wars as they lack both manpower and industrial resources. Thus in an unequal battle, acts of terrorism work as equalizers. It is also pointed out that much like modern day nuclear war, where the distinction between combatants and noncombatants gets completely blurred, terrorism comfortably fits within the heritage of total war.[34] In this regard, it is noteworthy that scholars like Schmid make a strong case for bringing terror acts within the purview of war crimes. He points out:

> What makes them different from soldiers ... is that they do not carry their arms openly and they do not discriminate between armed adversaries and non-combatants. Since they do not fight by the rules of war they turn themselves into war criminals. Terrorism distinguishes itself from conventional and to some extent also from guerrilla warfare through the disregard for the principles of chivalry and humanity contained in the Hague Regulations and Geneva Conventions.[35]

In this regard, Wheeler notes that even conventional armies break rules of war with impunity and contemporary terrorists in preferring civilian targets merely emulate the heritage of modern total war.[36] Paul Wilkinson recognizes this paradox when he admits, 'it is in practice extremely difficult to draw boundaries between war and terror'.[37]

In their seminal book *Political Terrorism*, Alex Schmid and Albert Jongman after scrutinizing the observations of researchers and analysts in the field, identified more than 100 definitions of terrorism.[38] While eighty-three per cent of a sample of 109 definitions agreed that violence was a defining feature of terrorism, only 5 per cent were willing to label such violence as criminal, and just 30 per cent could view such violence in martial terms. For the majority, terrorism was unmistakably a kind of political violence. In this regard, it is noteworthy that the issue of *state terrorism* – terrorist acts of government towards its own citizens – figured significantly in several of these definitions. Another interesting revelation was that, while there was a willingness to include state terrorism within the ambit of terrorism, there was a clear reluctance to view terrorism as warfare. However, the inclusion of state terrorism within the broader discourse of terrorism marks a clear departure from the past. Terms like 'wholesale' and 'retail', suggestive of the distinction between state terrorism and oppositional terrorism, have also gained currency and it is argued that the 'retail' terrorism of oppositional groups is provoked by the 'wholesale' terrorism of the state.[39]

Scholars like Newman and Lynch, point at the fundamental difference between terrorism and other forms of violence. In their words, 'the one feature that distinguishes terrorism from other forms of violence is an established, often elaborate ideology that is used to justify the act or acts of violence'.[40] The existence of such ideology is significant and is mainly derived from theories that explain human, social and political conditions. Implicit is the conviction that terrorism has a *morality,* that raises serious questions and articulates deep beliefs such as: 'One person's terrorist is another person's freedom fighter'; 'Kill one, terrorize a thousand'; 'Extremism in defense of liberty is no vice'; and 'It became necessary to destroy the town to save it'.[41] These quotations, clearly represent an uncompromising belief in the righteousness of the espoused cause, while simultaneously justifying and glorifying the hardships that violence may inflict on both perceived enemies and members of the terror outfits. According to Paul Wilkinson, what differentiates terrorism from other forms of organized violence are the features of amorality. In his words:

> What fundamentally distinguishes terrorism from other forms of organized violence is not simply its severity, but its features of amorality and antinomianism. Terrorists either profess indifference to existing moral codes or else claim exemption from all such obligations. Political terror, if it is waged consciously and deliberately, is implicitly prepared to sacrifice all moral and humanitarian consideration for the sake of some political end.[42]

Taking this debate further, Jeff Goodwin differentiates terrorism from both guerilla warfare and state terrorism. He introduces the concept of 'revolutionary terrorism', which is described as strategic use of violence and threats of violence by a revolutionary movement against civilians or noncombatants, aimed at influencing several audiences. The 'revolutionary movement', he points out, can be any organization or network that seeks to alter the political and in some cases the socio-economic order in fundamental ways.[43] More often than not, these groups are oppositional political groups, which view terrorism as a political strategy. Goodwin further differentiates between 'selective' or 'individualized' terrorism and 'categorical terrorism'. 'Selective' or 'individualized' terrorism is essentially a strategy of 'targeted assassination', directed against noncombatants singled out on account of their individual identities and are generally identified as government collaborators. They may include politicians, state officials, political activists, unsympathetic intellectuals, journalists and others.[44] Categorical terrorism, on the other hand, is defined as 'the strategic use of violence and threats of violence, usually intended to influence several audiences, by oppositional political groups against civilians or noncombatants who belong to a specific ethnicity, religious or national group, social class or some other collectivity without regard to their individual identity or role'.[45] The victims of the categorical terrorist assault are described as 'complicitous civilians', who routinely benefit from aggressive state policies against the revolutionaries and their presumed constituents.[46]

While there is no universally accepted definition of terrorism, it is abundantly clear, that it is the interplay of different factors that shape perspectives of the participants in a terrorist environment. Regardless of the official and scholarly definitions crafted, participants have a tendency to draw their own conclusions that is often coloured by factors such as individual experiences, group identity, culture and history. For the practitioners and patrons of terrorist violence, terrorists are revered freedom fighters and terror acts are no more than unfortunate consequences of a just war against an oppressive powerful opponent. The broad audience to the terrorist incident, would predictably react differently. While direct audiences in all likelihood would easily connect with the physical victims of violence, indirect audiences, being far removed from the immediate theatre by virtue of physical distance as well as their identities, would be more of spectators. Analysts too, as interpreters of incidents, shape perspectives and thus emerge as key participants. Two assumptions, however are central to the understanding of the phenomenon of terrorism. *First,* is the acceptance that violence, which in general is understood as behaviour that disrupts values and expectations, is an integral part of the political process and is aimed at maximizing uncertainty[47] and power, particularly in its psychological dimension, increases with uncertainty.[48] *Second*, is the understanding that the maximization of uncertainty results in conditions of extreme fear and anxiety and is considered as an achievement of great power. In the words of David Fromkin: 'the threat of violence and the use of fear to coerce, persuade or gain public attention aims at one psychological result: to increase the probability of compliance'.[49] Terrorism, thus is 'a form of behaviour which is not susceptible to a single definition; that it is a type of behaviour, policy, tool or instrument used by individuals, groups and nations, attests to the fact that its definition depends on the perspective from which it is viewed'.[50]

Clearly, the prevalent definitions of terrorism entail conceptual and syntactical difficulties and this partly explains why alternative concepts with more positive connotations – guerrilla movements, underground movements, national liberation movements, separatists, rebels and so forth – are preferred to both describe and characterize terrorist outfits. The choice of concepts is significant and is mainly aimed at providing acceptability to such outfits, by glossing over the brutalities of terrorism.

The focus for the purpose of this analysis, is specifically on political terrorism, as a strategy of violence within a broader political context. Political terrorism in this sense, would mean the 'systematic use of murder and destruction, and the threat of murder and destruction to terrorize individuals, groups, communities or governments into conceding to the terrorists' political aims'.[51] It is significant, that although within the larger discourse on terrorism there are several areas of divergence over pertinent questions, such as who can practice terrorism, under what circumstances and with what consequences, some common features in most formal definitions clearly stand out. These may be thus enumerated:

- **Terrorism is exemplary.** Terrorist acts are selective and often pre-emptive enforcement of compellence or deterrent postures that serves to obtain both compliance and modification of collective behaviour patterns.[52]
- **Terrorism is unpredictable.** Extreme uncertainty and lack of anticipation on the part of the victim serve to enhance the aggressor's

power and thereby impact the adversary's ability to both anticipate and react.[53]

- **More often than not, 'Targets' are of a non-military nature.** Contemporary acts of terrorism are mostly of an indiscriminate variety, with the victims being normally accessible and unexpected targets. As in non-conventional warfare, the distinction between the frontline and the 'civilian population' is barely there. The anonymity of the victim, serves as a warning to the population at large about the likelihood of each individual being a potential target. To use the terminology of nuclear warfare, terrorism is 'counter value' rather than 'counter force'.[54]
- **There is an apparent consensus at the 'moral' unacceptability of terrorism.** Across differing ideologies and regimes, there is the official rejection of terrorism as a 'legitimate' means for achieving political aims. What is lacking however, is a global consensus on 'whose' terrorism and what kinds of terror are to be eradicated through concerted global action.
- **Terrorism, mainly though not exclusively, is a tactic in the struggle of the weak against the strong.** Acts of extreme violence are sometimes committed to 'even up' the balance of forces in an unequal political and military battle.
- **Terrorism is a dramatic symbol of hostility involving a symbolic selection of 'targets'.** 'Targets' tend to get selected because of their association to a certain social, economic, ethnic or political category. Inanimate objects symbolizing a government's power, often get targeted.
- **The relatively low use of force adds to the attractiveness of terrorism as a favoured strategy among both state and non-state actors.** The low cost and relatively high yield technique of terrorism, makes it an attractive tactical option for both established governments and non-state groups looking for flexible responses and 'limited war' strategies. Consequently, terrorism has become an immoral surrogate for general war.[55]
- **Terrorism is a form of costly signaling.** Terrorism in this sense would mean the 'purposeful use of violence by the precipitator against an instrumental target in order to communicate to a primary target a threat of violence so as to coerce the primary target into behaviour or attitudes through intense fear or anxiety in connection with a demanded power outcome'.[56] Signaling in terrorist campaigns would include: attrition, intimidation, provocation, spoiling and outbidding.[57]

Motivating Factors

The understanding of the complexities of terrorism entails the identification of both non-psychological and psychological instrumental bases of terrorist actions. According to Martha Crenshaw, motivations behind terrorism are driven by numerous factors, ranging from the socialization of individuals who become 'terrorists' to its purpose, continuity with other nonviolent forms of political action and also availability of opportunities.[58] Typical explanations for terrorism in much public discourse, revolve either around *grievances* or on the theories of *political order*. Grievances, in this regard, are believed to be the outcome of social disorganization witnessed in traditional societies experiencing sudden economic transformations. In such societies, it is pointed out, that growing inequalities, presence of non-locals, erosion of social norms coinciding with the planting of new institutions, encourage disquiet which subsequently results in the creation of ideal recruiting environment for terrorist outfits.[59] The theories of *political order*, on the other hand, argue that the semi-open nature of quasi-authoritarian and partial democracies, make them more prone to internal armed conflicts and civil wars by creating opportunities for dissident mobilization. Inadequate fiscal and administrative capacities in many of these states, clearly work in favour of terrorists.[60]

Terrorism as a strategic option

Scholars who subscribe to the *non-psychological perspective*, believe that terror activity is a calculated response to circumstances and is opted by its practitioners from a range of perceived alternatives, the relative effectiveness of which is assessed through observation and experience. Terrorism, thus cannot be dismissed as pathological or inexplicable and is an outcome of intentional choice, involving regularized decision making processes. The goals pursued, clearly aim at changing the status quo and consequently preserving threatened privileges. In this, terrorist groups are quick to learn from the experiences of other similar outfits and this explains patterns of contagion in terrorist incidents.[61]

Terrorism, appears to be the preferred tactic of small and weak organizations in their quest to compensate for what they lack in numbers. In the words of Martha Crenshaw:

> The observation that terrorism is a weapon of the weak is hackneyed but apt. At least when initially adopted, terrorism is the strategy of a minority that by its own judgment lacks other means. When the group perceives its options are limited, terrorism is attractive because it is a relatively inexpensive and simple alternative, and because it's potential reward is high.[62]

The lack of numbers can be attributed to several factors. One possibility may be the lack of appeal among the masses, for the extreme ideological position taken by the challengers of the regime. Failure to mobilize support may also be attributed to the inability or unwillingness of the cadres to devote time to organizational work. In this regard, it is noteworthy that no matter how widespread popular dissatisfaction is, mobilization is imperative for the masses to rise.[63] Fear of negative sanctions from the regime, coupled with the misreading of the ground situation in regard to the presumed strength of the rebels, are other factors that deter people from coming out in open support for the insurgent cause. Turk, emphatically argues that terrorism need not always be the weapon of the weak. In his words: 'Because any group may adopt terror tactics, it is misleading to assume either that "terrorism is the weapon of the weak" or that terrorists are always small groups of outsiders – or at most a "lunatic fringe" ... Terror is organized violence, but the nature of the organization cannot be specified in defining terror'.[64] Clearly, there are very good reasons why rebel groups employ or reject a strategy of terrorism.

Time factor is crucial in the choice of terrorist means. External factors, both psychological and organizational, have the potential to trigger immediate action. A change in the ground situation may offer opportunities to organizations to compensate for its inferiority viz-à-viz the government. This may be due to the regimes' inability to protect the life and property of its citizens, or it may be because the regime has made itself morally and politically susceptible by adopting excessive force against its own people. Government repression is known to work in two ways: it may discourage dissent and may also ignite a moral backlash.[65]

International environment is no less critical a factor. If global opinion goes against the legitimacy of the targeted regime, rebels are encouraged to act aggressively, hoping that their cause would get greater visibility and support. Factors like, personalities of leaders, competition among rivals within the organization and pressure from followers, also have a bearing on the decision to use terror tactics.

Availability of new resources, often impact the situation to the advantage of the challengers. These assets may be secured through an alliance with a foreign government or through linkages with more established outfits or through criminal means such as extortions, robberies and kidnapping for ransom. This is imperative, because supporting full-time terrorist activities require uninterrupted funding. Efforts towards this end get augmented by strategic innovations. Careful selection of targets considered taboo, and locales where violence is unexpected such as schools, hospitals and places of worship are clear examples of such innovations.[66]

The *cost and benefit calculation* is central to the decision to use terrorist methods. Terrorism is both defensive as well as opportunistic, determined by calculations of resources and opportunities. Occasional violence is known to serve useful purpose. Not only does it give the outfit greater visibility, it also results in the consolidation of its power base. And at times, given the urgency of the situation, superior government resources and the likelihood of other methods not being able to make a desired impact, terrorism becomes the only workable option. However, the use of terrorism is not without a cost. As a domestic strategy, it invariably invites punitive government reaction, fear of which may weaken the fervour for confrontation. Indiscriminate terrorist violence also holds the risk of provoking a moral outrage that may result in the distancing of the citizenry. However, in ethnically divided societies, the risk of popular alienation is minimum, as in such societies the government of the majority appears illegal to the challenging minority and hence commands little support.[67]

There are obvious *advantages* of terrorism that the terrorist organizations fully recognize. The agenda setting function clearly stands out. By skillfully articulating the compulsions to resort to violence, terrorism powerfully puts the issue of political change in the public imagination. The ensuing disarray, not only poses a serious challenge to the authority of the government, but also has the potential to deflate its administrative institutions – its police, military and the courts. Terrorist success serves another useful purpose. In a potent way, it maintains the confidence and zeal of the supporters and sympathizers of the terrorist cause. These gains however, are subject to two factors: the lengths to which the government is willing to go to reclaim its authority and on the population's forbearance to insecurity and suppression.[68]

Terrorism's constituencies are diverse and are central to its changing dynamics. Besides sympathizers, antagonists and 'neutrals', a host of other actors such as the government, the political parties, churches, trade unions, intellectuals, social movements and also the mass media are a component of this matrix. These actors are a part of an interactive process, where they not only react to one another's decisions but even anticipate them. Terrorism thus, as Michel Wieviorka points out, fits into a set of relations that can be subjected to a synchronic or structural analysis.[69]

Terrorism as an offshoot of psychological behaviour

Scholars who subscribe to this view, attribute a special psycho-logic to rationalize violent acts that terrorists are psychologically compelled to commit. This special logic gets clearly reflected in the polarizing and absolutist 'us versus them' rhetoric that defines most of their violent acts. In this regard, the striking uniformity of the rhetoric, despite the diversity of causes that terrorists espouse, is clearly revealing. While 'they', denote the establishment and in the psycho-logic reasoning of the terrorists are responsible for all discord and hence deserve to be exterminated, 'us' are the freedom fighters whose just and moral acts are the outcome of justified rage.[70] Crenshaw attempts an explanation of the terrorist psychology:

> The actions of terrorist organizations are based on a subjective interpretation of the world rather than objective reality. Perceptions of the political and social environment are filtered through beliefs and attitudes. It is clearly mistaken, however, to assume that terrorist act in terms of a consistent rationality based on accurate representation of reality. In fact, one of the aims of the terrorist organizations is to convince

> skeptical audiences to see the world in between governments and terrorists concerns for the definition of the conflict.[71]

Although people with diverse backgrounds are known to tread the terrorist path, it is pointed out, that individuals with certain kind of personality attributes are dis-proportionately oriented towards a career in terrorism. By all indication, excitement seeking, action-oriented and aggressive people are more likely to choose this path. In this regard, the psychological mechanism of 'externalization' and 'splitting' that characterize individuals with narcissistic and borderline personality disturbances, assumes significance.[72] 'Splitting' is a personality trait, that is an outcome of a particular type of psychological damage inflicted during childhood. The resultant narcissistic wounds, lead to the development of what clinicians describe as 'the injured self'.[73] An individual with such personality assemblage, displays a behaviour pattern that obsessively centres around his idealized self and projects onto others, all the devalued weaknesses within him. Such individuals, instinctively connect with the polarizing and absolutist ideologies of terrorism, as it provides a powerful explanation for what has gone wrong in their lives, besides helping them chart out a path for establishing an identity for themselves.

Studies on the lives of terrorists have also revealed linkages between the demographic characteristics of a society, levels of employment and terrorism. Rapid population growth is known to redistribute resources, resulting in economic grievances. Consequently, there is a tendency for unattached, unemployed youth with free time, high energy levels and a zeal for adventure to get attracted to radical causes.[74] Membership of such groups prove to be comforting, as it powerfully contributes to the consolidation of a psychosocial identity at a time of great societal flux. Even educated youth tend to get drawn towards radical causes. This is particularly evident in developing societies, where students in formal education find themselves culturally caught between two worlds, one traditional and the other modern.

Although each terrorist group operates in a unique historical setting and cannot be studied in isolation from its national cultural milieu, available data does provide interesting insights into the psychology of the terrorist mind, particularly in regard to group membership. In a very powerful way, group membership help members overcome personal feelings of inadequacy and insecurity. Submergence and allegiance could be to an individual, an organization, a divine force, real or imaginary motherland, conscience or even a psychic compulsion. In exchange of such submergence, the individual experiences an elevated sense of pride, confidence and also a sense of self worth and security – both physical as well as security against the torture of doubt.[75] Within the group, however, there are two opposing forces in play. Forces that Bion persuasively describes as – the *work group* and the basic *assumption group*. While the work group is goal oriented, the basic assumption group suffers from three identifiable psychological symptoms: the *fight-fight*, the *dependency* and the *pairing* symptoms.[76] Within the assumption group, the *fight-fight* group delineates itself in relation to the outside world, which both justifies and threatens its existence. The *dependency* group looks up to an all-powerful leader for guidance and the *pairing* group awaits the arrival of a messiah for salvation. In varying degrees, terrorist groups are known to manifest all three psychological symptoms.[77]

Within the group environment, doubters are dealt with absolute firmness.[78] Particularly so in case of underground organizations, where the group becomes the ultimate interpreter of ideology, the sole source of information and confirmation, and in the face of external threats, the only dependable refuge.[79] Consequently, what emerges is a group mind that exerts tremendous pressure on the group to commit acts of violence. The rationalist and the psychological line of reasoning attribute different reasons for the pressure. While the rationalists argue that political violence is clearly a tactic to achieve the group's political goals, the psychological line of reasoning points at the risks and dangers of inaction for action driven people. They argue that periodic violence is imperative to *justify the existence of terrorist groups*. Janis describes it as a manifestation of 'group think', which clearly is based on the one dimensional perception of the enemy as evil. This coupled with illusions of invulnerability, not only leads to excessive optimism but also excessive risk taking, that often manifest in the form of brutal violent acts.[80] Terrorists, whose only sense of significance comes from being terrorists, have a compelling reason to wage what Ferracuti describes as 'fantasy war' – a war that is real only in the mind of the terrorist.[81] Ironically, success to the espoused cause is not entirely welcomed, as it holds the risk of making the group irrelevant.

Terrorism in Contemporary International Relations

The phenomenon of terrorism underwent drastic transformation after the Second World War, and as a result emerged a new type of terrorism that was international in character. International terrorism came to be understood as 'acts of violence across national boundaries, or with clear international repercussions, often within the territory or involving the citizens of a third party to a dispute'.[82] Scholars have identified following characteristics of the contemporary 'strain' of terrorism: [83]

- There is a clear movement towards the 'transnationalization' of terror, resulting in a shift from vertical forms of organization to horizontal networking structures.
- A clear shift in strategy from calculated to random murder, that often gets manifested in terrorist operations away from the immediate theatre of conflict, in areas understood as 'neutral territory'.
- Broad co-ordination among widely disparate groups, coupled with the opportunities provided by the privatization of violence and its

instruments, contributes to the success of the technique. Diaspora support has emerged as an important factor in the support structure of terrorist outfits.

- Another noteworthy feature of cotemporary terrorism, is its ability to effectively undercut the state's monopoly of violence and acquire greater visibility, by successfully availing opportunities created by technological globalization.

Mary Kaldor uses the term 'regressive globalization' to describe the character of the new terrorist groups.[84] She argues that many of these groups have emerged in reaction to the upheavals generated by globalization, as well as, due to disenchantment with the secular ideologies of the state. The opportunities created by globalization, in the form of increased funding from transnational criminal groups and diaspora and also through the media, give a fillip to these groups to aggressively espouse their chosen cause. A noteworthy feature, is that these groups, differ significantly from classical terrorist groups in ideology, tactics and organization. What characterizes them is the pursuit of modern political agenda with anti-modern symbols and their acts are justified as a part of a great war against the 'other'. In case of religious groups, it is a 'cosmic war' against 'evil' and in case of nationalist groups, it is all about avenging historic injustices.[85]

In the fabric of contemporary international relations, terrorism has come to be recognized as a significant factor, severely threatening national sovereignty by undermining the 'territorial function' of the nation state.[86] Such recognition, clearly is an outcome of a number of profound and mutually reinforcing changes in the global order. 'Trans-nationalization' of economic relations, elites and communications, evidently are some such factors. Another factor is the 'globalization' of military alliances, that clearly has resulted in the erosion of the traditional concept of 'neutrality'. The accentuation of the nuclear stalemate, is believed to be another compelling factor that encourages the development of non-conventional forms of warfare. In this setting, terrorism as a general phenomenon, skillfully adapts to the new transnational conditions and emerges as a potent political weapon that much like the transnational corporations, has the ability to 'shop' for jurisdiction. In this regard, Barry Buzan makes insightful observations, within the prevalent set of theories on international relations, on the implications of the phenomenon on international relations.[87]

The *neorealist* perspective, according to him is state-centric and is driven by the argument that an understanding of the changes effected on the global power structure, resulting from the end of bipolarism, is critical to the understanding of the international security environment. The discourse mainly centres around the distribution of material power in the global political structure, and its interplay with the balance of power logic.[88] Neorealists would argue, that events like the 11 September, 2001 attack on the US, are the direct outcome of unipolarism and the response to it being an instance of the unipolar power structure in action. The most obvious impact of 9/11, was the repositioning of relationships amongst the great powers and the intensification of territorial politics, manifested in the form of increased security controls and a general upgrading of the state's right to surveillance.[89] It is further argued, that the reality of global terrorism brings into focus three major staples of the realist/security studies agenda – the issue of proliferation of weapons of mass destruction (WMDs); security challenges emerging on account of the revolution in military affairs and; the controversial idea that the world is all set for a clash of civilization, defined in cultural and civilizational terms.[90] These factors have not only widened the gulf between the capability of the sole superpower and all other actors in the system, but have also generated a scenario, where the weak are being pushed, either towards 'submission' or 'pursuit' of alternative military means. Both terrorism and WMDs are thus options, that get explored.[91]

The *Globalists* argue, that with the de-territorialization of world politics, globalization's clearest guiding theme is the independent role of both transnational entities – corporations, non-governmental social and political organizations – and intergovernmental organizations and regimes.[92] Consequently, the network of interactions involving varied actors at different levels, has been dramatically impacted and the state is merely one of the players with little control over the outcome of these interactions. Globalization, thus has complicated the security debate by focusing on its two interrelated aspects, the first highlighting the unequal, exploitative and coercive aspects of the centre-periphery relationship and the second acknowledging the effectiveness of globalization as the most effective and swiftest way to overcome the same.[93] Globalists argue, that cracks in the global Westphalian political fabric, evident in the form of failed states, has created spaces for non-state actors on the murky side of world society to operate aggressively, and what has emerged can be understood as the subaltern variant to the notion of *globalization from below*. It involves the cementing of ties amongst 'dubious groups' and escalation of 'shadowy activities', ranging from smuggling of commodities, illicit production and trading of small weapons and drugs, money laundering, trafficking in human and other illegal activities, that steer across national, ethnic and even religious associations.[94] Global terrorism, according to globalists, is clearly a powerful manifestation of the subaltern non-state successfully organizing and reproducing its acts at the global level.

The *regionalist* perspective argues that with the transformation of great powers into 'lite powers', in the aftermath of the Cold War, there is a discernible reduction in the ability of global powers to have a sustained interest in the affairs of the world. It is the pulls and pressures of domestic policy, that is dictating their foreign policy choices and also impacting their ability to strategically and militarily engage in world trouble spots. The changed scenario provides ample space to local states, to engage in military-political interactions, in their respective regions with less outside interference.[95] The regionalist perspective, emphatically holds that barring few exceptions in history, regional security dynamics have always been vital to the overall security constellation in the international system.[96] In the context of global terrorism, regionalists argue that although cotemporary terrorist organizations manifest themselves as de-territorialized transnational players, they are intimately connected with the political dynamics of their respective regions, and their motives, organizational goals and pattern of operation have to be understood within the regional context. The study of regionalism, thus has to take into account, the cultural, the functional and the structural variants in the contexts to be examined.[97] A noteworthy feather in the context of regionalism, according to Bozeman, is the institutionalization of violent regional conflicts that clearly is a complex mixture of intra-national, intra-regional and extra-regional conflicts. This provides sufficient scope for regionally different ways of managing tensions. In his words:

> Studies of the world's numerous strife-torn regions show conclusively that moral, intellectual, social, or political conflicts are experienced in greatly varying ways: that levels of conflict tolerance are not convergent; and the allowance must be made, therefore, for culturally or regionally different ways of managing tensions and disputes.[98]

A related perspective by Buzan on *regional security complexes*, powerfully supports the observation on the complexity of regional conflicts. Buzan defines such a complex as 'a group of states whose primary security concerns link together sufficiently closely that their national securities cannot realistically be considered apart from one another. Security complexes tend to be durable, but they are neither permanent nor internally rigid'.[99] However, in the context of regional conflicts, it needs to be stated that the nature of borders have an impact on war propensity. Although every state aims at wielding effective control within its territory, peripheral societies present peculiar challenges to state control. The heterogeneous nature of such societies in almost every sense - ethnic, linguistic, religious and ideological - creates pressures to establish new autonomous units and consequently the world's peripheries witness cycles of violence and counter violence.

Insurgency and Terrorism

Both semantically and conceptually, insurgency and terrorism denote different situations. However, in the context of violence against the state, with most of the insurgent groups opting to use systematic terror in pursuit of their goals, the line separating the two stands clearly blurred. The Oxford English Dictionary describes insurgency as 'a heaving or rising; an upheaval; the action of rising against authority; a revolt'.[100] Two facts stand out from its dictionary meaning that sets it apart from other related concepts – it is a *revolt* directed against a political authority with an unwavering will to *change* the status quo. Terror, according to the Oxford English Dictionary, in an apparent reference to 'the reign of terror' in France, is 'government by intimidation as directed and carried out by the party in power in France during the revolution of 1784-1794'. It is 'a policy intended to strike with terror those against whom it is adopted; the employment of methods of intimidation; the fact of terrorizing or condition of being terrorized'.[101] While insurgency, mainly understood as a 'rise in revolt against an established authority', indicates an objective, terrorism is more of a strategy geared towards the achievement of certain objectives. Insurgents may or may not adopt terrorism as a strategy. Another noteworthy difference between the two terms is that, while insurgent acts are always against a political authority, terror as a strategy may be used either by a political authority or against it. It is noteworthy, that in either case, scholars have failed to evolve universally acceptable definitions and hence both these concepts are plagued by definitional controversies.

To comprehend most terrorism, it becomes imperative to understand insurgency. Often understood as a political legitimacy crisis, insurgency mainly gets manifested as a struggle between a non-ruling group and the ruling authorities. In the ensuing struggle, the non-ruling group willfully uses political resources and violence to demolish, reformulate or uphold the basis of legitimacy of those aspects of politics that are sacrosanct to one or the other warring side. With a lot being at stake for the warring parties, the struggles often take the form of protracted conflicts. This is particularly evident in the Third World, where the mismatch between political and cultural boundaries are particularly glaring.[102] Even in societies where the legitimacy of the political community is not an issue, there are other grounds for internal conflicts, centring around the legitimacy of salient values that steer and limit the making and execution of binding decisions in the political system.[103] Insurgency also gets viewed as a 'little' revolution. This is mainly because, almost all aspects of a revolution – theory, ideology and tactics – are present in it, though the proportion varies from group to group.

Terror, on the other hand 'entails the threat or use of symbolic violent acts aimed at influencing political behaviour'.[104] In the words of Walter Laqueur, terrorism is:

> the use of covert violence by a group for political ends, is usually directed against a government, but it is also used against other ethnic groups, classes or parties. The aims may vary from the redress of specific grievances to the overthrow of a government and the seizure of power, or to the liberation of a country from foreign rule. Terrorists seek to cause a political, social and economic disruption and for this purpose frequently engage in planned or indiscriminate murder ... It has been waged by national and religious groups, by the left and by the right, by

> national as well as internationalist movements and it has been state sponsored.[105]

Attempts at defining insurgency and terrorism have not been without challenges. Since 1970, when the General Assembly adopted the declaration on Principles of International Law Concerning Friendly Cooperation Among States, the international community has been struggling to define these two terms within the ambit of the aims and objectives of the United Nations (UN) Charter, which states:

> Every State has the duty to refrain from organizing, assisting or participating in acts of civil strife or terrorist acts in another State or acquiescing in organized activities within its territory directed towards the commission of such acts, when the acts referred to in the present paragraph involve a threat of use of forces.

However, it is noteworthy that the Principle of Equal Rights and Self-determination of Peoples, expressed in the later part of the same UN declaration, creates an ambivalence. The Principle states:

> Every state has the duty to refrain from any forcible action which deprives people referred to above, in the elaboration of the present principles of their right to self-determination and freedom and independence. In their actions against, and resistance to such forcible action in pursuit of the exercise of their right to self-determination, such peoples are entitled to seek and receive support in accordance with the purpose and principles of the charter.[106]

The Adhoc Committee on International Terrorism, set up by the UN in 1973, added to the existing ambivalence by unambiguously stating that every instance of insurgency was not an act of terrorism. Exemptions were provided to activities that derived from:

> ... the inalienable right to self-determinate and independence of all peoples under colonial and racist regime and other forms of alien domination and the legitimacy of their struggle, in particular the struggle of national liberation movements, in accordance with the purposes and principles of the charter and the relevant resolutions of the organs of the United Nations.[107]

It 1974, in the context of aggression, the UN General Assembly once again made attempts to define terrorism. Article 3(g) of the declaration states:

> The sending by or on behalf of a State of armed bands, groups, irregulars and mercenaries, which carry out acts of armed force against another State of such gravity as to amount to the acts listed above, or its substantial involvement therein.[108]

However, Article 7 of the same declaration compounds the ambivalence by expressing desire to protect both, a state against subversive aggression from another, and also citizens and social groups from terror of the state. The declaration states:

> Nothing in this definition, and in particular Article 3 (inventory of acts that qualify as aggression) could in any way prejudice the right to self-determination, freedom and independence, as derived from the Charter, of peoples forcibly deprived of that right and referred to in the Declaration of Principles of International Law concerning friendly relations and cooperation among States in accordance with Charter of the United Nations, particularly people under colonial and racist regimes or other forms of alien domination; nor the rights of these people to struggle to that end and to seek and receive support, in accordance with the principles of the Charter and in conformity with the above mentioned Declaration.[109]

It is noteworthy that it was only on 9 December 1985, that the UN General Assembly unanimously adopted a resolution condemning all acts of terrorism as criminal. However, the issue is far from resolved with little consensus on what acts actually constitute terrorism. In this regard, it is significant that way back in 1937, the League of Nations made attempts to come up with a definition of terrorism. A convention (that never came into existence) was drafted describing terrorism as: 'All criminal acts directed against a state and intended or calculated to create a state of terror in the minds of particular persons or a group of persons or the general public.'[110]

Clearly, both insurgency and terrorism are multi-dimensional phenomenon and hence evolving a commonly agreed definition for them is fraught with difficulties. However, two very apparent dimensions of the phenomenon are political and security, to which may also be added an international dimension. This is particularly in regard to the tendency of some states, to use insurgency and terrorism as instruments of state policy in its war against rival countries. In case of Third World countries, insurgencies mainly take the form of internal ethnic wars and clearly are serious hostile events, largely revolving around the issues of nation building and economic undevelopment. Socio-economic, religious and ideological dimensions add to the complexities of the phenomenon. This is particularly evident in fractured societies, where there is a clear disinclination to transcend parochial loyalties.[111] In such societies, there is little ambiguity in regard to the competing goals of the participants – structural change versus maintenance of status quo, establishment of a separate political system versus reinforcement the existing one, and changing the incumbent political authority versus continuing with the same.[112]

The violent aspect of insurgencies get manifested in different forms of warfare, such as terrorism, guerrilla war and conventional warfare.[113] With insurgent movements frequently undergoing goal transformations, categorizing insurgencies is not without challenges. However, the goals fluctuate between long-term, intermediate and short-term goals. While the long term goals are clearly geared towards changing the political system, the intermediate goals aim at eroding, both internally and externally, the government's psychological support base.[114] The proximate objectives are situational and may vary according to the demands of the circumstances. These often manifest in the form of occasional violence, mainly aimed at extracting political concessions from a demoralized government, in an environment of widespread disarray. Need for greater visibility, coupled with power struggle among specific factions within an insurgent organization, may also provoke insurgents to act violently.[115] What is obvious is the belief in 'propaganda by deed'.[116] This clearly involves a deep understanding of the psychology of fear and its likely impact on the society. The outcome of such fear, in the words of an observer 'destroys the solidarity, cooperation and interdependence on which social functioning is based, and substitutes insecurity and distrust'.[117] This clearly generates suspicion, against the government and its capacity to fulfill primary security functions for its citizens. Consequently, it results in a level of disorientation, where the source of the victims fear lies outside his field of experience.[118]

A striking feature of insurgency driven conflicts is the power asymmetry between the warring sides. The legal asymmetry between the legitimate sovereign government, with access to enormous resources to prosecute the war, and the rebels is particularly profound.[119] Consequently, an understanding of the dynamics of insurgency environment, both in its physical and human dimension, is critical to its evaluation. In regard to physical environment, A. H. Shollom makes an interesting observation. In his words:

> One of the main factors contributing to the development of a partisan movement was the presence of suitable terrain in which to operate. We include in such terrain: swamps, mountains and forests where mobility is limited to movement on foot and in light vehicles. The fact that the partisan operates in such terrain will be to his advantage, for in an environment of this nature, the regular forces lose the use of their vehicles and artillery as well as the ability to mass superior members. In essence, the terrain reduces the better equipped, better trained, and better-armed regular force to a level where the partisan is its equal.[120]

Added to the physical setting and the societal cleavages is the perception of relative deprivation, as manifested in the form of institutionalized discrimination against certain groups in relation to socio-economic benefits. The relative deprivation theory gives explanations of the socio-economic dimension of political violence and has been expanded from the frustration-aggression theory, expounded in 1939 by John Dollard of USA.[121] According to this theory, a sense of deprivation or injustice, real or perceived is often a major precondition for political violence. Wilkinson argues: 'collective rage and violence are not necessarily a rumination of individual frustrations but may, in large part, be a function of changing ideologies, beliefs and historical conditions which so materially affect social conceptions of justice and legitimacy'.[122]

The role of determined leaders, capable of politically and militarily mobilizing domestic and external support, remains a critical factor in the emergence and sustenance of insurgencies. In this, the role of intellectuals in providing strategic vision and contextualizing perceived social, economic and political injustices, is particularly crucial. In the words of Gurr: 'discontent people act aggressively only when they become aware of the supposed source of frustration or someone with whom they associate frustration'.[123] He further states, that men's susceptibility to beliefs that rationalize violence is mainly a function of their discontent.[124]

Popular support, both in its passive and active form, is thus significant for the sustenance and success of insurgencies. In this regard, the Vietminh manual on guerrilla war aptly sums:

> Without the "popular antennae" we would be without information; without the protection of the people we could neither keep our secrets nor execute quick movement; without the people the guerrillas could neither attack the enemy nor replenish their forces and, in consequence, they could not accomplish their mission with ardour and speed .... The population helps us fight the enemy by giving information, suggesting ruses and plans, helping us to overcome difficulties due to lack of arms, and providing us with guides. It also supplies liaison agents, hides and protects us, assists our actions near posts, feeds us and looks after our wounded .... Cooperating with guerrillas, it has participated in sabotage acts, in diversionary actions, in encircling the enemy, and in applying the scorched earth policy .... On several occasions and in cooperation with guerrillas, it has taken part in combat.[125]

External patron support, in the form of sanctuaries, weapon supply, financial assistance, training and so forth, is mainly motivated by instrumental factors such as strategic interests or enhancement of regional and global clout.[126] Such support may come from sympathetic neighbours, other insurgent groups or from organizations and institutions based outside the country. In regard to the role of sanctuaries, Bernard B. Fall makes a significant observation. In his words: 'in brutal fact, the success or failure of all rebellions since World War II depended entirely on whether the active sanctuary was willing and able to perform its role'.[127] Cross border linkages ensure a steady supply of resources that facilitate weapons' procurement, political and propaganda support, besides opportunities for training, recruiting and trafficking in illegal commodities.[128] Evidently, countries with weak institutional capacities are more likely to emerge as potential safe havens.

A chronology of armed conflicts in the post 1945 period, reveal a global upsurge in insurgencies, mostly intrastate in nature, waged by entirely disparate groups over the question of state versus nation.[129] A major characteristic of these insurgencies is the widespread use of terror, both by the insurgents and by the military and paramilitary forces pitted against them. It is noteworthy, that front lines in such wars get blurred and there is little regard for the Geneva conventions.[130] Another defining feature of these conflicts, is that, it is of a low-intensity variety. Low Intensity Conflict (LIC), for the purpose of the present study may be defined as:

> ... a politico-military confrontation between the established authority (state) and organized group(s) of people with or without external assistance, beyond the scope of legitimate, route, peaceful contest/ agitation. Being on the low end of the conflict spectrum, it imposes an undefined restraint on the execution of military operations.[131]

Mary Kaldor describes these conflicts as 'New Wars'. Although most of these new wars appear to be localized, they involve innumerable transnational connections. Consequently, the distinction between internal and external, aggression and repression and even between local and global gets blurred. A defining feather of most of these wars, is the centrality of identity politics with criminality, corruption and inefficiency being other factors impacting its dynamics.[132]Another defining characteristic of these 'new wars', are its linkages with poverty.[133] Consequently, the affected countries become incubators for virtually every type of transnational threat – infectious disease, environmental degradation, international crime and drug syndicates, arms proliferation and terrorism.

The empirical focus of this book is on the dynamics of terrorism in North East India – a region of great differences and complexities. The region, comprising the states of Arunachal Pradesh, Assam, Manipur, Meghalaya, Mizoram, Nagaland, Sikkim and Tripura represents much diversity, ethnically, linguistically, culturally, economically and even topographically. However, the imperatives of geography and history so impact this heterogeneous periphery of India, that the fallouts of events in one part of the region powerfully resonate in the other. This is particularly so in case of conflicts. The conflicts, spread across a wide canvas, have engulfed almost the entire region, mainly manifesting as multiple insurgencies with terrorism as its defining feature. It is noteworthy, that conflicts of varying intensity exist in almost every state of the region. The geo-strategic location of the region – between what is now Bangladesh, Tibet, Burma and Bhutan – creates a context in which the multiplicity of ethno-territorial identities achieve political salience. This is mainly due to the fact, that in most cases, the political boundaries do not coincide with the social boundaries. Concepts such as uneven development, differential modernization, regional deprivation, lack of assimilation, internal colonialism and cultural oppression, only partially explain the nature of the ethnic turmoil. However, in the context of comprehending the trajectory of the terrorist phenomenon in the region, there are glaring similarities in the pattern of insurgent politics, that warrants a holistic understanding of the phenomenon in all its dimensions. With most of the insurgent groups, across the spectrum, increasingly adopting terrorist techniques, the fine line separating insurgency and terrorism stands erased. A primary feature underlying terrorist behaviour in the region is political extremism, which clearly implies: 'taking a political idea to its limits, regardless of unfortunate repercussions, impracticalities, arguments, and feelings to the contrary, and with the intention not only to confront, but to eliminate opposition .... intolerance toward all views other than one's own'.[134] Actors taking recourse to terrorism, consider themselves as champions of groups within society, defending and preserving an identity which otherwise stands the risk of being assimilated.

The analysis of terrorism in North East India, is mainly concerned with non-state groups having an unambiguous agenda of confronting the state. The objectives mainly oscillate between extracting significant political concessions from the state - moral, legal or material - to replacing the state itself. They are primarily linked to national bases and are thus examples of *domestic political terrorism,* although many of them have strong cross-border linkages. While ethnicity remains the primary paradigm around which conflicts revolve in the region, its linkages to organized crime, drug trafficking and proliferation of small arms is well established. It goes without saying, that given the porous nature of the international borders and also the present context of globalization, internal conflicts in the region are no longer localized. The internationalization of these local insurgencies has serious national security ramifications. The following two sections of the book will delve into the pertinent issues, that dominate the security landscape of India's fragile North Eastern borderlands, and profoundly impacts the internal and foreign policy choices of the Indian State.

Part II

INDIA'S NORTH EASTERN BORDERLANDS AND THE DYNAMICS OF TERRORISM

Background

Located between South and South East Asia, India's North East is indisputably Asia's oldest trouble spot[1]. A conglomerate of distinct political units, the region, a 'colonial construct'[2], is placed between what is now Bangladesh, Tibet, Burma[3] and Bhutan, with a thin land corridor connecting it with the rest of India – the Siliguri Corridor which is an area of 12,203 sq. kms connecting mainland India with the outlying border states of the North Eastern frontiers.[4] Often referred to as the 'seven sisters', these states are Assam – the biggest state in terms of population – Arunachal Pradesh (the former North Eastern Frontier Agency or NEFA), Mizoram, Nagaland, Meghalaya, Tripura and Manipur (the last two being princely states).[5] With ninety-eight per cent of the borders of North East India being international borders, the region's geo-strategic significance clearly stands out.[6] These borders have been involved in at least three major wars (in 1962, 1965 and 1971), besides numerous other security skirmishes.[7] Given the fragile nature of the geographical and political connectivity of the region to mainland India the political and security challenges emanating from these remote frontiers, have proved to be intractable. The combined area of the region (inclusive of Sikkim) comprises 7.9 per cent of the country's territory (about 263,179 sq.kms), and according to the 2001 Census of India, is inhabited by 3.8 per cent of the national population (Table I). Characterized by unparalleled ethnic, cultural, religious and linguistic diversity, the region is inhabited by three distinct groups of people – the hill tribes, the plain tribes and the non-tribal population of the plains.[8]

North East India's first encounter with British colonialism began in 1826, with the conclusion of the Treaty of Yandaboo. The treaty, concluded between the defeated Burmese invaders and the British, paved the way for aggressive colonial penetration into the region on a large scale. By virtue of the treaty, the Burmese renounced claims on the territories of Assam, Manipur and its neighbouring areas. Tenasserim and Arrakan were also ceded to the British.[9] After a brief spell of puppet regimes, the whole of Assam along with the adjoining hilly tracts were brought under the direct administrative umbrella of the Bengal Presidency. Prospects for the exploitation of extractive minerals such as coal and oil, triggered the case for a 'forward policy' on the hills. Profits from the cultivation of cash crops, such as tea and rubber proved to be an added attraction.[10] It is noteworthy, that until the British advent, the notion of territorial or political authority was unheard of in the hills. It was only in 1914, with the drawing of the McMahon Line, that the frontier between the sub-Himalayan and Himalayan British territory and Tibet was demarcated for the first time.[11]

The historical connectedness of the region was systematically eroded by the extra-ordinary administrative policies of progressive segregation that came into place between 1873 and 1934. These policies led to the categorization of the tribal populated areas into 'non-regulated', 'backward' or 'excluded' areas.

Table: I
Basic Facts about North East India, 2001

States of North East India	Capital	Year of Statehood	No. of Lok Sabha Constituencies	Area in sq.kms	Literacy Rate
1	2	3	4	5	6
Arunachal Pradesh	Itanagar	20 February 1987	2	83743	54.3
Assam	Dispur	20 February 1947	14	78438	63.3
Manipur	Imphal	21 January 1972	2	22327	70.5
Meghalaya	Shillong	21 January 1972	2	22429	62.6
Mizoram	Aizwal	20 February 1987	1	22081	88.8
Nagaland	Kohima	1 December 1963	1	16579	66.6
Sikkim	Gangtok	16 May 1975	1	7096	68.8
Tripura	Agartala	1 December 1972	2	10486	73.2
NER				263179	68.5
All India	Delhi			3287263	64.8

Note: i) NER = North East Region
ii) *Excludes Mao Maram, Paomata & Purul sub-division of Senapati District.

Source: Basic Statistics of NER, 2006.

The Inner Line Regulation of 1873, prohibited access to these areas to all 'outsiders' except those with special permission from the government. The extension of the Regulation to most of the hill areas, resulted in the creation of 'a frontier within a frontier' that consequently accentuated the already existing political and cultural rift between the tribal areas and the plains. In continuation of this policy, the Government of India Act, 1935, made most of the hill areas in the region 'excluded areas', outside the jurisdiction of the provincial legislature. The Act invented the phrase 'tribal areas', which was defined as 'the areas along the frontiers of India or in Baluchistan which are not part of British India or of Burma or of any Indian State or of any foreign State' [Section 311(1)]. 'India' was defined in the same Section as 'British India together with all territories of any Indian Ruler under the sovereignty of His

Majesty, all territories of any Indian Ruler under the suzerainty of such an Indian Ruler, the tribal areas, and, any other territories which His Majesty in Council may, from time to time ... declare to be part of India'.[12] The political ramifications of these exclusionary policies, put in place by the 'alien administration' were far reaching. It resulted in a glaring disconnect between the pattern of administration prevailing in the tribal areas and the rest of the country. The tribal communities in the region, thus remained disengaged from the momentous social and political developments taking place elsewhere in India, and consequently the heterogeneous character of the region remained unaltered even after the British had quit the country.[13] The nation building strategies - political, economic and cultural - adopted in independent India, could do precious little to alter this reality. It proved to be 'internally subversive' and came to be viewed in the dominant perception as tools of domination and subjugation. Such perception, observers point out, has been a critical factor in igniting and sustaining 'rebel consciousness' in the region. Rationalizing the complexity of the ethnoscape of North East India, Sanjib Baruah writes: 'Every where in the world those areas that did not go through the process of standardization associated with the rise and consolidation of nation states, e.g. the emergence of the print media, national languages, widespread literacy, and national educational systems, are perhaps significantly more diverse than areas that did'.[14]

The 'rebel consciousness' that so powerfully defines the politics of North East India, challenges the state-centric notion of Indianness from a position of autonomy rooted in cultural distinctness that largely revolves around primordial identities. Claims of nationhood - sovereignty, territory and institutional authority - orbit mainly around ethnic lines and are expressed in both non-violent and violent forms.[15] In this context, it is significant that narratives of 'internal colonization' define the anti-state 'decolonization struggles', being waged in the region since the early 1950s.[16] More often than not, the uprisings are spearheaded by the 'neo-class' or the 'ethno-class'[17] among the ethnic groups. Claims on the state and political processes vary, ranging from special representative rights to enhanced autonomy and even self-determination. Demands for special cultural rights, including affirmative action aimed at enhancing the socio-economic status of groups that perceive themselves as disadvantaged, figure high in the agenda. These demands however, have not remained unheeded. Through special acts and agreements, new states have been carved[18] and through the constitutional mechanism of the Sixth Schedule, autonomous districts and autonomous regions within the districts, identified with particular tribes, have been created.[19] The approval of the idea of 'exclusive homelands', in no small measure legitimizes cultural politics intrinsically linked to the cycle of violence and ethnic cleansing so rampant in the region.

The operation of the principle of 'protective discrimination', within the liberal democratic federal political arrangement of the Indian Constitution, creates its own dynamics that only adds to the complexity of the situation. It results in a de-facto second class citizenship for excluded groups, living within the shared space, and thus accentuates the cleavages along which ethnic battles are waged in the region. With a majority of the ethnic groups being designated as Scheduled Tribes (STs), economic rights in regard to landownership, trade licenses and business are restricted. Even access to elected offices is not open.[20] This raises the crucial constitutional question of the status and rights of non-tribals living in the region.[21] It is noteworthy that the Constitution of India of 1950, makes a distinction between tribal areas of Assam (a state in North East) and those in other parts of India. While the Fifth Schedule provides for the administration of the tribal people in other parts of India, in case of Assam, it is the Sixth Schedule.[22] The Sixth Schedule, however does not provide protection to all the STs of the areas where it is applicable. A notable exclusion are the plain tribes.[23] Unequal economic and political opportunities coupled with unequal access to resources, aggravate perceptions of being deprived among the disadvantaged, who clearly feel discriminated against in a setup that does not depend upon institutions but culture. This, along with the complications generated by the ethnic geography of the region, artificially constructed political borders and weak political institutions, make violent confrontations, the accepted grammar of politics in North East India.[24]

The Nature of Terrorism in North East India

The term 'North East', clearly fails to encompass the differences, diversity and the complexities that India's North Eastern frontiers represent. However, in regard to contextualizing terrorism, there are sufficient commonalities and linkages among the states that comprise the region to justify such a grouping.[25] The region is characterized by widespread conflicts, mainly revolving around the geography of the region, the multi ethnic character of its people, and the political and economic feeding grounds of discontent. Political expediency coupled with abundance of examples for imitation, are some other factors that add to the complexities of the ever-changing conflict dynamics. The conflicts may be broadly categorized as:

Tribal Groups versus the State. These conflicts are mainly triggered by a concept of distinct and separate nationhood, aimed at renegotiating and readjusting relationship with the Indian Union.[26]

Tribal versus Tribal. These conflicts mainly emerge out of the resistance of numerically smaller and less dominant cultural and political groups, living within a shared space, to the homogenizing pressures of the dominant groups. Identity assertion of the smaller groups, consequently result in violent conflicts both with the dominant group and other contesting groups sharing the same geographical space.[27]

Tribal versus Non-Tribals. Movements such as these, mainly revolve around sub-national aspirations and are mostly directed against the Union Government, having the constitutional authority to accommodate such aspirations through necessary amendments. The brunt of such uprisings are mainly borne by the state governments, who are constitutionally bound to maintain law and order in their respective states.[28]

A noteworthy feature of the conflict situation in the region is the factor of *criminality,* that operates within the framework of identity politics and powerfully manifests as 'retrograde set of relationships' posing a serious challenge to the economic and administrative authority of the state.

Aggressive engagement with the politics of identity, characterize nearly every state of North East India. Espoused by sub-national ethnic groups, insurgency inspired ethnic violence in the region, has unmistakably blurred the thin line distinguishing insurgency from terrorism. Best understood as examples of *ethnic terrorism*, the phenomenon can be described as deliberate violence employed by its practitioners, as a part of a proto-guerrilla movement 'against symbolic targets', designed largely to 'foster identity as well as to advance standard political goals'.[29] The politics of identity that triggers the phenomenon is believed to give:

> individuals ... a connection to political projects based on elements that are very basic to their self-conceptions. Members of these groups see themselves as having in common certain important characteristics that set them apart from the larger population – a commonality that is based on difference.[30]

Although different contexts and concerns shape the perception of the social forces that drive identity politics, 'for a separatist movement to emerge, it is imperative that people are convinced that they share something in common against an enemy.'[31] It is here, that the ethnic terrorists, in comparison to other extremist groups, have a far greater capacity to mobilize support as they already have a 'built-in audience' among a well-defined group of people. Consequently, their actions get interpreted as expressions of retaliation against subjugation and domination.[32] Mobilizations, in such scenario, mainly arise against a backdrop of social 'markers' that individuals have not consciously opted for. Consequently, claims of group uniqueness fall on receptive ears, with communities willing to believe that they possess singular culture with a distinctive set of repressed and neglected traditions. Such a belief, results in the acceptance of 'difference' as an inescapable reality of social and political life. In the words of Bohman:

> If new forms of cultural diversity have now produced conflicts and disagreement so deep and troubling that even our standard liberal

> solutions, modeled on religious liberty and tolerance, no longer seems adequate or stable. To borrow a distinction from David Hume, many current disagreements are not merely conflicts of interest but conflicts of principle.[33]

A defining feature of ethnic mobilizations is the restrictive nature of the membership of organizations that spearhead such movements. Rarely does it extend beyond the specific ethnic group. The objective clearly is to foster ethnic unity through aggressive mobilization and to 'win the census' by engineering demographic changes that result in ethnic homogenization.[34] However, it is worth noting that 'cultural identity', the premise on which ethnic ties stand, is a fluid concept. It is situational and hence subject to being 'redefined', 'invented' and 'imagined'.[35]

In the context of the ethno-nationalist discourse, two factors particularly stand out. First, is the continued salience of ethnic distinctiveness, shaped by shared values, history, culture and language, as a resilient and potent instrument of mobilization and identity formation. Second, is the colossal mismatch between the legally demarcated sovereign frontiers of the modern international state system and the demographic map of the distinct national identities. Other significant factors, that fuel the ethno-nationalist fire include: availability of dynamic leaders capable of mobilizing ethnic constituencies; availability of tools of terror, and availability of political and military support from external actors and other ethnic groups.[36] Evidently, politicization of cleavages once regarded as arbitrary and non-political have become a fixture on the political landscape of contemporary times, generating a brand of politics that severely challenges the established familiar ideologies and political alignments of almost every society.[37] Central to the creation of such a climate, is the designation of a person or a group – religious, ethnic or political as 'the enemy' and giving a strident call for its suppression and marginalization if not annihilation. Contempt for opponents, according to Stanley J. Tambiah, is inherent in the glorification of one's own nationality. In his words: 'when any group or community constructs its own myths of origin, stories of victories and conquests, and the lives of exemplary culture heroes, it also directly or indirectly denigrates and blackens the traditions of the opponent neighbours and contestants against whom its accomplishments are measured'.[38] Such an exclusive identity based political discourse, according to Mary Kaldor, 'necessarily generates a minority' which in its least involves 'psychological discrimination' against those labeled as the 'others' and at its worst results in 'population expulsion and genocide'.[39] Narratives of a glorious past, historical injustices and real and imagined threat perceptions from communities identified as the 'other', sustain such exclusionary politics.

As in most fractured parts of the world, perceived discrimination along economic, political and cultural lines, have triggered scores of insurgencies throughout the landscape of North East India. It is a dynamic process in which contesting ethnic groups with seemingly different ethno-ideological and value structure, strive to consolidate their identities and promote their material interests from invalidating behaviour of other groups. The ensuing inter-ethnic competition is plainly a 'struggle for power', between groups that control power and its institutions and others seeking a similar position. These conflicts have some defining features: more often than not, they tend to be asymmetrical; they are ambiguous in character and as such complicate differentiations between a friend and a foe; they are fought unconventionally using political and psychological means and methods; and these conflicts often get transformed into protracted wars of attrition. The agenda aggressively pushed forward are mainly three: political independence or autonomy, economic liberation and the preservation of 'cultural identity'. It is noteworthy, that within the umbrella of the larger conflict, there persist struggles at several levels. Within the ethnic group, the tussle mainly revolves over the control of symbolic and material resources. This clearly involves defining the group's margins and its rules of exclusion and inclusion. The second set of struggle is between the legitimacy claims of contesting groups and mainly manifest as competition for rights, privileges and control over resources. The third level of struggle is primarily between the state and groups that control its governing structures on the one hand, and the population that inhabits its territory on the other.[40] Violence plays a vital part in fanning and sustaining these struggles by polarizing communities in more ways than one. The classic 'security dilemma', clearly is a defining feature of the conflict situation in most ethnically polarized societies.[41] The arming of one ethnic group, provokes rival groups to make similar security arrangements, which paradoxically triggers an escalation and consequently the language of terrorism in the name of cultural defense and self protection does not go unheeded. One groups' haste to deploy defensive forces appear intimidating to others, and thus the notion of 'innocent bystanders' becomes meaningless and as the situation in North East India suggests, groups 'inevitably get politicized and militarized'.[42]

Conflicts in the North-East: An Overview

With no less than 100 armed rebel groups of varying intensity present in the region, North East India clearly has the distinction of being one of the most volatile areas of the world. Certain specificities are worth noting. First, barring a few exceptions, most of the states of the region have experienced long drawn violent uprisings seeking either secession from the Indian Union or greater autonomy within the Union. Second, conflict in some manifestation or the other is visible in each state of the region. Besides discord between the states and the central government, disputes of varying intensity and nature are known to exist among the constituent states of the region, between one tribe and another, between tribal and non-tribal groups and between indigenous groups and 'outsiders', who have moved in from other parts of India and from neighbouring countries such as Bangladesh and Nepal. While Nagaland, Manipur, Assam and Tripura rank among the most violent states in the region, Arunachal Pradesh, Meghalaya and Mizoram have also been witnessing proliferation of ultra outfits that clearly have the potential of waging violent conflicts with the Indian State.[43] The names of the rebel outfits, in most cases, prove to be very revealing both in terms of their social base as well as their agendas. However, the speed of proliferation raises pertinent questions, both about the political clout and organizational strength of many of these outfits.[44] The fact remains that these politicized and militarized outfits serve important agenda setting functions, that profoundly impact the course of politics in their respective areas of operation. Another unique feature of the ethnic situation in North East India, is the existence of influential student organizations in almost every state. These bodies determine the political agenda in their respective states and are a powerful political force to reckon with.[45]

Nagaland

The Naga flare up, that began in 1952, inaugurated North East India's first face-off with the Indian State. The genesis of this uprising can be traced to the period before independence when a memorandum was submitted to the British administration in 1926, forcefully articulating sovereign status for Nagaland comprising both sides of the hilly border region between India and Burma – i.e. the North East Indian states of Nagaland, Manipur, Assam and Arunachal Pradesh and Burma's Sagaing Division and Kachin state.[46] According to the NSCN (IM) website, Nagaland or Nagalim, occupying a compact area of 120,000 sq.kms, lying at the tri-junction of China, India and Burma, always had a sovereign existence. The website states:

> Nagalim without the knowledge and consent of the Naga people, was apportioned between India and Burma after their respective declaration of independence. The part that India illegally claims is subdivided and placed under four different administrative units, viz., Assam, Arunacal Pradesh, Manipur and Nagaland state. The eastern part, which Burma unlawfully claims, is placed under two administrative units, viz., Kachin state and Sagaing Division (formerly known as the Naga Hills). Nagalim however transcends all these arbitrary demarcations of boundary.[47]

In the aftermath of the Treaty of Yandaboo in 1826, the Naga territory, in stages, came under British control. By 1866, the Naga Hills acquired the status of a separate district under the Lieutenant Governorship of Bengal and with the separation of Assam from Bengal in 1874, the Hills Districts became a part of Assam.[48] In 1919, when Assam became a Governorship, the Naga Hills were declared a 'Backward Tract'. In 1929, the Naga Club, an organization of 20 Naga's submitted a memorandum to the Simon Commission – a commission that was considering political reforms in India in response to the rising anti-colonial tide.[49] Describing the Nagas as 'unvanquished people', the memorandum expressed strong sentiments against the inclusion of the Nagas in any reform scheme that was likely to be proposed by the Commission. Given their small population and limited educational endowments, the Nagas expressed apprehensions about the efficacy of the number based electoral system that was likely to come into place in Independent India.[50]

The British policy of granting relative autonomy to the Nagas viz-à-viz other parts of North East, contributed in no small measure to the independence claim of the Nagas. On 1 November 1873, a regulation marking the 'inner line' was introduced that clearly prohibited all British subjects and 'any persons, sending in or passing through, such districts, from going beyond such line without a pass under the hand and seal of the executive officer to such district, or such officer as he may authorize from time to time cancel or vary such prohibition'. [51] The Government of India Act of 1935, based on the recommendations of the Simon Commission, declared the 'Naga Hills' as 'Excluded Areas'. This explicitly meant that no act of the Federal Legislature or Assam Legislature was to apply to the Naga Hills. Under Section 92 of the 1935 Act, although the executive authority of the province of Assam extended to the Naga Hills district, but as 'excluded area' the Governor exercised his discretion in all matters relating to the hills district.[52]

The arrival of the Christian missionaries in the Naga Hills, proved to be a critical factor in the creation of the idea of a single Naga community. The proselytizing efforts of the American Baptist Mission, linked Christianity inextricably to Naga identity.[53] The Christian missionaries played a remarkable role in the educational and cultural upliftment of the Naga people. Their contribution in the form of giving the Nagas, a written script and language, both Roman and English, contributed hugely in creating a sense of group identity. [54] Such an identity, made the Nagas culturally distinct from the mainly Hindu and Muslim population of mainland India and thus added a cultural and to some extent a religious dimension to their ongoing resistance.[55] In this regard, the comment of Angami Zapu Phizo, the moving spirit behind the Naga uprising, proves to be quite revealing. In his words:

> We wish to remain within the fold of the Christian nations and of the Commonwealth. If great Russia and mainland China are proud to feel that they follow the ideology of the German Karl Marx, tiny Nagaland is happy to be a follower of Jesus Christ, whom we have come to believe in as our Saviour.[56]

Naga accounts suggest, that M. K. Gandhi was extremely sympathetic to the Naga cause and literally endorsed their point of view on Independence by stating: 'Nagas have every right to be independent ... if you do not wish to join the Union of India, nobody will force you to do that. The Congress Government will not do that'.[57] Jawaharlal Nehru, the first prime minister of India, on the other hand was more cautious and realistic in his approach. In

1946, in his communication to T. Sakhrie, a prominent member of the Naga National Council (NNC), the apex body of the Nagas, he plainly stated:

> Naga territory in Eastern Assam is much too small to stand by itself politically or economically. It lies between two huge countries, India and China, and part of it consists of rather backward people who require considerable help ... Inevitably, therefore, this Naga territory must form part of India and of Assam with which it has developed such close association.[58]

Subsequently, the Nagas were brought to accept the independence of India on 15 August 1947, and also became a part of the Union through what came to be known as the Hydari Agreement – after Sir Akbar Hydari, the then Governor of Assam. The Nine-Point Agreement between the Government of India (GOI) and NNC was signed on 29 June 1947.[59] The ninth clause of the declaration was most significant. It assigned the Union of India with special responsibility for the Naga areas for a period of ten years after which with the consent of the NNC, the future of the agreement would be decided upon – an extension or a renegotiation. Nagas point out, that Clause 9 of the Hydari Agreement held out to them the option of freedom. The GOI on its part argued, that the inclusion of the 'Sixth Schedule' in the Indian Constitution, with clear provisions for the formation of autonomous district councils aimed at giving greater autonomy to tribal minorities in the region, made the ninth clause of the Hydari agreement redundant. The divergence in perception, resulted in the launching of an armed 'independence struggle' under the aegis of the NNC leader Phizo. Phizo is credited for creating an underground government called the Naga Federal Government (NFG) in 1954 and a Naga Federal Army of around 15,000 armed guerrillas, based loosely on the hierarchical lines of the Indian Army.[60] Recruitment for this army was carried out from amongst the local population, from desertions engineered within the Assam Police, Assam Rifles (police and paramilitary forces) and ex-soldiers from the area. The necessary expertise that this army swiftly acquired of waging a modern war, may be attributed to numerous factors. One of them clearly was the military exposure acquired by the Naga's in the Second World War, as they fought alongside with the British. This along with their basic hunting skills, equipped them for a long drawn guerrilla war against the Indian State. The rifles given by the British and the significant stockpile of weapons left behind by the retreating Japanese forces, provided them with the necessary hardware for waging the struggle. The supply of weapons was further augmented from across the border, mainly from East Pakistan. Following the induction of the Indian Army in the Naga Hills in April 1956, Phizo fled to Pakistan and thereafter, to London in June 1960. Subsequently the Armed Forces (Special power) Act, 1958 was invoked and North East India witnessed massive deployment of the army.

In July 1960, a 6-point agreement between the GOI and a section of the Naga leadership, resulted in the creation of the State of Nagaland on 1 December 1963.[61] Immediately afterwards, elections to the state legislature were held.[62] On 11 November 1975, another agreement called the Shillong Accord was signed. This accord, in effect, related to the end of hostilities between the GOI and the Naga groups.[63] However, the accord was denounced by the more radical elements among the Naga leadership including Isak Swu and Thuingaleng Muivah, who went on to lead the National Socialist Council of Nagaland, NSCN (IM) on 2 February 1980. As an organization, the NSCN (IM) not only aggressively spearheaded the Naga militancy but also actively aided other separatist groups in the region. Clannish divisions however led to the split of the NSCN in 1988, resulting in the formation of NSCN (K) (Khaplang) under the leadership of Khole Konyak Khaplang. Tribal affiliations powerfully dominate and dictate insurgent politics in Nagaland and this split clearly revealed the divisions between the Nagas of the East (Burma, Eastern Nagaland and Arunachal Pradesh) and those of the West and South (Nagaland, Eastern Assam and Manipur). Ever since, both these groups have been involved in the worst kind of internecine clashes resulting in the killing of their own cadres. The contest between the rival factions of the NSCN, remains one of the most intricate problems of the Naga insurgency.

Although the NSCN (IM) continues to demand sovereignty for the Nagas, since 25 July 1997, a ceasefire agreement between the GOI and the NSCN (IM) has created scope for the two sides to carry on a process of fitful negotiations. The year 2001, saw an important development when the GOI established a formal ceasefire agreement with the Khaplang faction of the NSCN.[64] As per terms agreed upon, talks commenced between the GOI and the NSCN (IM) at neutral locations, outside India. The agreements, have placed restrictions on the security forces in making arrests, and limit their activities mainly to patrolling international and state boundaries. Apparently, it also restricts the NSCN factions from carrying out violent activities such as extortions, raids and recruitments. However, such activities still continue. Although both factions have signed ceasefires with the GOI, they increasingly launch attacks against each other in their struggle for political influence and recognition. Other stresses and strains have also surfaced in regard to the Naga problem. Clash of interests between warring factions, and the traditional rivalries of the tribes in the Naga inhabitant parts of the region, add their own imprint on the ongoing conflict. Added to it, is the cry of the Naga Students' Federation (NSF) against 'outsiders' and foreigners. The concept of Greater Nagaland or Nagalim, covering all Naga inhabited parts of Arunachal Pradesh, Assam and Manipur, has led to inter-state tensions.[65] Of late, as a result of splits in both factions of the NSCN, a third armed faction has emerged – the National Socialist Council of Nagaland (Unification) or the NSCN (U). Ever since the inception of this faction on 23 November 2007, the state has witnessed a surge in violence, mainly between the three groups.[66]

Currently, the active insurgent groups in Nagaland are the NSCN (IM), NSCN (K) and NSCN (U).[67]

Manipur

The primary conflict in Manipur involves a variety of insurgent groups constituted along tribal identities and demanding sovereign homelands. Politicisation of ethnic identities in the post-independence era, and internal rivalries in state politics along religious and ethnic lines, has profoundly impacted the polity and administration of the state and also the course of insurgent politics. Tensions between ethnic and tribal sub-groups, over pattern of land tenure and distribution have triggered a multiplicity of secondary conflicts. A number of accumulated grievances, several of which are historical in nature, fuel Manipuri discontent. The circumstance of Manipur's merger with India in October 1949, continues to cast its shadow on the post-colonial politics of Manipur.[68] The resentment centres around the perception, that the independent Kingdom of Manipur was not incorporated into the Indian Union as an equal member state of the Union.[69] The fact that full statehood was conferred to Manipur only in 1972 (nine years after Nagaland), despite Manipur having the distinction of holding the first ever elections to a state assembly, continues to be a sore point in Manipur till this day. Language is also an extremely emotive and explosive issue. Notwithstanding its distinguished history, it was only in 1992 that the Manipuri language was accorded the status of an official language in the Eighth Schedule of the Indian Constitution.[70] The issue of the Kubaw valley is yet another factor. The valley (spread over some 7000 square miles), historically a part of Manipur, was handed over by the British to Burma as a gesture of goodwill in the aftermath of the signing of the Treaty of Yandaboo in1826. In 1953, Jawaharlal Nehru during a visit with the Burmese premier U Nu, gave up Manipur's claim over it. This decision was not received very well in the troubled state and continues, till this day, to rankle the psyche of significant sections of the Manipuri population. These instances have come to be interpreted as examples of extreme insensitivity and apathy of the central government to Manipuri culture, heritage and sentiments. In recent years, the issue of Bangladeshi and Nepalese migration and the Assamese and Naga irredentism, have also been a source of increasing unrest in the state. Another source of anxiety, is the fear that the territory of Manipur may be radically spilt by the GOI, to accommodate the Greater Nagaland demand of the Naga insurgents.

The turmoil in Manipur, is aggravated by the various 'internal' quarrels between its explosive ethnic mix.[71] The population of the state is broadly divided between those who live in the hills and those who live in the Imphal valley. The Meiteis, the largest ethnic group in the state constituting more than half of the total population, live in the valley which covers only 10 per cent of the state's geographical area.[72] While the hill tribes are classified as scheduled tribes and qualify for reservations in education and government employment, the Meiteis do not.[73] Meiteis argue that the hill tribes have used this unfair advantage to dominate the administrative setup of the state.[74] The insurgency in Nagaland has further complicated the situation in Manipur, with Manipur sharing long and hostile borders with Nagaland. Four hill districts in Manipur have large Naga population and in the past two decades, there has been a growing trend of inter-tribal unrest. As the push for 'Greater Nagaland' has intensified, militant Naga groups have launched violent operations in Manipur claiming almost half the territory of Manipur as part of Nagaland.[75] This has triggered demands for the amendment of the Indian Constitution to guarantee the inviolability of Manipur's borders, much on the lines of guarantee given to Jammu and Kashmir.[76] Another issue providing ammunition to the turmoil is the provision of the Manipur Land and Revenue Regulation Act of 1960, which debars Meiteis from buying land in the hills, while no such restriction exists for the hill people.[77] The politics of recognition that defines and sets the parameter of ethno-nationalism elsewhere in the region, has not left Manipur untouched. It powerfully manifests in contradictory visions of nationhood, between the hill and the valley people. The complexities of the situation, both in cultural and political terms, have clearly resulted in the creation of numerous stakeholders, aggressively contesting for legal and illegal spoils. The situation is exploited to the hilt by rival militant groups aspiring to get a foothold in their identified spaces, for political and material gains. Over the years, these non-state actors have become so indispensable, that even mainstream political actors do not refrain from seeking their services and support in their bid to win electoral battles.

From amongst nearly 40 insurgent groups that have registered their presence in Manipur, as many as 15 are known to be active. Five Muslim militant organizations have emerged to protect the interest of Manipur muslims who constitute around seven per cent of the population of the state.[78] The prominent militant outfits are the United National Liberation Front (UNLF), People's Liberation Army (PLA), People's Revolutionary Party of Kangleipak (PREPAK) (these three groups operate from a unified platform called the Manipur People's Liberation Front), the Kangleipak Communist Party (KCP), People's Republican Army (PRA), the Kanglei Yawol Kunna Lup (KYKL), Hmar People's Convention-Democracy (HPC-D), Kuki Liberation Army (KNA), Kuki National Front (KNF), Kuki Revolutionary Army (KRA), People's United Liberation Front (PULF), United Kuki Liberation Front (UKLF), Zomi Revolutionary Army (ZRA) and the National Socialist Council of Nagaland (NSCN-IM).[79]

Assam

Sharing boundaries with all other states of the region, Assam in a geographical sense, is the core state of North East India. The states of Arunachal Pradesh,

Meghalaya, Mizoram and Nagaland were carved out of Assam in an attempt to address some of the ethnic challenges of the region – mainly to resolve, contain and pre-empt independentist insurgencies. Insurgency in the state primarily emerged out of one main issue i.e. the deportation of illegal immigrants from Bangladesh. The roots of this problem can be traced to the colonial period when for commercial reasons, the administration encouraged migration from thickly populated neighbouring regions as well as from other parts of the country. The establishment of the first tea garden in Assam in 1835, laid the foundation of a thriving tea industry largely oriented towards export. A few decades later, the discovery of oil in Upper Assam resulted in the setting up of the first oil refinery at Digboi in 1890. These developments, generated a pressing need for cheap and easily accessible labour force to work both in the tea plantations and the oil fields. The decision to bring large tracts of unutilized land under cultivation, coupled with the imperative for expanding the communication network in the region, created an even bigger demand for labour. As the labour requirements could not be fulfilled with the available manpower in the state, cheap labour was brought in from Sylhet and Mymensingh districts of East Bengal (present day Bangladesh) and from Bihar, Orissa, the Central Provinces (present day Madhya Pradesh), the United Provinces (present day Uttar Pradesh) and Madras (in Tamil Nadu). The aggressive expansion of commerce necessitated a more direct administrative intervention and by 1857, the region came to be administered directly by the representatives of the British government. The need for educated people to staff the administration resulted in an influx from Bengal, mainly the English educated Bengali to man clerical and lower administrative positions. For the indigenous population, it was clearly a paradoxical situation where opportunities for economic progress came at the cost of dilution of identity.

The partition of the country, only added to the complexities of the situation. Along with the burden of history, it also brought into focus strategic concerns that put heavy pressure on the traditional linkages that had sustained trade and commerce in the region, particularly with present day Bangladesh and Burma. The ethnic, linguistic, religious and economic demarcations, compounded the existing complexities and fueled centrifugal tendencies in more ways than one. Against this background, the issue of unabated influx of population from across the international borders, notably Bangladesh, came to be viewed in the popular perception, as demographic invasion aimed at altering the cultural, linguistic and religious profile of the region. It is noteworthy, that from time to time, powerful movements triggered by popular sentiments, have sought proactive steps to tackle the issue. While some groups have demanded greater autonomy and statehood for preserving their identity, others have aggressively articulated the urgent need for the detection and deportation of illegal immigrants to their country of origin.[80]Protests against the unabated violation of the international borders have manifested in different forms. One such protest movement commenced in 1979, under the leadership of the All Assam Students' Union (ASSU), and lasted six years (1979-85) until an 'accord' was signed between the GOI and the leaders of the movement. Rated as independent India's 'biggest mass uprising', the movement soon turned violent.[81] The fundamental issue raised was the pressing need for 'a national response to what was called a national problem'.[82] The key demands of the agitationists: detection and deportation of foreigners from Assam; deletion of names of foreigners from the electoral rolls; identity cards to bona fide citizens and; constitutional safeguards to Assam, are issues that still dominate and dictate the politics of the state. The Assam Accord between the GOI and the AASU in 1985, however failed to resolve the crisis. The Asom Gana Parishad (AGP), the newly formed regional party that swept the elections to the state legislature in the aftermath of the 'accord', could do precious little to implement the terms of the 'accord'. The task of identifying 'foreigners' proved to be extremely difficult. This, coupled with the judiciary's interference in regard to the revision of the electoral rolls, only added to the complexities of the situation.

Separatist violence in the state is mainly led by the United Liberation Front of Assam (ULFA), an outfit that came into existence in 1979 with the declared goal of leading a full-scale liberation struggle. Within a decade, the group had achieved critical mass in terms of support base, training and organizational infrastructure. Linkages with other ultra organizations in the region and cross border ties were also in place.[83] Rejecting a solution within the constitutional parameters, the group continues to demand sovereign status for Assam, outside the Indian Union.

The problem of separatism in Assam is not specific only to the ULFA. The *Bodos*, a major tribe, believed to be among the earliest settlers in the state, initiated multiple insurgencies on issues ranging from the dispossession of their traditional lands by outside settlers to the marginalization of their language and culture viz-a-viz the dominant Assamese nation.[84] The Bodo assertion, clearly is a multidimensional phenomenon. The contestations that define the parameter of the rebellion are primarily against the Indian State and against the dominance of the Assamese nation. Clash with other peripheral and dominant identities, such as the Adivasi, Bengalis and Kochs have deepened the complexities of the conflict dynamics. In the early years, the Bodo movement, spearheaded by the All Bodo Students' Union (ABSU), found synergy with the AASU led movement in the rest of Assam. The Assam Accord, between the AASU and the GOI proved to be a turning point in the history of the Bodo struggle. The complete exclusion of the Bodo concerns in the 'accord', generated a sense of serious betrayal and thereafter the Bodo movement took a violent turn. Their initial demand for autonomy changed into a demand for an independent state, forcefully articulated by radical groups like the National Democratic Front of Bodoland (NDFB).[85] The signing of the Memorandum of Settlement on 20 February 1993, between the Government of Assam, the ABSU and the Bodo People's Action Committee (BPAC), provided for the setting up of a Bodo Autonomous Council (BAC). However, the nature, extent and degree of powers to be vested in the BAC, became a bone of contention and protests erupted in violent forms. On 10 February 2003, another 'accord' in the form of a tripartite agreement was signed between the GOI, the Government of Assam and the Bodo Liberation Tiger Force (BLTF).[86] As this accord does not have the approval of the NDFB, its fate remains uncertain.

The culture of violence propagated by the ULFA and the Bodos – the key outfits in the state – has led to the mushrooming of 'copycat rebel groups', mobilized along tribal, religious, and cultural fissures. Currently there are over two dozen active insurgent groups listed in the state, the ULFA[87] being the leading player followed by the NDFB and the Bodo Liberation Tigers (BLT). Out of the 37 outfits having presence in the state, the active ones are the NDFB, the ULFA, the Adivasi Cobra Force (ACF), Dima Halim Daogah (DHD), Hmar People's Convention-Democracy (HPC-D), Kamptapur Liberation Organization (KLO), Muslim United Liberation Tigers of Assam (MULTA), the United People's Democratic Solidarity (UPDS), Black Widow, All Adivasi National Liberation Army and Karbi Longri North Cachar Hills (KLNLF).[88]

Tripura

The state of Tripura has international borders along its entire south-western, western, north-western and northern stretch. Contiguous with present day Bangladesh, the princely state of Tripura peacefully acceded to the Indian Union on 13 August 1947 and thereafter chose to fully integrate on 15 October 1949. It was accorded the union territory status on 1 November 1956 and on 21 January 1972, became a full-fledged state of the Indian Union. Similar to Assam, the major problem in Tripura is the changing demographics and its ramifications, conspicuous by the altered ethno- religious profile of the state. In a span of a few decades, the dramatic population shift of Bengali Hindu refugees and migrants from East Pakistan, marginalized the aboriginal hill tribes comprising about twenty-one different groups, including Hindus, Buddhists and Christians, into a minority. The magnitude of the incessant demographic and cultural pressure, had far reaching political consequences resulting in the state's institutions and economic activities becoming the preserve of the non-natives or 'outsiders'. This transformation barely took time and within a few decades, the demographic profile of the state stood completely altered – the percentage of the tribal population shrunk from two-thirds to one-third. The most obvious fallout, of this demographic invasion manifested in the form of land encroachment and alienation, that put a severe strain on the fragile resource base of the state.[89] The compulsions of electoral politics in the post-independence era, encouraged political parties to garner migrant vote bank and the problems thus remained largely unattended. As political control slipped out of the hands of the 'natives', a process of radicalization began. This became evident with the formation of the Tripura Upajati Juba Samity (TUJS) or Tripura Tribals Youth League in June 1967.[90] The TUJS demanded the creation of an autonomous district council under the provisions of the Sixth Schedule of the Constitution, adoption of Kok Borak (the language of the Tripuris) as the official language, restoration of the alienated tribal lands and the overall economic development of the state.

Militancy began in earnest in 1978, with the formation of the Tripura National Volunteer Force (TNVF) and its declaration to win 'Tripura's freedom'. Another tribal militant organization that emerged was the All Tripura People's Liberation Organization (ATPLO). The struggles within the state, both violent and non-violent, revolve mainly around the issues of the restoration of tribal lands, immigration controls, the expulsion of foreigners, and the reservation of seats in the legislative assembly for the tribals. In 1988, a peace accord was signed between TNV and the GOI, which resulted in the TNV agreeing to accept the Indian Constitution and disarm its cadres. The government on its part, promised to take proactive steps to address the core issues fermenting the unrest - alienation of tribal lands and lack of opportunities for gainful employment among the tribal youth. It was hoped that the creation of development centres across the state, would contain further alienation among the tribals. However, for a variety of reasons, militancy continues to flourish and the state has the distinction of being one of the most violent states in the region. With the formation of the All Tripura Tiger's Force (ATTF) in 1989 and the National Liberation Front of Tripura (NLFT) in 1990, two more rebel oufits emerged in the insurgency landscape of the state. In addition, there are over a dozen groups actively offering their services as guns for hire. The insurgency in Tripura that emerged primarily over issues of identity and land alienation, has over the years degenerated into the politics of ethnic cleansing and rampant lawlessness.[91]

Among the two dozen rebel outfits having a presence in the state, the active ones are the All Tripura Tiger Force (ATTF), the National Liberation Front of Tripura (NLFT), Tripura Liberation Organization Front (TLOF), United Liberation Bengali Front (ULBF) and the Borok National Council of Tripura (BNCT).[92]

Spillover Insurgencies in Mizoram, Meghalaya and Arunachal Pradesh

The fallouts of the insurgency inspired violence in the immediate neighbourhood, have significantly impacted the politics in the states of Mizoram, Meghalaya and Arunachal Pradesh. Inter-tribal strife and acrimony against 'outsiders', have led to the emergence of multiple militant outfits, constituted along exclusionary tribal identities. The resultant law and order issues have generated considerable turmoil. The violence, though much lower in intensity compared to other states, mainly targets other ethnic groups or is related to mounting criminal and extortion racquets. Mizoram, clearly is a special case. Peace was restored in 1986, after a 20-year long insurgency, when a settlement was reached between the militant Mizo National Front (MNF) and the GOI, resulting in the granting of full statehood to Mizoram. Subsequently, the MNF got transformed into a regional political party and its leader was appointed the first chief minister of the state.[93] Presently, there are two active militant groups in the state, the Bru National Liberation Front (BNLF) and the Hmar People's Convention-Democracy (HPC-D). The BNLF emerged to defend the interests of the Bru community (also known as Reangs), who are predominantly Hindus and came to Mizoram in the 1950's from the Chittagong Hill Tracts (CHT) in Bangladesh. The assertion of Bru identity assumed disturbing proportion in the late 1990s, leading to severe ethnic clashes resulting in the displacement of thousands of Brus. The Brus feel increasingly persecuted by the mainly Christian Mizos and are demanding an Autonomous District Council within Mizoram.[94] The HPC-D has also been demanding an autonomous status for the 15,000 H'mar's living in Southern Mizoram.[95]

Meghalaya, one of the less troubled state in the region, has been experiencing turbulence since the 1980s, mainly spearheaded by the influential Khasi Students' Union (KSU) and the Federation of Khasi, Jantia and Garo People (FKJGP).[96] The active militant groups in the state are the Achik National Volunteer Council (ANVC), the Hynniewtrep National Liberation Council (HNLC) and the People's Liberation Front of Meghalaya (PLFM).[97]

The state of Arunachal Pradesh, believed to be the 'most peaceful state' in North East India, has its own share of turbulence, much of it, clearly 'spillovers' from the events unfolding in the immediate neighbourhood. While the Assam and Nagaland militants, use the western part of the state bordering Bhutan as hideouts, its eastern flank has emerged as an effective transit route to Burma and also a huge source for extortion, illegal trade and recruitment. The Changlang and Tirap districts of Arunachal Pradesh, located between Nagaland and the northwestern corner of the Burmese Sagaing Division, have fallen prey to the increasing criminalization of the Naga and Assamese ultras.[98] As elsewhere in North East India, Arunachal Pradesh is also witnessing the consolidation of the Arunachalese identity, which more often than not manifest as struggles against the non-indigenous populations, the representatives of the GOI and the immigrants, particularly the Chakma and Hajong refugees. An important militant outfit in the state is the Arunachal Dragon Force (ADF), formed in 1996.[99]

Small Conflicts

A distinct feature of the conflict dynamics in North East India is the makeover of the dominant ethnic movements, shaped around the struggle for greater political space, into 'hegemons' over the smaller ethnic groups. This has resulted in the proliferation of ethnic conflicts between the dominant and minority communities, living within the same space.[100] The strategy of the dominant to discipline the smaller groups, thus prepares the ground for the emergence of innumerable smaller conflicts most of it in retaliation to the domination. A striking fallout is the manifestation of a psychology that perceives the 'other' in the vicinity responsible for all problems. The mindset gets manifested in brutal acts of violence, that is more often a calculated strategy to gain greater visibility for the group and its cause.[101] In this war of the 'insiders' against the 'insiders', chauvinist mythmaking plays a significant role. According to Boyd Shafer, such mythmaking is a hallmark of nearly all ethno-national movements and primarily manifest in three ways: 'self-glorifying', 'self-whitewashing', and 'other maligning'.[102] The outcome manifests as endless narratives of bloodshed with more and more indigenous communities getting sucked into it. The reasons range from language to politics over territory and resources. The clash between the Karbis and Dimasas tribes in Assam's Karbi Anglong district, is an example of turf war that has plagued the region in recent times.[103] Another ethnic battleground has been Manipur, where thousands of people were killed between 1992 and 1998 in the Naga-Kuki clashes and the Kuki-Paitte violence. In both cases the clashes were over the control of land and extortion areas. Tripura has its own share of ethnic flare-ups, between tribal and non-tribal groups. In Mizoram, the Mizos and Brus are locked in gory battles, resulting in largescale migration of Brus to the neighbouring state of Tripura.[104] The mismatch between ethnic and the geographical boundaries, clearly widens the area of the conflict and results in a scenario where no state in the region is free from militancy. As a natural corollary, the all prevailing turmoil propels a string of new violent insurgencies, on a regular basis that profoundly impacts the course of insurgent politics.

An appraisal of the ethnic assertions in the region, powerfully drives home the point that apprehensions about the loss of identity remains the primary motivating force behind most of the uprisings. A feeling of neglect and dispossession resulting from the national decision-making process in the Centre, where the region figures only remotely, also fuels the logic for resentment.[105] The basic issues reverberating in the entire region, as aptly highlighted by an observer, are 'land, migration and fears of loss of identity' – insecurities that provide the ideological shield for the most brutal crimes committed against humanity.[106]

Cross-border Linkages

Post-partition, the geopolitics of South Asia altered drastically and India found itself flanked by hostile neighbours, fiercely competing for a share in the geopolitical space. Wedged between a rising People's Republic of China in the northern flank and a hostile East Pakistan on the eastern side, India's situation was clearly unenviable. Tensions on the north-western frontiers, loudly resonated in the east and given the history of India's uneasy relationship with most of its neighbours, North East India emerged as a theatre for foreign involvement. The ultra groups of the region, found willing patrons in the immediate vicinity, as they waged a protracted war against the Indian State. In due course, the territories of Burma, Bangladesh, Bhutan and Nepal also got involved in anti-India campaigns. Weak internal controls combined with fragile border controls, aided cross border connections that mainly manifested in financial and organizational support, weapons supply, training, operational co-operation, smuggling of arms and drugs and also movement of population. With 98 per cent of the borders of the region being international, the task of establishing linkages proved to be relatively simple. In this regard, it is significant that the timing of some major insurgencies in the region almost coincided with India's wars with China and Pakistan in 1962 and 1965 respectively.

The China Factor

China's ideological and technical support to the North East ultras, is believed to date back to the 1950s. However, it was only after the 1962 war with India over contested borders, that China's involvement in the region became more unconcealed.[107] Destabilizing India, by undermining the fragile ethnic framework of its northeastern frontiers, perfectly served China's strategic objective of containing India within the natural boundaries of South Asia, i.e. within the Himalayas and the Indian Ocean. There is sufficient evidence to suggest, that over the years, China has successfully consolidated its presence in and around North East India. The growing Chinese influence in Burma and in the Indian Ocean, since the late 1980s, especially after the Junta assumed power in that country in 1988, has direct bearing on the turbulence obtaining in North East India.[108] In this regard, it is significant that China's three largest arms clients are Pakistan, Burma and Bangladesh. Confessions of surrendered militants reveal, that ultra groups in both Assam and Nagaland have received major arms consignments from China.[109]

Apart from the Nagas, the Chinese have also extended moral and material support to Mizo and Meiti insurgents of Mizoram and Manipur respectively. There are reports to suggest that the Naga militants have a liaison office in Chinese territory, across the borders with Arunachal Pradesh. Naga liaison officers are believed to be based in Kunmin (the capital of Yunan province of China, geographically located closest to North East India) and in Lhasa (Tibet), and it is understood that Naga cadres have established contacts with the Yunanese military intelligence.[110] The ULFA rebels are also known to have crossed over to China via Bhutan in the 1990s, to negotiate arms deal. Confessional statements of surrendered ULFA militants, have revealed close military interactions between the outfit and China. The Chittagong arms haul of April 2004, a major arms seizure in Bangladesh, exposed the intricacies of the Chinese, NSCN (IM) and ULFA linkages.[111]

Although observers believe, that over the years, China's strategic priorities in South Asia have visibly shifted from a position of blatant hostility towards

India to 'passive hostility', there are indications to suggest that ties between China and the North Eastern insurgent and criminal outfits are not dormant. With critical differences between India and China still remaining unresolved, India's apprehensions about Chinese intentions in the region, continue to be a cause of strategic concern.[112] From time to time, the Indian political establishment has candidly articulated concerns over security issues emanating from China and taken extremely serious view on Chinese political positions and claims in regard to matters concerning the borders.[113]

Pakistan

The fierce rivalry between India and Pakistan, as manifested in three full fledged wars (1947-48, 1965 and 1971) and serious escalations (the Kargil conflict of 1999 and the 2002 mobilization of forces on the borders), have over the years been waged in different ways and at different theatres. North East India, did not remain untouched from the fallouts of the animosity between the two South Asian neighbours. As events unfolded, it became clear that India's sensitive and extensive north-eastern frontiers figured hugely in Pakistan's strategic calculations against India. In his book, 'The Myth of Independence', the one time Prime Minister, Zulfikar Ali Bhutto wrote:

> One (of the problems) at least is nearly as important as the Kashmir dispute; that of Assam and some districts of India adjacent to East Pakistan. To these, East Pakistan has very good claims, which should not have been allowed to remain quiescent ... The eviction of Indian Muslims into East Pakistan and the disputed borders of Assam and Tripura should not be forgotten.[114]

Bhutto, in his book, was openly supportive of a policy that would cement a special relationship with the non-Hindu population of Assam, until the wrong about Assam being an integral part of India could be undone. Observers have often construed Bhutto's forthright views, as an open confession of Pakistan's designs of converting Assam into a Muslim majority state by engineering demographic invasions. However, there is an underlying deeper context to Pakistan's involvement in the region, given its history of hostility with India. The tactical effort, clearly aims at securing a favourable balance of power, by pinning down the Indian armed forces within the Indian soil and successfully creating 'systemic crisis' across India, particularly in 'its borderlands'.[115] It is noteworthy, that Pakistan was the first nation to offer moral and material assistance to the nascent ethno-nationalist separatist movements that emerged in the political landscape of North East India, starting with the establishment of the Naga National Council in 1956.[116] Pakistan's role in internationalizing the Naga cause was also crucial.[117] The Mizo insurgents, united under the banner of the Mizo National Front (MNF), also found constructive support from Pakistan.[118] Though the emergence of Bangladesh in 1971, with active Indian support, proved to be a setback for the Naga and Mizo separatists, it did not deter them from traveling to West

Pakistan and strengthening their linkages with that country. Ties were also strengthened with the Burmese Communist Party, and as a result a conduit to the Yunan province of China was made available through the Kachin passage.[119] The Chinese overt support to the Naga and Mizo rebels, encouraged Pakistan to design a strategy of linking separatist outfits of North East India under a 'joint command'. The strategy was largely geared to even up Pakistan's loses in Kashmir, by encouraging turmoil in the troubled north-eastern frontiers of India and consequently weakening India's internal security system.[120] This clearly meant, the expansion of the scope of activities of Pakistan's Inter Services Intelligence (ISI) in the region.[121] ISI's support to elements antagonistic to the Indian State, mainly manifest in the form of supply of arms and ammunitions, research developed high explosives (RDX), technical advise, training as well as arranging transborder sanctuaries.

The covert operations of the ISI in the region, increased manifold during the 1980s. Reports suggest that the ISI was instrumental in operating training camps in Bangladesh, where separatist rebels of the North East, collectively know as the 'United Liberation Front of Seven Sisters' were trained in subversive activities. The included groups were, the National Socialist Council of Nagaland, People's Liberation Army, the National Liberation Front of Tripura, the United Liberation Front of Assam and the National Democratic Front of Bodoland.[122]

Some ULFA cadres are believed to have been trained directly by Pakistani soldiers and the Mujahideen in the Afghanistan-Pakistan border areas.[123] ISI's subversive activities are widespread and include: overt and covert financial and material support to the local militia; indiscriminate violence against civilians; creation of new ultra outfits along ethnic and communal lines; provide logistical support to ultra groups such as fake passports, visa and other documents; deliver weapons and counterfeit currency; engage and encourage drug transfer and trade; sabotage oil and gas pipelines and other key installations, communication lines, railways and roads and; accentuate communal cleavages by way of disinformation campaigns.[124] In this endeavour, the role of the 'resident agents' in providing reconnaissance support is particularly crucial.[125] Much of ISI's terror activities, through skillful coordination, have been outsourced to the local groups in the region. Towards this objective, it has not hesitated to tap the resources of Islamic financial and educational institutions, as well as those of other non-governmental bodies.[126] The mushrooming of the Islamic fundamentalist groups in the region, is believed to be the direct outcome of the ISI's patronage and support.

Bangladesh

The creation of Bangladesh in 1971, contrary to Indian expectations, only marginally altered the hostile international environment around North East India. The assassination of Mujibur Rahman, the first President of Bangladesh, once again altered the ground situation in favour of the North East insurgents and the successive regimes in Bangladesh have not been averse to supporting the Indian ultras.[127] The presence of Indian rebels in Bangladesh, has been a major irritant in the bilateral ties between India and Bangladesh. In his memoirs, India's former Foreign Secretary late J.N. Dixit writes:

> We had reliable information that ULFA and some Bodos were being provided sanctuary and bases by Bangladesh intelligence authorities, who in turn, were being guided by the Inter Services Intelligence of Pakistan. We had sufficient details of the mechanisms and sources through which these separatists were being financed at Dhaka. I personally conveyed this information to the Bangladesh Foreign Secretary and Home Secretary during my two bilateral visits to Dhaka between the second half of 1992 and end of 1993 ... Their response were always non-committal and bland apart from proforma denials.[128]

Viewed in the context of increased engagement between China and Bangladesh and the revival of the ISI networks, the presence of North East ultras in Bangladesh is a serious cause of concern to the Indian security establishment. A report aptly puts the scenario in perspective. It states:

> China's role as a defence education provider has also been on the rise in South Asia, a region traditionally dominated by India. The rise of anti-Indian sentiment in Bangladesh, coupled with the rise of Islamic fundamentalism, has led the Bangladeshi government to seek closer ties with China. In the past few years, literally hundreds of Bangladeshi officers graduated from PLA educational institutions. China is currently the main supplier of weapons to its armed forces, supplying it with frigates, fighter jets, tanks, armoured personnel carriers and other equipments sold at "friendly prices".[129]

Bangladesh clearly has emerged as an important patron of the North East rebel groups. Several reports point to the presence of militant camps and hideouts in that country, with over a hundred camps located in the border areas alone. The camps, run by the prominent North East ultra groups, are more than safe havens. They are known to facilitate arms shipments in transit to India.[130]

India believes that the ISI and Bangladesh's security establishment, the Directorate General of Forces Intelligence (DGFI), work in coordination in backing North East rebels and in propping jihadi groups in the region.[131] The support comes in the form of financial assistance, ideological indoctrination and logistic backup.[132] The anti-India operations of these two intelligence agencies, is believed to be largely facilitated by the overwhelming presence of the illegal immigrant Bangladeshi population, in and around the porous borders between Bangladesh and the Indian states of Assam, West Bengal, Mizoram, Tripura and Meghalaya. For the insurgents, it makes strategic sense to have bases in Bangladesh as it provides them proximity to the Cox Bazaar port – the key receiving point of weapon consignments shipped from the black markets of South East Asia. A factor believed to have played a role in the proliferation of militant bases in Bangladesh, has been the growing ties between the Research and Analysis Wing (RAW) – the Indian Intelligence Agency – and the Burmese rebel groups such as the Kachin Independence Army (KIA), the Chin National Front (CNF) and the National Unity Party of Arakans (NUPA). The objective of forging these ties have primarily been strategic – of denying a corridor to the North East insurgents. In response to this development (in the mid-1990s), rebel bases in both Bangladesh and Bhutan emerged in a big way. North East insurgents are also known to have hired safe houses in a number of cities and towns of Bangladesh, such as Dhaka, Chittagong and Sylhet. The National Liberation Front of Tripura (NLFT), is believed to be the second largest insurgent group present in Bangladesh. Some Manipuri outfits are also based in Bangladesh.

The issue of militant bases in Bangladesh, figured prominently in the talks between the Indian Prime Minister Manmohan Singh and the then Bangladesh Prime Minister Khaleda Zia, during the March 2006 New Delhi visit of Khaleda Zia. India expects Bangladesh to emulate the examples of Bhutan and Burma and clear rebel bases from its territory.[133]

Burma (Myanmar)

Bordering the Indian states of Arunachal Pradesh, Manipur and Mizoram, in and around the lightly administered areas of Burma, separatist camps are known to exist.[134] The historical-cultural affinities, between groups on both sides of the borders, facilitate forging of linkages that prove valuable to the Indian rebels in their war against the Indian State. Rebel groups, notably the Nagas, the Mizos, the Meitis and the Tripuris, have found training facilities and safe havens in Burma with relative ease. The Kachins of North Burma have for long been suppliers and trainers to the Nagas and a host of other North Eastern ultras, notably the ULFA, the PREPAK from Manipur and the PLA from Tripura. This association has helped the Indian rebels in more ways than one. It provides them with easy access to the arms market of Cambodia, besides making them stakeholders in the lucarative drug trade.[135] The location of the region on the western corner of Burma's infamous Golden Triangle, one of the two largest opium producing regions in the world, naturally attracts the rebels into the drug trade. According to the International Narcotics Control Bureau (INCB) report, countries around the Golden Triangle, particularly Burma produce more than 70 per cent of the amphetamines available globally.[136] This explains, the routing of the drug channels from the Golden Triangle to North East India.[137] The Burmese rebel groups, KIA, the Burmese Communist Party (BCP), and the Arakan Liberation Party (ALP) have developed linkages with Indian rebel groups such as NSCN and ULFA. Drugs are brought upto Tamu in the Indo-Burma border and also the Bangladesh-Burma border, under the protection of Burmese ultras, where from the North Eastern insurgent groups and Bangladesh syndicates take over and push the drugs further inland.

The porous Indo-Burma border is eminently suitable for the free movement of insurgent groups as well as contraband. The free passage between the border towns of Moreh in Manipur and Tamu in Burma, facilitate the process. It is believed that the ultras on both sides of the border, control the entire illicit traffic on the Ledo road, between Assam and the Yunan province of China. Ethnic connectivity as well as shared underground economic interests, sustain the mutually beneficial illegal enterprise. Collusion, complicity and inefficiency of security personnels on both sides, are other contributory factors that integrate North East India into the network of regional drug trafficking.[138]

The 'rebel factor', profoundly impacts the political and security environment of North East India and has emerged as the most significant issue in India-Burma relationship.[139] Over the years, the bases in Burma have served important functions for the North East rebels: offered sanctuaries particularly after the bifurcation of Pakistan; served as a crucial contact point between the rebels and China for weapon procurement and training and; emerged as a regrouping and guerrilla warfare training zone for new recruits.[140] Though in the past one decade, ties between India and Burma have improved considerably and security irritants such as cross-border terrorism, narcotic trade and arms smuggling have figured highly on the official agenda of the two countries, given the nature of the deep-rooted cultural, economic and political interconnections in the peripheries of the two nations, it is unlikely for solutions to emerge anytime soon .[141]

Thailand, Nepal and Bhutan

Thailand is another country in India's extended neighbourhood, frequently visited by the North East militants – the attraction mainly being the thriving underground arms bazaar, located in the Three Pagoda Pass opposite the Karen state of Burma and the Ranong coast adjoining the Tenasserim Division of the country. These areas, close to the loosely administered Burmese borders, provide convenient routes for gun running. The NSCN was the first group to establish its presence in Thailand in 1987. Thereafter, several ULFA activists traveled to Thailand to negotiate arms deal. Some leaders of the ultra groups have also established commercial interests in the Thai capital.[142]

Besides Thailand, Bhutan and Nepal, in varying degrees, have found themselves sucked into the matrix of North East insurgency. The North East separatist groups, have used the territories of these two countries as safe havens and transit corridors. Bhutan, strategically positioned between China and the Brahmaputra valley of Assam, till very recently was an important base for the militants. In view of its porous borders, weak security forces and the formidable strength of the militants', Bhutan got embroiled into the turbulence affecting the region. Militant camps were in operation since 1992.[143] The counter-insurgency operations launched by the Indian security forces against the ULFA in 1991 and 1992, forced them to establish bases in Bhutan. Later the ULFA was joined by the NDFB and KLO. It is estimated that by 2003, an estimated

3000 militants, representing major and minor groups including criminal gangs, were residing in Bhutan.[144] On 15 December 2003, under pressure from the Indian Government and also to reinforce the Kingdom's sovereignty that was being openly challenged by the ultras, the Royal Bhutanese Army launched a military offensive named 'Operation All Clear'.[145] The Operation, which lasted for over two weeks, resulted in the killing of about 200 militants and the surrender of over 500. However, several hundred militants managed to escape through the porous borders to Bangladesh, Burma and even China. Some of them even managed to enter Arunachal Pradesh in India. It is believed that the militants have once again regrouped and have established some bases in Bhutan, though their strength has been considerably weakened.[146] There are also reports suggesting, that some of the camps have been relocated in Nepal with the help of the Nepalese Maoists.[147]

Of all the insurgent groups, the Nagas have been the most active in enlisting foreign support. Besides Pakistan, China, and Bangladesh, the Nagas have developed links with insurgents in Burma as well as the Liberation Tigers of Tamil Eelem (LTTE) in Sri Lanka. There are reports indicating that the NSCN (IM) has maintained offices in Bangladesh, Nepal, Pakistan, Singapore, Sweden and Thailand. From time to time, the NSCN (K), a rival to the NSCN (IM), has used Bangladesh and Upper Burma to regroup militarily. As a part of the peace process, on several occasions, Indian leaders have met with Naga leaders abroad – a clear pointer to the formidable external linkages of the outfit.[148]

The role of umbrella organizations as coordinating agencies, forging alliances and strategic combines between disparate ultra groups, both within the region and across, is significant to the conduct of insurgency in the region. Issues in regard to the security of insurgent bases, finances, transit corridors, arms supply and training, fall within the purview of these coordinating bodies. Bereft of ideology, these organizations create their own dynamics that profoundly impact the course of insurgent politics in the region. By forging mutually beneficial links between large and small groups, within the same theatre of conflict and across theatres, these organizations provide a semblance of stability in an environment that is permanently in flux.[149] The first umbrella organization to be established in the region was the Indo-Burma Revolutionary Front (IBRF), formed in May 1990 by the ULFA, the NSCN, the United National Liberation Front of Manipur (UNLFM) and some Burmese rebels. The name clearly signified its sphere of operations and the areas that its constituents proposed to unify – the North Eastern States of India and North Western Burma.[150] In 1993, a wider insurgent network including all the North East states came into existence, with the formation of the National Liberation Front of the Seven Sisters (NLFSS). This organization underwent a transformation in 1994, to become the Self-Defence United Front of the South East Himalayan Region (SDUFSHR).[151]

Arms Supply

Similar to other parts of the world inflicted with ethnic conflicts, the acquisition of illegal small arms and light weapons by ultra outfits, is a vital factor in the conduct and duration of the conflict in North East India.[152] Easy availability of the same, aided by the region's geo-political contiguity to Burma and South-East Asia, is a critical factor that encourage rebel groups, across the spectrum, to adopt militant postures against the Indian State. In 1956, when the Naga separatists, clearly the most heavily armed group in North East India, started their violent campaigns, their weapon stock comprised mainly of the World War II weapons left behind by the Japanese and the Allied forces.[153] Subsequently, supplies from Pakistan and China augmented the stock. The role of Burmese rebels, notably the Kachins, in providing weapons, training, sanctuary and access to the clandestine arms market of South East Asia was particularly significant.[154] By the mid 1980s, as active Chinese support started dwindling, the rebels started exploring the black markets of South East Asia. India's effort at cultivating the Kachins, to deny the North East separatists the corridor to reach China, is believed to be a contributory factor that pushed the rebels to look for alternative channels for uninterrupted weapon supply. The market, that mainly emerged after the fall of the Khmer Rouge, was first accessed by the LTTE and subsequently the NSCN, the ULFA, the Bodo, the Manipuri and Tripuri militants gained access to it.[155] Thereafter, arms from this market found its way to different parts of North East India. The role of the LTTE, in regard to gun running in the region is particularly noteworthy. There is sufficient evidence to suggest that they are actively engaged in weapon transfers through the high seas, in self owned cargo vessels, braving detection by the Indian and Sri Lankan naval patrol guards.[156] The LTTE operated training camps are known to exist in the Burmese jungles, particularly in the Arakan state and Sagaing Division. These camps are the trading point where drugs are swapped for weapons.[157] It is noteworthy, that the LTTE has successfully utilized the presence of the Tamil population residing in India's North East, to establish contact with the local militia in need of arms. It is believed, that the over 17,000 Tamils living in the vicinity of Moreh in Manipur and also across Burma, have control over the legitimate as well as the smuggling trade of the area.[158]

Towards the end of 1990s, another significant source of weapons supply had been successfully tapped by the North East insurgents – the Yunan mafia. The mafia, with access to Chinese state run ordinance factories, has emerged as active players in the illegal arms trade. The fact that these weapons are priced much lower than the ones procured from Thailand, has found favour among the North East ultras.[159] According to Indian intelligence reports, the ULFA has become a major conduit for these arms to a host of client rebel groups not just in the North East but also in other parts of South Asia, ranging from the Nepali and Indian Maoists to the Jihadis in Bangladesh.[160] The weapons are transported through land and sea routes – through Burmese territory and through the Bay of Bengal on trawlers. Thailand's flourishing underground arms bazaar, located in the Three Pagoda Pass area opposite Karen state in Burma, offers weapons of every description – from assault rifles of the Automatic Kalashnikov (AK) series, M-16 type of weapons and ammunitions, Chinese hand-grenades, Cambodian and Vietnamese landmines, rocket launchers and communication material. The weapons purchased from this market are trans-shipped from Southern Thailand via the Three Pagoda Pass and the Rangong coastline, by Burmese insurgents in fishing vessels, through Andaman sea to Cox Bazaar in Bangladesh – a port that has emerged as a major supply point of illegal arms.[161] From here, the arms are routed to destinations in Burma and North East India, through different routes. The Naga Hills in Burma's Chin state, adjoining Manipur and Mizoram, is one of the prominent routes through which arms sneak into North East India. Some of the arms move up the CHT and enter India through Tripura, Assam, Meghalaya and Nagaland. It is noteworthy that Shillong, the capital of Meghalaya and Dimapur in the Assam-Kohima border, have emerged as important chains in this underground arms network. Besides smuggled arms, country-made weapons also contribute towards the proliferation in a significant way.

The global origins of the weapons in the inventory of the North Eastern insurgents, reveal the massive spread of the networks involved in the procurement and delivery of the same. The weapons come from countries such as China, Pakistan, Belgium, Thailand, Russia, United States of America, United Kingdom, Czechoslovakia, Afghanistan, Bangladesh, Cambodia, Burma and even Israel. South Asian militant and extremist groups, criminal groups operating elsewhere in India, pilferage from legal gun and ordinance factories, are some other sources that augment the supply.[162] Although the factors dictating the choice of weapons vary from group to group, the primary factor remains flexibility in the face of varying tactics adopted by the security agencies battling them. AK-47s, 56s, M-16s and G-3s are the most common weapons in use. Semi-automatic rifles, such as the M-21 and self-loading rifles, including .303 calibre weapons, Russian Dragunov sniper rifles, have also been in usage. Captured government stocks of FN-MAG machine guns, RPG-7s and 57mm RCL M18 anti-tank weapons are some other weapons. Improvised explosive devices, mines, rocket propelled grenades, rocket launchers and Chinese hand grenades are also a part of the arsenal.[163]

Although most of the rebel groups have established separate networks with arms suppliers, the entire project, right from the ordering stage to its delivery and collection involves the active participation of several actors. Autonomous mafia modules are the mainstay of these networks. Large arms collections are believed to be joint operations between the concerned insurgent group on the Indian side and rebel groups across the borders. The role of the Chin National Front Army, the Arakan Revolutionary Front and the Kachin Independence Army in Burma, particularly stand out. The region's inhospitable topography, its ever-changing porous borders, geographical proximity to South East Asia and presence of anti-India elements, are other factors that aid the proliferation of illegal small arms and light weapons.[164]

Interwined to the proliferation of arms in the region is the issue of narco-insurgency. The long international borders of North East India, touching several nations and running through difficult porous terrain, makes the problem insurmountable. The success of the drug syndicate in effectively roping within its fold wide sections of the society, ranging from politicians, insurgents, common citizens and even security personnel, prove beyond doubt the deep rooted nature of problem.[165] The 1,643 kms Burmese border with India, stretching through dense forests, is impossible to patrol. The National Highway 39 (that runs through both Imphal and Dimapur), lying at the intersection of Burma, Thailand and Laos, is precariously close to Asia's notorious Golden Triangle.[166] From here, heroin is trafficked into Manipur and then to other parts of India and abroad. Smugglers have the option of shipping unprocessed opium to laboratories near the border, where they get easily processed at very low costs.[167] The International Narcotics Control Board (INCB) has identified the North Eastern States of Mizoram, Manipur and Nagaland as extremely fragile areas along the drug trafficking route.[168] Officials of the Narcotics cell and Customs enforcement in Manipur believe that most of the trafficking is done by cross-border tribes like the Kuki, Chin and Zomi, who have access to both India and Burma. Besides the commercial value, drugs are also used as an effective instrument to acquire control over rival tribal groups.[169] Drug peddling and control of the drug corridors, thus have become a major preoccupation of the insurgent outfits. Interestingly, many ultra groups in the region, including some prominent ones, have taken tough public posturing against drug peddlers and abusers, declaring drugs to be a grave social menace.[170]

In recent years, synthetic drugs like methmphetamines, including ecstasy, produced in Burma have found significant markets in the North East.[171] There are reports suggesting that ephedra, a medicinal plant legally cultivated in Arunachal Pradesh, is illegally exported to Burma to be converted into Amphetamine Type Stimulant tablets (ATS), in private transportable laboratories. The increasing seizure of these tablets by the Indian security agencies on the Indo-Burma border, is a pointer to the popularity of this drug.[172] With most of the North East insurgents drawing their strategic and tactical inspiration from across the borders, notably from Burma, the benefits of involving full time into the drug trade network is an attractive venture. However, the fallouts of drug trafficking in the region are too telling to be ignored. According to the Indian Council of Medical Research (ICMR), the region's drug addict population is estimated at round 1, 20,000. The 2006

Report of the United Nations Office on Drug and Crime (UNODC) states, that the use of drugs in the region has reached an 'epidemic proportion'. In the last three decades, the method of drug use has changed – from smoking cannabis and opium to injecting drugs. The addicts have taken to injecting dextropropoxyphene, a synthetic powder that is emptied from spasmopropoxyphene or proxyvon capsules, procured from medicine shops. While the use of dextropropoxyphene is common in Mizoram and Nagaland, the injecting drug users in Manipur are hooked to heroin. Cannabis users are common in Assam, Meghalaya and Tripura. With addicts using intravenous injections to push drugs, the number of HIV positive cases in the region has risen drastically. Ethnic separatists taking to drug trade, are also known to encourage tribal farmers to cultivate poppy, particularly in parts of Arunachal Pradesh, Manipur, Nagaland and Assam. In the absence of gainful agricultural alternatives, the likelihood of the region falling prey to poppy cultivation cannot be ruled out. Much like the broad geography of the region and the diverse range of drugs in circulation, the people involved in this trade are equally diverse. Politicians, merchants, professional criminals and even ordinary folks are chains in this vast commercial enterprise, predominantly defined on ethnic, religious, linguistic and cultural lines. In recent times, items such as gems and cannabis have found a place in the smuggling list, with Burma being one of the world's richest sources of precious stones.[173]

Terrorism as Criminal Enterprise

The prevailing insurgency environment in the region, encourages and sustains the creation of a powerful well entrenched subterranean economy, that generates complex intersections which impinge the course of politics in the region. The consequences are serious and is mainly evident in the form of weak enforcement of law and order, mainly resulting from the subversion and hijacking of state institutions. The 'terrorist economy', characterized by complex nexus between armed rebel outfits and organized criminal groups, is sufficiently powerful to subjugate and subvert the legitimate economy of the region. The maintenance of a terror enterprise, run by over 100 insurgent groups, is a costly affair that clearly demands an uninterrupted supply of funds.[174] Given the extremely narrow ethnic character of most rebel outfits, there is no scope for diaspora support. This creates a compelling need to generate resources within the region, and thus provides the logic for the extensive spread of resource generating criminal activities across North East India. Institutionalized as the underground 'parallel economy', these activities thrive on extortion racquets, kidnappings for ransom, drug and gun running, 'tax collection' and siphoning of development funds through intimidation or collusion with the implementing state authorities. So pervasive is its spread, that even corporate houses and state institutions have come around its pattern of operations. The all pervading poverty, combined with slow economic growth, inadequate unemployment opportunities, particularly for the educated youth and the crisis of governance, create a favourable context for non-state actors, including militant groups, to seize and consolidate their legitimacy.[175]

The progressive erosion of the state authority, mainly reflected in the government's inability or perceived inability to protect the life and property of its citizens, to enforce the ordinary laws of the land (starkly evident from the excessive reliance on extra-ordinary laws), to carry out its financial responsibilities with credibility and to enforce compliance among its employees, provides ample scope for the ultras to take over as providers of 'critical' services in their zones of influence. In this regard, it is noteworthy that state interventions - both military and developmental - have not been wanting. However, for a host of reasons it has failed to have the desired effect. Deep-rooted administrative decline in the afflicted state, infiltration of militant sympathizers in the state police and administrative machinery, and the perception of the security forces being the 'oppressive occupiers', prove to be major stumbling blocks.[176] The easy passage to safe sanctuaries across the porous borders, enable militants to lie low and wait for an opportune time to regroup and re-emerge after the army operations have subsided. The developmental interventions have proved to be equally inadequate in arresting the turmoil in the region, and in creating an investment friendly environment conducive to economic development. In a scenario of near complete administrative collapse, devoid of accountability and transparency, funds meant for development conveniently flow into the coffers of the rebels, through a mutually reinforcing collusive arrangement with the legitimate power elites. The devastating affect of this collusion, inhibits the emergence of a legitimate economy and results in swift exodus of capital from the region. Developmental targets, as a rule, are never achieved and given the unacceptable risks confronted by local officials in executing these projects, there is a clear lack of initiative and commitment.[177]

The techniques of fund mobilization follow a familiar pattern in almost every theatre of conflict, with 'cooperation and competition' with the existing state administration being its defining features. With the rebels actively making money out of state sponsored welfare projects, the slogan of 'dismantling' or 'replacing' the state apparatus is more of rhetoric. One clear example is the illegal proceeds earned (running into millions of Indian Rupees) from the subversion of the Public Distribution System (PDS), through the diversion of commodities meant for the weaker sections of the society into the open market.[178] Controlling and levying 'toll tax' on vehicles plying on the major routes running through the region, is another resource generating venture. With groups having demarcated their respective zones of influence on the highways, such taxes are levied at several points.[179] The hold of the militants on virtually every illegal trade and its routes - drugs and arms - is an established fact, and significantly follows the same course as the route for Acquired Immune Deficiency Syndrome (AIDS). The increasing incidence of AIDS in the region has become a serious health issue, closely connected with drug abuse. It is noteworthy, that about 30 per cent of intravenous drug users (IDU) reside in North East India alone. This is a big number, considering the fact that the total population of the region is around 3.8 per cent of India's population.[180] Besides health, the insurgency environment has also adversely impacted the fragile *eco-system* of the region, mainly resulting from the destruction of precious forest cover for setting up militant hideouts and camps. Wild life parks and sanctuaries, with its endangered flora and fauna, have borne the brunt of such assaults. Poachers in league with militants are involved in wildlife contraband in Assam's world famous Kaziranga sanctuary, home to the endangered one horned rhino.[181] Militants are also known to have established sanctuaries in the Manas Reserve Forests and the Manas Game Sanctuary in lower Assam, from where they move into the contiguous border areas of Bhutan.[182]

Extortion, levying of 'taxes' and protection money on corporate houses, businessmen and salaried class, is another significant resource generating channel that funds the terror enterprise in North East India. So pervasive is its hold and reach that no section of the society has escaped its grip – migrants, non-tribals and even indigenous people. Tea gardens, public sector enterprises such as the Oil and Natural Gas Corporation (ONGC), Oil India Limited (OIL), North Eastern Electric Power Corporation (NEEPCO), Bongaigoan Refineries and Petrochemical Limited (BRPL) and even the Indian Railways have come under the extortion net. In some states, the spread has so impacted the day to day political and social life, that the local administration stands completely paralyzed. Contracts are secured at gunpoint and development projects get stalled mid-way, mainly due to the inability of the administration to cope with the pressure and intimidation of the militants.[183] Another noteworthy trend defining the criminal enterprise is the practice of outsourcing criminal activities by bigger outfits to the smaller ones. The profits get shared, the proportion varies depending upon the nature of linkages and the extent of dependence of the smaller groups on the larger ones.[184] A decent chunk of the resources thus generated, get diverted into legitimate businesses such as construction and transport, travel agencies and the hospitality business. However, the actual beneficiaries of these businesses are the top rung leaders, who generally reside and direct their 'freedom struggles' from outside India.[185] Examples abound in each state of increasing criminality, extortion drive, indiscriminate violence, individual rackets, morality campaigns and fratricidal clashes. The trajectory of the terror discourse in Manipur,[186] Assam[187] and Nagaland,[188] clearly the most violent states in the region, present interesting insights.

The states of Arunachal Pradesh, Meghalaya and Mizoram, have not remained untouched by the increasing criminalization of the outfits of

Nagaland, Manipur and Assam. The Tirap and Changlang districts of Arunachal Pradesh, the main gateways to Burma, have become important centres for illegal trade and recruitment.[189] Groups like the Hynniewtrep National Liberation Council (HNLC) and the A'chik Liberation Matgrik Army (ALMA), spearhead the criminal drive in Meghalaya. These outfits run an extensive underground domain, specializing in the smuggling of counterfeit currency and extortion, that mainly target businessmen, members of rival tribes, government and army officials, as well as immigrant workers.[190] The prospects, of making easy money has given birth to many smaller militant outfits, such as the Retrieval Indigenous Unified Front (RIUF), the Hynniewtrep National Special Red Army (HNSRA) and the People's Liberation Front of Meghalaya (PLF-M), to name a few.[191]

The relatively peaceful state of Mizoram has emerged as a turf for both nacro-terrorism and gun running.[192] The southernmost part of the state, often referred as the 'tri-junction' due to its close proximity to the 'no man's land' of Indo-Burma-Bangladesh border, has become a haven for militants and gun runners having easy access to Bangladesh's Cox Bazaar, from where arms are smuggled into the state. Close proximity to the infamous Golden Triangle, provides easy access to drugs and has generated huge illegal business opportunities for militants not just in Mizoram but all over the region.[193] In Tripura, the terror network has spread its tentacles both in urban and rural areas. The operations range from abduction, murder, extortion and sex trade. There are reports that suggest the involvement of ultra groups in pornography and trafficking of women. Women from the region, are believed to be supplied via Burma to Thailand to work in sex parlours.[194]

Although the state agencies are seen locked in battling the ultras, in the contemporary politics of the region, the nexus between the mainstream politicians and the militants is far too entrenched to go unnoticed.[195] Elections are won and lost depending on the predisposition of parties towards the ultras. Political parties of every hue, need the ultras to influence the outcome of the elections. Militants get involved both ways: either to help one candidate win or to ensure the defeat of another.[196] With every political party stacked with funds, the militants are more than willing to offer their services.

The surrender schemes pushed through the region, do very little to dismantle the terror enterprise. The scheme officially called the 'Scheme for Surrender-Cum-Rehabilitation of Militants in the North East', is more of a politico-military strategy aimed at 'buying' militants away from subversive acts, through amnesty and attractive financial packages. Evidently, it comes at an enormous social and political cost'.[197] The attractive financial rewards that the scheme entails, get much more attractive by the state's disinclination to take cognizance of serious crimes committed by the surrendering rebels. Although the broad idea was to ensure gainful employment for the surrendered militant, the social and economic costs of such a policy has proved to be enormous. As most of the surrendered ultras retained their arms, weapons continued to be in circulation, resulting in the complete obliteration of the thin line dividing political and non-political violence. Like in Assam, the government's rehabilitation package for surrendered militants in Tripura has also proved to be deceptive. By all accounts, surrender schemes have become a lucrative 'cottage industry' for unemployed youths to earn quick money. It is estimated that in the last two decades, the number of those surrendered far exceeded the actual number of underground militants of all outfits. It is common knowledge, that unemployed tribal youth are often hired by militant leaders to show off their strength during surrender ceremonies. The structural loophole of the rehabilitation policy does not come in the way of specifically preventing a militant from surrendering twice or even thrice.[198] Clearly, wrong strategies, misuse of rehabilitation policies and irresponsible politics result in a kind of durable anarchy, characterized by a democracy deficit that is too stark to go unnoticed.[199] With criminal groups being informally co-opted into the normal political process, the practice of gun for hire to the 'highest bidder' has become an accepted part of the electoral culture. Threat of violence and actual violence, clearly reinforce the diversified network of illegal and quasi-legal ventures that has come to overlook the political landscape of North East India.[200] 'Accords' between conflicting parties only marginally alter the ground situation. As conclusion of 'accords' is 'necessarily preceded by ethnic discords', they embody a 'battle that is protracted and indecisive' and thus cannot in any substantial way guarantee a resolution.[201] Emerging out of the 'de facto' and 'de jure' bargains between militant factions and the government, it contributes towards the enveloping 'crisis of democracy', evident in the form of scant regard for rule of law and the principles of accountability and transparency. An increase in human rights abuse and a rise in all the categories of killing – of civilians, security forces and of militants is evidence of it.[202]

With the instrument of violence paying rich economic dividends, the message goes loud and clear to the ever increasing number of unemployed youth, that violence pays by offering 'illegal' opportunities in the 'legal mainstream' and hence is a viable career option. Clearly, insurgency fuels criminality and criminality provides access to huge financial resources, that in turn create entrenched interests determined not to disturb the vicious cycle. The Annual Report of the Home Minister of the Government of India (2000-2001), made a striking remark about the nature of insurgency in the region, when it stated that insurgency had become a 'cottage industry', 'bereft of ideology', with the sole purpose of 'making money'.[203]

Illegal Migration from Bangladesh and Islamic Militancy

Transformed demography of North East India, in terms of changed ethnic, linguistic and religious profile, is a direct outcome of the large scale movement of population from across its borders – mainly from Bangladesh. The genesis of this phenomenon can be traced to the first half of the nineteenth century, when as a result of the signing of the Treaty of Yandaboo in 1826, Assam came directly under the British rule. The confirmation of the viability of large-scale cultivation of tea in Assam and the discovery of oil around the same time, triggered profound economic changes that provided sufficient grounds to the colonialists to encourage migration (including forced migration) into Assam, a trend that grew more intense in the subsequent years. Migrants came in big numbers – workers for Assam's tea plantation from present-day Bihar, Bengal, Orissa, the Central Provinces (present day Madhya Pradesh), the United Provinces, Madras and landless peasants from the districts of Sylhet and Mymensingh in East Bengal (present day Bangladesh).[204] Needless to say, the massive migration significantly altered the demographic structure of the region. Demographers have observed that Assam's rate of population growth during 1901-51 was phenomenal.[205] Significantly in 1921, when the population growth was negative for India, Assam had shown an alarmingly higher growth rate, that is 20.47 per cent. The gap of growth between India and Assam was as high as 20.77 per cent.[206]

Although the 'Line System' was put in place to contain the adverse impact of migration, it had limited utility.[207] Commenting on the alarming influx scenario, in 1931, the Census Commissioner for Assam, C.S. Mullen candidly stated: 'the most important event' in Assam over the past quarter century 'has been the invasion of a vast horde of land hungry Bengali immigrants, mostly Muslims from the districts of Eastern Bengal and in particular Mymensingh'. The influx, he feared would 'alter permanently the whole future of Assam and would destroy more surely than did the Burmese invaders ... the whole structure of Assamese culture and civilization'.[208] The tacit encouragement of migration, by Assam's Premier Mohammad Saadullah of the Muslim League (who was at the helm most of the years between 1937 and 1946), was a critical factor in propelling the phenomenon on a scale that was unprecedented. His July 1941 Land Settlement policy, was an open invitation to immigrants, 'allowing them to settle on Government land anywhere in Assam and enabling them to seize as much as thirty "bighas" of land and more for each homestead'.[209] A policy such as this, preceding the Partition of India in 1947, clearly was not devoid of politics. The observation of the 1941 census report was more than telling. The report observed: 'The most noticeable rise in the Muslim population in Assam once again represents immigration from Mymensingh and East Bengal generally. The policy of colonization of Assam by Muslims of Bengal was continued under the joint auspices of Sir Saadulla in Assam and Mr Nazimuddin in Bengal ...'[210] The drastic change in status of the landless migrant from sharecropper to landowners, subsequent to the implementation of the settlement policy was not without consequences – political, social and economic. Clearly, the changing demographics of the region with religious and ethno-nationalistic roots, was to impinge on the politics of the host society in more ways than one. Nazli Choukri makes a significant observation in regard to such dramatic demographic transformation in any given society. In his words:

> Population size may function as a political parameter when, for example, it generates population pressures upon resources that lead to expansionist tendencies. Population composition may be a parameter of a conflict when it sets the cleavages in a society generating tensions that result in ethnic or religious conflict. So too, the population distribution may be a political parameter when, for instance, tribal allegiance crosses national boundaries and generates overt conflict, or when the migration of population changes the ethnic composition of the receiving community and results in nativist reaction.[211]

Clearly, the transformed socio-economic structure of North East India, consequent to penetration of foreign capital, gave a fillip to migration into the region as never before. These migrations, apart from creating the ground for cultural and linguistic flareup, triggered economic and political competition among diverse groups of people over jobs and other privileges. In the ensuing competition, the 'outsiders' – the English educated Bengali Hindus, the enterprising Marwari businessmen and the Bengali Muslim peasants – had a clear edge. The ground clearly was being laid for the emergence of 'nativist' movements that would in due course envelope the entire region. 'Nativism' as an ideology is exclusionary, for it seeks to exclude non members from residing or working in a territory that they are non local to. Subsequently conflicts erupt, mainly resulting from competition between 'natives' and 'non-natives', for control and access to available economic, political and social resources.[212] However in determining 'nativism', the notion of time assumes significance, for longer the duration of residence of an ethnic community in a particular geographical territory, the greater its entitlement. In North East India, it is noteworthy, that the nativist reaction is targeted not just against immigrants from another country but also against so called 'foreigners' from other cultures within the country.[213]

Post-1947, the movement of people from Bangladesh became illegal with the changed political boundaries of the sub-continent. This illegal influx, first from East Pakistan and then Bangladesh, into different parts of India was triggered by a variety of multi-dimensional and inter-related factors – religious, political, ethnic, economic and environmental. For example, millions of Hindus fled from East Pakistan to India, to escape communal violence following the partition of India in 1947. Similarly, about 10 million Bengalis took refuge in India during the liberation war of Bangladesh in 1971. Again, thousands of Chakmas fled to India on account of ethic conflicts in the CHT during the 1970s and the 1980s.[214] These examples of forced migrations have mainly been incident specific and have taken place at a particular point of time in recent history. However, sustained and uninterrupted movement of people from Bangladesh to India, has been taking place for reasons other than political, religious and ethnic. One of the major driving forces behind this influx, clearly is the environmental crisis that plagues most of rural Bangladesh. Bangladesh, according to an observer, presents a 'Malthusian nightmare, with too many people on too little land'.[215] In the last fifty years, the population in Bangladesh has increased at a rapid rate, although there seems to be substantial improvement in the recent years. According to the census data, from 42.16 million in 1952, the population of Bangladesh increased to 129.2 million in 2001, a net addition of 87.04 million people. During 1970-90, the population increased at an annual average rate of 2.5 per cent, which declined to 2.3 per cent per annum during 1990-2003.[216] Over the last fifty years, the population density has increased from 285 to 975 persons per sq. km. This increase in population, if viewed against the background of available resources, presents an alarming scenario that is strikingly evident in the ecological and economic marginalization of the poor – particularly the rural poor. The country represents an environmental pressure point, with intense population pressure on a very limited natural resource base, resulting in scarcities triggered by both environmental change and unequal access to available resources. Recurring natural disasters such as cyclones, riverbank erosion and floods, only add to the prevailing crisis and amplify the vulnerability of the poor to episodic change. The incapacity of the existing urban-industrial economy of the country, to provide avenues to such a large population, pushes people to look elsewhere for survival alternatives. One of the major consequences of the environment induced spatial and economic marginalization of the poor in Bangladesh, is their movement to other regions – both within the country and in the immediate neighbourhood, across international borders as environmental migrants.[217]

Politicization of demographic issues, clearly has the potential to generate severe political, social, economic, ethnic and communal turmoil in any given society.[218] North East India is no exception. Estimates on illegal migration to Assam vary widely from 10-14 million to 4-5 million, although there has hardly been any systematic study on the extent of migration to Assam.[219] While some authors feel that the extent of illegal migration from Bangladesh to Assam and other North Eastern states are grossly exaggerated in public debates, doubts have also been expressed about the authenticity of the census data on migration. However, some important aspects of the demographic changes in the states of North East India need to be discussed here.

Firstly, states of North East India have experienced a comparatively high growth rate of population in the post independence period (Table II). While there are various factors responsible for these high growth rates, immigration in general and illegal immigration from neighbouring countries in particular, are widely considered to be one of the underlying causes of such high rates of population growth.[220] The increased growth rate of population in Tripura during 1951-61 (78.71 per cent), for example, can be explained in terms of migration of Hindu refugees from East Pakistan (now Bangladesh), in the aftermath of partition. *Secondly*, in Assam, the percentage share of Hindus in the total population has come down from 72.51 in 1971 to 67.13 per cent in 1991, while that of Muslims and Christians has increased from 24.56 and 2.61 per cent in 1971 to 28.43 and 3.32 per cent in 1991 respectively. While the high growth rate of Christians in the state (95.37 per cent) during 1971-91, may have been contributed to some extent, by conversion, the high growth rate of Muslims (77.42 per cent) is attributed to migration of Muslim population from Bangladesh.[221] In other states of North East India too, there has been a rise in the share of Muslim population during the past decades. *Thirdly*, in many of the districts of Assam, bordering Bangladesh, an unusually high growth of Muslim population has been noted and their share in the total population has increased appreciably, particularly during the post-1971 period.[222] A survey report has come up with alarming figures of the abnormal rise in population in the border districts of Assam. Comparing the 1971-81 and 1981-91 census figures of Bangladesh, the report expressed concern over the ten million 'missing' people in Bangladesh.[223] Demographically, Assam has been the fastest growing area in the Indian subcontinent. The growth in its population has been by 676 per cent, from 3.3 million to 22.3 million, during the period 1909 to 1991. During the same period, the growth in India as a whole was 354 per cent, from 23.4 million in 1901 to 843.9 million in 1991.[224]

Table: II
Growth Rate of Population in the States of North-East India: 1951-2001

Sate	Growth Rate of Population				
	1951-1961	1961-1971	1971-1981	1981-1991	1991-2001
1	2	3	4	5	6
Assam	34.98	34.95	23.36**	24.24**	18.85
Arunachal Pradesh*	-	38.91	35.15	36.83	26.21
Manipur	35.04	37.53	32.46	29.29	30.02
Meghalaya	27.03	31.50	32.04	32.86	29.94
Mizoram	35.61	24.93	48.55	39.70	29.18
Nagaland	14.07	39.88	50.05	56.08	64.41
Tripura	78.71	36.28	31.92	34.30	15.74
North East Region	38.04	35.04	26.40	27.46	22.02
India	21.51	24.80	24.69	23.82	21.34

Source: Census of India, various years and Bhuyan, 2002
Notes: *Census was conducted for the first time in 1961.
**Since census was not conducted in Assam in 1981, the rates for 1971-81 and 1981-91 are estimated on the basis of interpolation

Other states in the region are also waging their own struggles against the onslaught of illegal migration. Manipur has been a destination for illegal migrants pouring in from Bangladesh, Nepal and Burma. Nagaland has also emerged as another favoured Bangladeshi destination.[225] In case of Tripura, the increased influx of outsiders around the time of partition, resulted in the massive shrinkage of the indigenous tribal population from 53.16 per cent in 1941 to 37.50 per cent in 1951.

The illegal immigrant in North East India, in the words of Myron Weiner, is clearly an 'unwanted' element, forced to cross the international borders for economic and environmental reasons. Their presence enhances the threat perception of the host community, of becoming socially and politically marginalized in their own land and hence they are rejected.[226] While a comprehensive estimate of illegals is not forthcoming,[227] the data provided in a report prepared by the then Governor of Assam, S.K. Sinha, highlights the magnitude of the problem posed by illegal immigrants. According to the report, submitted by the Governor to the President of India on 8 November 1998, there were 5.4 million Bangladeshi migrants in West Bengal, 4 million in Assam, 0.8 million in Tripura, 0.5 million in Bihar, 0.5 million in Maharastra, 0.5 million in Rajasthan and 0.3 million in Delhi.[228]

Social responses in North East India to the population influx has been destabalizing, ranging from complete hostility to xenophobic intolerance, that more often than not manifest as violent insurgencies intrinsically linked to the politics of ethnic cleansing. Even Arunachal Pradesh, believed to be the 'most peaceful state' in the strife ridden North East, has not escaped this xenophobic fervour. It began with the arrival in India of the Buddhist and the Hajong refugees from the Chittagong Hill Tracts and the Mymensingh districts of East Pakistan, in the aftermath of the submergence of their traditional lands, post construction of the Kaptai dam and also owing to religious persecution. The decision to settle these refugees in Arunachal Pradesh was taken in 1964 and a total of 2,748 families of Chakma and Hajong refugees, comprising 14,888 persons were settled in three districts, of Arunachal Pradesh.[229] The local population in these districts, vehemently resented the government's decision to settle the refugees in their land as it impinged on their customary laws and traditional rights. This was the start of a bitter anti-refugee agitation in the frontier state, under the leadership of the state's powerful student body, the All Arunachal Pradesh Students' Union. The grant of citizenship rights to these refugee groups is being strongly resisted, despite the 9 January 1996 Supreme Court judgment in support of the refugees. The lack of a refugee-specific legislation in India, clearly comes in the way of settling this issue in the state and elsewhere in the region.[230]

Islamic Militancy

A grave fallout of the population surge from across India's porous eastern borders, has been the mushrooming of Islamic militant activities in North

East India. As a complex security challenge, observers believe, 'it has come to plague governance and peace in the North East and its ethnic and religious composition makes it difficult to comprehend and address'.[231] The radicalization of Bangladeshi society together with easy access to arms and sanctuaries, remains a critical factor in fueling and sustaining these fundamentalist operations. The fall of the Taliban, consequent to the US led 'Operation Enduring Freedom', not only triggered the eastward surge of the Jihadis but also provided an impetus to home grown variant of Islamic extremism inside Bangladesh.[232] Reports suggestive of the presence of Al-Qaeda elements in Bangladesh, after the descend of the Taliban in Afghanistan in 2002, has clearly added a new dimension to the ongoing security discourse in South Asia.[233] Viewed against this background, illegal migration from Bangladesh into India, has strategic implications that transcend the immediate region.[234] From the Indian perspective, Bangladesh has emerged as a convenient 'proxy war base' against India and elements hostile to the Indian State are aggressively engaged in activities detrimental to Indian interests. Geo-strategically several factors facilitate this process:

- *Firstly*, the two countries – India and Bangladesh – share a land border of 4,096.7 kms and a maritime border of 180 kms that is geographically porous. The riverine configurations in the west and hilly terrain in the east, makes close surveillance of these borders an extremely difficult task, that gets compounded by the shifting course of the rivers that run through them. Soil erosion and frequent floods make the task of border demarcation even tougher, especially with the formation of numerous river islands and *chars*.[235] That the demarcation of borders would raise future complications was amply clear even in 1947, when the Head of the Bengal Boundary Commission, Cyril Radcliffe wrote in his report: 'The province (Bengal) offers few, if any, satisfactory natural boundaries, and its development has been on lines that do not well accord with a division by contiguous majority areas of Muslim and non-Muslim majorities'.[236] The boundaries so demarcated, continue to be afflicted with several unsettled border disputes, one of which is over the issue of 'enclaves' and 'adverse' possessions. There are 111 Indian enclaves (17,158 acres) in Bangladesh and 51 Bangladeshi enclaves in India (7,110.02 acres), besides 34 places (2,892.31 acres) of Indian land under adverse possession of Bangladesh and 40 places (2,251.66) of Bangladesh land under adverse possession of India.[237]

- Geographically, several Indian states such as West Bengal, Assam, Meghalaya, Tripura and Mizoram share border configuration with Bangladesh, resulting in the availability of numerous ingress routes into Indian territory through Bangladesh.[238] This clearly has serious security implications for the 'Bangladesh locked' North Eastern states as well as the slender 'Siliguri Corridor', the sole link between mainland India and its eastern frontiers. The presence of sizable illegal migrant population, in and around the areas adjoining the Bangladesh borders, present its own set of security challenges. These habitats, provide the necessary supportive structure to fundamentalist outfits seeking inroads into the Indian side. The socio-religious commonality between the populations on either side, prove to be a crucial factor in cementing such cooperative endeavours. The porous land and maritime borders, create a congenial smuggling environment that sustains a thriving underground economy. Besides arms and ammunitions and a host of consumer items, the biggest smuggled item is cattle. Over hundred cattle corridors open all along the Indo-Bangladesh border, where cattle are transported from several Indian states, notably Punjab, Rajasthan, Uttar Pradesh, Madhya Pradesh and Bihar. It is estimated that around 1.7 million cattle annually cross over to Bangladesh.[239]

- Bangladesh's emergence as a bastion of Islamic militancy is mainly fuelled by the political-religious factors that have come to define its politics and society in recent times.[240] With the ascendancy of the four party coalition government led by the Bangladesh National Party (BNP) in 2001, violence as an instrument of political domination, emerged as a critical factor in the politics of Bangladesh. Surviving on the support of Islamic fundamentalist parties such as the Jamaat-I-Islami (JIJ) and the Islami Oikya Jote (IOJ), the government succumbed to the Islamic agenda of its coalition partners. Other fundamentalist Islamist organizations like Jamaat, Shibir IOJ, Jagrat Muslim Janata Bangladesh (JMJB) and the Harkat-Ul-Jihad-al-Islami Bangladesh (HUJIB), have also ensured their imprint by infiltrating into the institutions of governance. Over the years, Bangladesh's armed forces have also increasingly come under the influence of Islamists. There are evidences to suggest, that the Jamaat and its front organizations maintain close links with terrorist outfits operating in South Asia and Afghanistan and also act on their behalf. These organizations draw their rank and file from the private madrassas that have mushroomed across the country.[241] It is noteworthy, that a booming fundamentalist economy sustains the terror enterprise. Besides donations from the Gulf countries, profits from investments in business enterprises such as banking, insurance, pharmaceuticals, real estate and education contribute to the yearly net profit of Tk 12 billion.[242]
- Post 9/11, Bangladesh has emerged as the new theatre for Taliban and Al-Qaeda operations. The geo-strategic location of Bangladesh coupled with the ineffective nature its state structures, provide perfect conditions for such elements to flourish. Terrorist activities from Bangladesh, can be coordinated in countries as distant as Spain and Indonesia. The growth of organizations affiliated with Al Qaeda in countries such as

> Thailand, Malaysia, Singapore and Indonesia prove beyond doubt that the entire region has emerged as a favoured destination for Islamic terror groups. Within India, illegal Bangladeshi migrants are believed to harbour terrorists and criminals on the run.[243] Currently, there are over a dozen well-established fundamentalist militant organizations in North East India, most of them mainly active in Assam. The Muslim United Liberation Tigers of Assam (MULTA), formed in 1996, spearheads Islamic Jihad in the region. Prior to September 2001, its cadres are believed to have received training at the Qawa Islamic Institute of Islamabad in Pakistan. According to confessions of arrested militants, some of its cadres were trained in the use of explosive devices by the Pakistan based terrorist outfit, the Harkat-Ul-Mujahideen (HuM).[244] Besides the MULTA, the other Islamic outfits in the region are Harkat-ul-Mujahidden (HuM), Muslim United Liberation Front of Assam (MULFA), Muslim Volunteer Force (MVF), Independent Liberation Army of Assam (ILAA), Liberation Islamic Tiger Force (LITF), Islamic Security Force of India (ISFI), Students' Islamic Movement of India (SIMI), People's United Liberation Front (PULF), Students' Islamic Organisation (SIO), the Islamic Liberation Army (ILA), the Islamic Force No. 786-Islam and the Islamic Revolutionary Army of Manipur.[245]

The dramatic demographic changes within Bangladesh, viz-a-viz its minorities, has also seriously impacted the nature and course of politics in that country. According to the 1941 Census of India, Hindus comprised 11.88 million or 28.3 per cent of the population of the then East Bengal. In a span of twenty years, in East Pakistan, the number had shrunk to 18.5 per cent. The figure drastically fell further during the liberation war in 1971 and by 1974 only 13.5 per cent of the population of Bangladesh remained Hindu. Recent estimates suggest, that the figure has come down to below 10 per cent.[246] The plight of the non-Bengali hill people residing in the CHT has been no different. About 200,000 of them had to flee in the 1960s and 1970s, with several thousands making an exodus after the emergence of Bangladesh. The 1979 settlement policy of the Bangladesh government, geared at settling people from the plains in the CHT, resulted in the settlement of 400,000 Bengali Muslims in the original tribal habitat. The makeover of Bangladesh from an ethnically and religiously diverse country to a Muslim majority nation (90 per cent of the population), has been mainly at the expense of its religious minorities such as the Hindus, the Buddhists and the Ahmadiyyas.[247]

The transformation in Bangladesh and the concomitant security implications for the entire South Asian region and beyond, has been aptly summed by Bertil Litner in the following words:

> A revolution is taking place in Bangladesh that threatens trouble for the region and beyond if left unchallenged. Islamic fundamentalism, religious intolerance, militant Muslim groups with links to international terrorist

> groups, powerful military with ties to the militants, the mushrooming of Islamic schools churning out radical students, middle-class apathy, poverty and lawlessness – all are combining to transform the nation.[248]

Clearly with the growing radicalization of Bangladesh, particularly in the last decade, social violence and religious extremism have come to shape the larger context of politics in the country. Bangladesh's complex Jihad infrastructure comprises of: the Jamaat-e-Islami, a political party which dates back to the British colonial era; the Islamic Chhatra Shibir (ICS), which is the Jamat-e-Islami's youth organization and a member of the International Islamic Federation of Students' Organization and also the World Assembly of Muslim Youth; the IOJ, which was a part of the four-party alliance led by the Bangladesh Nationalist Party, voted to power in October 2001; the Harkat-ul-Jihad-al-Islami (HUJI), which is Bangladesh's main militant Islamic outfit having extensive contacts with Islamic groups in the Indian states of West Bengal and Assam. This outfit figures in the US State Department's list of terrorist organizations.[249] It's recruits, mainly from the Madrassas spread throughout the country, at one time proudly identified themselves as 'Bangladeshi Taliban';[250] the Jihad Movement, which is a common name for several Islamist groups in Bangladesh of which the HUJI is the largest;[251] Hizb ut-Tahrir (HT), which is an international Islamist movement with branches in the former republics of the Soviet Union, Indonesia and even Denmark; Arakan Rohingya National Organization (ARNO), a political group among Rohingya migrants from Burma, who live in the Chittagong Cox's Bazaar area and are fighting for an autonomous Muslim region in Burma's Arakan state; Rohingya Solidarity Organization (RSO); the Jagrata Muslim Janata Bangladesh(JMJB), an Islamist organization established on the lines of the Taliban; and the Jama'atul Mujahideen Bangladesh (JMB). Some of the major violent incidents in the past few years, would reveal the reach, potency and determination of these outfits in carrying out their terror acts, that mainly target places and people labeled as 'un-Islamic', such as cinema theatres, cultural gatherings and political rallies.[252]

The growing Islamisation of Bangladesh, clearly has direct consequences for entire South Asia, especially for the region it 'strategically borders'.[253] The border areas of both West Bengal and Assam, have become dens for fundamentalist Islamist operations.[254] A report in the *Hindustan Times* of 7 November 2003, quoting a document by India's Intelligence Bureau, meant for presentation at the 38th Conference of State Directors General of Police at Delhi, stated that the surge in Islamic fundamentalism in Assam was largely the outcome of continuing influx of Bangladeshi's into the state, where Muslims had come to account for 33 per cent of the population in 2003 against 12 per cent in 1947. Similar sentiments were expressed in a conference of the Directors General of Police of North East India, in November 2006.[255] The magnitude of the influx can be assessed from the fact that the outcome of elections in about 30 of the state's 126 Assembly seats, is directly influenced by the demographic change.[256]

More recently, the Guwahati High Court in a judgment and order passed on 25 July 2008, observed: 'Bangladeshis in Assam have become king makers' and 'strong political will to free Assam from illegal Bangladeshis is the need of the hour coupled with public activism in that direction'.[257] Increasingly, hundreds of Madrassas have sprung up along the entire stretch of the India-Bangladesh border.[258] In 2000, a startling report from the Assam Chief Minister's Office gave details of the misuse of Madrassas and its funds for subversive and extremist activities.[259] Similar anxieties, were expressed by the West Bengal Chief Minister in 2002.[260] With the population of illegal migrants being estimated to be around 15 million, the fallouts on the electoral politics of the bordering Indian districts is more than obvious.[261]

It is in this context, that the emergence of Bangladesh as the 'largest clandestine arms supplier' in South Asia assumes significance.[262] In early April 2004, a huge arms consignment described as the 'largest single illegal arms cache' in Bangladesh's history, was confiscated from the Chittagong port area – a principle conduit for trafficking small arms into Bangladesh and beyond. The south-eastern district of Bandarban in the CHTs, spread over 4,479 sq. kms, has also emerged as an important centre of both gun and drug running.[263] Sharing 129 kms international boundary with Burma, Bandarban's hostile geography, characterized by mountain ranges and dense forest cover, as well as its distant location (187 kms away from capital Dhaka), makes it a preferred destination of militant groupings – groupings of the Arakans and the Rohingyas from Burma, Bangladeshi radical Islamist forces and the North Eastern militants. Uncomplicated access to the sea through the Cox's Bazaar district, makes Bandarban an advantageous destination. In addition to opportunities for trafficing in illegal arms and explosives, the district is also known for poppy cultivation.[264]

In North East India, Islamic militancy spearheaded by fundamentalist groups gained visibility around the early 1990s. Triggered mainly in retaliation to the sustained violent campaigns over the issue of illegal migration from Bangladesh, Islamic militant groups mainly emerged as self-defence apparatus to 'protect and defend' muslim interests. In due course, the agenda expanded to the Islamisation of the region, aimed at creating an independent political and living space for the Muslims. The conservative ascendancy in Bangladesh coupled with the demographic invasion underway in the region, clearly aided the process. The ideological inspiration, necessary training and other logistical support, came from Bangladesh, the ISI and the global Islamic fundamentalist networks.[265] Within the region, as a well thought out strategy these organizations have avoided direct engagement with the Indian security forces, rather they have discreetly registered their presence in the society. The objective clearly is to polarize the society on communal lines, by engineering religious riots, conducting misinformation campaigns and targeting public spots such as market places, railway and bus stations. It is noteworthy, that these outfits face very little resistance from the local ethnic militant groups. A cooperative arrangement defines their ties, with members of the Islamist groups often serving as conduits between rebel groups in the region and their patrons across the border.[266]

The dilution of ideology, bordering on renunciation, by one of the most acclaimed ethnically based militant outfit in the region, the ULFA, testifies to the changed social and political reality obtaining in North East India. It is believed, that this complete turn around by an outfit that came into existence mainly to protect the identity of the indigenous people, has much to do with the altered demographics of the region and the increased dependence of the ULFA on Bangladesh. Bangladesh along with Burma and till very recently Bhutan, is a country where the liaison camps, safe houses and the commercial interests of the ULFA are located. The top brass of the ULFA leadership, according to Indian intelligence reports, are under the protection of the DGFI and the ISI. Besides, a large number of training camps are also located in Bangladesh that train and house militants from North East India.[267] A new dimension has been added to the conflict dynamics in the region, with the targeting of the 'enemies of Assam' – the Hindi speaking population, identified as the symbols of the Indian State. Such assaults, make strategic sense, as it provides both visibility and legitimacy to the outfit that is hard pressed to justify its softened stand on the issue of influx from Bangladesh.[268] In this context, the statement of the ULFA in regard to the immigrants from Bangladesh assumes significance. Describing the immigrants from East Bengal, as 'a major part of the national life of the people of Assam', the ULFA reportedly stated: 'Our freedom struggle can never be successful without these people ... the masses who earn their living through hard physical labour can never be our enemies. All the labouring masses are our friends and the main motive force of our freedom revolt'.[269] Like the ULFA, the Naga militants have also gone soft on the issue of demographic influx from Bangladesh. Clearly, the politics of altered demographics has impacted the power equations between the outfits and their patrons across the borders.

For the Indian security establishment, the challenges emanating from the eastern neighbourhood are multiple and vexed. The security impacts of the international migration flow from Bangladesh are multiple and interrelated and profoundly impact the Indian State's ability to maintain its sovereignty. With the migrants increasingly living lives 'stretched across national borders', they form contested constituencies, vulnerable to mobilizations by different actors, resulting in divided and ambiguous loyalties that challenge the conventional ideas on citizenship.[270] In this regard, the views expressed by the former US Secretary of State Henry Kissinger, in his memoirs, *The White House Years*, is significant. Mr Kissinger wrote:

> The inevitable emergence of Bangladesh – which we postulated – presented India with fierce long-term problems. For Bangladesh was in fact East Bengal separated only by religion, from India's most fractious and India's most separatist state of West Bengal. They share language, tradition, culture and above all a volatile national character. Whether it is turned nationalist or radical, Bangladesh would over time accentuate India's centrifugal tendencies.[271]

The Illegal Migrants (Determination by Tribunals) Act, 1983 (IMDT)

The IMDT Act, enacted by the Indian Parliament in 1983 to detect and deport illegal migrants from Assam, was a legislation that had a direct bearing on the migration discourse in the state. The Act encountered popular criticism that profoundly impacted the politics of the state.[272] The Act, a federal legislation, was introduced in the state on 15 October 1983, at the height of the 'anti-foreigner' (anti-Bangladeshi) uprising spearheaded by the AASU, to provide protection to 'genuine citizens', who it was feared would be harassed in the absence of adequate legal protection. What made the Act controversial was the fact that it applied only to the state of Assam. In this regard, it is noteworthy that schedule 5 of the Assam Accord, defines 'Illegal migrants' as persons who entered Assam after 24 December 1971.

The Act was viewed to be strongly discriminatory, as Assam was the only state which had this law, whereas the rest of the country followed the Foreigners Act of 1946.[273] The Act was considered to be 'migrant friendly', as under the Act, the onus of establishing nationality rested not on the illegal migrant, not even on the government, but on the private individual who had to pay a fee to lodge a complaint and do so under a stipulated jurisdiction, i.e. within three kms from the place where a suspected illegal migrant was residing. The Foreigners Act, thus found favour with the anti-migrant groups as it vested the burden of proof on the accused. That the IMDT Act proved to be ineffective, was evident from the fact that in a period of 22 years only about 1538 persons were deported. The five tribunals set up under this Act, in the districts bordering Bangladesh, from January 1983 registered 423,021 cases, dealt with 65,000 cases, disposed 23,420 cases and had till the end of 2004, declared 12,424 people as illegal migrants. Out of this, only 1,538 of them had been deported.[274] The first official attack on the IMDT Act and the illegal migration in the region, came from Lt.Gen (Retd) S.K. Sinha, a former Governor of Assam, in the form of a 42-page report submitted to the President of India in 1998.The report cautioned, that the North East region could eventually slip out of India's political control, because massive infiltration was not just upsetting the demographic balance of the region but also diluting the identity of the people. The Governor observed:

> The unabated influx of illegal migrants from Bangladesh into Assam and the consequent perceptible change in the demographic pattern of the State, has been a matter of grave concern. It threatens to reduce the Assamese people to a minority in their own State, as happened in Tripura and Sikkim. It's more dangerous dimension of greatly undermining our national security is ignored. The long cherished design of Greater East Pakistan/Bangladesh, making inroads into the strategic land link of Assam with the rest of the country, can lead to severing the entire land mass of the North East, with all its rich resources from the rest of the country. This will have disastrous strategic and economic consequences.[275]

Since 1998, when the All India Lawyers Forum for Civil Liberties filed a public interest litigation (PIL) in the Supreme Court, seeking a direction to the central and state governments in Assam, Meghalaya, West Bengal, Mizoram, Tripura and Delhi to deport all illegal migrants from Bangladesh living in India, efforts were on to quash the Act. Finally, on a PIL filed by a former student leader turned AGP member of the parliament in 2000, the Supreme Court struck down the IMDT Act as unconstitutional. The apex court in its 114-page order observed that illegal migration was an aggression on Assam that was adversely impacting the state's economic growth. The IMDT Act was 'ultra varies' of the Constitution of India, as it prevented the Union of India from discharging its constitutional duty under Article 355, of protecting the constituents of the Union from external aggression and internal disturbance. The judgment also held the IMDT Act violative of Article 14 of the Constitution containing the equality clause, since the Act was made applicable only to the state of Assam. The court also reaffirmed that the burden of proof in all democracies lay with the accused who had to prove that he/she was a citizen of the country.[276] The Court ordered for the transfer of all cases pending before the IMDT tribunals to Foreigners (Tribunal) Order, where it would be decided under the Foreigners Act.

It is significant, that for over two decades in Assam – a state of 26 million people – the politics of citizenship has sustained vote-bank politics. Elections have been won and lost on the stand taken by political parties on the controversial IMDT Act. With Muslims (mostly settlers) being a deciding factor in more than half of Assam's 126 State Assembly constituencies, the issue of illegal migration continues to be an explosive issue in the politics of the state.[277] Clearly, the movement of people from Bangladesh into India – not merely into states bordering Bangladesh – has created an irreversible shift in the balance of forces. Although from time to time, the judiciary has taken a serious view of it, the ground situation remains largely unchanged.[278] In this regard, a significant observation was made by the Guwahati High Court on 25 July 2008. Expressing alarm at the magnitude of influx, the Court stated: 'It is no longer a secret or in the domain of 'doubt' that illegal Bangladeshis have intruded every nook and corner of Assam, including forest land'. If the trend continued, the court warned 'the day is not far off when the indigenous people of Assam, both Hindus and Muslims and other religious groups will be reduced to minorities in their own land ... and Bangladeshis will intrude upon the corridors of power'.[279] It is noteworthy, that both legal and 'informal' methods have failed to substantially alter the situation on the ground, because given the compulsions of vote bank politics, governments shy away from acknowledging the gravity of the situation. Clearly, the sensitivity of this issue in India sends a message to Bangladesh that it is dealing with a soft state. It is in this context that the statement of Bangladesh's, then foreign minister Mohammad Morshed Khan, assumes significance. Speaking at an event organized in Dhaka by the Bangladesh Enterprise Institute on 7 September 2004, the foreign minister reportedly said: 'Bangladesh is India-locked. Delhi has also to remember that the seven North Eastern Indian states are Bangladesh locked'.[280]

Border Management

The issue of illegal immigration is intrinsically linked to that of border management and is central to a state's 'interdependence sovereignty' – its ability to control transborder movements and its domestic sovereignty.[281] In the Indian context, due to the absence of a comprehensive strategy towards border management, despite the overwhelming presence of multiple agencies at the borders, detection and deportation of infiltrators remain an insuperable problem. Recognizing the challenges of border management, the Kargil Review Committee, set up after the 1998 Kargil war[282] noted:

> Border Management has become immensely more complex over the years and the entire issue needs detailed study in order to evolve force structures and procedures that ensure improved border management and a reduction, if not the elimination, in the inflow of narcotics, illegal migrants, terrorists and arms.[283]

Similarly, the Report of the Group of Ministers (GoM) set up after the Kargil war, emphasized on the pressing need to adopt a holistic approach towards border management. The Report stated:

> The term border management must be interpreted in its widest sense and would imply co-ordination and concerted action by political leadership and administrative, diplomatic, security, intelligence, legal, regulatory and economic agencies of the country to secure our frontiers and subserve the best interests of the country. Looked at from this perspective, the management of borders presents many challenging problems.[284]

The report recognized in unambiguous terms, the fluidity of the concept of border management and its dependence, not simply on the configuration of the borders but on a host of other factors, ranging from political and diplomatic relations between the countries involved, to economic and ethno-religious linkages between people across the borders.[285] In the context of India-Bangladesh borders, the non-demarcation of land borders, changing nature of the maritime borders and the disputes over the non-exchange of enclaves, pose major challenges for border management.[286]

Table: III
Borders of India

Items	Distance in Kms
Total Land Borders	15600
Indo-Pakistan Border	3147
Actual Ground Position Line	110
Line of Control	740
International Border Jummu & Kashmir	199
International Border Punjab	533
Rajasthan	1037
Gujarat	508
International Border-Nepal	1751
International Border-Bhutan	699
International Border-Bangladesh	4351
International Border-Myanmar	1643
Indo-China Border	4056
Western Sector	2176
Middle Sector	554
Eastern Sector	1326

Source: Prakash Singh, Border Management, *BSF Journal*, 2 July 2001, (1) pp. 11-23

In 1987, India opted to build fences along the Indo-Bangladesh border as an effective measure to check illegal migration and smuggling activities. The first stage of the fencing project (which includes construction of border roads and bridges besides fencing) started in 1987 and continued till 1999. The second phase of the project was approved by the GOI in June 2000, and comprises a far greater component of fencing (2,429 kms), roads (797 kms) and bridges (4,062 metres) in different states.[287] Although the effectiveness of fences in preventing population movements remain doubtful, the process itself has been plagued by problems, such as the complex procedure of land acquisition and the non-availability of adequate forces to guard the borders and help erect fences.[288] Besides, there are severe logistic challenges, particularly in the hilly terrain of Tripura, Mizoram and Meghalaya. The ambiguity of jurisdiction on the borders, in turn compounds the problem of both guarding and fencing. In some cases, the jurisdiction extends to 5 kms while in other cases it is 15 kms. The inability of the deployed forces to keep the area sanitized from human habitation and cultivation, only adds to the complexities of the situation. Insufficient floodlighting due to limited supply of electricity seriously impacts the efficacy of night patrolling. Destruction of barbed wires by smugglers and criminals also impact the pace of border fencing. Collusion of the population residing in the border areas with the infiltrators present its own set of unique challenges. This is particularly so in the 'enclaves', where the weak jurisdiction of the law of the land has transformed these areas into dens of crime. As an effective strategy, women and children are often used as carriers in smuggling operations, and in the absence of women police on the borders, their detention becomes very difficult.[289]

Cooperation from Bangladesh authorities has been lacking as they see the border-fencing move as 'unfriendly and unfair'.[290] Bangladesh considers the fencing move as a 'military wire obstacle', that clearly violates the Indo-Bangladesh Border Agreement of 1974.[291] The Border Guidelines that emerged out of the agreement states, that neither side should have any security forces, permanent or temporary, within 150 yards on either side of the international border, nor defensive works of any nature including trenches in the stretch of 150 yards on each side of the boundary. Bangladesh regards the ongoing construction activities as a violation of the Border Guidelines.[292]

The multiplicity of agencies working on the same borders, inevitably results in the lack of accountability as well as problems of command and control.[293] Very often, the services of the forces meant for guarding the borders get diverted for security related counter-insurgency operations, resulting in borders being virtually unmanned.[294] Thus, in the absence of adequate border management policies, illegal flow of population from across the border continues unabated and the likelihood of the phenomenon being substantially contained remains slim.[295]

The patronage of local politicians in creating enabling conditions, for infiltrators to procure ration cards and other such legal documents to enlist as voters, seriously comes in the way of detection and deportation. It is an open secret, that the skillfully played game of 'settlement for vote' has the approval stamp of the criminal-police-administration triumvirate. Through established routes, assisted by middlemen, infiltrators slip into India – to the North Eastern States, West Bengal, Delhi and even Mumbai. The 'self-perpetuating dynamism' of the process, is too obvious to go unnoticed.[296] And in the insurgency struck landscape of North East India, the immigrant population, often perceived as a conservative force, ends up being a counter-weight to the separatists and thus a potential support base for the State.

Conclusion

The armed assertions in North East India have tested the might of the Indian political establishment for over five decades. The linkages between the prominent ethnic militant groups and their patrons, in the neighbourhood, are far too real to be ignored. So is the surge in fundamentalist activities, informed by events and ideas from across the borders. However till date, the state policies in place have proved to be inadequate in effectively dealing with the situation. At best they can be described as belated and adhoc. Though there have been several political initiatives, resulting in 'accords' between the state and the conflicting parties, most of these 'accords' have had limited success. The degeneration of the political process into the 'electoral process', in the aftermath of these agreements, serve to legitimize identity politics and consequently, electoral politics far from ironing out differences, consolidate ethnic loyalties. Prejudices, misconceptions and suspicions, sustain this brand of politics. Within the rebel groups, the sequence of emergence, decline and splitting continue to replicate itself and the longer the insurgency, the easier it is to cross the already blurred line between insurgency and terrorism. More and more militant groups are treading the path of terrorism, signified by the growing use of explosives against soft targets, indiscriminate killings and ethnic cleansing. However, 'insurgency fatigue' seems to have set in, which is evident in the steady erosion of popular base of most ultra groups and the growing public restlessness for peaceful settlement. Negotiations, however, present their own set of challenges. In a scenario, where multiplicity of outfits are operating, negotiations with some provoke violent reactions from others. The ensuing escalation of violence only adds to the complexities of the situation. The continuous demographic destabilization, on account of unchecked migration, is the most vexed issue dominating the politics of the region. It is not migration per se that is an issue, but continued migration in a situation of stagnation and underdevelopment that brings things to a boil. Indiscriminate external patronage to rebel outfits, irrespective of ideology, create further barriers to conflict resolution. The lucrative criminal economy of terrorism and a counter-terrorism policy that seems to reward or ignore criminal activities, only adds to the prevailing lawlessness.

Part III

THE ROAD AHEAD

Introduction

Governmental response, clearly stands out as the most important variable impacting the outcome of insurgencies anywhere in the world. In this regard, Walter Sonderlund opines: 'As soon as the challenge is in the open, the success of the operation depends not primarily on the development of insurgent strength, but more importantly on the degree of vigour, determination and skill with which the incumbent regime acts to defend itself, both politically and militarily'.[1] In case of North East India, the dilemma involved in the formulation of counter-insurgency and counter-terrorism policies, present challenges that are not easy to resolve. Terrorist violence in the region, manifest in a variety of complex forms and governments and security agencies have to deal with multiple adversaries. Consequently, as else where in the world, the state response to the phenomenon often gets susceptible to 'emotional judgments, misperceptions and oversimplification'.[2] Although control over the instruments of coercion and high degree of political institutionalization, invariably give governments an edge in fashioning a response, the urgency for an informed and comprehensive understanding of the ground situation clearly stands out. Given the fact that the threat posed by insurgents varies in scope and complexity from case to case, key questions that need to be addressed are: How would government policies impact the perceptions and actions of rebel groups being battled? Is terrorist violence, fundamentally an act of provocation or a defensive response to perceived injustice? Do concessions stimulate further violence? Does negative public reaction, discourage terrorist violence? What are the implications of continued counter-insurgency and counter-terrorism operations on the constitutional rights and civil liberties of the citizens?[3] However, it has to be borne in mind that there is no universally applicable policy, as each conflict involving terrorism varies both in structure and dynamics and has its own defining features. Consequently, it becomes necessary to tailor state policies keeping in view the historical, cultural and political specificities of the groups involved. The preparedness value of the intelligence agencies, an effective anti-terrorism legislation, a responsive judicial system and the availability of military forces to aid civil power, are some other factors that vitally impact the state response. Central to any such policy, is the response of the rebels to government initiatives, forceful or conciliatory. However, in democratic societies terrorism has its own dynamics, profoundly impacted by the opportunities that democracy provides for self-expression. In the words of Bealey, terrorism in a democracy is:

> The violence of desperate men [sic] ... small groups of armed assassins and saboteurs ... the last resort of those who cannot achieve their aims by persuasion and the ballot box ... the deployment or threat of terrorist violence represents the ultimate failure of conventional channels of political expression and legitimate forms of authority.[4]

The State Response

The 'moral economy' of violence, that characterize the political and social environment in North East India revolves around the acceptance of: 'violence as an historical inevitability; violence as self defence; violence as intrinsic to politics; violence as emancipation and violence as bargaining'.[5] Consequently, violence in the region manifests as, what Nieburg would describe : 'as acts of disruption, destruction, injury whose purpose, choice of targets or victims, surrounding circumstances, implementation, and/or effects have political significance, that is, tend to modify the behaviour of others in a bargaining situation that has consequence for the social system'.[6] Evidently, in fractured societies such as the North East, where the mismatch between the level of social mobilization and the capacity of the political structure to provide avenues for participation is too glaring, violence becomes the accepted grammar of politics. More often than not, violence clearly is the outcome of 'rapid social change and the rapid mobilization of new groups into politics coupled with the slow development of political institutions'.[7] In such a scenario, however, the ability of rebel groups to wield power is directly proportional to the extent to which they exercise control over the 'normative', 'coercive' and 'utilitarian' resources within their identified theatre of operation.[8] Combination of deep-seated grievances, along with the capability of group leaders to effectively highlight them, accentuates the overall climate of disquiet.[9] That violence will be confronted with violence, is an accepted reality in the insurgency struck environment of North East India. From the point of view of the state, unreasonable concessions to secessionists would result in a domino effect, triggering similar demands in other parts of the country and thus severely compromising the government's credibility and moral worth at performing its foremost duty of securing the unity and integrity of India. On the other hand, in the rebel imagination, use of force against the government is both an act of self defence as well as a pre-emptive strategy of leveling the play field, in an environment where violence has come to be accepted as the only effective method of communication.

It is noteworthy, that since independence the Indian State has been striving to put into place a complex set of values, rules and institutions, to delineate power sharing arrangements between the Union and its constituents. These may be broadly summed up as: 'liberal constitutionalism, civic nationalism, the devolution of power in a layered federalism and group rights'.[10] It is within these clearly defined parameters that policies of counter-insurgency and counter-terrorism coupled with programmes of political, economic and social interventions, are expected to operate. Political initiatives towards this end have not been wanting. North East India, clearly is a test case. Political interventions have manifested in the form of restructured institutions, grant of specific legal concessions, increased financial flow, periodic democratic elections and special amnesty and rehabilitation schemes for surrendered ultras. The political reorganization of the region on the basis of language, in the post independence period, was an effective strategy to accommodate ethnic aspirations. Thus in 1963, Nagaland was carved out of Assam, covering the Naga Hill District of Assam and the Tuensang Frontier Division of NEFA. Mizo aspirations were accommodated with the creation of the union territory of Mizoram in 1972 and finally a full fledged state in 1987, after a prolonged armed uprising by the Mizos. The state of Meghalaya was formed in 1972, comprising the Khasi Jaintia Hills and the Garo Hills district of Assam. Presently, the truncated state of Assam comprises of the Brahmaputra and the Barak valleys and the two hill districts of Karbi Anglong and the North Cachar Hills. The princely states of Manipur and Tripura acquired the status of union territory in 1963 and became full fledged states in 1972. Under the Sixth Schedule of the Constitution, the concept of Autonomous District Councils was introduced in the region, mainly to enable tribal communities to govern themselves as per their customary laws in matters pertaining to: land; forest; water resources; agricultural practices; village and town administration; property; marriage and divorce and other social customs.[11] Through special provisions, restrictions have been placed on the rights of the non-tribals and people from other states of India to own property in these areas. The system of Inner Line Permit, prohibits entry of non-natives into the states of Arunachal Pradesh, Mizoram and Nagaland, without a valid permit issued by the respective state government. Within the plain areas, tribal belts and blocks have been constituted to prevent land alienation from tribals living in those areas.

However, despite attempts to politically seek solutions for the vexed problems of the eastern frontiers, there is heavy military presence in the region.[12] Understandable national security concerns, necessitate a military intervention. Given the volatile political landscape of the region, with porous borders that allow rebels to procure arms and a hostile neighbourhood willing to provide sanctuaries and logistic support, these concerns are clearly grounded in reality. Consequently, as part of the counter insurgency operations, special laws get invoked to assist military operations. The Armed Forces Special Act (1958), the National Security Act (1980), the Disturbed Areas Act (1976), and the Terrorism and Disruptive Activities Prevention Act [TADA] (1985), have been part of the counter-insurgency operations in the region. In its operations, the Indian Army is assisted by other central paramilitary forces such as the Central Reserve Police Force (CRPF), the Border Security Force (BSF), the Assam Rifles[13] and the various intelligence bureaus and the police forces of each state of the region. In Assam, the counter-insurgency establishment is described as the Unified Command and under this arrangement all forces including the state police, come under the operational command of the army.[14] In regard to the counter-insurgency operations, the top decision-making node is the Union Home Ministry and the operational node consists of the Indian Army and other para-military, police and intelligence units, controlled by the central and state governments. Elected members of the political leadership and senior bureaucrats of the affected states are also a part of the counter-insurgency apparatus. A noteworthy feature is the practice of appointing people from the security establishment as governors of states, resulting in serious aspersions being cast on the office itself.[15]

Central to any counter-insurgency and counter-terrorism policy is the evolution of legal mechanisms. Most legal instruments used by the Indian government to tackle the challenge, have been situational and have emerged more in the context of emergency situations. The term 'terrorism' still evades a definition. The National Security Act (1980), is believed to be the first Act in Indian history to be aimed at organized terrorism. The Act, applicable across India, allowed both the central and the state government to put anyone in preventive detention for a year, if there was sufficient reason to believe that lockup was necessary to prevent the person from 'acting in any manner prejudicial to the defense of India, the relations of India with foreign powers, or to the security of India'.[16] A serious criticism of the Act was that, the understanding of terrorism was kept ambiguous, thus leaving it open to the charge of government abuse. The first serious attempt to define terrorism was made in 1984 by the Terrorist Affected Areas (Special Courts) Act (1984).[17] A terrorist under this Act was defined as:

> any person who indulges in wanton killing of persons or in violence or in the disruption of services or means of communication essential to the community or in damaging property with a view to: putting the public or any section of the public in fear; adversely affecting the harmony between various religious, racial, language or regional groups or castes or communities; coercing or overawing the government established by law and; endangering the sovereignty and integrity of India.[18]

Arguably, the definition was 'maximalist' in the sense that it included a precise break-up of the activities that would be considered as terrorism. The Terrorist and Disruptive Activities Act of 1985 (TADA), only slightly modified the definition of terrorism. The singular difference was the inclusion of an element of 'motive' leading up to a terrorist act. The Act clearly stated that any attempt to 'strike terror in the people or a section of the people' was in effect an act of terrorism.[19] The Prevention of Terrorism Ordinance (2001) went a step further in defining terrorism. According to this controversial law:

> Whoever (a) with intent to threaten the unity, integrity, security or sovereignty of India or to strike terror in the people or any section of the people does any act or thing ... in such a manner as to cause or likely to cause both death or injury or detains any person or threatens to kill any person ... (b) or is or continues to be a member of an association

> declared unlawful under the Unlawful Activities (Prevention) Act ... commits a terrorist act.

This expanded definition of terrorism, clearly included the 'act of association' with a terrorist group within its purview. This ordinance, which replaced the TADA after it was allowed to lapse in May 1995 amidst criticism of being unduly unfair to the accused, became the Prevention of Terrorism Act (POTA) in 2002.[20] In September 2004, POTA was also allowed to lapse.

In the context of the above discussion, it is noteworthy that the urgency for stringent anti-terrorism laws as an antidote against terrorism, was first articulated in 2000 by the National Law Commission in the following words:

> An extraordinary situation calls for an extraordinary law, designed to meet and check such extraordinary situations. It is one thing to say that we must create and provide internal structures and safeguards against possible use and abuse of the act and altogether a different thing to say that because a law is liable to be misused, we should not have an act at all.[21]

No anti-terrorism law has replaced POTA and acts of terrorism fall under the purview of the Unlawful Activities (Prevention) Act, 1967, as amended on 21 September 2004 by a Presidential ordinance, further amended in December 2008, in the aftermath of the 26/11 Mumbai terror attacks.[22]

Counter insurgency operations in North East India, have clearly been in tune with the Indian conceptual model for counter-insurgency, which for all practical purpose as noted by an observer, is reactive rather than proactive.[23] The approach and methodology follow a linear pattern of first dealing with the situation as a law and order problem, followed by full-scale counter-insurgency operations. The army is deployed at the behest of the Union Government after the failure of the concerned state government to effectively deal with the situation. The role of the army is primarily to create an environment which would bring the insurgents to the negotiation table and pave the way for a ceasefire declaration. Successful negotiations, often lead to political outcomes that result in the grant of statehood, union territory, autonomous district council or some other political concession, that would presumably preserve and safeguard the identity and culture of the indigenous population. Failed negotiations, often result in resumption of operations by both sides. Commenting on the important features of the Indian counter-insurgency strategy, an observer notes:

> ... the use of drift, the art of tiring down the insurgent leadership through unending negotiations ... India has used its army and para-military forces to soften up the rebels and forced them to the table. It has used clan and tribal rivalries to split ... It has used huge fund flow to neutralize the hostility ... with favours and concessions, positions of power and financial benefits ....[24]

A strategy such as this, lacks vision and serves very limited purpose. The need for a holistic national counter-insurgency and counter-terrorism policy, with an in depth understanding of its national, international, strategic, technology and information ramifications, has been forcefully articulated by security experts. Even within the Army, there is a call for an integrated political and military response to internal violence. The central thesis of the Indian Army's doctrine on sub-conventional warfare states:

> The management and final resolution, of such [sub-conventional] conflicts necessitates a multi-pronged thrust by all elements of national power to address the root causes. The application of Armed forces in the initial stages is aimed at providing a secure environment, wherein various institutions of government can function devoid of any inimical interference. Having provided this environment, the Armed Forces, thereafter, function in a manner that strengthens the hands of the civil authorities.[25]

There is also a recognition that 'any tendency to resort to quick and seemingly efficient military-like actions which may appear to resolve an immediate local issue but, in all probability, may seriously hurt long-term objectives and future stability should be curbed without exception'.[26]

With several parts of North East India being perpetually under military operations, the costs in terms of democracy deficit has been glaring. Consequently, suspension and abrogation of basic rights have become a routine affair in many parts of the region. The Armed Forces Special Powers (Assam and Manipur) Act (1958), that covers several parts of the region, implies temporary suspension of some basic 'Fundamental Rights' guaranteed by the Indian Constitution.[27] Such a scenario, clearly calls for putting into place innovative political initiatives that would contain the rhetorical appeal of the rebels and secure civilian cooperation.

Illusive Peace

With most conflicts in North East India, being transformed into protracted struggles of attrition, peace continues to be a far-fetched dream. The inherent contradictions in the counter-insurgency policies, largely geared towards containment, only add to the prevailing chaos. Military operations only marginally impact the ground situation. The goals of these operations are limited to the creation of conditions for a particular rebel group to come forward for negotiations, surrender weapons and work towards a compromise. This however, may not inspire other groups to renounce violence nor does it discourage them from emulating the success of those who have acquired prominence and success through the short-cut route of violence. To top it, the policy of co-opting former militants in the counter-insurgency operations sustains the climate of mistrust, resulting in a vicious cycle of violence between anti and pro-government rebel groups. Consequently, democracy deficit in the form of complete disregard for rule of law and human freedom become non issues.[28] Issues of human rights, do not figure highly in the political discourse of the region – at best it is selective. Most of the victims of human rights abuse are clearly civilians and in the power dynamics of a deeply polarized region, their plight seldom gets the attention it deserves. Moreover, a counter-terrorism policy willing to strike deals with anti-system elements, causes irreparable damage to the legitimacy of legal and political institutions. Interestingly, while elections are held at regular intervals, the lack of basic democratic values is strikingly evident.[29]

The question of durable peace in the region, raises complex issues critical to the creation of what may be described as 'basic procedural justice'. Justice in this sense implies, fair procedures of negotiation and arbitration that forms the basis for the recognition of untidy and temporary compromises between incompatible visions of dignified existence. Such a notion of justice makes possible a minimally decent life independent of any wider conception of good.[30] It is the first concrete step towards the semblance of a social order, where every voice is given a hearing and some visibility is ensured even for the most marginalized, during the process of negotiations. Critical to this process, is the recognition and acceptance that the ongoing conflict has had victims and silence on collective wrongs limits justice with a powerful message going to the victim on 'his marginality and irrelevance'.[31] Clearly, it implies that appropriate engagement with the past, at the level of reason and emotion, is crucial to the prevention of wrong doing in the future.[32] In the context of the multi-ethnic landscape of North East India, there is no escape from the acceptance that dominant communities maintain their cultural and political dominance, by wresting away from smaller identities their respective right to cultural self-determination.

The approach of the Indian State towards North East India, particularly acquires meaning when viewed within the ambit of the dominant paradigms that drives it's response towards the region. Four paradigms, mainly stand out: cultural, security, politics and development.[33] The 'cultural paradigm', that dominated much of the 1950s and the early '60s, mainly focused on the preservation of the cultural diversity of the region. The 1962 Indo-Chinese war, dramatically altered this perception and North East India became strategically important both in the geographical and geopolitical sense. In the early '70s, the 'security paradigm' was replaced by the 'politics paradigm'. It was felt that political representation of the diverse tribal cultures and sub-nationalities of the region, through the instrument of representative, pluralist parliamentary democracy, would create stakeholders in the 'mainstream' democratic process. Consequently, a number of new states were carved out in anticipation that adequate political representation would quell the upheaval. The 'development paradigm', marked by phenomenal increase in public expenditure, made its appearance in the '80s, and continues to capture the imagination of the policy makers till this day. Increased expenditure in physical and social infrastructure, in the form of special economic packages, it is believed, will prove to be a cure for all ailments that plague the region.[34] In the face of facts, if the 'neglect' theory is to mean economic neglect in the form of developmental assistance, the statistics clearly reveal an altogether different story. Between 1990-91 and 2002-03, the region received an amount of about IR 1,08,5040 million from the Central Government. While Assam received about IR 43,0000 million from the Centre, Arunachal and Manipur received about IR 9,9000 million and IR 11,5000 million respectively. During the same period, Nagaland and Mizoram received IR 12,0000 million and 9,0000 million respectively and the states of Tripura and Meghalaya received IR 14,0000 and 9,0000 million each. Although a portion of this gross amount came back to the Central Government as repayment on loans and interest payments, the cumulative net devolution from the Centre to the North East region for the period between 1990-91 and 2002-03 remained at about IR 92,0000 million. During this period, the grant portion alone stood at IR 65, 0000 million.[35] Part of the problem, by all accounts is the surplus pumping of funds that seldom reach the people for whom it is intended.

Against this background, it becomes increasingly evident that the road to peace in the region, is plagued with multiple challenges and has much to do with the kind of interactions that actors involved have with one another. Kenneth Boulding argues that there are three basic ways in which humans relate to each other – by means of *threats*, *exchange*, and *integration*.[36] These interactions, seriously impact the notion of peace in any society. While the threat system may result in a hegemonic or deterrent peace, the exchange system results in functional peace. Similarly the outcome of integration is integrative peace. Of the three, peace achieved through threat is fragile as it cannot be pursued beyond a point. Exchange centric peace has its own limitations because it encounters the issue of relative gains. In the given circumstances, the most durable path to peace is through the integrative path of community building, resulting from ethical respect and moral convergence with communities, who not very long ago were described as the 'other'. This however, does not imply the absence of conflict but rather an arrangement that facilitates the resolution of conflict, short of war. Karl Deutsch describes this arrangement as the 'pluralist security community'.[37] Such a community has at least two autonomous centres of political authority and there exits an enduring expectation for the peaceful resolution of conflict. The founding of such a community, however, depends upon certain background conditions. First, is the compatibility of the key political values applicable to the decision making process. Second, the ability and the willingness of participating actors to respond to each other's 'needs, messages and actions', without taking recourse to violence. The third important condition is the 'mutual predictability of behaviour' of the actors involved. This would imply a reliable understanding of what motivates the other side. Evidently, it is the linkages between values, institutions and habits that set the stage for the acceptance of a pluralist and democratic conception of society.[38] Civil society institutions, thus become crucial to the creation of such a society. This is particularly so in societies plagued with ethnic conflicts, where the cult of violence results in a certain externalization of 'truth'. Consequently, the notion of *social capital* as a critical societal ingredient to the larger peace process assumes significance.

Social Capital can best be understood, as the 'moral resource' of a society that contributes to 'public good' by facilitating solutions. It refers to features of social organization, such as trust, norms and networks that contribute to the efficiency of society by encouraging coordinated action.[39] Locating social capital, within the civil society discourse, is thus critical to the understanding of the role of civil society in creating democratic space. This is particularly so in societies experiencing protracted conflict. In such societies, the civil society provides value and stability to the ongoing political discourses by exposing to its constituents the views and opinions of others. Standing between the state and family, civil society represents an autonomous space that provides room for new social movements to operate and form public-private partnerships in the social sector. It is in these spaces, through networks and associational life among citizens that social capital is created. It is noteworthy, that the concept of social capital has come to be understood as a sister concept to concepts such as democracy, civil society and good governance - concepts that are central to the democratic functioning of institutions. The concept has redefined the very idea of development with the argument, that economic development cannot be merely equated with the expansion of the gross national product (GNP), but must also include *non-economic factors* and their impact on enhancement of human capabilities vital for development, such as education, womens' empowerment, social justice and equal opportunities for all.[40] One of the most direct outcomes of social capital is *associationalism,* that thrives best among weak interpersonal ties arising out of shared solidarities that link members of different groups, cutting across social cleavages.

Central to the crisis that North East India finds itself in, is the notion of connectedness in social and political terms. Connectedness, in this regard, would mean the enabling processes that build trust, cooperation and associationalism. This however, can be understood at four different levels. The first, being at the level of emotional and psychological connectivity with the rest of India. Second, at the level of inter-state ties within the region. Third, at the level of value consensus that defines, shapes and regulates inter group ties. And finally, at the level of integrative behaviour that would motivate people to come forward for greater common good.

A characteristic unique to the state and society in North East India, is the co-existence of a strong sense of identity and shared community values. The absence of ascriptive traditional hierarchies, combined with minimum differences in land ownership, education and income, contributes to a strong sense of communal bonding. Intense feelings of nationalism, however does exist among the communities, founded mainly on the idea of a homeland attached to a definite territory and its past memories. It is a phenomenon that is described as the 'territorialization of memory', drawn mainly from experiences and narratives associated with a particular ethnoscape.[41] Narratives and perspectives on this past, present and future get reflected in folk memories, literature, culture and even political polemics about identity assertion and relations viz-à-viz the rest of India. Clearly, these factors underlie the fierce feeling of nationalism that characterize ethnic assertions in the region.

However, in contrast to other parts of India, North East India has a vibrant civil society that impacts upon the functioning of the state and its institutions. The absence of traditional ascriptive hierarchies, provides enhanced space for egalitarianism and a culture of oneness, in turn provides greater scope for public action. This, coupled with higher levels of literacy and relatively higher status of women in decision-making, in both private and public arena, contributes towards the greater visibility of civil society institutions. A noteworthy feature, is the role of civil society actors such as the church and other cultural and social associations in the political and social life of the region. The Church in particular, has played an impressive role in the spread of modern education across the region and thereby powerfully contributes to the pattern of interest articulation.[42] Given the co-existence of multiple tribal and non-tribal identities, the church has emerged as an important point of convergence for the diverse cultural groups. This is particularly evident in tribal majority states like Nagaland, Mizoram and Meghalaya, where the Church is actively engaged in imparting values and norms that facilitate collective action. The state of Assam also has a history of rich associational life, amply reflected in the activities of the Assam Sahitya Sabha and the Bodo Sahitya Sabha.[43] In the state of Nagaland, the activities of associations like the Naga Hoho, Naga Mothers' association and theYoung Naga have significantly impacted the course of politics in the state. In each state of the region, there is a powerful student association actively involved in the social and political life of the state.

Paradoxically in North East India, social capital born out of ethnic, tribal and cultural affiliations exists in abundance, but only within the narrow confines of the community. A number of narrow divisions exist between communities that cause distrust, alienation and a multiplicity of conflicts visible at different levels. The first, is the *low level of integration* with the rest of the country, which is evident in the new revisionist historiography of the the region that de-emphasizes the region's connections with the rest of India and privileges its historical and cultural links to South East Asia.[44] The attitude of the mainland towards the region, in the popular perception, is believed to be coloured by 'ignorance', 'arrogance', 'discrimination', 'coercion' and 'cooptation'.[45] Another visible level of division in the region is between the constituent states themselves. This is manifested in forms such as territorial disputes, competition for resources and restrictions on employment opportunities and other economic avenues, to people from the neighbourhood. Closely connected is the absence of value integration, both within and between ethnic groups. The region, thus is characterized with scant social capital between the contesting groups and also between the tribals and the non-tribals. The non-tribals believe, that the principle of 'protective discrimination' deprives them with a level playing field by severely limiting their economic opportunities as well as opportunities for political participation. The cumulative impact of such divisions is the lack of integrative behaviour, that prevents the inhabitants of the region from working together for common objectives.

'Eastward ho' diplomacy

The mismatch between the social and political boundaries in North East India, has had a two-fold impact on the politics of the region. First, it has made the region vulnerable to external intrigues, mainly at the behest of hostile neighbours. Second, given the historical continuities between the region and the countries across, there is unabated movement of people from across the borders. External interventions in the region have manifested in different forms – ranging from arms transfer and training to diplomatic support and studied silence on the presence of Indian ultras in foreign territory. The demands of peripheral communities, for the redrawing of international boundaries in tune with their ethnic social continuities, provide ample opportunities for external involvement.[46] Closely connected is the emotive issue of cross-border population movement, that brings into centrestage serious questions in regard to the constitutional rights of citizens and matters pertaining to the preservation of language and cultural rights of the indigenous population. It also brings the issue of human rights to the centrestage of the ongoing political discourse in the region. It is significant, that in the ethnically fractured polity of North East India, the discourse on 'human rights' assumes special meaning. This is mainly because, social boundaries unlike political boundaries are believed to be sacrosanct and for most ethnic groups, the right to live in their own community is a right far superior to other rights. Viewed from this perspective, the Indian State becomes the external agency encroaching on the living spaces of the smaller communities and thereby violating their human rights. The discourse on rights in North East India, thus rests on three complex premises: doing away with international boundaries; regarding rights as 'ends' in themselves and; the acceptance of an extremely abstract and situational nature of the concept. And in the complete absence of 'rational deliberations' on the concept within the society at large, the eventuality of an ethnic bloodbath is a foregone conclusion.[47] The inability of the state to contain the ethnic outrage, is clearly not without serious consequences. With the transformation of the conflicts into full blown wars between rival communities, the issue of human rights gets completely sidelined. Cross border migration adds its own dynamics to the ongoing turmoil. A disturbing trend since the early 1990s, is the consolidation of Islamic militant outfits. Several of these groups are informed by experiences across the borders and echo sentiments not very different from the Muslim Volunteers' Force, a radical outfit raised in Assam with a clear agenda:

> ... to impart in the Muslims for self-defence, to form "death squads" to enroll people and train them for protecting the people belonging to the Muslim community in buses, trains and in public places, to take suitable measures against those who by virtue of their power and high ranks are condemning the Muslims, torturing and killing them, to take counter-measures then and there, to take steps for restoring Muslim interests wherever they are in jeopardy.[48]

India's declared policy of dealing with the neighbours on these contentious issues has been through the framework of bilateralism.[49] However, in regard to bilateralism, the lack of quid pro quo presents its own set of problems. The refusal by one of the two sides to recognize a problem impacting the neighbourhood, can prove to be very damaging. This is particularly evident on the issue of cross border influx from Bangladesh. Bangladesh continues to be in denial and as a result the ties between the two countries have come under severe strain.[50]

Diplomacy, communications, economics and military means are other options, that India has explored in varying degrees. While on the one hand, through sustained campaigns India has sought to focus global attention on the nature and extent of external involvement in its troubled frontiers, on the other, it has also been trying to aggressively engage its eastern neighbours through its *Look East Policy*. The idea is to revive the historical and geographical links between North East India and the immediate neighbourhood. Post-partition, the disruption of the communication network with East Pakistan – rail, road and river links – put an end to the geographical advantage that the region enjoyed, located at the crossroad of the newly emerging nations of Asia. The 1962 border war with China and the increasing hostilities with Pakistan, transformed the region sharing 4500 kms of border with the newly emerging nations of Asia, namely, China, Burma, East Pakistan, Bhutan and Nepal, into a landlocked outpost of a large continental economy.[51] The 'Look East' policy aims at paying adequate attention to both the strategic challenges and opportunities in the North East, through the creation of multiple options on regional free trade. The initiative was launched in the early 1990s by the then Prime Minister, Narasimha Rao and covered mainly the countries of South East Asia. In the late 1990s, Prime Minister, A.B. Vajpayee expanded the policy to cover much of Asia, including the

Association of South East Asian Nations (ASEAN), China, Japan, Australia and New Zealand. The main focus of the 'Look East' policy in the first phase, was on forging commercial and institutional links with Asia. The second phase was more ambitious, as it aimed at political partnership, physical connectivity, free trade arrangements and defence cooperation. The strategy, it is believed will open a range of new possibilities for North East India, that would end the 'remoteness' of the region, give a push to economic growth and create better conditions to effectively address the problems of insurgency in the region.[52] Clearly, the focus hinges upon North East India becoming the *gateway* to South East Asia. The advocates of this policy argue, that regional integration through the North East corridor holds the key to the resolution of the major ills of the region – the problem of economic stagnation and the containment of the social and political turmoil that has destabilized the region for several decades. This calls for an appropriate socio-economic strategy, that would transform the region into a strategic base for domestic and foreign investors, to tap the contiguous markets of China, Myanmar, Bangladesh, Laos, Thailand, Vietnam, Cambodia, Malaysia, Indonesia and beyond. The future of North East, it is argued, lies in its 'political integration with India and economic integration with South East Asia'.[53]

Within the North East, the 'Look East' policy would involve opening continental connections through several points along the 1643 kilometre international border with Burma, covering the Indian states of Mizoram, Manipur, Nagaland and Arunachal Pradesh. Notwithstanding the fluctuations in Indo-Burmese ties, transport corridors through Burma make both strategic and economic sense. Firstly, without the support of the Burmese military junta, India's hope of dismantling the bases of the North East rebels in Burmese territory cannot be realized.[54] Secondly, by engaging Burma in a big way, India hopes to balance Chinese presence in that country, which incidentally coincided with the lull in Indo-Burmese relationship between 1977-1988. This has to be particularly understood in the context of India's discomfort with the Sino-Pakistan ties in its western frontiers. In this context, it is significant that issues of better connectivity and trade figured in a big way in the official discussions with General Maung Aye of Myanmar, during his March 2008 visit to New Delhi.[55] Third, economic imperatives, propel India to make inroads not only in its near abroad but also beyond, to make the most of the fast changing trade and investment climate in an increasingly globalized world. Towards this end, India's 'Eastward ho' project has been working at two levels. First, India has been trying to chart its way into the East Asia Club, through eventual membership in the Asia Pacific Economic Cooperation (APEC).[56] Secondly, by forging sub-regional economic cooperation among the countries of the region, India hopes to have a firm presence in the region. The fallouts of the financial crisis, that engulfed the country in the early 1990s and the collapse of Soviet Union in December 1991, necessitated the need for such an eastward thrust in foreign policy. The idea, clearly was to enlarge the sphere of economic engagement through the renewal of ties with civilizational neighbours in South East and East Asia.[57]

In the entire scheme of 'Eastward ho', North East India figures as the gateway to South East Asia. A gateway can be best understood as:

> a place acting as a conduit or itself giving rise to the transmission of ideas, people, goods, services, knowledge, expertise, and other appurtenances of civilization from one place (including the area of the gateway itself), to another, internationally. The gateway should serve not merely a physical function of providing for the transit of goods, services and persons, but it should also provide for the positive irradiation of one area by the other in terms of higher levels of thought, activity and living.[58]

A Gateway, thus by definition is expected to play a lead role in development relative to its hinterland. This clearly requires the *gateway* to be politically stable, show relatively higher rate of economic growth than the hinterland, be endowed with high levels of human resources and technology and have the ability to proactively react to global change by improving the quality, diversity and relevance of the services offered. These are no easy goals and by all indications, North East India has a long way to go before it can play the role of a *gateway*, in any real sense of the term. However, some significant initiatives have been taken towards this end. Two forms of cooperation are currently underway: those involving India and the South Asian countries of Nepal, Bhutan and Bangladesh. Among these projects are the South Asia Growth Quadrangle (SAGQ), supported by the South Asian Association for Regional Cooperation (SAARC)[59] and the South Asia Sub-regional Economic Cooperation programme (SASEC), supported by the Asian Development Bank; and those that promote co-operation between South Asian countries and countries across North East India.

The proposed SAGQ, promoted by the SAARC, offers valuable investment opportunities in unexploited arenas such as hydro-electricity, natural gas, crude oil, port facilities, forest, tourism, mineral resources, health, information technology, education, human resource development and commodities and products such as jute, leather, fishery and horticulture. Although the level of cooperation among the participating countries, does not demand a change in their ideological profile or their macro policies in regard to their socio-economic development, SAGQ has not been able to make much headway. The SAARC Free Trade Agreement, concluded on 6 January 2004 was the first meaningful step taken by the South Asian nations to enhance collective prosperity through regional economic integration. Similarly, the *Association of South East Asian Nations* (ASEAN), set in the 1960s, has been crucial in promoting wide ranging dialogue process with several regional and non-regional countries. A novel concept pioneered by the forum, was that of triangles and quadrilaterals, to identify and coordinate complementary projects in contiguous regions of adjacent countries and then create conditions for accelerated growth through mutual cooperation among those regions.[60] Acknowledging the sound logic for developing greater economic integration with India's Southeast neighbours, in October 2004, Prime Minister Manmohan Singh, proposed the idea of an Asian community grouping including the ASEAN and the countries of Northeast Asia (China, Japan, Korea and India). Such a grouping, he hoped would create an 'arc of advantage' to rival the European Union.[61] It is noteworthy, that as a part of its 'Look East' policy, India is a summit level partner of ASEAN along with China, Japan and Korea. India is also the signatory of the free trade area agreement with Thailand and Singapore and plans to sign a similar treaty with Brunei, Indonesia and Malaysia by 2011 and with the other ASEAN countries such as the Philippines, Cambodia, Laos, Myanmar and Vietnam by 2016. Clearly, through initiatives that forge closer Indo-ASEAN ties, India hopes to eventually make it to the APEC. The continuous Indo-ASEAN dialogue, since the early 1990s, have thus paved the way for multi-lateral relations between India and the countries of South East Asia in a significant way. The Bangladesh-India-Myanmar-Sri Lanka-Thailand Economic Cooperation (BIMST-EC) and Mekong-Ganga Cooperation (MGC) are examples of this endeavour. Initially the BIMST-EC grouping, launched in 1997, consisted of India, Bangladesh, Burma, Sri Lanka and Thailand. Nepal and Bhutan acquired membership at a later date. The forum was designed to economically integrate countries of the Bay of Bengal basin through arrangements, that would promote trade, investment and cooperative measures in crucial areas such as trade and investment, technology, energy, transport and communications, tourism, environment and disaster management, public health, agriculture, poverty alleviation, counter-terrorism and transnational crimes. The BIMSTEC-FTA is believed to have a trade potential between US$ 33 to 59 billion.[62] Towards its stated objective of linking the Indian subcontinent and Indo-China, the forum has initiated steps in the direction of infrastructure development, notably the Trans-Asia Highway that would link North East India to Bangkok. The *Mekong-Ganga Cooperation* (MGC) was launched in July 2000 by India, the riparian country of the Ganges and Cambodia, Laos, Myanmar, Vietnam and Thailand, the riparian states of the Mekong river. The main plank of the multi-lateral cooperation of the MGC is cultural, aimed at forging people-to-people link between the inhabitants of the two river valley civilizations. There is also the Bangladesh-China-India-Myanmar Regional Economic Forum (BCIM), an outcome of the *Kunming Initiative* of 1999.[63]

Creating better connectivity, both via land and waterways, is critical to the creation of India's continental ties with South East Asia. Towards this end, GOI has consented to an inter-governmental agreement on Asian Highways and has also become a party to the 1,40,000 kilometre network.

The network, which extends to 32 countries, aims at providing connectivity between capitals of member-countries, main industrial and agricultural centres, major sea and river ports, depots and places of major tourist attractions.[64] There are also suggestions that the opening of two routes – *Southern Silk Road* and the *Ledo Road* – both of which are geographically and economically complementary to each other, is critical to India's 'Look East' policy. While the Southern Silk Road traditionally connected China to the Indian Ocean, from its Sichuan and Yunan province to Yangon (Rangoon) in Burma, the Ledo Road connects the Ledo town in Upper Assam to Yunan in China. This road is also known as the Stilwell road, named after the American General Joe Stilwell who took the initiative to rebuild the road, to facilitate the movement of the allied forces fighting the Japanese army during the Second World War. This road holds the promise of economic boost for the entire region.[65] A third road that is proposed, is fairly ambitious. This Trans-Asia Highway aims at connecting Saurashtra in Gujarat to Singapore via North East India. However, given the difficult terrain of the region, the completion of the project is clearly not without perils.[66] Another project called the Kolodyne project aims at upgrading port facilities at Sittwe, located about 250 kms away from the border between Mizoram and Burma. Sittwe is located on the mighty Kolodyne river, which flows through Mizoram and Burma before finding its way into the Bay of Bengal. Once completed, the Kolodyne waterway will offer better connectivity between mainland India and North East, by providing a cheaper and quicker alternative route.[67] This scheme is likely to dramatically expand the weight of Burma in India's neighbourhood diplomacy.[68] A significant start in this direction was the signing of the border agreement between India and Burma in 1994. The agreement became operational in 1995, through Moreh in Manipur to Tamu in Burma's Sagaing division. In February 2001, a 160-kilometre Kalay-Kalaywa-Kyiong-Tamu road in Sagaing division of Burma, was inaugurated. This 'Friendship Road', constructed by India's Border Road Organization, provides connectivity between Indian border outposts and Central Burma. In April 2002, India, Burma and Thailand agreed to work towards the construction of a trilateral highway that would link these countries. Such collaborative arrangements, clearly benefit the parties involved. While India liberates North East India from its geographic isolation, Burma benefits from Indian investment in its infrastructure and for Thailand it means road connectivity to a huge market of over a billion people.[69] There is also a considered move to boost Indo-Bangladesh road links. In this regard, India has proposed to the Economic and Social Commission for Asia and the Pacific of the United Nations, to amend the Asian Highway Route – 2 and 48. Such an amendment of the route, will provide connectivity of the Asian Highway Route through Bhutan to India as well as to Bangladesh and Nepal.[70]

Although, economic diplomacy clearly holds the key to much of the economic ills of the North East region, there are other variables that are no less critical. A combination of both external and internal factors present bottlenecks in the way of economic integration. The external factors include the ambiguous nature of the status of India's relationship with Burma, one of its neighbours in the region. The balancing act of maintaining ties with both the military junta and the pro-democracy forces within Burma has proved to be a tough act.[71] India is also wary of the growing economic and military cooperation between China and Burma. Clearly, these ties have strategic implications for India, more so against the background of Sino-Indian border dispute still evading resolution. The security anxieties have resulted in the lack of synchronization of India's policies with China, ASEAN and Burma. Consequently, it has impacted the pace of the 'Look East' policy. The extreme sensitivity of the region to the issue of migration is also a factor that needs urgent attention. Clearly, there are no easy solutions to this problem. Any restrictions on internal migration hits at the very foundation of the Constitution of India, which is obliged to guarantee its citizens the right to live and work within the territory of India. The most effective strategy, in the given circumstances, would be to initiate measures aimed at changing attitudes towards migration. It has to be appreciated that migrants in their own way, enrich the host population with their labour, skills, and ways of life.[72]

However on the issue of cross border migration, there is scope for far greater intervention. Clearly this would involve a mix of several policy formulae, realistic enough to be implemented. The first step towards this end would be to enlist the services of demographers and social scientists, to get credible statistics on migration so as to facilitate rational discussions on the subject. Suggestions have ranged from issuing temporary work permits to fencing the borders. There are also suggestions that India should actively assist countries like Bangladesh, Nepal and Bhutan to deal with the challenges of under-development. Towards this end, it is believed that a massive programme of infrastructure building, mainly focusing on transport through the waterways, roads and railways lines, would generate huge capacity for employment and a vast range of ancillary industries. The industry leaders, economists, and foreign policy think-tanks from eastern India, Bangladesh and Bhutan have envisioned the Greater Ganga-Brahmaputra-Meghna Initiative – an eastern South Asian sub-regional economic cooperation initiative.[73] Development of transnational trade, including border trade, in this neighbourhood is expected to boost up strong regional growth linkages that would percolate deeper down. Along with gradual integration of capital, and output and input markets, thickly populated countries like Bangladesh would like to have formal access to the Indian labour market.[74] Given the difficulties in prohibiting illegal migration and the need for developing mutually beneficial framework for economic cooperation in the region, it would be in India's long-term interest to establish viable institutional mechanisms to effectively regulate and control cross-border population movements.

The internal factors that impede the integration of North East India to the dynamic economies of South East Asia, are several. These range from non-existent infrastructure to non-conducive investment opportunities within the region, mainly on account of the prevailing insurgency environment. Restrictions on labour movement, due to inner line regulations in at least three states of the region – Arunachal Pradesh, Nagaland, and Mizoram – does precious little to improve the situation. With nearly two-thirds of the land area under community ownership, little remains for the market. Such rigid barriers are contrary to the processes of contemporary globalization as it halts the penetration of market forces. However, it has to be borne in mind, that the region's integration to the larger transnational region may not necessarily tone down ethnic assertions. Market forces are known to have their own specificities and globalization in the region cannot be divorced from distributive performance.[75] As long as there are communities that feel marginalized, the potential of a flare always remains. This clearly calls for a long term strategic vision, that not only addresses the immediate concerns of the region but also explores future possibilities that go beyond the region. In this regard, the North Eastern Region Vision 2020 Document, released by the Prime Minister on 2 July 2008 is significant. The vision statement emphasizes on three non-economic sectors, complimenting the ongoing economic initiatives for the overall development of the region – internal security, good governance and cooperative initiatives with neighbouring Bangladesh and Burma, within the overall framework of the 'Look East' policy. In this regard, the resolve of the Ministry of External Affairs to be actively involved in the development of the North Eastern region, as a strategic extension of India's foreign policy objectives, is significant. The idea is to bring 'India's foreign policy to its borders', by working out a 'new development-foreign policy equation' that would be driven by the imperatives of economic development. The clear thrust would be towards infrastructure development and better physical connectivity with the neighbours – Bangladesh, Burma, Thailand and even China.[76]

Peace Processes

In the context of the conflict situation in North East India, there is an increasing acceptance of the reality, that though the state may not be the sole security providing agency in the region, its role is critical in the resolution of conflicts. The role particularly assumes significance, considering the fact that insurgents seldom speak in a unified voice and left on their own, communities have proved to be singularly incapable of governing their own affairs. The problem gets compounded when a plurality of insurgent outfits claim to be champions of the same community. This invariably calls for greater intervention by the state and more often than not, result in the state's transformation into a party to the conflict. With both sides contesting the representative character of the other, the question of representation assumes significance. This puts serious questions on the state's ability to act as a neutral and credible arbitrator. Observers have categorized the conflicts in the region into two: *zero-sum* and *non-zero-sum*. While non-zero-sum conflicts lend themselves to compromises and have fair chances of resolution, the zero-sum conflicts, based on mutually incompatible positions between the warring sides evade resolution.[77] Understandably, the second category of conflict provides scope for civil society initiatives to blunt the sharpness of the strife. Paradoxically, no social initiative in the region becomes viable unless it confers recognition to the 'identity' of the communities and their right to be different from the other. Implicit to this, is the conceptual distinction between the 'threatening other' and the 'fraternal other'. The challenge for the civil society is to transform the 'threatening other' to the 'fraternal other', by engaging the multiple social forces in a continuous process of dialogue and a critical process of social audit.[78] The ongoing peace processes in the region, an outcome of unprecedented civil society initiative, is clearly a pointer towards this end. This process-oriented approach to conflict resolution, is a clear departure from the previous approaches that largely emphasized on events, personalities and group-oriented behaviour. It seeks to comprehend political developments through social and political processes, that underlie such phenomenon. It is noteworthy, that 'culture' and 'identity' are being understood as products of highly interactive socio-political and economic processes, and thus not unalterable and immutable concepts. Consequently, the process of peace making in the region has invariably entailed a change, not only in the agenda of ethnic communities or organizations claiming to represent them, but also in the contending subjects involved in the process. The experiment currently underway in Nagaland and Assam offer interesting insights.

The Naga Peace Process

The future of insurgent politics in the entire North East region, to a large extent, hinges on the outcome of the talks between the GOI and the NSCN (IM), underway since mid-1997, after a formal ceasefire declaration between the GOI and the NSCN. Subsequently in 2001, the GOI also signed a ceasefire agreement with the breakaway Khaplang faction of the NSCN. Ever since, within Nagaland, an uneasy calm persists between the security forces and the Naga rebel groups. The acknowledgement of the impossibility of a military solution to the problem, by the parties to the conflict, is seen in many quarters as a historic step towards seeking a credible resolution of the conflict. The roots of the current peace initiatives go back to September 1964, when the first ceasefire between the GOI and the Federal Government of Nagaland (FGN) took place. The ceasefire declaration was an outcome of the tireless efforts of the Peace Mission, consisting of Jayprakash Narayan, Rev. Michael Scott and B.P. Chaliha – illustrious individuals representing different walks of public life. The initiative of the Peace Mission, often regarded as the first civil society initiative, clearly heralded the beginning of a new perspective to the complex Naga issue. The highpoint of the initiative was Clause 10 of the Peace Mission's proposal, which while accepting the right to self-determination of all 'subject peoples', called upon the NFG to accept the 'historical processes that have taken place to give birth to the Union of India and to the great concepts and ideals underlying the Indian Constitution'.[79] As the Mission's proposal did not adequately address the core issues of sovereignty and territoriality, it was rejected by the NFG.

The present process, which began in right earnest after the mutually accepted ceasefire came into force in Nagaland on 1 August 1997, is clearly an outcome of civil society initiatives by organizations such as the Church represented by the Council of Baptist churches, the Naga Mothers' Association and the Naga Hoho – the apex civil body of the Nagas. These organizations played a significant role in mobilizing public opinion in favour of the peace process. Drawing strength from both traditional linkages and modern institutional ideas, civil society institutions in Nagaland have emerged as a powerful force in the politics of the state. It is these institutions that are exerting pressure on the underground factions and the over ground groups, to sink in their differences and work out a settlement with the GOI.[80]

The peace talks between the GOI and the NSCN (IM), spanning over several years, have been mainly held outside the country in venues like Amsterdam and Bangkok. The one notable exception was the talks held in New Delhi in 2003. The two major issues on which the future of these talks hinge, are the issue of *sovereignty* and *territoriality*. These issues are highly emotive and have the potential to not only derail the peace process, but also engulf the entire North East region in flames. Central to the issue of territoriality is the conviction of almost all Naga groups, both underground and over ground, to live in a composite homeland. This composite homeland or Nagalim would eat into large stretches of territory of the neighbouring states of Manipur, Assam and Arunachal Pradesh. If the large-scale violence that engulfed the region in 2001, after the GOI agreed to declare ceasefire without territorial limits, is any indication, there are no easy solutions to this vexed issue. The problem gets compounded due to the confusions about the representative character of some of the outfits that claim to represent the Nagas. As things stand today, no single insurgent group can claim to be the sole representative of the Naga people. The diversity within the Naga society, clearly hits at the root of such claims. A recent development has added a new angle to the ongoing factional violence in the state. A new armed outfit, the National Socialist Council of Nagaland (Unification) or the NSCN (U) emerged on 23 November 2007, including within its fold break away members from both the NSCN factions.[81] The resulting internecine conflicts between the three Naga rebel outfits, NSCN (IM), the NSCN (Khaplang) and the

NSCN (U), raises serious questions on the durability of the peace process.[82] It is noteworthy, that the turf wars between the factions of the NSCN have claimed more lives than the insurgency itself.[83] In the given situation, it becomes abundantly clear that any GOI proposal for the resolution of the Naga imbroglio would make little headway, without meaningful negotiations with other Naga groups.

At the core of the question of *territoriality* is the idea of Greater Nagaland or Naglim, covering 120,000 kms of land claimed to be the traditional homeland of different Naga tribes, dispersed throughout the area. The mismatch between the political boundaries, put forth by the colonial administration after the advent of the British, and the social boundaries, have become the main point of contention between the different nationalities inhabiting the area. For instance, Greater Nagaland would include the three Naga populated districts of Manipur, namely Ukhrul, Tamenglong and Senapati. Any such merger, would mean an encroachment on Manipur's territory by more than half. Similarly, both Assam and Arunachal Pradesh would have to part with its territories. Clearly, it is a sensitive issue having the potential to trigger a major flare up in the entire region. On the issue of *sovereignty*, it is apparent, that an understanding has emerged among the rebel groups that the GOI does not have the mandate to concede a demand that would invariably stimulate secessionist tendencies elsewhere in India. There is also an acknowledgement that international opinion would not endorse such a move. A solution that focuses on integration and not disintegration, clearly is the favoured option. In the given situation, the feasibility of a separate independent Nagaland outside the Indian Union seems a remote possibility. A realistic solution would be to settle for maximum autonomy within the Indian Union, through structural arrangements that would maximize internal self-determination.[84] On the issue of sovereignty, way back in 1965, Rev. Michael Scott, a member of the Peace Mission, made some pertinent observations that are relevant even today. In a note titled *Bearings on the Future of Nagaland*, Scott had observed:

> What does India require of Nagaland other than the security of the border? Far from exacting tribute from the Nagas, the flow is rather from India to Nagaland in the form of a large proportion of its annual revenue ... As compared with African or colonial territories, Nagaland under the present set-up has the ownership of land and settlement under its control. Nagas cannot be forcibly or constitutionally deprived of their land as the indigenous people of South Africa for example have been deprived ... Education, health and finance are subjects under Naga jurisdiction ... If Nagaland in its, present stage of development, has not the economic resources enabling it to be independent in this real sense of the word, Naga leaders would be honest and realistic if they face these facts of life and pursue a policy which, while bringing peace to the people, will also give a reasonable prospect of achieving progress ...[85]

Given the current state of inter-tribal strife in Nagaland, it is difficult to predict the likely course of the peace process. However, the significance of the fact that over the years, the Nagas have participated in elections conducted by the GOI through its Election Commission, cannot be lost out. The decision of the NSCN (IM) to let the February 2003 state legislature elections pass by without a boycott call, is a clear indication of the changed realities. Even the March 2008 elections to the state legislature passed off without any major disturbance.[86] Clearly the acceptance of the democratic process within the ambit of the Indian Constitution, by an outfit believed to have the best fighting apparatus in the entire North East region, is an indication of the changed global geo-strategic environment. There also seems to be a resigned acceptance that every uprising has only a limited time span and beyond a point it becomes increasingly difficult to sustain the momentum. It is a slippery pitch on which both sides are navigating. Even if the NSCN (IM) dilutes its stand on sovereignty by eventually settling for greater autonomy, its uncompromising position on Greater Nagaland, that calls for the restructuring of the political boundaries of Arunachal Pradesh, Assam and Manipur, has the potential to derail the entire peace process. By all indications, pressure seems to building up on the GOI by both the rebels and the civil society groups, who clearly have become wary of the periodic extension of the ceasefire without any conclusive political action.[87] Warnings to the GOI, that the breakdown of talks would mean the end of ceasefire and resumption of hostilities, unmistakably reflects the yearning of the common Naga for peace.[88]

Peace Talks in Assam

Since October 2005, largely at the behest of the civil society, a semblance of a dialogue was initiated between the GOI and the armed separatist group ULFA nominated 11-member People's Consultative Group (PCG). The process, it was hoped would create a conducive environment, through the initiation of 'confidence building measures' (CBMs) that would eventually pave the way for direct negotiations between the GOI and the proscribed outfit. A shroud of secrecy surrounded the outcome of the three rounds of talks, that took place between the GOI and the PCG between October 2005 and June 2006. The talks were held at the highest level with the Prime Minister attending the first meeting. The second meeting, that took place against the background of a series of violent incidents in the run-up to the Republic day celebration, was between the PGC and the National Security Adviser.[89] The third Centre-PCG talks, once again held against the backdrop of a spate of bomb blasts and explosions, was presided by the Home Minister.[90] The ULFA, however refrained from directly participating in the talks and insisted on the fulfillment of certain preconditions before directly engaging the Centre. The preconditions included the immediate suspension of the army operations, impartial inquiry into cases of human rights violation by the security forces and the release of its leaders and cadres relinquishing in prisons, many of whom charged with serious crimes. The talks could not inch forward and as expected, the stumbling block was the issue of sovereignty. While the GOI expected the ULFA to situate its grievances within the framework of the Constitution and abjure violence, the ULFA in turn expected the GOI to prove its sincerity by initiating CBMs. Even after three rounds into the talks, the modalities for direct talks with the separatist outfit could not be worked out.[91] The lack of representative character of the ULFA nominated PCG, clearly raised serious questions both on its credibility and ability to push forward the talks. The continuing violence in the state, manifested through killings and bombings and the extortion drive of the ULFA, jeopardized the outcome of the talks. Consequently, the army operations that stood suspended as a goodwill gesture from 14 August 2006 was once again resumed on 24 September 2006. However, once again efforts were revived to provide direction to the seemingly directionless peace process. The PCG, again reopened channels and there was another initiative led by the Peoples' Committee for Peace Initiatives in Assam (PCPIA), clearly with the clearance of the ULFA. Relentless pressure from the military and the state police has led to a rift in the ULFA camp, with cadres pressurizing the leadership to hold talks with the GOI. It is significant that two companies of the 28th battalion, believed to be the most potent striking force of the ULFA, have declared a unilateral ceasefire, subsequent to which a good number of ULFA cadres have surrendered.[92] On its part, the GOI is being cautions and seeking opinion from the various agencies engaged in the counter-insurgency operations, before initiating any moves for the resumption of talks.

Besides Nagaland and Assam, the clamour for peace is also evident in the other states of the region.[93] Peace, communal harmony and scrapping of the oppressive Armed Forces (Special Powers) Act, are the general aspirations of the people in the other militancy ravaged parts of North East India. Human rights and developmental issues figure high in the peace agenda. So does the issue of drugs and AIDS, which manifestly is resulting in the decimation of the working age population in several parts of the region. The cry is for lasting peace through a political solution – a peace that is not at the cost of dilution of another community's cultural and territorial claims.[94] The governmental response continues to be three pronged: counter-insurgency operations by the security forces; diplomatic efforts to persuade neighbours to flush out the ultras and; negotiations towards a peace dialogue that would result in a comprehensive peace agreement with the rebels.

Towards a Comprehensive Regional Security Framework

In the South Asian context, acrimony in inter-state interactions is one of the most direct fallouts of terrorism. Violence bordering on actual terror, defines nearly every conflict in the region, be it an insurgency, an ethnic assertion, state-led security operations and even interstate proxy war. Examples abound where an attitude of consent and tacit support has driven one state's approach towards terrorist violence in a neighbouring state. Consequently, mistrust and suspicion define inter-state ties.[95] However, the intense global focus on South Asia in the aftermath of the 11 September attacks on the US, triggered a clear strategic shift in security thinking within the region. An understanding emerged, that combating terror in all its manifestations, required a holistic approach towards global and regional security, entailing cooperation at all levels – international, regional and national.[96] The coalition against terrorism, put together in the aftermath of post 9/11, released processes that profoundly impacted the conflict resolution strategies in South Asia.

Combating international terrorism is one of the stated objectives of the US in South Asia. Towards this goal, it has made a determined effort to enlist the support of both India and Pakistan. Growing military cooperation, intelligence sharing, softening of non-proliferation constrains, easing the debt burden of Pakistan and the Indo-US civilian nuclear deal, clearly indicate the US seriousness in building enduring strategic alliances in the region. However, the tone and texture of the global coalition against terrorism, put together by the US, have come under severe strain. Four intersecting areas of disagreement have adversely impacted coalition relations. The first, is the issue of *global overreach,* resulting from the vision of an open-ended conflict offered by the US. The second is the blatant *unilateralist impulse,* displayed by the US in its conduct of the war. *Value disorientation,* is the third contentious issue. Within the US government and the academic community, there is increasing recognition, that the US has only limited capabilities to impose its policies on its coalition partners and is more dependent on the support of its potential allies.[97]

Against this background, it becomes increasingly clear that regional institutions have a critical role to play in developing a cooperative security framework for dealing with both regional and global security threats. A fine example is the *Organization for Security and Cooperation in Europe* (OSCE) – clearly the largest regional security organization in the world, with states representing Europe, the Caucasus, Central Asia and North America. The OSCE's approach to security is comprehensive and cooperative and its activities mainly revolve around conflict prevention, crisis management and post-conflict rehabilitation. Wide range of security-related issues, including arms control, preventive diplomacy, confidence and security building measures, human rights, democratization, election monitoring and economic and environmental security, figure among its concerns.[98] However, an important tool that South Asia can emulate from the OSCE, is the establishment of an early warning system. 'Early warning', as an information system, is a well developed database that can predict, forecast and extrapolate on future conflict scenarios and provide timely information to decision makers.[99] However, such mechanisms will have to be located within the broadened comprehensive security framework, that clearly would mean looking beyond the traditional notions of security.

It is abundantly clear, that meeting the challenge of terrorism calls for a pragmatic set of countermeasures that would effectively contain its menace. Commitment to human security, preventive diplomacy, compliance with humanitarian law and human rights law, are essential ingredients in this endeavour. This certainly calls for a protocol among the countries of the region, declaring rejection of cross-border support for terrorism in any form. In the light of the foregoing discussion, it becomes self-evident, that the absence of an institutionalized security mechanism for South Asia has been a serious impediment in the path of trust and confidence building in the region, though efforts in this direction have not been wanting. *The SAARC Convention on Suppression of Terrorism* was adopted at the third SAARC summit in Kathmandu, in November 1987. This convention, 'required that each state should refrain from organizing, instigating, assisting or participating in acts of civil strife or terrorist acts in another state or acquiescing in organized activities within its territory directed towards the commission of such acts'.[100] The difficulty with this Convention was that, not only did it require each country to separately ratify the Convention, it also made it mandatory for member states to enact enabling legislation domestically, so as to facilitate the implementation of its critical provisions. With these goals not been pursued seriously enough, the success of the Convention (based on UN General Assembly Resolution 2625) is mainly premised on the SAARC nations displaying the political will to proceed unilaterally, bilaterally and multilaterally, towards this end. With terrorist outfits in the region having meaningful transnational linkages among themselves, the need for this Convention to be pushed forward cannot be over emphasized. To give teeth to the 1987 Convention on Terrorism, an Additional Protocol was signed among the member countries in the Islamabad Summit (6 January 2006), by the foreign ministers of SAARC. Signed against the backdrop of post 9/11, the Protocol deals with the measures to suppress and eradicate the financing of terrorism; exchange of information; extradition of terrorists and promotion of technical cooperation among member states. However, with the definition of terrorism being contested by the member countries, the hurdles in the path of its implementation remain.[101] The Fifteenth SAARC Summit held in Colombo on 2-3 August 2008, once again reiterated the resolve of the member states to combat the menace of terrorism through proactive steps. Describing terrorism as the 'single biggest threat to stability and progress' in the region, the Indian Prime Minister, urged upon the member states to evolve mechanisms to combat it.[102] The Summit Declaration, released towards the conclusion of the meet, reiterated the commitment of the member states: 'to strengthen the legal regime against terrorism, including by undertaking to implement all international conventions relating to combating terrorism to which Member States are parties, as well as the SAARC Regional Convention on Suppression of Terrorism and the Additional Protocol to the SAARC Regional Convention on the Suppression of Terrorism'.[103] In this regard, the approval of the SAARC Convention on Mutual Legal Assistance Treaty (MLAT) is significant. The treaty is believed to be path breaking, as it will facilitate greater cooperation among security forces of the SAARC member states to track, arrest and handover criminals and terrorists. The objective of the treaty, is to strengthen the two SAARC conventions on terrorism and drug trafficking.[104]

Conclusion

While the final outcome of the peace processes in North East India remains uncertain, clearly there are both expectations and apprehensions at the level of the civil society. Over the years, civil society institutions have played a significant role in breaking the 'mutually hurting stalemate' between the warring sides, shaping expectations and also setting higher standards against which the state's sincerity is evaluated. On the issue of talks with rebels, the GOI has categorically spelled out its official position on several occasions. It is willing to negotiate with any separatist/militant/insurgent/rebel/terrorist outfit, provided it locates its demands within the framework of the Indian Constitution and shuns violence. However, there have been instances when depending on the strength, durability and the perceived need to secure a settlement, the GOI has adopted flexible postures. Despite the changed international scenario, the positions taken by the rebels clearly resonate among significant sections of the population they claim to represent. This factor, in no small measure, keeps these movements alive and puts a lot of pressure on the government to negotiate. However, the intended and unintended consequences of long drawn violence in the region, heavily casts its shadow on the outcome of these negotiations. Harmonizing differences between the competing factions of the insurgents, in an environment surcharged with suspicion, proves to be the biggest challenge. To top it, a feeling of 'entrapment' by either side only adds to the complexity of the situation.

In the absence of effective governence, resulting from the breakdown of 'normal politics', the need for a viable political solution clearly stands out. However, given the nature of the turmoil in the region, the task is wrought with serious difficulties. Although none of the existing movements pose a strategic challenge of a magnitude that would impinge on the unity and integrity of India, they clearly have the capacity to seriously undermine the overall security environment of the country. India, all poised to make a massive economic leap, cannot afford to have a troubled periphery. The threat that these multiple insurgencies pose on the democratic fabric of India, is even more severe. The mutation, fracturing and transformation of these movements into criminal bands, only add to the scale of the prevailing chaos and the convergence of the political and financial motives of violence. In the face of this reality, conventional political and security interventions serve little purpose. The pattern of violence, mainly manifesting as xenophobic killings and financially driven criminal acts, thrive in a scenario of weak or non-existent implementation of the rule of law. The existing formal institutions have proved to be ineffective and the artificially imposed stability by virtue of military operations is only a mirage. Government campaigns devoid of administrative competence result in faulty, misguided policy responses. A striking example is the down playing of human rights violations, resulting in the accentuation of the social distance between the region and the rest of India and also between communities and thereby legitimizing the discourse on marginality, alienation and sub-nationalism. The situation prevailing in most states of the region, may thus be described as 'blocked'. This implies the persistence of an institutional setup, that is incapable of carrying out its duties except in a repetitive manner. The challenge clearly is to deal with this block. In the highly heterogeneous and diverse society of North East India, even if some semblance of normalcy gets restored in the near future, it will take a while for communities deformed by xenophobic politics and burdened by criminalized economies to successfully work out durable social and political contract among themselves.

Part IV

APPENDICES

APPENDIX A

10 Year Akbar Hydari Agreement: June 1947

That the right of the Nagas to develop themselves according to their expressed wishes is recognized.

1. Judicial - All cases, whether civil or criminal, arising between Nagas in Naga Hills will be disposed of by duly constituted Naga Courts according to the Naga customary laws or such as may be introduced with the consent of the duly recognized Naga representative organizations save that where a sentence of transportation or death has been passed there will be the right to appeal to the Governor.

In cases arising between Nagas and Non-Naga in (a) Kohima and Mokokchung Town areas, and (b) The judge in the neighbouring plain districts, if not Naga, will be assisted by a Naga assessor.

2. Executive - The general principle is accepted that what the Naga National Council is prepared to pay for, the Naga National Council should control. This principle will apply equally to the work done as well as the staff employment. While the Naga District Officer will be appointed at the discretion of the Governor, sub-divs of the Naga Hills should be administered by a sub-divisional council, who would be responsible to the District Officer for all matters falling within the latter's responsibility and to the Naga National Council for all matters falling within their responsibility.

In regard to:

(a) Agriculture - The Naga National Council will exercise all the powers now vested in the District Officers.

(b) C.W.D. - The Naga National Council will take over full control.

(c) Education and Forest Department - The Naga National Council is prepared to pay for all the services and staff.

3. Legislative - That no law passed by the provincial or Central Legislature which would materially affect the terms of this agreement or the religious practices of the Nagas shall have legal force in the Naga Hills without the consent of the Naga National Council. In case of dispute as to whether any law did so affect this agreement, the matter would be referred by the Naga National Council to the Governor who then may direct the law in question should not have legal force in the Naga Hills pending the decision of the Central Government.

4. **Land** – That with all its resources, the Naga Hills should not be alienated to a non-Naga without the consent of the Naga National Council.

5. **Taxation** – That the Naga National Council will be responsible for the imposition, collection and expenditure and land revenue and house-tax and of such other taxes as may be imposed by the Naga National Council.

6. **Boundaries** – That the present administrative division should be modified so as (1) to bring back to the Naga Hills District all the forest areas transferred to the Sibsagar and Nowgong Districts in the past; and (2) to bring under one unified administrative unit, as far as possible, all Naga areas so included would be within the scope of the present proposed Agreement. No areas should be transferred out of the Naga Hills without the consent of the Naga National Council.

7. **Arms Act** – The District Officer will act on the advice of the Naga National Council in accordance with the provision of the Arms Act.

8. **Regulations** – The Chin Hills Regulations and the Bengal Eastern Frontier Regulations will remain in force.

9. **Period of Agreement** – The Governor of Assam as the agent of the Government of Indian Union will have a special responsibility for a period of 10 years to ensure the due observance of this agreement; at the end of this period, the Naga National Council will be asked whether they require the above Agreement to be extended for a further period, or a new agreement regarding the future of the Naga people be arrived at.

APPENDIX B

The Shillong Agreement of November 11, 1975

1. The following representatives of the underground organizations met the Governor of Nagaland, Shri L.P.Singh representing the Government of India, at Shillong on 10th and 11th November 1975.

1. Shri I. Temjenba
2. Shri S. Dahru
3. Shri Veenyiyi Rhakhu
4. Shri Z. Ramyo
5. Shri M. Assa
6. Shri Kevi Yally

2. There was a series of four discussions. Some of the discussions were held with the Governor alone; at others, the Governor was assisted by the two Advisors for Nagaland, Shri M. Ramunny, and Shri H. Zopianga, and Shri M. L. Kampano, Joint Secretary in the Ministry of Home Affairs. All the five members of the Liaison Committee, namely Rev. Longri Ao, Dr M. Aram, Shri L. Lungalang, Shri Kenneth Kerhuo, and Shri Lungshim Shaiza, participated in the discussions.

3. The following were the outcome of the discussions:

(i) The representatives of the underground organizations conveyed their decision, of their own volition, to accept, without condition, the Constitution of India.

(ii) It was agreed that the arms, now underground, would be brought out and deposited at appointed places. Details for giving effect to this agreement will be worked out between them and representatives of the Government, the security forces, and members of the Liaison Committee.

(iii) It was agreed that the representatives of the underground organizations should have reasonable time to formulate other issues for discussion for final settlement.

Dated Shillong
November 11, 1975
Sd/-(I. Temjenba)
Sd/-(S. Dahru)
Sd/-(Z. Ramyo)
Sd/-(M.Assa)
Sd/-(Kevi Yally)

On behalf of the representative of underground organizations.
Representative of the Government of India

Sd/-(L.P. Singh)
On behalf of the Government of India.

Supplementary Agreement of January 5, 1976

Implementation of Clause II of the Shillong Accord of November 11, 1975.

1. It was decided that the collection of arms, initially at collection centers, would commence as early as possible, and will be completed by 25th January 1976. Initial places of collection to be decided through discussion between Commissioner, representatives of underground organizations and the members of the Liaison Committee.
2. Once all arms are collected, these will be handed over to Peace Council team at the respective places of collection.
3. Peace Council team will arrange to transport the arms from collection centers to Chedema Peace Camp and arrange guards, etc., for safe custody of arms.
4. Similar arrangement at agreed place/places will be made in Manipur with the concurrence of the Manipur Government.
5. The underground may stay at peace camps to be established at suitable places, and their maintenance will be arranged only by the Peace Council. Any voluntary contribution from any source will be made to the Peace Council who will utilize the fund according to necessity.

Sd/-
(L.P. Singh)

1.Sd/-
(Biseto Medom Keyho)

2.Sd/-
(Pukrove Nakru)

3. Sd/-
(Z. Rambo)

4. Sd/-
(I. Temjenba)

Place: Shillong
Dated January 5, 1976

APPENDIX C

Manipur Merger Agreement, 1949

Agreement made this twenty first day of September, 1949 between the Governor General of India and His Highness, The Maharaja of Manipur.

Whereas in the best interests of the State of Manipur as well as the Dominion of India it is desirable to provide for the administration of the said State by or under authority of the Dominion Government.

IT IS HEREBY AGREED AS FOLLOWS:

Article I

His Highness The Maharaja of Manipur hereby cedes to the Dominion Government full and exclusive authority, jurisdiction and powers for and in relation to the governance of the State and agrees to transfer administration of the State to the Dominion Government on the fifteenth day of October 1949 (there in after referred to as ' the said day'). As from the said day the Dominion Government will be competent to exercise the said powers, authority and jurisdiction in such manner and through such agency as it may think fit.

Article II

His Highness the Maharaja shall continue to enjoy the same personal rights, privileges, dignities, titles, authority over religious observances, customs, usages, rites and ceremonies and institutions in charge of the same in the State, which he would have enjoyed had this agreement not been made.

Article III

His Highness the Maharaja shall with effect from the said day be entitled to receive for his lifetime from the revenue of the State annually for his Privy Purse the sum of Rupees three lakhs free of all taxes. This amount is intended to cover all the expenses of the Ruler and his family, including expenses on account of is personal staff and armed guards, maintenance of his residences, marriages and other ceremonies, etc. and the allowances to the Ruler's relations who on the date of execution of this agreement were in receipt of such allowances from the revenues of the State, and will neither be increased nor reduced for any reason whatsoever. The Government of India undertake that the said sum of Rupees three lakhs shall be paid to His Highness the Maharaja in four equal installments in advances at the beginning of each quarter from the State treasury or at such other treasury as may be specified by the Government of India.

Article IV

His Highness the Maharaja shall be entitled to the full ownership, use and enjoyment of all private properties (as distinct from State properties) belonging to him on the date of the agreement. His Highness the Maharaja will furnish to the dominion Government before the first January 1950, an inventory of all the immovable property, securities and cash balance held by him as such private property. If any dispute arises as to whether any items of properties, the private property of His Highness the Maharaja or State property, it shall be referred to a Judicial Officer qualified to be appointed as a High Court Judge, and the decision of that officer shall be final and binding on both parties. Provided that His Highness the Maharaja's right to the use of the residences known as 'Redlands' and 'Les Chatalettes' in Shillong, and the property in the town of Gauhati known as 'Manipuri Basti' shall not be questioned.

Article V

All the members of His Highness's family shall be entitled to all the personal rights, privileges, dignities and titles enjoyed by them whether within or outside the territories of the State, immediately before the 15th August, 1947.

Article VI

The Dominion Government guarantees the succession, according to law and custom, to the gaddi of the State and to His Highness the Maharajah's personal rights, privileges, dignities, titles, authority over religious observances, customs usage, rites and ceremonies and institutions in charge of the same in the State.

Article VII

No enquiry shall be made by or under the authority of the Government of India, and no proceedings shall lie in any Court in Manipur, against His Highness the Maharaja whether in a personal capacity or otherwise in respect of anything done or omitted to be done by him or under his authority during the period of his administration of that State.

Article VIII

The Government of India hereby guarantees either the continuation in service of the permanent members of the Public Services of Manipur on conditions which will be not less advantageous than those on which they were serving before the date on which the administration of Manipur is made over to the Government of India or the payment of reasonable compensation.

The Government of India further guarantees the continuance of pensions and leave salaries sanctioned by His Highness the Maharaja to servants of the State who have retired or proceeded on leave preparatory to retirement, before the date on which the administration of Manipur is made over to the Government of India.

The Government of India shall also undertake to make suitable provisions for the employment of Manipuris in the various branches of Public Services, and in every way encourage Manipuris to join them. They also undertake to preserve various laws, customs and conventions prevailing in the State pertaining to the social economic and religious life of the people.

Article IX

Except with the previous sanction of the Government of India no proceedings, civil or criminal shall be instituted against any person in respect of any act done or purporting to be done in the execution of his duties as a servant of the State before the day on which the administration is made over to the Government of India.

In confirmation whereof Mr Vapal Pangunni Menon, Adviser to the Government of India in the Ministry of State, has appended his signature on behalf and with the authority of the Governor General of India and His Highness Maharaja Bodh Chandra Singh, Maharaja of Manipur has appended his signature on behalf of himself, his heirs and successors.

BODH CHANDRA SINGH

Maharaja of Manipur

V.P. Menon	SRI PRAKASH	September 21, 1949
Governor of Assam	Adviser to the Government of India	
Shillong	(Ministry of State)	

APPENDIX D

Assam Accord

1. Government have all along been most anxious to find a satisfactory solution to the problem of foreigners in Assam. The All Assam Students Union (AASU) and the All Assam Gana Sangram Parishad (AAGSP) have also expressed their keenness to find such solution.
2. The AASU through their Memorandum dated 2nd February 1980 presented to the late Prime Minister Smt Indira Gandhi, conveyed their profound sense of apprehensions regarding the continuing influx of foreign nationals into Assam and the fear about adverse effects upon the political, social, cultural and economic life of the State.
3. Being fully alive to the genuine apprehensions of the people of Assam, the then Prime Minister initiated the dialogue with the AASU/AAGSP. Subsequently talks were held at the Prime Minister's and Home Minister's level during the period 1980-83. Several rounds of informal talks were held during 1984. Formal discussions were resumed in March 1985.
4. Keeping all aspects of the problem including constitutional and legal provisions, international agreements, national commitments and humanitarian considerations, it has been decided to proceed as follows.

Foreigners Issue

5.1 For purposes of detection and deletion of foreigners, 1.1.1966, shall be the base data and year.

5.2 All persons who came to Assam prior to 1.1.1966, including those amongst them whose names appeared on the electoral rolls used in 1967 elections shall be regularized.

5.3 Foreigners who came to Assam after 1.1.1966 (inclusive) and up to 24th March, 1971 shall be detected in accordance with the provisions of the Foreigners Act, 1946 and the Foreigners (Tribunals) Order 1964.

5.4 Names of foreigners so detected will be deleted from the electoral rolls in force. Such persons will be required to register themselves before the Registration Officers of the respective districts in accordance with the provisions of the Registration of Foreigners Act, 1939 and the Registration of Foreigners Rules, 1939.

5.5 For this purpose, Government of India will undertake suitable strengthening of the government machinery.

5.6 On the expiry of a period of ten years following the date of detection, the names of all such persons, which have been deleted from the electoral rolls, shall be restored.

5.7 All persons who were expelled earlier, but have since re-entered illegally into Assam shall be expelled.

5.8 Foreigners who came to Assam on or after March 25, 1971 shall continue to be detected, deleted and practical steps shall be taken to expel such foreigners.

5.9 The Government will give due consideration to certain difficulties expressed by the AASU/AAGSP regarding the implementation of the Illegal Migrants (Determination by Tribunals) Acts, 1983.

Safeguards and Economic Development

6. Constitutional, legislative and administrative safeguards, as may be appropriate shall be provided to protect, preserve and promote the culture, social, linguistic identity and heritage of the Assamese people.

7. The Government takes this opportunity to renew their commitment for the speedy all round economic development of Assam, so as to improve the standard of living of the people. Special emphasis will be placed on education and science and technology through establishment of national institutions.

Other Issues

8.1 The Government will arrange for the issue of citizenship certificates in future only by the authorities of the Central Government.

8.2 Specific complaints that may be made by the AASU/AAGSP about irregular issuance of Indian Citizenship Certificates (ICC) will be looked into.

9.1 The international border shall be made secure against future infiltration by erection of physical barriers like walls, barbed wire fencing and other obstacles at appropriate places. Patrolling by security forces on land and riverine routes all along the international border shall be adequately intensified. In order to further strengthen the security arrangements, to prevent effectively future infiltration, an adequate number of check posts shall be set up.

9.2 Besides the arrangements mentioned above and keeping in view security considerations, a road all along the international border shall be constructed as to facilitate patrolling by security forces. Land between border and the road would be kept free of human habitation, wherever possible. Riverine patrolling along the international border would be intensified. All effective measures would be adopted to prevent infiltrators crossing or attempting to cross the international border.

10. It will be ensured that relevant laws for prevention of encroachment of government lands in tribal belts and blocks are strictly enforced and unauthorized encroachers evicted as laid down under such laws.
11. It will be ensured that the relevant law restricting acquisition of immovable property by foreigners in Assam is strictly enforced.
12. It will be ensured that Birth and Death Registers are duly maintained.

Restoration of Normalcy

13. The All Assam Students Union (AASU) and the All Assam Gana Sangram Parishad (AAGSP) call off the agitation, assure full co-operation and dedicate themselves towards the development of the country.
14. The Central and the State Government have agreed to:
    a. Review with sympathy and withdraw cases of disciplinary action taken against employees in the context of the agitation and to ensure that there is no victimization;
    b. Frame a scheme for ex gratia payment to next of kin of those who were killed in the course of the agitation;
    c. Give sympathetic consideration to proposal for relaxation of upper age limit for employment in public services in Assam, having regard to exceptional situation that prevailed in holding of academic and competitive examinations etc, in the context of agitation in Assam;
    d. Undertake review of detention cases, if any, as well as cases against persons charged with criminal offences in connection with the agitation, except those charged with commission of heinous offences;
    e. Consider withdrawal of the prohibitory orders/notifications in force, if any.

15. The Ministry of Home Affairs will be the nodal Ministry for the implementation of the above.

Signed/-
(P.K. Mahanta)
President
All Assam Students Union

Signed/-
(R. D. Pradhan)
Home Secretary
Govt. Of India

Signed/-
(B. K Phukan)
General Secretary
All Assam Students Union

Signed/-
(Smt. P.P. Trivedi)
Chief Secretary
Govt. of India.

Signed/-
(Biraj Sharma)
Convenor
All Assam Gana Sangram Parishad

In the presence of
Signed/-
(Rajiv Gandhi)
Prime Minister of India

Date: 5th August 1985
Place: New Delhi

1. Election Commission will be requested to ensure preparation of fair electoral rolls.
2. Time for submission of claims and objections will be extended by 30 days, subject to this being consistent with Election rules.
3. The Election Commission will be requested to send Central Observers.

Signed/-
Home Secretary

1. Oil refinery will be established in Assam.
2. Central Government will render full assistance to the State Government in their efforts to re-open:
    i. Ashok Paper Mill
    ii. Jute Mills
3. I.I.T. will be set up in Assam

APPENDIX E

Memorandum of Settlement on Bodoland Territorial Council (BTC)

On February 10, 2003, the Assam government, the Union government and the Bodo Liberation Tigers signed the Memorandum of Settlement(MoS) on Bodoland Territorial Council (BTC), in New Delhi. The jurisdiction of the BTC shall extend over 3082 villages and the BTC has been given legislative powers over 40 subjects. The accord provides for an Executive Council comprising of a maximum of 12 Executive Members, including a Chief and a Deputy Chief, with adequate representation to the non-tribal population.

Presented below is the full text of the accord.

1. The Government of India and the Government of Assam have been making concerted efforts to fulfill the aspirations of the Bodo people relating to their cultural identity, language, education and economic development. Towards this end, a series of talks were held between Government of India, Government of Assam and Bodo Liberation Tigers (BLT) since March 2000. As a result, it is agreed to create a self-governing body for the Bodo Areas in the State of Assam as follows:

2. Objectives

The objectives of the agreement are: to create an Autonomous self governing body to be known as Bodoland Territorial Council (BTC) within the State of Assam and to provide constitutional protection under Sixth Schedule to the said Autonomous Body; to fulfill economic, educational and linguistic aspirations and the preservation of land-rights, socio-cultural and ethnic identity of the Bodos; and speed up the infrastructure development in BTC area.

3. Area

3.1. The area of proposed BTC shall comprise all the 3082 villages and areas to be so notified by the State Government. The above mentioned villages and areas shall be divided into 4 contiguous districts after reorganization of the existing districts of Assam within a period of 6 months of the signing of the agreement on the lines of the proposal given by BLT subject to clearance of the Delimitation Commission.

3.2 A committee comprising one representative each from Governments of India & Assam and BLT will decide by consensus on the inclusion of additional villages and areas in the BTC from out of 95 villages and areas on the basis of the criteria of tribal population being not less than 50%, contiguity or any other agreed relevant criteria within a period of three months of signing of this MoS.

4. Status of Bodoland Territorial Council

The provision of the Sixth schedule and other relevant Articles of the Constitution of India will apply to BTC, mutatis mutandis in terms of this agreement. The safeguards/modifications for the non-tribals in BTC area, inter-alia, will include the following:

4.1. Provision of para 1 (2) of Sixth Schedule regarding Autonomous Regions will not be applicable to BTC.

4.2. A provision will be made in para 2(1) of the Sixth Schedule for increasing the number of members for BTC up to 46 out of which 30 will be reserved for Scheduled Tribes, 5 for non-tribal communities, 5 open for all communities and 6 to be nominated by Governor of Assam from the unrepresented communities for BTC area of which at least two should be women. Nominated members will have the same rights and privileges as other members, including voting rights. Election from the 40 constituencies of BTC shall be on the basis of adult franchise. The term of the elected members of BTC shall be for 5 years.

4.3. Safeguards for the settlement rights, transfer and inheritance of property etc. of non-tribals will be suitably incorporated in para 3 of the Sixth Schedule. Any such law as may be made by the BTC in this regard will not, in particular:

(a) Extinguish the rights and privileges enjoyed by a citizen of India in respect of their land at the commencement of BTC, and

(b) Bar any citizen from acquiring land either by way of inheritance, allotment, settlement or by way of transfer if such citizens were eligible for such bonafide acquisition of land within the BTC area.

4.4. Provision will be added in para 6 of Sixth Schedule that in BTC area, language and medium of instruction in educational institutions will not be changed without approval of the State Government.

4.5. Provision of para 8 of Sixth Schedule regarding power to assess and collect land revenue and impose taxes shall be applicable to BTC.

4.6. Para 10 of the Sixth Schedule will not be applicable to BTC area.

4.7. Provision of Article 332(6) of the Constitution will be so modified that the existing status of representation of BTC area in the State Assembly is kept intact. After the creation of BTC, the Parliamentary and Assembly Constituencies shall be delimited by the Delimitation Commission in accordance with the provisions of the Constitution.

4.8. In the event, **Panchayati Raj** system ceases to be in force in the council area, the powers of the Panchayati Raj Institutions in such matters shall be vested with the Council.

The Amendments to the Sixth Schedule shall include provisions in such a manner that non-tribals are not disadvantaged in relation to the rights enjoyed by them at the commencement of BTC and their rights and privileges including land rights are fully protected.

5. Power and Functions

5.1. The Council shall have legislative powers in respect to subjects transferred to it as enumerated below. All laws made under this paragraph shall be submitted forthwith to the Governor and until assented to by him, shall have no effect. The BTC shall have executive, administrative and financial powers in respect of subjects transferred to it.

Subjects to be entrusted to BTC by Assam Government

1. Small, Cottage and Rural Industry; 2. Animal Husbandry & Veterinary; 3. Forest; 4. Agriculture; 5. PWD; 6. Sericulture; 7. Education (Primary Education, Higher Secondary Including vocational training, Adult Education, College Education (General); 8. Cultural Affairs; 9. Soil Conservation; 10. Co-operation; 11. Fisheries; 12. Panchayat and Rural Development; 13. Handloom and Textile; 14. Health & Family Welfare; 15. Public Health Engineering; 16. Irrigation; 17. Social Welfare; 18. Flood Control; 19. Sports & Youth Welfare; 20. Weights and Measures; 21. Library Services; 22. Museum & Archaeology; 23. Urban Development - Town and Country Planning; 24. Tribal Research Institute; 25. Land & Revenue; 26. Publicity/Public Relations; 27. Printing & Stationery; 28. Tourism; 29. Transport; 30. Planning and Development; 31. Municipal Corporation, Improvement Trust, District Boards and other local authorities; 32. Welfare of Plan Tribes and Backward Classes; 33. Markets and fairs; 34. Lotteries, Theatres, Dramatic performance and cinema; 35. Statistics; 36. Food and Civil supply; 37. Intoxicating liquors, opium and derivatives etc.; 38. Labour and employment; 39. Relief and Rehabilitation; 40. Registration of Births and Deaths.

5.2. There shall be an Executive Council comprising of not more than 12 Executive Members, one of whom shall be the Chief and another one the Deputy Chief of the said Executive Council. There shall be adequate representation for the non-tribal members in the Executive Council. The Chief and the Deputy Chief of the Council shall have the status equivalent to the Cabinet Minister and the other Executive Members equivalent to the Minister of the State of Assam for protocol purposes in BTC area.

5.3. The BTC shall have the full control over the officers and staff connected with the delegated subjects working in the BTC area and shall be competent to transfer officers and staff within the BTC area. ACRs of these officers shall also be written by the appropriated BTC authority.

5.4. BTC shall also be competent to make appointments for all posts under its control in accordance with the rules of appointment followed by the Government of Assam. However, the posts, where recruitment is made on the recommendation of APSC, shall not be covered under this provision. The Council may constitute a Selection Board for appointments to be made by it and may also make rules, with the approval of the Governor of Assam to regulate appointments and to ensure adequate representation for all communities living in the Council area.
5.5. No posts shall be created by BTC without concurrence of the Government of Assam and it shall also abide by the decision of the Government of Assam in respect of abolition of/temporarily keeping vacant any post.
5.6. Development functions and bodies within the competence of BTC shall be transferred to BTC. In respect of DRDA, concurrence of Government of India will be obtained.
5.7. The offices of the Dy. Commissioner and Superintendent of Police will be outside the superintendence and control of BTC.
5.8. The State Government would provide an amount, to be decided every year on population ratio basis, as grants-in-aid in two equal installments to the BTC for executing development works. The proportionate share for the BTC shall be calculated on the basis of the plan funds available after setting aside the funds required for earmarked sectors and the salary. This amount may be reduced proportionately if the state plan allocation is reduced or there is plan cut due to resource problem. In addition, the Council will be paid a suitable amount of plan funds and non-plan funds to cover the office expenses and the salaries of the staff working under their control. The BTC shall disburse the salaries of the staff under their control and would ensure strict economy in the matter.
5.9. BTC authority shall prepare a plan with the amounts likely to be available for development works, both under State share and Central share, covering any or all the activities of the departments under their control. The Council shall have full discretion in selecting the activities and choosing the amount for the investment under the same in any year covering all groups of people in a fair and equitable manner. This plan will be a sub set of the State plan and would be treated as its integral part. Once the plan of the State, including BTC plan, gets the approval of the Planning Commission the BTC authority will start execution of their plan in the BTC area. Modifications, if any, made by the Planning Commission in the BTC proposal, shall be binding on the BTC authority. The State Government shall not divert the funds allocated to the BTC to other heads and also ensure its timely release. BTC may have Planning Department to prepare the plans for BTC area to be submitted to Planning Commission through the Government of Assam.
5.10. The executive functions of the BTC shall be exercised through its Principal Secretary who shall be an officer of the rank not below of Commissioner/ Secretary to Government of Assam. The sanctioning powers of the

Government of Assam shall be vested with the Principal Secretary of BTC and sanctioning powers of head(s) of the Department(s) including for technical sanction shall be conferred on the senior most officer of that Department preferably not below the rank of Additional Director, who may be designated as Director of BTC for that department. The Principal Secretary and other officers shall exercise their powers under the overall guidance and supervision of BTC.

6. Law and Order
To strengthen the Police Administration, Government of Assam shall appoint an IGP for 4 districts of BTC and the jurisdiction of the DIG Kokrajhar shall also be modified to cover these 4 districts.

7. Revision of list of ST
Consequent to the inclusion of BTC area into the Sixth Schedule, the list of ST for the State of Assam shall be so modified so as to ensure that the tribal status of Bodos and other tribals living outside the BTC area does not get affected adversely.

8. Grant of ST status of Bodo Kacharis of Karbi Anglong and NC Hills districts
The Government of India agrees to consider sympathetically the inclusion of the Bodo Kacharis living in Karbi Anglong and NC Hills Autonomous Council area in the ST (Hill) List of State of Assam.

9. Development of Bodo Language
9.1. The Government of India agrees to consider favourably the inclusion of Bodo Language in Devnagri Script in the Eighth Schedule of the Constitution.
9.2. Bodo language shall be the official language of BTC subject to the condition that Assamese and English shall also continue to be used for official purpose.

10. Additional Development Package for BTC
10.1. The State Government, within the limitation of financial and other constraints, may offer or allow the Council to offer, possible and sustainable additional incentives for attracting private investment in the Council area and would also support projects for external funding.
10.2. In order to accelerate the development of the region and to meet the aspirations of the people, the Government of India will provide financial assistance of Rs 100 crores per annum for 5 years for projects to develop the socio-economic infrastructure in BTC areas over and above the normal plan assistance to the State of Assam. The size of the Corpus will be reviewed after a period of 5 years. Suitable mechanism will be built in the system to ensure that the funds are transferred to BTC in time and at regular intervals. An

illustrative list of projects, which may be considered to be taken up in BTC are given below:

List of projects:

1. To establish a centre for development and research of Bodo language; 2. Upgradation of existing educational infrastructure by way of renovation/ addition of buildings, providing modern facilities for teaching such as computers, science laboratories etc. from primary level to college level in BTC area; 3. A cultural complex to be established at Kokrajhar to promote and develop Bodo tradition and cultural heritage; 4. To establish a super-specialty hospital with all modern facilities at Kokrajhar Government Hospitals shall be established in all district, sub-divisional and block headquarter; 5. To establish sports complexes in all the district headquarters; 6. Food processing plants and cold storage facilities at Kokrajhar, Kajolgaon, Udalguri and Tamulpur; 7. Construction of a bridge over river Aai to connect Koilamoila, Amguri etc. with the rest of the district; 8. To build a Bodoland Bhawan in Delhi; 9. To set up integrated agro-processing park and textile-cum-apparel park; 10. Revitalization of Kokilabari Agricultural Farm; 11. To develop adequate infrastructure to promote Manas sanctuary as an international tourist spot; 12. To complete Champa, Suklai and Dhansiri irrigation projects; 13. To construct a highway on the Indo-Bhutan border from Jamduar to Bhairabkunda to connect remote places located adjacent to the border; 14. To set up model dairy, fishery, horticulture and poultry farms/training centres at different places in all the 4 districts to encourage youth for self-employment; 15. To enhance the existing facilities in veterinary hospitals in BTC area.

10.3. Government of India will provide necessary one time financial assistance required for development of administrative infrastructure in the newly created district headquarters, sub-divisional headquarters and book headquarters, besides the BTC Secretariat Complex at Kokrajhar

11. Centrally funded University

11.1. A centrally funded Central Institute of Technology (CIT) will be set up to impact education in various technological/vocational disciplines such as Information Technology, Bio-Technology, Food Processing, Rural Industries, Business Management, etc.

11.2. The CIT will be subsequently upgraded to a Centrally funded State University with technical and non-technical disciplines to be run by the BTC.

12. Relief & Rehabilitation

12.1. The BLT would join the national mainstream and shun the path of violence in the interest of peace and development. After the formation of the interim council of BTC, BLT will dissolve itself as an organization and surrender with arms within a week of swearing-in of the interim council. The State Government would provide full support to relief and rehabilitation of the members of BLT who would surrender with arms in this process in accordance with the existing policy of the State. Financial support in such cases, however shall be limited to be provisions of the scheme prepared and funded by the Government of India. Withdrawal of cases against such persons and those related to overground Bodo movement since 1987 shall be considered according to the existing policy of the State of Assam.

12.2. The Government of India will initiate steps for review of action against the Bodo employees of Government of India and subordinate officers as well as in respect of Central Government Undertakings. Similar action would be taken by the Government of Assam.

12.3. Bodo youth will be considered for recruitment in Police, Army and Paramilitary forces to increase their representation in these forces.

13. Special Rehabilitation Programme for the people affected by ethnic disturbances:

The Special Rehabilitation Programme (SRP) for the people affected by ethnic disturbances in Assam, who are at present living at relief camps in Kokrajhar, Bongaigaon etc. shall be completed by the Government of Assam with active support of BTC. Necessary funds for their rehabilitation shall be provided by the Government of India and lands which are free from all encumbrances required for such rehabilitation shall be made available by the BTC.

14. Interim Council

Immediately after signing of the agreement, Interim Executive Council for BTC shall be formed by Governor of Assam from amongst the leaders of the present Bodo movement, including the signatories to this settlement, and shall include adequate representation to the non-tribal communities in BTC area. The Interim Council shall not continue for a period beyond 6 months during which period election to the Council shall be held. Government of Assam shall dissolve the Bodoland Autonomous Council (BAC) and repeal the BAC Act.

15. Government of Assam will consider inclusion of all tribals including Bodos in RHAC/MAC/LAC in consultation with leaders of these Councils.

16. The Implementation of the provision of the Memorandum of Settlement shall be periodically reviewed by a Committee comprising representatives of Government of India, Government of Assam and BTC.

Signed on 10th February, 2003 at New Delhi in the presence of Shri L.K. Advani, Hon'ble Deputy Prime Minister of India and Shri Tarun Gogoi, Chief Minister of Assam.

Hagrama (Basumatary)	(P K Dutta)	(R C A Jain)
Chairman	Chief Secretary	Secretary (BM)
Bodo Liberation Tigers	Govt. of Assam	Ministry of Home Affairs
		Government of India

APPENDIX F

Memorandum of Understanding with TNV

The following is the text of the 'memorandum of understanding' to end insurgency in Tripura.

Preamble

Government of India has been making efforts to bring about a satisfactory settlement of the problems of tribals in Tripura by restoring peace and harmony in areas where disturbed conditions prevailed.

The Tripura National Volunteers (TNV), through their letter dated 4 May 1988, addressed to the Governor of Tripura signed by Shri Bijoy Kumar Harankhawl, stated that keeping in view the Prime Minister Shri Rajiv Gandhi's Policy of solution of problems through negotiations, TNV have decided to abjure violence, give up secessionist demand and to hold negotiations for peaceful solution for all the problems of Tripura within the Constitution of India. The TNV also furnished its by-laws which confirm to the laws in force. On this basis a series of discussions were held with representatives of TNV.

The following were the outcome of the discussions:

Deposit of Arms and Ammunition and Stopping of Underground Activities by TNV

The TNV undertakes to take all necessary steps to end underground activities and to bring out all undergrounds of the TNV with their arms, ammunition and equipment within one month of signing of this memorandum. Details for giving effect to this part of settlement will be worked and implemented under the supervision of the Central Government.

The TNV further undertakes to ensure that it does not resort to violence and to help in restoration of amity between different sections of the population.

The TNV undertakes not to extend any support to any other extremist group by way of training, supply of arms or providing of protection or in any other manner.

Rehabilitation of Undergrounds

Suitable steps will be taken for the resettlement and rehabilitation of TNV undergrounds coming overground in the light of the schemes drawn up for the purpose.

Measures to Prevent Infiltration

Stringent measures will be taken to prevent infiltration from across the border by strengthening arrangements on the border and construction of roads along vulnerable sections of the Indo-Bangladesh border in Tripura Sector for better patrolling and vigil. Vigorous actions against such infiltrators will also be taken under the law.

Reservation of Seats in the Tripura Legislative Assembly for Tribals

With a view to satisfying the aspirations of tribals of Tripura for a greater share in the governance of the State, legislative measures will be taken including those for the enactment of the Bill for the amendment of the Constitution.

The Constitutional amendments shall provide that notwithstanding anything in the Constitution, the Legislative Assembly of Tripura reserved for scheduled tribes shall be such number of seats, a proportion not less than the number, as on the date of coming into force of the constitutional amendment, of members belonging to the scheduled tribes in the existing Assembly bears to the total number of seats in the existing Assembly.

The Representation of People's Act, 1950, shall also be amended to provide for reservation of 20 seats for scheduled tribes in the Assembly of Tripura. However, the amendments shall not effect any representation in the existing Assembly of Tripura until its dissolution.

Restoration of Alienated Lands of Tribals

It was agreed that following actions will be taken:

1. Review of rejected applications for restoration of tribal land under the Tripura Land Revenue and Land Reforms Act, 1960;
2. Effective implementation of the law for restoration;
3. Stringent measures to prevent fresh alienation;
4. Provision of soil conservation measures and irrigation facilities in tribal area; and
5. Strengthening of the agricultural credit system so as to provide for an appropriate agency with adequate tribal representation to ensure easy facilities for both consumption and operational credit to tribals.

Redrawing of the Boundaries of Autonomous District Council Area

Tribal majority villages, which now fall outside the autonomous district council area and are contiguous to such area will be included in the autonomous district and similarly placed non-tribal majority villages presently in the autonomous district and on the periphery may be excluded.

Measures for Long-run Economic Development of Tripura

Maximum emphasis will be placed on extensive and intensive skills-formation of the tribal youths of Tripura so as to improve their prospects of employment including self employment in various trades such as motor workshops, pharmacies, electronic goods, carpentry, tailoring, stationary, weaving, rice and oil mills, general stores, fishery, poultry, piggery, horticulture, handloom and handicrafts.

Special intensive recruitment drives will be organized for police and paramilitary forces in Tripura with a view to enlisting as many tribal youth as possible.

All-India Radio will increase the duration and content of their programmes in tribal languages and dialects of Tripura. Additional transmitting stations will be provided for coverage even to the remoter areas of the State.

The demands relating to self-employment of tribals, issue of permits for vehicles to tribals for commercial purposes, visits of tribalmen and women to such places in the country as may be of value from the viewpoint of inspiration, training and the experience in relevant fields will be considered sympathetically by the government.

At least 2,500 *Jhumia* families will be rehabilitated in five centers or more in accordance with model schemes based on agriculture, horticulture including vegetable growing, animal husbandry, fisheries and plantations, with a view to weaning them away from *Jhum* cultivation. The scheme would also provide for housing assistance.

In the autonomous district council area of Tripura, rice, salt and kerosene oil will be given at subsidized rates during lean months for a period of three years.

Conscious effort will be made for effective implementation of the provisions of the Sixth Schedule of the Constitution insofar as it relates to Tripura.

APPENDIX G

The Armed Forces (Special Powers) Act, 1958
Act 28 of 1958, 11th September, 1958

An Act to enable certain special powers to be conferred upon members of the armed forces in disturbed areas in the State of [1][Arunachal Pradesh, Assam, Manipur, Meghalaya, Mizoram, Nagaland and Tripura].

Be it enacted by Parliament in the Ninth Year of the Republic of India as follows:

1. Short Title and Extent – (1) This Act may be called[2] [The Armed Forces (Special Powers) Act, 1958].

[3][(2) It extends to the whole of the State of [4][Arunachal Pradesh, Assam, Manipur, Meghalaya, Mizoram, Nagaland and Tripura].

2. Definitions – In this Act, unless the context otherwise requires:

(a) "Armed forces" means the Military forces and the air forces operating as land forces, and includes any other armed forces of the Union so operating;

(b) "Disturbed area" means an area which is for the time being declared by notification under section 3, to be a disturbed area;

(c) All other words and expressions used herein, but not defined and defined in the Air Force Act, 1950 (45 of 1950), or the Army Act, 1950 (46 of 1950) shall have meanings respectively assigned to them in those Acts.

3. Power to Declare Areas to be Disturbed Areas – If, in relation to any State or Union territory of which the Act extends, the Governor of that State or the Administrator of that Union territory or the Central Government, in either case, if of the opinion that the whole or any part of such State or Union territory, as the case may be, is in such a disturbed or dangerous condition that the use of armed forces in aid of the civil powers is necessary, the Governor of that State or the Administrator of that Union territory or the Central Government, as the case may be, may, by notification in the Official Gazette, declare the whole or such part of such State or Union territory to be a disturbed area].

4. Special Power of the Armed Forces – Any commissioned officer, warrant officer, non commissioned officer or any other person of equivalent rank in the armed forces may, in a disturbed area –

(a) If he is of opinion that it is necessary so to do for the maintenance of Public order, after giving such due warning as he may consider necessary, fire upon or otherwise use force, even to the causing of death, against any person who is acting in contravention of any law or order for the time being in force in the disturbed area prohibiting the assembly of five or more persons or the carrying of weapons or of things capable of being used as weapons or of fire-arms, ammunition or explosive substances;

(b) If he is of opinion that it is necessary so to do, destroy any arms dump, prepared or fortified position or shelter from which armed attacks are made or are likely to be made or are attempted to be made, or any structure used as a training camp for armed volunteers or utilized as a hide-out by armed gangs or absconders wanted for any offence;

(c) Arrest, without warrant, any person who has committed a cognizable offence or against whom a reasonable suspicion exists that he has committed or is about to commit a cognizable offence and may use such force as may be necessary to effect the arrest;

(d) Enter and search without warrant any premises to make any such arrest as aforesaid or to recover any person believed to be wrongfully restrained or confined or any property reasonably suspected to be stolen property or any arms, ammunition or explosive substances believed to be unlawfully kept in such premises and may for that purpose use such force as may be necessary.

5. Arrested Persons to be made over to the Police – Any person arrested and taken into custody under this Act shall be made over to the officer-in-charge of the nearest police station with the least possible delay, together with a report of the circumstances occasioning the arrest.

6. Protection to Persons acting under Act – No persecution, suit or other legal proceeding shall be instituted, except with the previous sanction of the Central Government, against any person in respect of anything done or purported to be done in exercise of the powers conferred by this Act.

7. Repeal and Saving – [Repealed by Amending and Repealing Act, 1960 (58 of 1960), First Schedule, sec. 2 (26-12-1960)]

1. Subs. By Act 69 of 1986, sec. 43, for "Assam, Manipur, Meghalaya, Mizoram, Nagaland and Tripura and the Union Territory of Arunachal Pradesh" (w.e.f. 20-2-1987).
2. Subs. By Act 7 of 1972, sec. 3, for "the Armed Forces (Assam and Manipur) Special Powers Act., 1958" (w.e.f. 5-4-1972).
3. Subs. By Act 7 of 1972, sec. 4 (w.e.f. 5-4-1972).
4. Subs. By Act 69 of 1986, sec. 43, for "Assam, Manipur, Meghalaya, Mizoram, Nagaland and Tripura and the Union territory of Arunachal Pradesh" (w.e.f. 20-2-1987).

APPENDIX H

Disturbed Areas (Special Courts Act), 1976

An Act to Provide for the Speedy Trial of Certain Offences in Certain Areas

1. Short title, extent and commencement.

(1) This Act may be called the Disturbed Areas (Special Courts) Act, 1976.

(2) It extends to the whole of India except the State of Jammu and Kashmir.

(3) It shall come into force on such date as the Central Government may, by notification in the Official Gazette, appoint and different dates may be appointed for different States or for different

Parts thereof

2. Definitions. In this Act, unless the context otherwise requires, -

(a) "Code" means the Code of Criminal Procedure, 1973; (2 of 1974)

(b) "Disturbed area" means an area declared as a disturbed area under section 3;

(c) Period of disturbance in relation to a disturbed area, means the period during which it is to be a disturbed area for the purposes of section 3;

(d) "Scheduled offence" means an offence specified in the Schedule being an offence forming part or arising out of, or connected with, any such disturbance as is referred to in section 3;

(e) "Special Court" means a Special Court constituted under section 4;

(f) Words and expressions used but not defined in this Act, and defined in the Code shall have the meanings respectively assigned to them in the Code.

3. Declaration or an area as disturbed area. (1) Where a State Government is satisfied that- (i) there was, or (ii) there is, in any area within a State extensive disturbance of the public peace and tranquility, by reason of differences or disputes between members of different religious, racial, language or regional groups or castes or 4. 15-8-1976: Vide Notification S.O. 549(E), dt. 13-8-1976. Communities, it may, by notification in the Official Gazette, declare such area to be a disturbed area. (2) A notification issued under sub-section (1) in respect of any area shall specify the period during which the area shall, for the purposes of this section, be a disturbed area and where the State Government is satisfied that there was such disturbance of public peace and tranquility as is referred to in sub-section (1) in that area from any date prior to the issue of such notification, the period specified in the notification may commence from that date: Provided that – (a) no period commencing from a date earlier than three months before the date of publication of the notification shall be specified therein ; and (b) so much of the period specified in such notification as is subsequent to the date of publication of the notification shall not, in the first instance, exceed three months but the State Government may amend such notification to extend such period from time to time by any period not exceeding three months at any one time if in the opinion of the State Government there continues to be in such area such disturbance of public peace and tranquility as is referred to in sub-section (1): Provided further that where the State Government is satisfied that there is no longer such disturbance of public peace and tranquility as is referred to in sub-section (1) in such area, it shall amend the notification issued under that sub-section in respect of that area to limit the period specified therein (whether originally or by amendment under the preceding provison) accordingly.

4. Constitution of Special Courts. (1) The State Government may, for the purpose of providing speedy trial of scheduled offences committed in disturbed areas, by notification in the Official Gazette, constitute as many Special Courts as may be necessary in or in relation to such disturbed area or areas as may be specified in the notification. (2) A Special Court shall consist of a single judge who shall be appointed by the High Court upon a request made by the State Government. Explanation.-In this sub-section, the word "appoint" shall have the meaning given to it in the Explanation to section 9 of the Code. (3) A person shall not be qualified for appointment as a judge of a Special Court unless – (a) he is qualified for appointment as a judge of a High Court, or (b) he has, for a period of not less than one year, been a Sessions Judge or an Additional Sessions Judge. (4) Notwithstanding anything contained in sub-section (3), a person shall not be eligible for being appointed as, and for being, a Judge of a Special Court in any State after he has attained the age at which Sessions Judges in that State have to retire from service.

5. Jurisdiction of Special Courts. (1) Notwithstanding anything contained in the Code or any other law, a scheduled offence committed in any disturbed area at any time during the period during which it is a disturbed area shall be triable, whether during or after such period, only by the Special Court constituted in or in relation to the disturbed area in which the offence has been committed. (2) When trying any scheduled offence, a Special Court may also try any offence other than the scheduled offence with which the accused may, under the Code, be charged at the same trial if the offence is connected with the scheduled offence.

6. Procedure and powers of Special Courts. (1) Every scheduled offence shall be cognizable. (2) A Special Court may take cognizance of any scheduled offence- (a) where under the Code such offence is an offence triable exclusively by a Court of Session, upon its being committed to it under section 209 of the Code as if the Special Court were a Court of Session; (b) in any other case, upon a police report of the facts together with a certificate from the public prosecutor to the effect that the offence is triable exclusively by the Special Court. (3) Where a scheduled offence is an offence triable exclusively by a Court of Session under the Code, a Special Court shall have all the powers of a Court of Session and shall try such offence as if it were a Court of Session, so far as may be in accordance with the procedure prescribed in the Code for trial before a Court of Session. (4) Where a scheduled offence is an offence which is punishable with imprisonment for a term exceeding three years but which, according to the provisions of the Code, is not an offence triable exclusively by a Court of Session, a Special Court may on taking cognizance of the offences perform the functions of a Magistrate under section 207 of the Code and thereafter try such offence so far as may be in accordance with the procedure prescribed in the Code for trial before a Court of Session as if the Special Court were a Court of Session and the case had been committed to it for trial under the provisions of the Code. (5) Where a scheduled offence is punishable with imprisonment for a term not exceeding three years or with fine or with both, a Special Court may, notwithstanding anything contained in sub-section (1) of section 260 or section 262 of the Code, try the offence in a summary way in accordance with the procedure prescribed in the Code and the provisions of sections 263 to 265 of the Code, shall so far as may be, apply to such trial: Provided that when, in the course of a summary trial under this sub-section, it appears to the Special Court that the nature of the case is such that it is-undesirable to try it summarily, the Special Court shall recall any witnesses who may have been examined and proceed to rehear the case in the manner provided by the provisions of the Code for the trial of such offence and the said provisions shall apply to and in relation to a Special Court as they apply to and in relation to a Magistrate: Provided further that in the case of any conviction in a summary trial under this section, it shall be lawful for a Special Court to pass a sentence of imprisonment for a term not exceeding two years. (6) A Special Court may, with a view to obtaining the evidence of any person suspected to have been directly or indirectly concerned in, or privy to, an offence, tender a pardon to such person on condition of his making a full and true disclosure of the whole circumstances within his knowledge relating to the offence and to every other person concerned whether as principal or abettor in the commission thereof and any pardon so tendered shall, for the purposes of section 308 of the Code, be deemed to have been tendered under section 307 thereof.

7. Power to transfer cases to regular courts. Where, after taking cognizance of any offence, a Special Court is of opinion that the offence is not a scheduled offence, it shall, notwithstanding that it has no jurisdiction to try the case, transfer the case for trial, to any court having jurisdiction under the Code and the court to which the case is transferred may proceed with the case as if it had taken cognizance of the offence.

8. Appeal and revision. The High Court may exercise, so far as they may be applicable, all the powers conferred by Chapters XXIX and XXX of the Code on a High Court, as if a Special Court is a Court of Session trying cases within the local limits of the jurisdiction of the High Court.

9. Overriding effect of Act. (1) The provisions of this Act shall have effect notwithstanding anything contained in the Code or any other law, but save as expressly provided in this Act, the provisions of the Code shall,, in so far as they are not inconsistent with the provisions of this Act apply to the proceedings before a Special Court; and for the purposes of the said provisions of the Code, the Special Court shall be deemed to be a Court of Session and the person conducting a prosecution before a Special Court shall be deemed to be a public prosecutor. (2) In particular and without prejudice to the generality of the provisions contained in sub-section (1), the provisions of sections 326 and 475 of the Code shall, so far as may be, apply to the proceedings before a Special Court, and for this purpose references in those provisions to a Magistrate shall be construed as references to the Special Court.

10. Savings. (1) Nothing in this Act shall affect the jurisdiction exercisable by, or the procedure applicable to, any court or other authority under any law relating to the naval, military or air forces or any other armed forces of the Union. (2) For the removal of doubts, it is hereby declared that for the purposes of any such law as is referred to in sub-section (1), a Special Court shall be deemed to be a court of ordinary criminal Justice

THE SCHEDULE

[See section 2 (d)]

1. Offences under the following provisions of the Indian Panel Code:

(45 of 1860)

Section 120B;

Sections 143 to 145, 147, 148, 151 to 155, 157, 158 and 160;

Sections 182, 183, 186 to 190;

Sections 193 to 195, 199, 201 to 203, 211 to 214, 216, 216A and 225

Sections 295 to 298;

Sections 302, 303, 304, 307, 308, 323 to 335, 341 to 348, 352 to 358, 363 to 369 and 376;

Sections 379, 380, 382, 384 to 387, 392 to 399, 402, 411, 412, 426, 427, 431, 435, 436, 440, 447 to 462;

Sections 504 to 506 and 509.

2. Offences under the following provisions of the Arms Act, 1959: (54of 1959) Sections 25 to 30.

3. Offences under the following provisions of the Indian Explosives Act, 1884, Sections 6(3) and 8(2).

APPENDIX I

The National Security Act, 1980
Enactment Date: [27th December, 1980]

1. Act Objective: An Act to provide for preventive detention in certain cases and for matters connected therewith. BE it enacted by Parliament in the Thirty-first Year of the Republic of India as follows: –

2. Definitions. In this Act, unless the context otherwise requires, –

(a) "Appropriate Government" means, as respects a detention order made by the Central Government or a person detained under such order, the Central Government, and as respects a detention order made by a State Government or by an officer subordinate to a State Government or as respects a person detained under such order, the State Government;

(b) "Detention order" means an order made under section 3;

(c) "Foreigner" has the same meaning as in the Foreigners Act, 1946 (31 of 1946);

(d) "Person" includes a foreigner;

(e) "State Government", in relation to a Union territory, means the administrator thereof.

3. Power to make orders detaining certain persons. (1) The Central Government or the State Government may, – (a) if satisfied with respect to any person that with a view to preventing him from acting in any manner prejudicial to the defence of India, the relations of India with foreign powers, or the security of India, or (b) if satisfied with respect to any foreigner that with a view to regulating his continued presence in India or with a view to making arrangements for his expulsion from India, it is necessary so to do, make an order directing that such person be detained. (2) The Central

Government or the State Government may, if satisfied with respect to any person that with a view to preventing him from acting in any manner prejudicial to the security of the State or from acting in any manner prejudicial to the maintenance of Public order or from acting in any manner prejudicial to the maintenance of supplies and services essential to the community it is necessary so to do, make an order directing that such person be detained. Explanation - For the purposes of this sub-section, "acting in any manner prejudicial to the maintenance of supplies and services essential to the community" does not include "acting in any manner prejudicial to the maintenance of supplies of commodities essential to the community" as defined in the Explanation to sub-section (1) of section 3 of the Prevention of Black-marketing and Maintenance of Supplies of Essential Commodities Act, 1980 (7 of 1980), and accordingly, no order of detention shall be made under this Act on any ground on which an order of detention may be made under that Act. (3) If, having regard to the circumstances prevailing or likely to prevail in any area within the local limits of the jurisdiction of a District Magistrate or a Commissioner of Police, the State Government is satisfied that it is necessary so to do, it may, by order in writing, direct, that during such period as may be specified in the order, such District Magistrate or Commissioner of Police may also, if satisfied as provided in sub-section (2), exercise the powers conferred by the said sub-section: Provided that the period specified in an order made by the State Government under this sub-section shall not, in the first instance, exceed three months, but the State Government may, if satisfied as aforesaid that it is necessary so to do, amend such order to extend such period from time to time by any period not exceeding three months at any one time. (4) When any order is made under this section by an officer mentioned in sub-section (3), he shall forthwith report the fact to the State Government to which he is subordinate together with the grounds on which the order has been made and such other particulars as, in his opinion, have a bearing on the matter, and no such order shall remain in force for more than twelve days after the making thereof unless, in the meantime, it has been approved by the State Government: Provided that where under section 8 the grounds of detention are communicated by the officer making the order after five days but not later than ten days from the date of detention, this sub-section shall apply subject to the modification that, for the words "twelve days", the words "fifteen days" shall be substituted. (5) When any order is made or approved by the State Government under this section, the State Government shall, within seven days, report the fact to the Central Government together with the grounds on which the order has been made and such other particulars as, in the opinion of the State Government, have a bearing on the necessity for the order.

4. Execution of detention orders. A detention order may be executed at any place in India in the manner provided for the execution of warrants of arrest under the Code of Criminal Procedure, 1973 (2 of 1974).

5. Power to regulate place and conditions of detention. Every person in respect of whom a detention order has been made shall be liable – (a) to be detained in such place and under such conditions, (b) including conditions as to maintenance, discipline and punishment for breaches of discipline, as the appropriate Government may, by general or special order, specify; and (c) to be removed from one place of detention to another place of detention, whether within the same State or in another State, by order of the appropriate Government: Provided that no order shall be made by a State Government under clause (d) for the removal of a person from one State to another State except with the consent of the Government of that other State.

6. Detention orders not to be invalid or inoperative on certain grounds. No detention order shall be invalid or inoperative merely by reason – (a) that the person to be detained there under is outside the limits of the territorial jurisdiction of the Government or officer making the order, or (b) that the place of detention of such person is outside the said limits.

7. Powers in relation to absconding persons. (1) If the Central Government or the State Government or an officer mentioned in sub- section (3) of section 3, as the case may be, has reason to believe that a person in respect of whom a detention order has been made has absconded or is concealing himself so that the order cannot be executed, that Government or officer may – (a) make a report in writing of the fact to a Metropolitan Magistrate or a Judicial Magistrate of the first class having jurisdiction in the place where the said person ordinarily resides; (b) by order notified in the Official Gazette direct the said person to appear before such officer, at such place and within such period as may be specified in the order. (2) Upon the making of a report against any person under clause (a) of sub-section (1), the provisions of sections 82, 83, 84 and 85 of the Code of Criminal Procedure, 1973 (2 of 1974), shall apply in respect of such person and his property as if the detention order made against him were a warrant issued by the Magistrate. (3) If any person fails to comply with an order issued under clause (b) of sub-section (1), he shall, unless he proves that it was not possible for him to comply therewith and that he had, within the period specified in the order, informed the officer mentioned in the order of the reason which rendered compliance therewith impossible and of his whereabouts, be punishable with imprisonment for a term which may extend to one year, or with fine, or with both. (4) Notwithstanding anything contained in the Code of Criminal Procedure, 1973 (2 of 1974), every offence under sub-section (3) shall be cognizable.

8. Grounds of order of detention to be disclosed to persons affected by the

order. (1) When a person is detained in pursuance of a detention order, the authority making the order shall, as soon as may be, but ordinarily not later than five days and in exceptional circumstances and for reasons to be recorded in writing, not later than ten days from the date of detention, communicate to him the grounds on which the order has been made and shall afford him the earliest opportunity of making a representation against the order to the appropriate Government. (2) Nothing in sub-section (1) shall require the authority to disclose facts which it considers to be against the public interest to disclose.

9. Constitution of Advisory Boards. (1) The Central Government and each State Government shall, whenever necessary, constitute one or more Advisory Boards for the purposes of this Act. (2) Every such Board shall consist of three persons who are, or have been, or are qualified to be appointed as, Judges of a High Court, and such persons shall be appointed by the appropriate Government. (3) The appropriate Government shall appoint one of the members of the Advisory Board who is, or has been, a Judge of a High Court to be its Chairman, and in the case of a Union territory, the appointment to the Advisory Board of any person who is a Judge of the High Court of a State shall be with the previous approval of the State Government concerned.

10. Reference to Advisory Boards. Save as otherwise expressly provided in this Act, in every case where a detention order has been made under this Act, the appropriate Government shall, within three weeks from the date of detention of a person under the order, place before the Advisory Board constituted by it under section 9, the grounds on which the order has been made and the representation, if any, made by the person affected by the order, and in case where the order has been made by an officer mentioned in sub-section (3) of section 3, also the report by such officer under sub-section (4) of that section.

11. Procedure of Advisory Boards. (1) The Advisory Board shall, after considering the materials placed before it and, after calling for such further information as it may deem necessary from the appropriate Government or from any person called for the purpose through the appropriate Government or from the person concerned, and if, in any particular case, it considers it essential so to do or if the person concerned desires to be heard, after hearing him in person, submit its report to the appropriate Government within seven weeks from the date of Detention of the person concerned. (2) The report of the Advisory Board shall specify in a separate part thereof the opinion of the Advisory Board as to whether or not there is sufficient cause for the detention of the person concerned. (3) When there is a difference of opinion among the members forming the Advisory Board, the opinion of the majority of such members shall be deemed to be the opinion of the Board. (4) Nothing in this section shall entitle any person against whom a detention order has been made to appear by any legal practitioner in any matter connected with the reference to the Advisory Board; and the proceedings of the Advisory Board and its report, excepting that part of the report in which the opinion of the Advisory Board is specified, shall be confidential.

12. Action upon the report of the Advisory Board. (1) In any case where the Advisory Board has reported that there is, in its opinion, sufficient cause for the detention of a person, the appropriate Government may confirm the detention order and continue the detention of the person concerned for such period as it thinks fit. (2) In any case where the Advisory Board has reported that there is, in its opinion, no sufficient cause for the detention of a person, the appropriate Government shall revoke the detention order and cause the person concerned to be released forthwith.

13. Maximum period of detention. The maximum period for which any person may be detained in pursuance of any detention order which has been confirmed under section 12 shall be twelve months from the date of detention: Provided that nothing contained in this section shall affect the power of the appropriate Government to revoke or modify the detention order at any earlier time.

14. Revocation of detention orders. (1) Without prejudice to the provisions of section 21 of the General Clauses Act, 1897 (10 of1897), a detention order may, at any time, be revoked or modified, – (a) notwithstanding that the order has been made by an officer mentioned in sub-section (3) of section 3, by the State Government to which that officer is subordinate or by the Central Government; (b) notwithstanding that the order has been made by a State Government, by the Central Government.

15. Temporary release of persons detained. (1) The appropriate Government may, at any time, direct that any person detained in pursuance of a detention order may be released for any specified period either without conditions or upon such conditions specified in the direction as that person accepts, and may, at any time, cancel his release. (2) In directing the release of any person under sub-section (1), the appropriate Government may require him to enter into a bond with or without sureties for the due observance of the conditions specified in the direction. (3) Any person released under sub-section (1) shall surrender himself at the time and place, and to the authority, specified in the order directing his release or cancelling his release, as the case may be. (4) If any person fails without sufficient cause to surrender himself in the manner specified in sub-section (3), he shall be punishable with imprisonment for a term, which may extend to two years, or with fine, or with both. (5) If any person released under sub-section (1) fails to fulfil any of the conditions imposed upon him under the said sub-section or in the bond entered into by him, the bond shall be declared to be forfeited and any person bound thereby shall be liable to pay the penalty thereof.

16. Protection of action taken in good faith. No suit or other legal proceeding shall lie against the Central Government or a State Government, and no suit, prosecution or other legal proceeding shall lie against any person, for anything in good faith done or intended to be done in pursuance of this Act.

17. Act not to have effect with respect to detentions under State laws. (1) Nothing in this Act shall apply or have any effect with respect to orders of detention, made under any State law, which are in force immediately before the commencement of the National Security Ordinance, 1980 (11 of 1980), and accordingly every person in respect of whom an order of detention made under any State law is in force immediately before such commencement, shall be governed with respect to such detention by the provisions of such State law or where the State law under which such order of detention is made is an Ordinance (hereinafter referred to as the State Ordinance) promulgated by the Governor of that State and the State Ordinance has been replaced – (i) before such commencement, by an enactment passed by the Legislature of that State, by such enactment; or (ii) after such commencement, by an enactment which is passed by the Legislature of that State and the application of which is confined to orders of detention made before such commencement under the State Ordinance, by such enactment, as if this Act had not been enacted. (2) Nothing in this section shall be deemed to bar the making under section 3, of a detention order against any person referred to in sub-section (1) after the detention order in force in respect of him as aforesaid immediately before the commencement of the National Security Ordinance, 1980 (11 of 1980), ceases to have effect for any reason whatsoever. Explanation – For the purposes of this section, "State law" means any law providing for preventive detention on all or any of the grounds on which an order of detention may be made under sub-section (2) of section 3 and in force in any State immediately before the commencement of the said Ordinance.

18. Repeal and saving. (1) The National Security Ordinance, 1980 (11 of 1980), is hereby repealed. (2) Notwithstanding such repeal, anything done or any action taken under the said Ordinance shall be deemed to have been done or taken under the corresponding provisions of this Act, as if this Act had come into force on the 23rd day of September, 1980, and, in particular, any reference made under section 10 of the said Ordinance and pending before any Advisory Board immediately before the date on which this Act receives the assent of the President may continue to be dealt with by that Board after that date as if such Board had been constituted under section 9 of this Act.

1* Ins. by Act 60 of 1984, s. 2 (w.e.f. 21-6-1984).

APPENDIX J

Terrorist Affected Areas (Special Courts) Act, 1984

1. Objective: An Act to provide for the speedy trial of certain offences in terrorist affected areas and for matters connected therewith. BE it enacted by Parliament in the Thirty-fifth Year of the Republic of India as follows: –

2. Definitions: (1) In this Act, unless the context otherwise requires, –

(a) "Code" means the Code of Criminal Procedure, 1973 (2 of 1974);

(b) "High Court", in relation to a Special Court, means the High Court within the territorial limits of whose jurisdiction such Special Court is proposed to be, or is, established;

(c) "Judicial zone" means a judicial zone constituted under sub-section (1) of section 3;

(d) "Notification" means a notification published in the Official Gazette;

(e) "Public Prosecutor" means a Public Prosecutor or an Additional Public Prosecutor or a Special Public Prosecutor appointed under section 9 and includes any person acting under the directions of the Public Prosecutor;

(f) "Scheduled offence" means an offence specified in the Schedule being an offence committed in a terrorist affected area;

(g) "Special Court" means a Special Court or an Additional Special Court established under section 4;

(h) "Terrorist" means a person who indulges in wanton killing of persons or in violence or in the disruption of services or means of communications essential to the community or in damaging property with a view to – (i) putting the public or any section of the public in fear; or (ii) affecting adversely the harmony between different religious, racial, language or regional groups or castes or communities; or (iii) coercing or overawing the Government established by law; or (iv) endangering the sovereignty and integrity of India;

(i) "Terrorist affected area" means an area declared as a terrorist affected area under section 3;

(j) Words and expressions used but not defined in this Act and defined in the Code shall have the meanings respectively assigned to them in the Code.

(2) Any reference in this Act to the Code or any provision thereof shall, in relation to an area in which the Code or such provision is not in force, be construed as a reference to the corresponding law or the relevant provision of the corresponding law, if any, in force in that area.

3. Declaration of terrorist affected area: (1) If the Central Government is of the opinion that offences of the nature specified in the Schedule are being committed in any area by terrorists on such a scale and in such a manner that it is expedient for the purpose of coping with the activities of such terrorists to have recourse to the provisions of this Act, it may, by notification, – (a) eclare such area to be a terrorist affected area; and (b) constitute such area into a single judicial zone or into as many judicial zones as it may deem fit.

(2) A notification issued under sub-section (1) in respect of an area shall specify the period during which the area shall, for the purposes of this Act, be a terrorist affected area, and where the Central Government is of the opinion that terrorists had been committing in that area, from a date earlier than the date of issue of the notification, offences of the nature specified in the Schedule on such a scale and in such a manner that it is expedient to commence the period specified in the notification from such earlier date, the period specified in the notification may commence from that date: Provided that – (a) no period commencing from a date earlier than six months from the date of publication of the notification shall be specified therein; and (b) so much of the period specified in such notification as is subsequent to the date of publication of the notification shall not, in the first instance, exceed six months, but the Central Government may, by notification, extend such period from time to time by any period not exceeding six months at any one time, if the Central Government, having regard to the activities of terrorists in such area, is of the opinion that it is expedient so to do.

Explanation: For the avoidance of doubts, it is hereby declared that the period specified in a notification issued under this section may commence from a date earlier than the date of commencement of this Act.

4. Establishment of Special Courts: (1) For the purpose of Providing for speedy trial of scheduled offences committed in a judicial zone, the Central Government may establish, by notification, a Special Court in relation to such judicial zone - (a) within such judicial zone; or (b) if the Central Government having regard to the exigencies of the situation in such judicial zone considers it expedient so to do, at any place outside such judicial zone but within the State in which such judicial zone is situated.

(2) Notwithstanding anything contained in sub-section (1), if, having regard to the exigencies of the situation prevailing in a State, the State Government is of the opinion that it is expedient to establish in relation to a judicial zone, or in relation to two or more judicial zones, in the State, an Additional Special Court outside the State, for the trial of such scheduled offences committed in the judicial zone or judicial zones, the trial whereof within the State - (a) is not likely to be fair or impartial or completed with utmost dispatch; or (b) is not likely to be feasible without occasioning a breach of peace or grave risk to the safety of the accused, the witnesses, the Public Prosecutor and the Judge or any of them; or (c) is not otherwise in the interests of justice, the State Government may request the Central Government to establish in relation to such judicial zone or judicial zones an Additional Special Court outside the State and thereupon the Central Government may, after taking into account the information furnished by the State Government and making such inquiry, if any, as it may deem fit, establish, by notification, such Additional Special Court at such place outside the State as may be specified in the notification.

5. Composition and appointment of Judges of Special Courts: (1) A Special Court shall be presided over by a judge to be appointed by the Central Government with the concurrence of the Chief Justice of the High Court.

(2) The Central Government may also appoint, with the concurrence of the Chief Justice of the High Court, Additional judges to exercise jurisdiction in a Special Court.

(3) A person shall not be qualified for appointment as a Judge or an Additional judge of a Special Court unless he is immediately before such appointment a Sessions Judge or an Additional Sessions Judge in any State.

(4) For the removal of doubts, it is hereby provided that the attainment by a person, appointed as a Judge or an Additional Judge of a Special Court, of age of superannuation under the rules applicable to him in the Service to which he belongs, shall not affect his continuance as such Judge or Additional Judge.

(5) Where any Additional Judge or Additional Judges is, or are, appointed in a Special Court, the Judge of the Special Court may, from time to time, by

general or special order, in writing, provide for the distribution of business of the Special Court among himself and the Additional Judge or Additional Judges and also for the disposal of urgent business in the event of his absence or the absence of any Additional Judge.

6. Place of sitting: A Special Court may, if it considers it expedient or desirable so to do, sit for any of its proceedings at any place, other than the ordinary place of its sitting, in the State in which it is established: Provided that if the Public Prosecutor certifies to the Special Court that it is in his opinion necessary for the protection of the accused or any witness or otherwise expedient in the interests of justice that the whole or any part of the trial should be held at some place other than the ordinary place of its sitting, the Special Court may, after hearing the accused, make an order to that effect unless, for reasons to be recorded in writing, the Special Court thinks fit to make any other order.

7. Jurisdiction of Special Court: (1) Notwithstanding anything contained in the Code or in any other law, a scheduled offence committed in a judicial zone in a State at any time during the period during which such judicial zone is, or is part of, a terrorist affected area shall be triable, whether during or after the expiry of such period, only by the Special Court established for such judicial zone in the State: Provided that where the period specified under sub-section (2) of section 3 as the period during which an area declared by notification under sub-section (1) of that section to be a terrorist affected area commences from a date earlier than the date on which such notification is issued, then – (a) nothing in the foregoing provisions of this sub-section shall apply to a scheduled offence committed in such area in which the whole of the evidence for the prosecution has been taken before the date of issue of such notification; and (b) all other cases involving scheduled offences committed in such area and pending before any court immediately before the date of issue of such notification shall stand transferred to the Special Court having jurisdiction under this section and the Special Court to which such proceedings stand transferred shall proceed with such cases from the stage at which they were pending at that time.

(2) Notwithstanding anything contained in sub-section (1), if in respect of a case involving a scheduled offence committed in any judicial zone in a State, the Central Government, having regard to the provisions of sub-section (2) of section 4 and the facts and circumstances of the case and all other relevant factors, is of the opinion that it is expedient that such offence should be tried by the Additional Special Court established in relation to such judicial zone outside the State, the Central Government may make a declaration to that effect: Provided that no such declaration shall be made unless the State Government has forwarded to the Central Government a report in writing containing a request for making of such declaration.

Explanation: Where an Additional Special Court is established in relation to two or more judicial zones, such Additional Special Court shall be deemed, for the purposes of this sub-section, to have been established in relation to each of such judicial zones.

(3) A declaration made under sub-section (2) shall not be called in question in any court.

(4) Where any declaration is made in respect of any offence committed in a judicial zone in a State, any prosecution in respect of such offence shall be instituted only in the Additional Special Court established in relation to such judicial zone outside the State, and if any prosecution in respect of such offence is pending immediately before such declaration in any other court, the same shall stand transferred to such Additional Special Court and such Additional Special Court shall proceed with such case from the stage at which it was pending at that time.

8. Powers of Special Courts with respect to other offences: (1) When trying any scheduled offence, a Special Court may also try any offence other than the scheduled offence with which the accused may, under the Code, be charged at the same trial if the offence is connected with the scheduled offence.

(2) If, in the course of any trial under this Act, it is found that the accused person has committed any offence, the Special Court may, whether such offence is or is not a scheduled offence, convict such person of such offence and pass any sentence authorized by law for the punishment thereof.

9. Public Prosecutors: (1) For every Special Court, the Central Government shall appoint a person to be the Public Prosecutor and may appoint one or more persons to be the Additional Public Prosecutor or Additional Public Prosecutors: Provided that the Central Government may also appoint for any case or class of cases a Special Public Prosecutor.

(2) A person shall be eligible to be appointed as a Public Prosecutor or an Additional Public Prosecutor or a Special Public Prosecutor under this section only if he has been in practice as an Advocate for not less than seven years or has held any post, for a period of not less than seven years, under the Union or a State, requiring special knowledge of law.

(3) Every person appointed as a Public Prosecutor or an Additional Public Prosecutor or a Special Public Prosecutor under this section shall be deemed to be a Public Prosecutor within the meaning of clause (u) of section 2 of the Code, and the provisions of the Code shall have effect accordingly.

10. Procedure and powers of Special Courts: (1) A Special Court may take cognizance of any scheduled offence, without the accused being committed to it for trial, upon receiving a complaint of facts which constitute such offence or upon a police report of such facts.

(2) Where a scheduled offence is punishable with imprisonment for a term not exceeding three years or with fine or with both, a Special Court may, notwithstanding anything contained in sub-section (1) of section 260 or section 262 of the Code, try the offence in a summary way in accordance with the procedure prescribed in the Code and the provisions of sections 263 to 265 of the Code, shall, so far as may be, apply to such trial: Provided that when, in the course of a summary trial under this sub-section, it appears to the Special Court that the nature of the case is such that it is undesirable to try it in a summary way, the Special Court shall recall any witnesses who may have been examined and proceed to re-hear the case in the manner provided by the provisions of the Code for the trial of such offence and the said provisions shall apply to and in relation to a Special Court as they apply to and in relation to a Magistrate: Provided further that in the case of any conviction in a summary trial under this section, it shall be lawful for a Special Court to pass a sentence of imprisonment for a term not exceeding two years.

(3) A Special Court may, with a view to obtaining the evidence of any person supposed to have been directly or indirectly concerned in, or privy to, an offence, tender a pardon to such person on condition of his making a full and true disclosure of the whole circumstances within his knowledge relative to the offence and to every other person concerned whether as principal or abettor in the commission thereof, and any pardon so tendered shall, for the purposes of section 308 of the Code, be deemed to have been tendered under section 307 thereof.

(4) Subject to the other provisions of this Act, a Special Court shall, for the purpose of trial of any offence, have all the powers of a Court of Session and shall try such offence as if it were a Court of Session so far as may be in accordance with the procedure prescribed in the Code for the trial before a Court of Session.

(5) Subject to the other provisions of this Act, every case before an Additional Special Court shall be dealt with as if such case had been transferred under section 406 of the Code to such Additional Special Court.

11. Power of Supreme Court to transfer case: Whenever it is made to appear to the Supreme Court that an order under this section is expedient for the ends of justice, it may direct that any particular case be transferred from one Special Court to another Special Court.

12. Protection of witnesses: (1) Notwithstanding anything contained in the Code, all proceedings before a Special Court shall be conducted in camera: Provided that where the Public Prosecutor so applies, any proceedings or part thereof may be held in open court.

(2) A Special Court may, on an application made by a witness in any proceedings before it or by the Public Prosecutor in relation to such witness or on its own motion, take such measures as it deems fit for keeping the identity and address of the witness secret.

(3) In particular and without prejudice to the generality of the provisions of sub-section (2), the measures which a Special Court may take under that sub-section may include – (a) the holding of the proceeding at a protected place; (b) the avoiding of the mention of the names and addresses of the witnesses in its orders or judgments or in any records of the case accessible to public; (c) the issuing of any directions for securing that the identity and addresses of the witnesses are not disclosed.

(4) Any person who contravenes any direction issued under sub-section (2) shall be punishable with imprisonment for a term, which may extend to one year and with fine, which may extend to one thousand rupees.

13. Power to transfer cases to regular courts: Where after taking cognizance of any offence, a Special Court is of opinion that the offence is not a scheduled offence, it shall, notwithstanding that it has no jurisdiction to try such offence, transfer the case for trial of such offence to any court having jurisdiction under the Code and the court to which the case is transferred may proceed with the trial of the offence as if it has taken cognizance of the offence.

14. Appeal: (1) Notwithstanding anything contained in the Code, an appeal shall lie as a matter of right from any judgment, sentence or order, not being interlocutory order, of a Special Court to the Supreme Court both on facts and on law.

(2) Except as aforesaid, no appeal or revision shall lie to any court from any judgment, sentence or order of a Special Court.

(3) Every appeal under this section shall be preferred within a period of thirty days from the date of the judgment, sentence or order appealed from: Provided that the Supreme Court may entertain an appeal after the expiry of the said period of thirty days if it is satisfied that the appellant had sufficient cause for not preferring the appeal within the period of thirty days.

15. Modified application of certain provisions of the Code: (1) Notwithstanding anything contained in the Code or any other law, every scheduled offence shall be deemed to be a cognizable offence within the meaning of clause (c) of section 2 of the Code and "cognizable case" as defined in that clause shall be construed accordingly.

(2) Section 167 of the Code shall apply in relation to a case involving a scheduled offence subject to the modifications that – (a) the reference in sub-section (1) thereof to "Judicial Magistrate" shall be construed as a reference to "Judicial Magistrate or Executive Magistrate"; (b) the references in sub-section (2) thereof to "fifteen days", "ninety days" and sixty days", wherever they occur, shall be construed as references to "thirty days", "one year" and "one year", respectively; and (c) sub-section (2A) thereof shall be deemed to have been omitted.

(3) Sections 366 to 371 and section 392 of the Code shall apply in relation to a case involving a scheduled offence subject to the modifications that the references to "Court of Session" and "High Court", wherever occurring therein, shall be construed as references to "Special Court" and "Supreme Court", respectively.

(4) Nothing in section 438 of the Code shall apply in relation to any case involving the arrest of any person on an accusation of having committed a scheduled offence in a terrorist affected area.

(5) Notwithstanding anything contained in the Code, no person accused of a scheduled offence shall, if in custody, be released on bail or on his own bond unless – (a) the Public Prosecutor has been given an opportunity to oppose the application for such release, and (b) where the Public Prosecutor opposes the application, the court is satisfied that there are reasonable grounds for believing that he is not guilty of such offence and that he is not likely to commit any offence while on bail.

(6) The limitations on granting of bail specified in sub-section (5) are in addition to the limitations under the Code or any other law for the time being in force on granting of bail. [Ins. by Act 45 of 1985, S.2.]

*[15A. Abolition of certain Special Courts: – Where the area comprising a judicial zone has ceased to be a terrorist affected area and no cases are pending before a Special Court or an Additional Special Court established in relation to such judicial zone, the Central Government may, by notification in the Official Gazette, abolish such Special Court or Additional Special Court.]

16. Overriding effect of Act: (1) The provisions of this Act shall have effect notwithstanding anything contained in the Code or any other law, but save as expressly provided in this Act, the provisions of the Code shall, in so far as they are not inconsistent with the provisions of this Act, apply to the proceedings before a Special Court; and for the purpose of the said provisions of the Code, the Special Court shall be deemed to be a Court of Session.

(2) In particular and without prejudice to the generality of the provisions contained in sub-section (1), the provisions of sections 326 and 475 of the Code shall, as far as may be, apply to the Proceedings before a Special Court, and for this purpose any reference in those provisions to a Magistrate shall be construed as a reference to the Special Court.

17. Delegation: The Central Government may, by notification, delegate, subject to such conditions as may be specified, all or any of the powers exercisable by it under this Act [except the power under sub-section (2) of section 4 and the power under sub-section (2) of section 7] to the State Government.

18. Saving: (1) Nothing in this Act shall affect the jurisdiction exercisable by, or the procedure applicable to, any court or other authority under any law relating to the naval, military or air forces or any other armed forces of the Union.

(2) For the removal of doubts, it is hereby declared that for the purposes of any such law as is referred to in sub-section (1), a Special Court shall be deemed to be a Court of ordinary criminal justice.

APPENDIX K

(THE) TERRORIST AND DISRUPTIVE ACTIVITIES (PREVENTION) ACT, 1987

Commonly known as TADA, the act was the first and only legislative effort by the Union government to define and counter terrorist activities. It was formulated in the back drop of growing terrorist violence in Punjab which had its violent effects in other parts of the country too, including capital New Delhi. The Act, which was criticized on various counts by human rights organizations and political parties, was permitted to lapse in May 1995 though cases initiated while it was in force continue to hold legal validity. The full text of the Act follows

(Act No. 28 of 1987)
(Amended by Act 43 of 1993)

1[3rd September, 1987]

PART I
PRELIMINARY

1. Short title, extent, application, commencement, duration and savings.
2. Definitions.

PART II
PUNISHMENTS FOR, AND MEASURES FOR COPING WITH, TERRORIST AND DISRUPTIVE ACTIVITIES

3. Punishment for terrorist acts
4. Punishments for disruptive activities
5. Possession of certain unauthorized arms, etc. in specified areas.
6. Enhanced penalties.
7. Conferment of powers

7A. Powers of investigating officers

8. Forfeiture of property of certain persons.

PART III
DESIGNATED COURTS

9. Designated Courts
10. Place of sitting
11. Jurisdiction of Designated Courts
12. Power of Designated Courts with respect to other offenses
13. Public Prosecutors
14. Procedure and powers of Designated Courts
15. Certain confessions made to police officers to be taken into consideration
16. Protection of witnesses
17. Trial by Designated Courts to have precedence
18. Power to transfer cases to regular courts
19. Appeal

PART IV
MISCELLANEOUS

20. Modified application of certain provision of the code

20 A. Cognizance of offence

21. Presumption as to offences under Section 3
22. Identification of accused
23. Saving
24. Saving as to orders
25. Overriding effect
26. Protection of action taken under this Act.
27. Power of the Supreme Court to make rules
28. Power to make rules
29. Rules to be laid before Houses of Parliament
30. Repeal and saving.

An Act to make special provisions for the prevention of, and for coping with, terrorist and disruptive activities and for matters connected therewith or incidental thereto.

Be it enacted by Parliament in the Thirty-eighth year of the Republic of India as follows:

Part I

PRELIMINARY

1. Short title, extent, application, commencement, duration and savings.-

(1) This Act may be called the Terrorist and Disruptive Activities (Prevention) Act, 1987.

(2) It extends to the whole of India, and it applies also, -

a. To citizens of India outside India;

b. To persons in the service of the Government, wherever they may be; and

c. To persons on ships and aircraft registered in India, wherever they may be.

(3) Sections 5, 15, 21 and 22 shall come into force at once and the remaining provisions of this Act shall be deemed to have come into force on the 24th day of May, 1987.

(4) It shall remain in force for a period of **2**[eight years] from the 24th day of May, 1987, but its expiry under the operation of this sub-section shall not affect, -

a. The previous operation of, or anything duly done or suffered under this Act or any rule made there under or any order made under any such rule, or

b. Any right, privilege, obligation or liability acquired accrued or incurred under this Act or any rule made there under or any order made under any such rule, or

a. Any penalty, forfeiture or punishment incurred in respect of any offence under this Act or any contravention of any rule made under this Act or of any order made under any such rule, or

b. Any investigation, legal proceeding or remedy in respect of any such right, privilege, obligation, liability, penalty, forfeiture or punishment as aforesaid.

and any such investigation, legal proceeding or remedy may be instituted, continued or enforced and any such penalty, forfeiture or punishment may be imposed as if this Act had not expired.

2. Definitions - (1) In this Act, unless the context otherwise requires, -

(a) "*abet*", with its grammatical variations and cognate expressions, includes, -

i. The communication or association with any person or class of persons who is engaged in assisting in any manner terrorists or disruptionists;

ii. The passing on, or publication of, without any lawful authority, and information likely to assist the terrorists or disruptionists, and the passing on, or publication of, or distribution of, any document or matter obtained from terrorists or disruptionists;

iii. The rendering of any assistance, whether financial or otherwise, the terrorists or disruptionists;

(b) "*Code*" means the Code of Criminal Procedure 1973 (2 of 1974);

(c) "*Designated Court*" means a Designated Court constituted under Section 9;

(d) "*Disruptive activity*" has the meaning assigned to it in Section 4, and the expression "disruptionist" shall be construed accordingly;

(e) "*High Court*" means the High Court of the State in which a judge or an additional judge of a Designated Court was working immediately before his appointment as such judge or additional judge;

(f) "*notified area*" means such area as the State Government may, by notification in the official Gazette, specify;

(g) "*public prosecutor*" means a Public Prosecutor or an Additional Public Prosecutor or a Special Public Prosecutor appointed under Section 13, and includes any person acting under the directions of the Public Prosecutor;

3[(gg) "*property*" means property and assets of any description, whether corporeal or incorporeal, movable or immovable, tangible or intangible and deeds and instruments evidencing title to, or interest in, such property or assets, derived or obtained from the terrorist Act and includes proceeds of terrorism;]

(h) "*terrorist act*" has the meaning assigned to it in sub-section (1) of Section 3, and the expression "terrorist" shall be construed accordingly;

(i) words and expressions used but not defined in this Act and defined in the Code shall have the meaning respectively assigned to them in the Code.

(2) Any reference in this Act to any enactment or any provision thereof shall, in relation to an area in which such enactment or such provision is not in force, be construed as a reference to the corresponding law or the relevant provision of the corresponding law, if any, in force in that area.

PART II

PUNISHMENTS FOR AND MEASURES FOR COPING WITH,

TERRORIST AND DISRUPTIVE ACTIVITIES

3. Punishment for terrorist acts. – (1) Whoever with intent to overawe the Government as by law established or to strike terror in the people or any section of the people or to alienate any section of the people or to adversely affect the harmony amongst different sections of the people does any act or thing by using bombs, dynamite or other explosive substances or inflammable substances or lethal weapons or poisons or noxious gases or other chemicals or by any other substances (whether biological or otherwise) of a hazardous nature in such a manner as to cause, or as is likely to cause, death of, or injuries to, any person or persons or loss of, or damage to, or destruction of, property or disruption of any supplies or services essential to the life of the community, or detains any person and threatens to kill or injure such person in order to compel the Government or any other person to do or abstain from doing any act, commits a terrorist act.

(2) Whoever commits a terrorist act, shall, –

(i) if such act has resulted in the death of any person, be punishable with death or imprisonment for life and shall also be liable to fine;

(ii) in any other case, be punishable with imprisonment for a term which shall not be less than five years but which may extend to imprisonment for life and shall also be liable to fine.

(3) Whoever conspires or attempts to commit, or advocates, abets, advises or incites or knowingly facilitates the commission of, a terrorist act or any act preparatory to a terrorist act, shall be punishable with imprisonment for a term which shall not be less than five years but which may extend to imprisonment for life and shall also be liable to fine.

(4) Whoever harbours or conceals, or attempts to harbour or conceal, any terrorist shall be punishable with imprisonment for a term which shall not be less than five years but which may extend to imprisonment for life and shall also be liable to fine.

4[(5) Any person who is a member of a terrorists gang or a terrorist organization, which is involved in terrorist acts, shall be punishable with imprisonment for a term which shall not be less than five years but which may extend to imprisonment for life and shall also be liable to fine.

(6) Whoever holds any property derived or obtained from commission of any terrorist act or has been acquired through the terrorist funds shall be punishable with imprisonment for a term which shall not be less than five years but which may extend to imprisonment for life and shall also be liable to fine.]

4. Punishment for disruptive activities. – (1) Whoever commits or conspires or attempts to commit or abets, advocates, advises, or knowingly facilitates the commission of, any disruptive activity or any act preparatory to a disruptive activity shall be punishable with imprisonment for a term which shall not be less than five years but which may extend to imprisonment for life and shall also be liable to fine.

(2) For the purposes of sub-section (1), "disruptive activity" means any action taken, whether by act or by speech or through any other media or in any other manner whatsoever, -

(i) Which questions, disrupts or is intended to disrupt, whether directly or indirectly, the sovereignty and territorial integrity of India; or

(ii) Which is intended to bring about or supports any claim, whether directly or indirectly, for the cession of any part of India or the secession of any part of India from the Union.

Explanation – For the purposes of this sub-section, –

(a) "Cession" includes the admission of any claim of any foreign country to any part of India, and

(b) "Secession" includes the assertion of any claim to determine whether a part of India will remain within the Union.

(3) Without prejudice to the generality of the provisions of sub-section(2), it is hereby declared that any action taken, whether by act or by speech or through any other media or in any other manner whatsoever, which –

a. Advocates, advises, suggests or incites; or

b. Predicts, prophesies or pronounces or otherwise expresses, in such manner as to incite, advice, suggest or prompt, the killing or the destruction of any person bound by oath under the constitution to uphold the sovereignty and integrity of India or any public servant shall be deemed to be a disruptive activity within the meaning of this section.

(4) Whoever harbours or conceals, or attempts to harbour or conceal, any disruptionist shall be punishable with imprisonment for a term which shall not be less than five years but which may be extend to imprisonment for life and shall also be liable to fine.

2. Habeas Corpus – In habeas corpus proceedings if the detention is legal at the time of the disposal of the petition the Court cannot order release of the person detained by issuing a writ of habeas corpus. Therefore, the legality or otherwise of the detention shall also be considered on the date of final disposal of the petition. *Bacha Bora v. State of Assam*, 1991 Cr LJ 2782 (Gau).

5. Possession of certain unauthorized arms, etc. in specified areas – Where any person is in possession of any arms and ammunition specified in Columns

2 and 3 of Category I or Category III (a) of Schedule I to the Arms Rules, 1962, or bombs, dynamite or other explosive substances unauthorizedly in a notified area, he shall, notwithstanding anything contained in any other law for the time being in force, be punishable with imprisonment for a term which shall not be less than five years but which may extend to imprisonment for life and shall also be liable to fine.

6. Enhanced penalties – (1) If any person with intend to aid any terrorist or disruptionist, contravenes any provision of, or any rule made under the Arms Act, 1959, the Explosives Act, 1884, the Explosives Substances Act, 1908 or the Inflammable Substances Act, 1952, he shall, notwithstanding anything contained in any of the aforesaid Acts or the rules made thereunder, be punishable with imprisonment for a term which shall not be less than five years but which may extend to imprisonment for life and shall also be liable to fine.

(2) For the purposes of this section, any person who attempts to contravene or abets, or attempts to abet, or does any act preparatory to the contravention of any provision of any law, rule or order, shall be deemed to have contravened that provision, and the provision of sub-section (1) shall, in relation to such person, have effect subject to the modification that the reference to "imprisonment for life" shall be construed as a reference to "imprisonment for ten years".

7. Conferment of powers – (1) Notwithstanding anything contained the Code or in any other provision of this Act, the Central Government may, if it considers it necessary or expedient so to do, –

a. For the prevention of, and for coping with, any offence under Section 3 or Section 4; or

b. For any case or class or group of cases under Section 3 or Section 4;

In any State or part thereof, confer, by notification in the official Gazette, on any officer of the Central Government, powers exercisable by a police officer under the Code in such State or part thereof or, as the case may be, for such case or class or group of cases and in particular, the powers of arrest, investigation and prosecution of persons before any Court.

(2) All officers of police and all officers of Government are hereby required and empowered to assist the officer of the Central Government referred to in sub-section (1), in the execution of the provisions of this Act or any rule or order made thereunder.

(3) The provisions of the Code shall, so far as may be and subject to such

modifications made in this Act, apply to the exercise of the powers by an officer under sub-section (1).

5[7-A. Powers of investigating officers – If an officer investigating an offence committed under this Act has reason to believe that any property in relation to which an investigation is being conducted is a property derived or obtained from the commission of any terrorist act and includes proceeds of terrorism he shall, with the approval of the Superintendent of Police, make an order seizing such property and where it is not practicable to seize such property, he may make an order of attachment directing that such property shall not be transferred or otherwise dealt with except with the prior permission of the officer making such order, or of the Designated Court and a copy of such order shall be served on the persons concerned :

Provided that the investigating officer shall duly inform the Designated Court within forty-eight hours of the attachment of such property and the said Court shall either confirm or revoke the order of attachment so issued.]

8. Forfeiture of property of certain persons: (1) Where a person has been convicted to any offence punishable under this Act or any rule made thereunder, the Designated Court may, in addition to awarding any punishment, by order in writing, declare that any property, movable or immovable or both, belonging to the accused and specified in the order, shall stand forfeited to the Government free from all encumbrances.

(2) Where any person is accused of any offence under this Act or any rule made thereunder, it shall be open to the Designated Court trying him to pass an order that all or any properties, movable or immovable or both belonging to him, shall, during the period of such trial, be attached, and where such trial ends in conviction, the properties so attached shall stand forfeited to Government free from all encumbrances.

(3) (a) If upon a report in writing made by a police officer or an officer referred to in sub-section (1) of Section 7, any Designated Court has reason to believe that any person, who has committed an offence punishable under this Act or any rule made thereunder, has absconded or is concealing himself so that he may not be apprehended, such court may, notwithstanding anything contained in Section 82 of the Code, publish a written proclamation requiring him to appear at a specified place and at a specified time not less than fifteen days but not more than thirty days from the date of publication of such proclamation.

(b) The Designated Court issuing a proclamation under Clause (a) may, at any time, order the attachment of any property, movable or immovable or both, belonging to the proclaimed person, and thereupon the provisions of Sections

83 to 85 of the Code shall apply to such attachment as if such attachment were made under that Code.

(c) If, within six months from the date of the attachment, any person, whose property is, or has been, at the disposal of the Government under sub-section (2) of Section 85 of the code, appears voluntarily or is apprehended and brought before the Designated Court by whose order the property was attached, or the Court to which such Court is subordinate, and proves to the satisfaction of such Court that he did not abscond or conceal himself for the purpose of avoiding apprehension and that he had not received such notice of the proclamation as to enable him to attend within the time specified therein, such property or, if the same has been sold, the net proceeds of the sale and the residue of the property, shall, after satisfying therefrom all costs incurred in consequence of the attachment, be delivered to him.

(4) Where any shares in a company stand forfeited to the Government under this sub-section, then, the company shall, notwithstanding anything contained in the Companies Act, 1956, or the articles of association the company, forthwith register the Government as the transferee of such shares.

PART III

DESIGNATED COURTS

9. Designated Courts: (1) The Central Government or a State Government may, by notification in the official Gazette, constitute one or more Designated Courts for such area or areas, or for such case or class or group of cases as may be specified in the notification.

(2) Where a notification constituting a Designated Court for any area or areas or for any case or class or group of cases is issued by the Central Government under sub-section (1), and a notification constituting a Designated Court for the same area or areas or for the same case or class or group of cases has also been issued by a State Government under that sub-section, the Designated Court constituted by the Central Government, whether the notification constituting such Court is issued before or after the issue of the notification constituting the Designated Court by the State Government, shall have, and the Designated Court constituted by the State Government shall not have, jurisdiction to try any offence committed in that area or areas or, as the case may be, the case or class or group of cases, and all cases pending before any Designated Court constituted by the State Government shall stand transferred to the Designated Court constituted by the Central Government.

(3) Where any question arises as to the jurisdiction of any Designated Court,

it shall be referred to the Central Government whose decision thereon shall be final.

(4) A Designated Court shall be presided over by a Judge to be appointed by the Central Government or, as the case may be, the State Government, with the concurrence of the Chief Justice of the High Court.

(5) The Central Government or, as the case may be, the State Government may also appoint, with the concurrence of the Chief Justice of the High Court additional Judges to exercise jurisdiction in a Designated Court.

(6) A person shall not be qualified for appointment as a Judge or an additional Judge of a Designated Court unless he is, immediately before such appointment a Sessions Judge or an additional Sessions Judge in any State.

(7) For the removal of doubts, it is hereby provided that the attainment by a person appointed a judge or an Additional Judge of a Designated Court of the age of superannuation under the rules applicable to him in the service to which he belongs, shall not affect his continuance as such Judge or Additional Judge.

(8) Where any Additional Judge or Additional Judges is or are appointed in a Designated Court, the Judge of the Designated Court may, from time to time, by general or special order, in writing, provide for the distribution of business of the Designated Court among himself and the additional Judge or Additional Judges and also for the disposal of urgent business in the event of his absence or the absence of any Additional Judge.

10. **Place of sitting:** A Designated Court may, on its own motion or on an application made by the Public Prosecutor, and if it considers it expedient or desirable so to do, sit for any of its proceedings at any place, other than its ordinary place of sitting :

Provided that nothing in this section shall be construed to change the place of sitting of a Designated Court constituted by a State Government to any place outside that State.

11. **Jurisdiction of Designated Courts:** (1) Notwithstanding anything contained in the Code, every offence punishable under any provision of this Act or any rule made thereunder shall be triable only by the Designated Court within whose local jurisdiction it was committed or, as the case may be, by the Designated Court constituted for trying such offence under sub-section (1) of Section 9.

(2) If, having regard to the exigencies of the situation prevailing in a State, the Central Government is of the opinion that, –

(a) The situation prevailing in such State is not conducive to a fair, impartial or speedy trial, or

(b) It is not likely to be feasible without occasioning the breach of peace or grave risk to the safety of the accused, the witnesses, the Public Prosecutor and the Judge of the Designated Court or any of them, or

(c) It is not otherwise in the interests of justice,

It may, with the concurrence of the Chief Justice of India (such occurrence to be obtained on a motion moved in that behalf by the Attorney-General), transfer any case pending before a Designated Court in that State to any other Designated Court within that State or in any other State.

(3) Where the whole or any part of the area within the local limits of the jurisdiction of a Designated Court has been declared to be, or forms part of, any area which has been declared to be a disturbed area under any enactment for the time being in force making provision for the suppression of disorder and restoration and maintenance of public order, and the Central Government is of opinion that the situation prevailing in the State is not conducive to fair, impartial or speedy trial within the State, of offences under this Act or the rules made thereunder which such Designated Court is competent to try, the Central Government may, with the concurrence of the Chief Justice of India, specify, by notification in the official Gazette, in relation to such Court (hereafter in this sub-section referred to as the local Court) a Designated Court outside the State (hereinafter in this section referred to as the specified court), and thereupon, -

a. It shall not be competent at any time during the period of operation of such notification, for such local court to exercise any jurisdiction in respect of, or try, any offence under this Act or the rules made thereunder;

b. The jurisdiction which would have been, but for the issue of such notification, exercisable by such local court in respect of such offences committed during the period of operation of such notification shall be exercisable by the specified court;

c. All cases relating to such offences pending immediately before the date of issue of such notification before such local court shall stand transferred on that date to the specified court;

d. All cases taken cognizance of by, or transferred to, the specified court under Clause (b) or Clause (c) shall be dealt with and tried in accordance with this Act (whether during the period of operation of such notification or thereafter) as if such offences had been committed within the local limits of the jurisdiction of the specified court or, as the case may be, transferred for trial to it under sub-section (2).

Explanation 1. – A notification under this sub-section in relation to any local court shall cease to operate on the date on which the whole or, as the case may be, the aforementioned part of the area within the local limits of its jurisdiction, ceases to be a disturbed area.

Explanation 2. – For the purposes of this section, "Attorney-General" means the Attorney-General of India or, in his absence, the Solicitor-General of India or, in the absence of both, one of the Additional Solicitors-General of India.

12. Power of Designated Courts with respect to other offences: (1) When trying any offence, a Designated Court may also try any other offence with which the accused may, under the Code, be charged at the same trial if the offence is connected with such other offence.

(2) If, in the course of any trial under this Act of any offence, it is found that the accused person has committed any other offence under this Act or any rule made thereunder or under any other law, the Designated Court may convict such person of such other offence and pass any sentence authorized by this Act or such rule or, as the case may be, such other law, for the punishment thereof.

13. Public Prosecutors: (1) For every Designated Court, the Central Government or, as the case may be, the State Government, shall appoint a person to be the Public Prosecutor and may appoint one or more persons to be the Additional Public Prosecutor or Additional Public Prosecutors; provided that the Central Government or, as the case may be, the State Government, may also appoint for any case or class or group of cases a Special Public Prosecutor.

(2) A person shall not be qualified to be appointed as a Public Prosecutor or an Additional Public Prosecutor or a Special Public Prosecutor under this section unless he has been in practice as an Advocate for not less than seven years or has held any post, for a period of not less than seven years, under the Union or a State, requiring special knowledge of law.

(3) Every person appointed as a Public Prosecutor or an Additional Public Prosecutor or a Special Public Prosecutor under this section shall be deemed to be a Public Prosecutor within the meaning of clause (u) of Section 2 of the Code and the provisions of the Code shall have effect accordingly.

14. Procedure and powers of Designated Courts: (1) A Designated Court may take cognizance of any offence, without the accused being committed to it for trial, upon receiving a complaint of facts which constitute such offence or upon a police report of such facts.

(2) Where an offence triable by a Designated Court is punishable with imprisonment for a term not exceeding three years or with fine or with both, the Designated Court may, notwithstanding anything contained in sub-section (1) of Section 260 or Section 262 of the Code, try the offence in a summary way in accordance with the procedure prescribed in the Code and the provisions of Section 263 to 265 of the Code, shall, so far as may be, apply to such trial:

Provided that when, in the course of a summary trial under this sub-section, it appears to the Designated Court that the nature of the case is such that it is undesirable to try it in a summary way, the Designated Court shall recall any witnesses who may have been examined and proceed to re-hear the case in the manner provided by the provisions of the Code for the trial of such offence and the said provisions shall apply to and in relation to a Designated Court as they apply to and in relation to a Magistrate:

Provided further that in the case of any conviction in a summary trial under this section, it shall be lawful for a Designated Court to pass a sentence of imprisonment for a term not exceeding two years.

(3) Subject to the other provisions of this Act, a Designated Court shall, for the purpose of trial of any offence, have all the powers of a Court of Session and shall try such offence as if it were a Court of Session so far as may be in accordance with the procedure prescribed in the Code for the trial before a Court of Session.

(4) Subject to the other provisions of this Act, every case transferred to a Designated Court under sub-section (2) of Section 11 shall be dealt with as if such case had been transferred under Section 406 of the Code to such Designated Court.

(5) Notwithstanding anything contained in the Code, a Designated Court may, if it thinks fit and for reasons to be recorded by it, proceed with the trial in the absence of the accused or his pleader and record the evidence of any witness, subject to the right of the accused to recall the witness for cross-examination.

15. Certain confessions made to police officers to be taken into consideration: (1) Notwithstanding anything in the Code or in the Indian Evidence Act, 1872, but subject to the provisions of this section, a confession made by a person before a police officer not lower in rank than a Superintendent of Police and recorded by such police officer either in writing or on any mechanical device like cassettes, tapes or sound tracks from out of which sounds or images can be reproduced, shall be admissible in the trial of such person **6**[or co-accused, abettor or conspirator] for an offence under this Act or rules made there under:

7[Provided that co-accused, abettor or conspirator is charged and tried in the same case together with the accused].

(2) The police officer shall, before recording any confession under sub-section (1), explain to the person making it that he is not bound to make a·confession and that, if he does so, it may be used as evidence against him and such police officer shall not record any such confession unless upon questioning the person making it, he has reason to believe that it is being made voluntarily.

16. Protection of witnesses: 8[(1) Notwithstanding anything contained in the Code, the proceedings under this Act may be held in *camera* if the Designated Court so desires.]

(2) A Designated Court may, on an application made by a witness in any proceedings before it or by the Public Prosecutor in relation to such witness or on its own motion, take such measures as it deems fit for keeping the identity and address of any witness secret.

(3) In particular, and without prejudice to the generality of the provisions of sub-section (2), the measures which a Designated Court may take under that sub-section may include, -

a. The holding of the proceedings at a place to be decided by the Designated Court;
b. The avoiding of the mention of the names and addresses of the witnesses in it orders or judgments or in any records of the case accessible to public;
c. The issuing of any directions for securing that the identity and addresses of the witnesses are not disclosed.
d. That it is in the public interest to order that all or any of the proceedings pending before such a court shall not be published in any manner.

(4) Any person who contravenes any direction issued under sub-section (3) shall be punishable with imprisonment for a term, which may extend to one year and with fine, which may extend to one thousand rupees.

17. Trial by Designated Courts to have precedence: The trial under this Act of any offence by a Designated Court shall have precedence over the trial of any other case against the accused in any other court (not being a Designated Court) and shall be concluded in preference to the trial of such other case and accordingly the trial of such other case shall remain in abeyance.

18. Power to transfer cases to regular courts: Where, after taking cognizance of any offence, a Designated Court is of opinion that the offence is not triable by it, it shall, notwithstanding that it has no jurisdiction to try such offence, transfer the case for the trial of such offence to any court having jurisdiction under the Code and the court to which the case is transferred may proceed with the trial of the offence as if it had taken cognizance of the offence.

19. Appeal: (1) Notwithstanding anything contained in the Code, an appeal shall lie as a matter of right from any judgment, sentence or order, not being an interlocutory order, of a Designated Court to the Supreme Court both on facts and on law.

(2) Except as aforesaid, no appeal or revision shall lie to any court from any judgment, sentence or order including an interlocutory order of a Designated Court.

(3) Every appeal under this section shall be preferred within a period of thirty days from the date of the judgment; sentence or order appealed from:

Provided that the Supreme Court may entertain an appeal after the expiry of the said period of thirty days if it is satisfied that the appellant had sufficient cause for not preferring the appeal within the period of thirty days.

PART IV

MISCELLANEOUS

20. Modified application of certain provisions of the Code: (1) Notwithstanding anything contained in the Code or any other law, every offence punishable under this Act or any rule made thereunder shall be deemed to be a cognizable offence within the meaning of clause (c) of Section 2 of the Code, and "cognizable case" as defined in that clause shall be construed accordingly.

(2) Section 21 of the Code shall apply in relation to a case involving an offence punishable under this Act or any rule made thereunder subject to the modification that the reference to "the State Government" therein shall be construed as a reference to "the Central Government or the State Government".

(3) Section 164 of the Code shall apply in relation to a case involving an offence punishable under this Act or any rule made thereunder, subject to the

modification that the reference in subsection (1) thereof to "Metropolitan Magistrate or Judicial Magistrate" shall be construed as a reference to "Metropolitan Magistrate, Judicial Magistrate, Executive Magistrate or Special Executive Magistrate.

(4) Section 167 of the Code shall apply in relation to a case involving an offence punishable under this Act or any rule made thereunder subject to the modifications that,-

a. The reference in sub-section (1) thereof to "Judicial Magistrate" shall be construed as a reference to Judicial Magistrate or Executive Magistrate or Special Executive Magistrate;

b. The reference in sub-section (2) thereof to "fifteen days," "ninety days" and "sixty days," wherever they occur, shall be construed as references to "sixty days."9[one hundred and eighty days] and [8][one hundred and eighty days], respectively; and

(bb) sub-section (2-A) thereof shall be deemed to have been omitted.

10[(bbb) in sub-section (2), after the proviso, the following proviso shall be inserted, namely:-

> "Provided further that, if it is not possible to complete the investigation within the said period of one hundred and eighty days, the Designated Court shall extend the said period up to one year, on the report of the Public Prosecutor indicating the progress of the investigation and the specific reasons for the detention of the accused beyond the said period of one hundred and eighty days.]

(5) Section 268 of the Code shall apply in relation to a case involving an offence punishable under this Act or any rule made thereunder subject to the modifications that -

a. The reference in sub-section (1) thereof –

 i. To "the State Government" shall be construed as a reference to "the Central Government or the State Government";

 ii. To "order of the State Government" shall be construed as a reference to "order of the Central Government or the State Government, as the case may be"; or

b. The reference in sub-section (2) thereof, to "State Government" shall be construed as a reference to "Central Government or the State Government, as the case may be".

(6) Sections 366 to 371 and Section 392 of the Code shall apply in relation to a case involving an offence triable by a Designated Court subject to the

modifications that the references to "Court of Session" and "High Court", wherever occurring therein, shall be construed as references to "Designated Court" and "Supreme Court", respectively.

(7) Nothing in Section 438 of the Code shall apply in relation to any case involving the arrest of any person on an accusation of having committed an offence punishable under this act or any rule made thereunder.

(8) Notwithstanding anything contained in the Code, no person accused of an offence punishable under this Act or any rule made thereunder shall, if in custody, be released on bail or on his own bond unless, –

a. The Public Prosecutor has been given an opportunity to oppose the application for such release, and

b. Where the Public Prosecutor opposes the application, the Court is satisfied that there are reasonable grounds for believing that he is not guilty of such offence and that he is not likely to commit any offence while on bail.

(9) The limitations on granting of bail specified in sub-section (8) are in addition to the limitations under the Code or any other law for the time being in force on granting of bail.

11[20-A. Cognizance of offence: (1) Notwithstanding, anything contained in the Code, no information about the commission of an offence under this Act shall be recorded by the police without the prior approval of the District Superintendent of Police.

(2) No court shall take cognizance of any offence under this Act without the previous sanction of the Inspector-General of Police, or as the case may be, the Commissioner of Police.]

21. Presumption as to offences under Section 3: (1) In a prosecution for an offence under sub-section (1) of Section 3, if it is proved –

a. That the arms or explosives or any other substances specified in Section 3 were recovered from the possession of the accused and there is reason to believe that such arms or explosives or other substances of similar nature, were used in the commission of such offence; or

b. That by the evidence of an expert the fingerprints of the accused were found at the site of the offence or on anything including arms and vehicles used in connection with the commission of such offence.

c. **12**[* * *]

(2) In a prosecution for an offence under sub-section 3 of Section 3, if it is proved that the accused rendered any financial assistance to a person accused

of, or reasonably suspected of, an offence under that section, the Designated Court shall presume, unless the contrary is proved, that such person has committed the offence under that sub-section.

22. Identification of accused: Where a person has been declared a proclaimed offender in terrorist case, the evidence regarding his identification by witnesses on the basis of his photograph shall have the same value as the evidence of a test identification parade.

23. Saving: (1) Nothing in this Act shall affect the jurisdiction exercisable by, or the procedure applicable to, any Court or other authority under any law relating to the naval, military or air forces or other armed forces of the Union.

(2) For the removal of doubts, it is hereby declared that for the purposes of any such law as is referred to in sub-section (1), a Designated Court shall be deemed to be a Court of ordinary criminal justice.

24. Saving as to orders: Where an order purports to have been made and signed by any authority in exercise of any power conferred by or under this Act, a Court shall, within the meaning of the Indian Evidence Act, 1872, presume that such order was so made by that authority.

25. Overriding effect: The provisions of this Act or any rule made thereunder or any order made under any such rule shall have effect notwithstanding anything inconsistent therewith contained in any enactment other than this Act or in any instrument having effect by virtue of any enactment other than this Act.

26. Protection of action taken under this Act: No suit, prosecution or other legal proceeding shall lie against the Central Government or State Government or any other authority on whom powers have been conferred under this Act or any rules made thereunder, for anything which is in good faith done or purported to be done in pursuance of this Act or any rules made thereunder or any order issued under any such rule.

27. Power of the Supreme Court to make rules: The Supreme Court may, by notification in the Official Gazette, make such rules, if any, as it may deem necessary for carrying out the provisions of this Act relating to Designated Court.

28. Power to make rules: (1) Without prejudice to the powers of the Supreme Court to make rules under Section 27, the Central Government may, by notification in the Official Gazette, make rules for carrying out the provisions of this Act.

(2) In particular, and without prejudice to the generality of the foregoing

power, such rules may provide for all or any of the following matters namely:

(a) regulating the conduct of persons in respect of areas the control of which is considered necessary or expedient and the removal of such persons from areas.
(b) The entry into, and search of, –

(i) Any vehicle, vessel or aircraft; or

(ii) Any place, whatsoever, reasonably suspected of being used for committing the offence referred to in Section 3 or Section 4 or for manufacturing or storing anything for the commission of any such offence.

(c) Conferring powers upon, –

(i) the Central Government;

(ii) a State Government;

(iii) an Administrator of a Union Territory under Article 239 of the Constitution;

(iv) an officer of the Central Government not lower in rank than of a Joint Secretary; or

(v) an officer of a State Government not lower in rank than that of a District Magistrate,

To make general or special orders to prevent or cope with terrorist acts or disruptive activities;

(d) The arrest and trial of persons contravening any of the rules or any order made thereunder;
(e) The punishment of any person who contravenes or attempts to contravene or abets or attempts to abet the contravention of any rule or order made thereunder with imprisonment for a term which may extend to seven years or for a term which may not be less than six months but which may extend to seven years or with fine or with imprisonment as aforesaid and fine;
(f) Providing for the seizure and detention of any property in respect of which such contravention, attempt or abetment as is referred to in Clause (e) has been committed and for the adjudication of such seizure and detention, whether by any court or by any other authority.

29. Rules to be laid before Houses of Parliament: Every rule made by the Central Government under this Act shall be laid, as soon as may be after it is made, before each House of Parliament, while it is in session, for a total period of thirty days which may be comprised in one session or in two or more successive sessions, and if, before the expiry of the session immediately following the session or the successive sessions aforesaid, both Houses agree in making any modification in the rule or both Houses agree that the rule should not be made, the rule shall thereafter have affect only in such modified form or be of no effect, as the case may be; so, however, that any such modification or annulment shall be without prejudice to the validity of anything previously done under that rule.

30. **Repeal and Saving:** (1) The Terrorist and Disruptive Activities (Prevention) Ordinance, 1987 (2 of 1987) is hereby repealed.

(2) Notwithstanding such repeal, anything done or any action taken under the said Ordinance shall be deemed to have been done or taken under the corresponding provisions of this Act.

Notes:

1.Received the assent of the President on 3rd September, 1987; published in the Gazette of India, (Extra.), Part II, Section 1, pp. 1 to 15, dated 3rd September, 1987

2.Subs. by Act 16 of 1989, Section 2, for the words "two years", re-subs. by Act 35 of 1991, for "four years", (w.e.f. 2-5-1991) and again subs. by Act 43 of 1993, Section 2, for "six years".

3.Ins. by Act 43 of 1993, Section 3.

4.Ins. by Act 43 of 1993, Section 4.

5.Ins. by Act 43 of 1993, Section 5.

6.Ins. by Act 43 of 1993, Section 6(a).

7.Ins. by Act 43 of 1993, Section 6(b).

8.Ins. by Act 43 of 1993, Section 7.

9.Subs. by Act 43 of 1993, Section 8(a).

10.Ins. by Act 43 of 1993, Section 8(b)

11.Ins. by Act 43 of 1993, Section 9.

12.Clauses (c) and (d), omitted by Act 43 of 1993, Section 10.

APPENDIX L

Scheme for Surrender-Cum-Rehabilitation of Militants in the North-East: Government of Assam

[The following is the text of the scheme announced by the State Government of Assam in 1998 for the surrender and rehabilitation of the terrorists of various outfits. This incidentally was the second such package announced in the State, the first one being the brainchild of the Hiteswar Saikia government. The latter was called the '100 per cent Special Money Margin Scheme' and was implemented between June 1, 1992 and March 31, 1997]

Objectives of the Scheme

1. The objective of the Scheme is to wean away the misguided youth and hardcore militants that have strayed into the folds of militancy and now find themselves trapped into that net. The Scheme also seeks to ensure that the militants who have surrendered do not find it attractive to join militants again.

Eligibility Criteria

2. The Scheme is applicable to those militants who surrender at least with one weapon as mentioned in para 6. However, in exceptional and deserving cases, militants, who surrender without arms, may also be considered for rehabilitation under the Scheme. The names of such militants would be scrutinized by the Screening Committee and a final view taken by Unified Headquarters or similar body at the State Government headquarters.

Benefits under the Scheme

3. Persons eligible under the Scheme will be initially lodged in a Rehabilitation Camp where they will be imparted training in a trade/vocation of their liking or befitting their aptitude.

4. They shall be paid a monthly stipend for a period of 12 months. The stipend in respect of a surrenderee shall not exceed Rs. 2000/- per month. The scale of stipend for various categories of surrenderees will be decided by the State Government in consultation with the Government of India.

5. Board and lodging at the Rehabilitation Camp will be free.

Note 1. The stay of a surrenderee in a Rehabilitation Camp shall not exceed one year. All attempts shall be made to settle the surrenderees during this period. In case of settlement of any surrenderee before the expiry of one year, the stipend shall be stopped with effect from the date of settlement.

Note 2. Minor crime cases against successfully rehabilitated surrenderees will be withdrawn.

Note 3. The surrenderees who have committed heinous crimes like murder, rape, abduction etc. will be subject to the due process of law and surrender shall not imply amnesty from the crimes.

Note 4. They shall be paid a monthly stipend for a period of 12 months. The stipend in respect of a surrenderee shall not exceed Rs. 2000/- per month. The scale of stipend for various categories of surrenderees will be decided by the State Government in consultation with the Government of India.

Note 5. The agency for rehabilitation may be a suitable NGO and/or the State Government. In case it is an NGO, it will run the Rehabilitation Camp with support from the Security Forces and the Government where required. (A suitable NGO, which has good credentials and willing to work in this sphere, will have to be identified and provided necessary support from the Government). Necessary infrastructure for board, lodging and training of surrenderees shall be provided to the NGO at Government cost.

Incentives for weapons

6. The following incentives have been built into the Scheme for the surrendered weapons/ammunitions:

i)	Rocket Launchers/UMG/GPMG/PIMCA/ Sniper Rifle	Rs.25,000 per weapon
ii)	AK 47/56/74 Rifle	Rs.15,000 per weapon
iii)	.303 Rifles/Pistol/Revolver and other service weapon	Rs.3,000 per weapon
iv)	Rocket	Rs.1,000 per weapon

v) Grenade/Hand grenade/Stick grenade	Rs.500per grenade
vi) Remote Control device	Rs.3000 each
vii) Ammunition of all types	Rs.3 per round
viii) Wireless Sets : a. Short range, b. Long range	Rs.1000 each Rs.5000 each set
ix) IED	Rs.3000 each
x) Explosive material	Rs.1000 per kg.

However, the incentive given for surrender of the aforesaid arms shall be deposited in the form of a Fixed Deposit in the joint name of surrenderee and the NGO/State Government nominee and shall be given to the surrenderee at the time of his leaving the Rehabilitation Camp.

7. The State Governments of the North-East shall implement the Scheme. However, the Government of India shall provide 100% reimbursement for expenditure incurred on the rehabilitation of surrenderees. In view of the financial position of insurgency affected States and also the fact that the NGO's who may undertake rehabilitation work would immediately need some money in advance, it was felt that there shall be provision for giving a part of the rehabilitation money in advance and the rest as reimbursement. Details would be worked out by the Ministry of Home Affairs in consultation with the Ministry of Finance.

8. The Government of India shall have the right to inspect any of the Camps set up for rehabilitation or transit and to verify any record in this regard.

Procedure

9. The following agencies will be involved in the process of surrender and rehabilitation:

(i) IG (Special Branch) will act as the Surrender and Rehabilitation Officer (S&R Officer) under the Scheme

(ii) Army

(iii) Central Para Military Force

(iv) A nominated NGO

10. Each of the Security Forces will identify one officer of the rank of DIG or equivalent officer as the nodal officer for coordinating surrender and rehabilitation work of militants with respect to their organization.

11. A militant shall be free to surrender before any unit of the Army/CPMFs,

District Magistrate, District SP, Range DIG, IG (Ops), IG (Special Branch), DIG (Special Brach), SPs (Special Branch), SDM, Sub-Divisional Police Officers and other notified officers. The officers for this purpose shall be notified by the State Governments with due approval of the Government of India. A militant may also surrender before any unit if the Army or the CPMFs outside the State. The officer receiving the surrender shall get the details as informed by the surrenderee filled into a prescribed performa and send the same to the S&R Officer and to the nodal officer of the three forces. The nodal officer of each of the organizations will verify the antecedents of the militants from its own sources and his activities and send its specific recommendations to the S&R Officer stating whether the individual could be taken in as surrenderee or not.

12. The officer receiving the surrender will provide immediate security to the surrendered militant and, after getting necessary details for filling up the performa, send him to the Transit Camp to be maintained by the S&R Officer. The board and lodging expenses for the person lodged in the Transit Camp will be borne by the Government. The maximum period within which the decision about a person should be taken would be 15 days.

13. On receiving reports from the four organizations regarding the activities of surrendered person as militant, a Screening Committee headed by the S&R Officer and comprising nodal offices of the four organizations would formally consider the surrender of militant and if accepted, transfer him to the Rehabilitation Camp.

14. Impact assessment of the policy would be done every year to ensure corrective action if required. If the percentage of surrenderees who are successfully rehabilitated at the rehabilitation centre is below 80 per cent, the NGO should be changed.

15. The expenditure during the current financial year, i.e. 1998-99 will be meted out of the sanctioned Budget.

Date of Effect

16. The Scheme will be applicable to those militants who have surrendered/ surrender after 1-4-1998. However, the Scheme will have only prospective effect so far as the payment of monthly stipend to the surrenderees is concerned. Similarly, the facilities to be provided to the NGO will be with prospective effect.

Modification in the Scheme

17. The Ministry of Home Affairs may carry out such modifications in the Scheme as may be considered necessary in public interest. The Ministry of Finance will be consulted if any such modification involves financial implications

APPENDIX M

The Prevention of Terrorism Act, 2002
Act No. 15 of 2002

An Act to make provisions for the prevention of, and for dealing with, terrorist activities and for matters connected therewith.

BE it enacted by Parliament in the Fifty-third Year of the Republic of India as follows: –

- **Preliminary**
- **Punishment for, and measures for dealing with terrorist activities**
- **Terrorist Organizations**
- **Special Courts**
- **Interception of communication in certain cases**
- **Miscellaneous**
- **The Schedule**

CHAPTER I
Preliminary

1. Short title, application, commencement, duration and savings:

(1) This Act may be called the Prevention of Terrorism Act, 2002.

(2) It extends to the whole of India.

(3) Every person shall be liable to punishment under this Act for every act or omission contrary to the provisions thereof, of which he is held guilty in India.

(4) Any person who commits an offence beyond India which is punishable under this Act shall be dealt with according to the provisions of this Act in the same manner as if such act had been committed in India.

(5) The provisions of this Act apply also to –

(a) Citizens of India outside India;

(b) Persons in the service of the Government, wherever they may be; and

(c) Persons on ships and aircrafts, registered in India, wherever they may be.

(6) Save as otherwise provided in respect of entries at serial numbers 24 and 25 of the Schedule to this Act, it shall be deemed to have come into force on the 24th day of October, 2001 and shall remain in force for a period of three years from the date of its commencement, but its expiry under the operation of this sub-section shall not affect –

(a) The previous operation of, or anything duly done or suffered under this Act, or

(b) Any right, privilege, obligation or liability acquired, accrued or incurred under this Act, or

(c) Any penalty, forfeiture or punishment incurred in respect of any offence under this Act, or

(d) Any investigation, legal proceeding or remedy in respect of any such right, privilege, obligation, liability, penalty, forfeiture or punishment as aforesaid,

and, any such investigation, legal proceeding or remedy may be instituted, continued or enforced and any such penalty, forfeiture or punishment may be imposed as if this Act had not expired.

2. Definitions

(1) In this Act, unless the context otherwise requires –

(a) "Code" means the Code of Criminal Procedure, 1973 (2 of 1974);

(b) "Designated Authority" shall mean such officer of the Central Government not below the rank of Joint Secretary to the Government, or such officer of the State Government not below the rank of Secretary to the Government, as the case may be, as may be specified by the Central Government or, as the case may be, the State Government, by a notification published in the Official Gazette;

(c) "proceeds of terrorism" shall mean all kinds of properties which have been derived or obtained from commission of any terrorist act or have been acquired through funds traceable to a terrorist act, and shall include cash irrespective of person in whose name such proceeds are standing or in whose possession they are found;

(d) "property" means property and assets of every description, whether corporeal or incorporeal, movable or immovable, tangible or intangible and deeds and instruments evidencing title to, or interest in, such property or assets and includes bank account;

(e) "Public Prosecutor" means a Public Prosecutor or an Additional Public Prosecutor or a Special Public Prosecutor appointed under section 28 and includes any person acting under the directions of the Public Prosecutor;

(f) "Special Court" means a Special Court constituted under section 23;

(g) "terrorist act" has the meaning assigned to it in sub-section (1) of section 3, and the expression "terrorist" shall be construed accordingly;

(h) "State Government", in relation to a Union territory, means the Administrator thereof;

(i) Words and expressions used but not defined in this Act and defined in the Code shall have the meanings respectively assigned to them in the Code.

(2) Any reference in this Act to any enactment or any provision thereof shall, in relation to an area in which such enactment or such provision is not in force, be construed as a reference to the corresponding law or the relevant provision of the corresponding law, if any, in force in that area.

CHAPTER II

Punishment for, and measures for dealing with, terrorist activities

3. Punishment for terrorist acts

(1) Whoever, -

(a) with intent to threaten the unity, integrity, security or sovereignty of India or to strike terror in the people or any section of the people does any act or thing by using bombs, dynamite or other explosive substances or inflammable substances or firearms or other lethal weapons or poisons or noxious gases or other chemicals or by any other substances (whether biological or otherwise) of a hazardous nature or by any other means whatsoever, in such a manner as to cause, or likely to cause, death of, or injuries to any person or persons or loss of, or damage to, or destruction of, property or disruption of any supplies or services essential to the life of the community or causes damage or destruction of any property or equipment used or intended to be used for the defense of India or in connection with any other purposes of the Government of India, any State Government or any of their agencies, or detains any person and threatens to kill or injure such person in order to compel the Government or any other person to do or abstain from doing any act;

(b) is or continues to be a member of an association declared unlawful under the Unlawful Activities (Prevention) Act, 1967 (37 of 1967), or voluntarily does an act aiding or promoting in any manner the objects of such association and in either case is in possession of any unlicensed firearms, ammunition, explosive or other instrument or substance capable of causing mass destruction and commits any act resulting in loss of human life or grievous injury to any person or causes significant damage to any property, commits a terrorist act.

Explanation. – For the purposes of this sub-section, "a terrorist act" shall include the act of raising funds intended for the purpose of terrorism.

(2) Whoever commits a terrorist act, shall, –

(a) If such act has resulted in the death of any person, be punishable with death or imprisonment for life and shall also be liable to fine;

(b) In any other case, be punishable with imprisonment for a term which shall not be less than five years but which may extend to imprisonment for life and shall also be liable to fine.

(3) Whoever conspires or attempts to commit, or advocates, abets, advises or incites or knowingly facilitates the commission of, a terrorist act or any act preparatory to a terrorist act, shall be punishable with imprisonment for a term which shall not be less than five years but which may extend to imprisonment for life and shall also be liable to fine.

(4) Whoever voluntarily harbors or conceals, or attempts to harbour or conceal any person knowing that such person is a terrorist shall be punishable with imprisonment for a term which shall not be less than three years but which may extend to imprisonment for life and shall also be liable to fine:

Provided that this sub-section shall not apply to any case in which the harbour or concealment is by the husband or wife of the offender.

(5) Any person who is a member of a terrorist gang or a terrorist organization, which is involved in terrorist acts, shall be punishable with imprisonment for a term which may extend to imprisonment for life or with fine which may extend to rupees ten lakh or with both.

Explanation. – For the purposes of this sub-section, "terrorist organization" means an organization which is concerned with or involved in terrorism.

(6) Whoever knowingly holds any property derived or obtained from commission of any terrorist act or has been acquired through the terrorist funds shall be punishable with imprisonment for a term which may extend to imprisonment for life or with fine which may extend to rupees ten lakh or with both.

(7) Whoever threatens any person who is a witness or any other person in whom such witness may be interested, with violence, or wrongfully restrains or confines the witness, or any other person in whom the witness may be interested, or does any other unlawful act with the said intent, shall be punishable with imprisonment which may extend to three years and fine.

4. Possession of certain unauthorized arms, etc.

Where any person is in unauthorized possession of any –

(a) arms or ammunition specified in columns (2) and (3) of Category I or Category III (a) of Schedule I to the Arms Rules, 1962, in a notified area,

(b) bombs, dynamite or hazardous explosive substances or other lethal weapons capable of mass destruction or biological or chemical substances of warfare in any area, whether notified or not, he shall be guilty of terrorist act notwithstanding anything contained in any other law for the time being in force, and be punishable with imprisonment for a term which may extend to imprisonment for life or with fine which may extend to rupees ten lakh or with both.

Explanation – In this section, "notified area" means such area as the State Government may, by notification in the Official Gazette, specify.

5. Enhanced penalties

(1) If any person with intent to aid any terrorist contravenes any provision of, or any rule made under the Explosives Act, 1884 (4 of 1884), the Explosive Substances Act, 1908 (6 of 1908), the Inflammable Substances Act, 1952 (20 of 1952) or the Arms Act, 1959 (54 of 1959), he shall, notwithstanding anything contained in any of the aforesaid Acts or the rules made there under, be punishable with imprisonment for a term which may extend to imprisonment for life and shall also be liable to fine.

(2) For the purposes of this section, any person who attempts to contravene or abets, or does any act preparatory to the contravention of any provision of any law, rule or order, shall be deemed to have contravened that provision, and the provisions of sub-section (1) shall, in relation to such person, have effect subject to the modification that the reference to "imprisonment for life" shall be construed as a reference to "imprisonment for ten years".

6. Holding of proceeds of terrorism illegal

(1) No person shall hold or be in possession of any proceeds of terrorism.

(2) Proceeds of terrorism, whether held by a terrorist or by any other person and whether or not such person is prosecuted or convicted under this Act, shall be liable to be forfeited to the Central Government or the State Government, as the case may be, in the manner provided under this Chapter.

7. Powers of investigating officers and appeal against order of Designated Authority

(1) If an officer (not below the rank of Superintendent of Police) investigating an offence committed under this Act, has reason to believe that any property in relation to which an investigation is being conducted, represents proceeds of terrorism, he shall, with the prior approval in writing of the Director General of the Police of the State in which such property is situated, make an order seizing such property and where it is not practicable to seize such property, make an order of attachment directing that such property shall not be transferred or otherwise dealt with except with the prior permission of the officer making such order, or of the Designated Authority before whom the properties seized or attached are produced and a copy of such order shall be served on the person concerned.

(2) For the removal of doubts, it is hereby provided that where an organisation is declared as a terrorist organisation under this Act and the investigating officer has reason to believe that any person has custody of any property which is being used or is intended to be used for the purpose of such terrorist organization, he may, by an order in writing, seize or attach such property.

(3) The investigating officer shall duly inform the Designated Authority within forty-eight hours of the seizure or attachment of such property.

(4) It shall be open to the Designated Authority before whom the seized or attached properties are produced either to confirm or revoke the order of attachment so issued:

Provided that an opportunity of making a representation by the person whose property is being attached shall be given.

(5) In the case of immovable property attached by the investigating officer, it shall be deemed to have been produced before the Designated Authority, when the investigating officer notifies his report and places it at the disposal of the Designated Authority.

(6) The investigating officer may seize and detain any cash to which this Chapter applies if he has reasonable grounds for suspecting that –

(a) It is intended to be used for the purposes of terrorism;

(b) It forms the whole or part of the resources of an organisation declared as terrorist organisation under this Act:

Provided that the cash seized under this sub-section by the investigating officer shall be released not later than the period of forty-eight hours beginning with the time when it is seized unless the matter involving the cash is before the Designated Authority and such Authority passes an order allowing its retention beyond forty-eight hours.

Explanation – For the purposes of this sub-section, "cash" means –

(a) Coins and notes in any currency;

(b) Postal orders;

(c) Traveller's cheques;

(d) Banker's drafts; and

(e) Such other monetary instruments as the Central Government or, as the case may be, the State Government may specify by an order made in writing.

(7) Any person aggrieved by an order made by the Designated Authority may prefer an appeal to the Special Court and the Special Court may either confirm the order of attachment of property or seizure so made or revoke such order and release the property.

8. Forfeiture of proceeds of terrorism

Where any property is seized or attached on the ground that it constitutes proceeds of terrorism and the Special Court is satisfied in this regard under sub-section (7) of section 7, it may order forfeiture of such property, whether or not the person from whose possession it is seized or attached, is prosecuted in a Special Court for an offence under this Act.

9. Issue of show cause notice before forfeiture of proceeds of terrorism

(1) No order forfeiting any proceeds of terrorism shall be made under section 8 unless the person holding or in possession of such proceeds is given a notice in writing informing him of the grounds on which it is proposed to forfeit the proceeds of terrorism and such person is given an opportunity of making a representation in writing within such reasonable time as may be specified in the notice against the grounds of forfeiture and is also given a reasonable opportunity of being heard in the matter.

(2) No order of forfeiture shall be made under sub-section (1), if such person establishes that he is a bona fide transferee of such proceeds for value without knowing that they represent proceeds of terrorism.

(3) It shall be competent for the Special Court to make an order in respect of property seized or attached, –

(a) Directing it to be sold if it is a perishable property and the provisions of section 459 of the Code shall, as nearly as may be practicable, apply to the net proceeds of such sale;

(b) Nominating any officer of the Central or State Government, in the case of any other property, to perform the function of the Administrator of such property subject to such conditions as may be specified by the Special Court.

10. Appeal

(1) Any person aggrieved by an order of forfeiture under section 8 may, within one month from the date of the receipt of such order, appeal to the High Court within whose jurisdiction, the Special Court, who passed the order appealed against, is situated.

(2) Where an order under section 8 is modified or annulled by the High Court or where in a prosecution instituted for the contravention of the provisions of this Act, the person against whom an order of forfeiture has been made under section 8 is acquitted, such property shall be returned to him and in either case if it is not possible for any reason to return the forfeited property, such person shall be paid the price therefor as if the property had been sold to the Central Government with reasonable interest calculated from the day of seizure of the property and such price shall be determined in the manner prescribed.

11. Order of forfeiture not to interfere with other punishments

The order of forfeiture made under this Act by the Special Court, shall not prevent the infliction of any other punishment to which the person affected thereby is liable under this Act.

12. Claims by third party

(1) Where any claim is preferred, or any objection is made to the seizure of any property under section 7 on the ground that such property is not liable to seizure, the Designated Authority before whom such property is produced, shall proceed to investigate the claim or objection:

Provided that no such investigation shall be made where the Designated Authority considers that the claim or objection is designed to cause unnecessary delay.

(2) In case claimant or objector establishes that the property specified in the notice issued under section 9 is not liable to be forfeited under the Act, the said notice shall be withdrawn or modified accordingly.

13. Powers of Designated Authority

The Designated Authority, acting under the provisions of this Act, shall have all the powers of a civil court required for making a full and fair enquiry into the matter before it.

14. Obligation to furnish information

(1) Notwithstanding anything contained in any other law, the officer investigating any offence under this Act, with prior approval in writing of an officer not below the rank of a Superintendent of Police, may require any officer or authority of the Central Government or a State Government or a local authority or a bank, or a company, or a firm or any other institution, establishment, organization or any individual to furnish information in their possession in relation to such offence, on points or matters, where the investigating officer has reason to believe that such information will be useful for, or relevant to, the purposes of this Act.

(2) Failure to furnish the information called for under sub-section (1), or deliberately furnishing false information shall be punishable with imprisonment for a term which may extend to three years or with fine or with both.

(3) Notwithstanding anything contained in the Code, the offence under sub-section (1) shall be tried as a summary case and the procedure prescribed in Chapter XXI of the said Code [except sub-section (2) of section 262] shall be applicable thereto.

15. Certain transfers to be null and void

Where, after the issue of an order under section 7 or issue of a notice under section 9, any property referred to in the said order or notice is transferred by any mode whatsoever, such transfer shall, for the purpose of the proceedings under this Act, be ignored and if such property is subsequently forfeited, the transfer of such property shall be deemed to be null and void.

16. Forfeiture of property of certain persons

(1) Where any person is accused of any offence under this Act, it shall be open to the Special Court trying him to pass an order that all or any of the properties, movable or immovable or both belonging to him, shall, during the period of such trial, be attached, if not already attached under this Act.

(2) Where a person has been convicted of any offence punishable under this Act, the Special Court may, in addition to awarding any punishment, by order in writing, declare that any property, movable or immovable or both, belonging to the accused and specified in the order, shall stand forfeited to the Central Government or the State Government, as the case may be, free from all encumbrances.

17. Company to transfer shares to Government

Where any shares in a company stand forfeited to the Central Government or the State Government, as the case may be, under this Act, then, the company shall, on receipt of the order of the Special Court, notwithstanding anything contained in the Companies Act, 1956 (1 of 1956), or the articles of association of the company, forthwith register the Central Government or the State Government, as the case may be, as the transferee of such shares.

CHAPTER III

Terrorist organizations

18. Declaration of an organization as a terrorist organization

(1) For the purposes of this Act, an organisation is a terrorist organisation if –

(a) It is listed in the Schedule, or

(b) It operates under the same name as an organisation listed in that Schedule.

(2) The Central Government may by order, in the Official Gazette, –

(a) Add an organisation to the Schedule;

(b) Remove an organisation from that Schedule;

(c) Amend that Schedule in some other way.

(3) The Central Government may exercise its power under clause (a) of sub-section (2) in respect of an organisation only if it believes that it is involved in terrorism.

(4) For the purposes of sub-section (3), an organisation shall be deemed to be involved in terrorism if it –

(a) Commits or participates in acts of terrorism,

(b) Prepares for terrorism,

(c) Promotes or encourages terrorism, or

(d) Is otherwise involved in terrorism.

19. Denotification of a terrorist organization

(1) An application may be made to the Central Government for the exercise of its power under clause (b) of sub-section (2) of section 18 to remove an organisation from the Schedule.

(2) An application may be made by –

(a) The organisation, or

(b) Any person affected by inclusion of the organisation in the Schedule as a terrorist organisation.

(3) The Central Government may make rules to prescribe the procedure for admission and disposal of an application made under this section.

(4) Where an application under sub-section (1) has been refused, the applicant may apply for a review to the Review Committee constituted by the Central Government under sub-section (1) of section 60 within one month from the date of receipt of the order by the applicant.

(5) The Review Committee may allow an application for review against refusal to remove an organisation from the Schedule, if it considers that the decision to refuse was flawed when considered in the light of the principles applicable on an application for judicial review.

(6) Where the Review Committee allows review under sub-section (5) by or in respect of an organisation, it may make an order under this sub-section.

(7) Where an order is made under sub-section (6), the Central Government shall, as soon as the certified copy of the order is received by it, make an order removing the organisation from the list in the Schedule.

20. Offence relating to membership of a terrorist organization

(1) A person commits an offence if he belongs or professes to belong to a terrorist organisation:

Provided that this sub-section shall not apply where the person charged is able to prove –

(a) That the organisation was not declared as a terrorist organisation at the time when he became a member or began to profess to be a member; and

(b) That he has not taken part in the activities of the organisation at any time during its inclusion in the Schedule as a terrorist organisation.

(2) A person guilty of an offence under this section shall be liable, on conviction, to imprisonment for a term not exceeding ten years or with fine or with both.

21. Offence relating to support given to a terrorist organization

(1) A person commits an offence if –

(a) He invites support for a terrorist organisation, and

(b) The support is not, or is not restricted to, the provision of money or other property within the meaning of section 22.

(2) A person commits an offence if he arranges, manages or assists in arranging or managing a meeting which he knows is –

(a) To support a terrorist organisation, or

(b) To further the activities of a terrorist organisation, or

(c) To be addressed by a person who belongs or professes to belong to a terrorist organisation.

(3) A person commits an offence if he addresses a meeting for the purpose of encouraging support for a terrorist organisation or to further its activities.

(4) A person guilty of an offence under this section shall be liable on conviction, to imprisonment for a term not exceeding ten years or with fine or with both.

Explanation. – For the purposes of this section, the expression "meeting" means a meeting of three or more persons whether or not the public are admitted.

22. Fund raising for a terrorist organization to be an offence

(1) A person commits an offence if he –

(a) Invites another to provide money or other property, and

(b) Intends that it should be used, or has reasonable cause to suspect that it may be used, for the purposes of terrorism.

(2) A person commits an offence if he –

(a) receives money or other property, and

(b) intends that it should be used, or has reasonable cause to suspect that it may be used, for the purposes of terrorism.

(3) A person commits an offence if he –

(a) Provides money or other property, and

(b) Knows or has reasonable cause to suspect that it will or may be used for the purposes of terrorism.

(4) In this section, a reference to the provision of money or other property is a reference to its being given, lent or otherwise made available, whether or not for consideration.

(5) A person guilty of an offence under this section shall be liable on conviction, to imprisonment for a term not exceeding fourteen years or with fine or with both.

CHAPTER IV

Special Courts

23. Special Courts

(1) The Central Government or a State Government may, by notification in the Official Gazette, constitute one or more Special Courts for such area or areas, or for such case or class or group of cases, as may be specified in the notification.

(2) Where a notification constituting a Special Court for any area or areas or for any case or class or group of cases is issued by the Central Government under sub-section (1), and a notification constituting a Special Court for the same area or areas or for the same case or class or group of cases has also been issued by the State Government under that sub-section, the Special Court constituted by the Central Government, whether the notification constituting such Court is issued before or after the issue of the notification constituting the Special Court by the State Government, shall have, and the Special Court constituted by the State Government shall not have, jurisdiction to try any offence committed in that area or areas or, as the case may be, the case or class or group of cases and all cases pending before any Special Court constituted by the State Government shall stand transferred to the Special Court constituted by the Central Government.

(3) Where any question arises as to the jurisdiction of any Special Court, it shall be referred to the Central Government whose decision in the matter shall be final.

(4) A Special Court shall be presided over by a judge to be appointed by the Central Government or, as the case may be, the State Government, with the concurrence of the Chief Justice of the High Court.

(5) The Central Government or, as the case may be, the State Government may also appoint, with the concurrence of the Chief Justice of the High Court, additional judges to exercise jurisdiction of a Special Court.

(6) A person shall not be qualified for appointment as a judge or an additional judge of a Special Court unless he is, immediately before such appointment, a sessions judge or an additional sessions judge in any State.

(7) For the removal of doubts, it is hereby provided that the attainment, by a person appointed as a judge or an additional judge of a Special Court, of the age of superannuation under the rules applicable to him in the service to which he belongs, shall not affect his continuance as such judge or additional judge.

(8) Where any additional judge or additional judges is or are appointed in a Special Court, the judge of the Special Court may, from time to time, by general or special order, in writing, provide for the distribution of business of the Special Court among all judges including himself and the additional judge or additional judges and also for the disposal of urgent business in the event of his absence or the absence of any additional judge.

24. Place of sitting

A Special Court may, on its own motion, or on an application made by the Public Prosecutor and if it considers it expedient or desirable so to do, sit for any of its proceedings at any place other than its ordinary place of sitting:

Provided that nothing in this section shall be construed to change the place of sitting of a Special Court constituted by a State Government to any place outside that State.

25. Jurisdiction of Special Courts

(1) Notwithstanding anything contained in the Code, every offence punishable under any provision of this Act shall be triable only by the Special Court within whose local jurisdiction it was committed or, as the case may be, by the Special Court constituted for trying such offence under section 23.

(2) If, having regard to the exigencies of the situation prevailing in a State, –

(a) it is not possible to have a fair, impartial or speedy trial; or

(b) it is not feasible to have the trial without occasioning the breach of peace or grave risk to the safety of the accused, the witnesses, the Public Prosecutor and a judge of the Special Court or any of them; or

(c) it is not otherwise in the interests of justice,

the Supreme Court may transfer any case pending before a Special Court to any other Special Court within that State or in any other State and the High Court may transfer any case pending before a Special Court situated in that State to any other Special Court within the State.

(3) The Supreme Court or the High Court, as the case may be, may act under this section either on the application of the Central Government or a party interested and any such application shall be made by motion, which shall, except when the applicant is the Attorney-General of India, be supported by an affidavit or affirmation.

26. Power of Special Courts with respect to other offences

(1) When trying any offence, a Special Court may also try any other offence with which the accused may, under the Code, be charged at the same trial if the offence is connected with such other offence.

(2) If, in the course of any trial under this Act of any offence, it is found that the accused person has committed any other offence under this Act or under any other law, the Special Court may convict such person of such other offence and pass any sentence or award punishment authorized by this Act or such rule or, as the case may be, under such other law.

27. Power to direct for samples, etc.

(1) When a police officer investigating a case requests the Court of a Chief Judicial Magistrate or the Court of a Chief Metropolitan Magistrate in writing for obtaining samples of handwriting, finger-prints, foot-prints, photographs, blood, saliva, semen, hair, voice of any accused person, reasonably suspected to be involved in the commission of an offence under this Act, it shall be lawful for the Court of a Chief Judicial Magistrate or the Court of a Chief Metropolitan Magistrate to direct that such samples be given by the accused person to the police officer either through a medical practitioner or otherwise, as the case may be.

(2) If any accused person refuses to give samples as provided in sub-section (1), the Court shall draw adverse inference against the accused.

28. Public Prosecutors

(1) For every Special Court, the Central Government or, as the case may be, the State Government, shall appoint a person to be the Public Prosecutor and may appoint one or more persons to be the Additional Public Prosecutor or Additional Public Prosecutors:

Provided that the Central Government or, as the case may be, the State Government, may also appoint for any case or class or group of cases, a Special Public Prosecutor.

(2) A person shall not be qualified to be appointed as a Public Prosecutor or an Additional Public Prosecutor or a Special Public Prosecutor under this section unless he has been in practice as an Advocate for not less than seven years or has held any post, for a period of not less than seven years, under the Union or a State, requiring special knowledge of law.

(3) Every person appointed as a Public Prosecutor or an Additional Public Prosecutor or a Special Public Prosecutor under this section shall be deemed to be a Public Prosecutor within the meaning of clause (u) of section 2 of the Code, and the provisions of the Code shall have effect accordingly.

29. Procedure and powers of Special Courts

(1) Subject to the provisions of section 50, a Special Court may take cognizance of any offence, without the accused being committed to it for trial, upon receiving a complaint of facts that constitute such offence or upon a police report of such facts.

(2) Where an offence triable by a Special Court is punishable with imprisonment for a term not exceeding three years or with fine or with both, the Special Court may, notwithstanding anything contained in sub-section (1) of section 260 or section 262 of the Code, try the offence in a summary way in accordance with the procedure prescribed in the Code and the

provisions of sections 263 to 265 of the Code, shall so far as may be, apply to such trial:

Provided that when, in the course of a summary trial under this sub-section, it appears to the Special Court that the nature of the case is such that it is undesirable to try it in a summary way, the Special Court shall recall any witnesses who may have been examined and proceed to re-hear the case in the manner provided by the provisions of the Code for the trial of such offence and the said provisions shall apply to and in relation to a Special Court as they apply to and in relation to a Magistrate:

Provided further that in the case of any conviction in a summary trial under this section, it shall be lawful for a Special Court to pass a sentence of imprisonment for a term not exceeding one year and with fine which may extend to rupees five lakh.

(3) Subject to the other provisions of this Act, a Special Court shall, for the purpose of trial of any offence, have all the powers of a Court of Session and shall try such offence as if it were a Court of Session so far as may be in accordance with the procedure prescribed in the Code for the trial before a Court of Session.

(4) Subject to the other provisions of this Act, every case transferred to a Special Court under section 25 shall be dealt with as if such case had been transferred under section 406 of the Code to such Special Court.

(5) Notwithstanding anything contained in the Code, but subject to the provisions of section 299 of the Code, a Special Court may, if it thinks fit and for reasons to be recorded by it, proceed with the trial in the absence of the accused or his pleader and record the evidence of any witness, subject to the right of the accused to recall the witness for cross-examination.

30. Protection of witnesses

(1) Notwithstanding anything contained in the Code, the proceedings under this Act may, for reasons to be recorded in writing, be held in camera if the Special Court so desires.

(2) A Special Court, if on an application made by a witness in any proceeding before it or by the Public Prosecutor in relation to such witness or on its own motion, is satisfied that the life of such witness is in danger, it may, for reasons to be recorded in writing, take such measures as it deems fit for keeping the identity and address of such witness secret.

(3) In particular, and without prejudice to the generality of the provisions of sub-section (2), the measures which a Special Court may take under that sub-section may include –

(a) The holding of the proceedings at a place to be decided by the Special Court;

(b) The avoiding of the mention of the names and addresses of the witnesses in its orders or judgments or in any records of the case accessible to public;

(c) The issuing of any directions for securing that the identity and address of the witnesses are not disclosed;

(d) A decision that it is in the public interest to order that all or any of the proceedings pending before such a Court shall not be published in any manner.

(4) Any person who contravenes any decision or direction issued under sub-section (3) shall be punishable with imprisonment for a term which may extend to one year and with fine which may extend to one thousand rupees.

31. Trial by Special Courts to have precedence

The trial under this Act of any offence by a Special Court shall have precedence over the trial of any other case against the accused in any other court (not being a Special Court) and shall be concluded in preference to the trial of such other case and accordingly the trial of such other case shall remain in abeyance.

32. Certain confessions made to police officers to be taken into consideration

(1) Notwithstanding anything in the Code or in the Indian Evidence Act, 1872 (1 of 1872), but subject to the provisions of this section, a confession made by a person before a police officer not lower in rank than a Superintendent of Police and recorded by such police officer either in writing or on any mechanical or electronic device like cassettes, tapes or sound tracks from out of which sound or images can be reproduced, shall be admissible in the trial of such person for an offence under this Act or the rules made thereunder.

(2) A police officer shall, before recording any confession made by a person under sub-section (1), explain to such person in writing that he is not bound to make a confession and that if he does so, it may be used against him:

Provided that where such person prefers to remain silent, the police officer shall not compel or induce him to make any confession.

(3) The confession shall be recorded in an atmosphere free from threat or inducement and shall be in the same language in which the person makes it.

(4) The person from whom a confession has been recorded under sub-section (1), shall be produced before the Court of a Chief Metropolitan Magistrate or the Court of a Chief Judicial Magistrate along with the original statement of confession, written or recorded on mechanical or electronic device within forty-eight hours.

(5) The Chief Metropolitan Magistrate or the Chief Judicial Magistrate, shall, record the statement, if any, made by the person so produced and get his signature or thumb impression and if there is any complaint of torture, such person shall be directed to be produced for medical examination before a Medical Officer not lower in rank than an Assistant Civil Surgeon and thereafter, he shall be sent to judicial custody.

33. Power to transfer cases to regular courts

Where, after taking cognizance of any offence, a Special Court is of the opinion that the offence is not triable by it, it shall, notwithstanding that it has no jurisdiction to try such offence, transfer the case for the trial of such offence to any court having jurisdiction under the Code and the Court to which the case is transferred may proceed with the trial of the offence as if it had taken cognizance of the offence.

34. Appeal

(1) Notwithstanding anything contained in the Code, an appeal shall lie from any judgment, sentence or order, not being an interlocutory order, of a Special Court to the High Court both on facts and on law.

Explanation – For the purposes of this section, "High Court" means a High Court within whose jurisdiction, a Special Court which passed the judgment, sentence or order, is situated.

(2) Every appeal under sub-section (1) shall be heard by a bench of two Judges of the High Court.

(3) Except as aforesaid, no appeal or revision shall lie to any court from any judgment, sentence or order including an interlocutory order of a Special Court.

(4) Notwithstanding anything contained in sub-section (3) of section 378 of the Code, an appeal shall lie to the High Court against an order of the Special Court granting or refusing bail.

(5) Every appeal under this section shall be preferred within a period of thirty days from the date of the judgment, sentence or order appealed from:

Provided that the High Court may entertain an appeal after the expiry of the said period of thirty days if it is satisfied that the appellant had sufficient cause for not preferring the appeal within the period of thirty days.

35. Transitional provisions and transfer of pending proceedings

(1) The jurisdiction conferred by this Act on a Special Court, shall, until a Special Court is constituted under section 23, in the case of any offence punishable under this Act, notwithstanding anything contained in the Code, be exercised by the Court of Session of the division in which such offence has

been committed and it shall have all the powers and follow the procedure provided under this Chapter.

(2) On and from the date when the Special Court is constituted under section 23, every trial under the provisions of this Act, which would have been required to be held before the Special Court, shall stand transferred to that Court on the date on which it is constituted.

CHAPTER V

Interception of communication in certain cases

36. Definitions

In this Chapter, unless the context otherwise requires, –

(a) "electronic communication" means any transmission of signs, signals, writings, images, sounds, data or intelligence of any nature transmitted in whole or in part by a wire, radio, electromagnetic, photo electronic or photo optical system that affects inland or foreign commerce but does not include –

(i) The radio portion of a cordless telephone communication that is transmitted between the wireless telephone hand-set and the base unit; or

(ii) Any wire or oral communication; or

(iii) Any communication made through a tone only paging device; or

(iv) Any communication from a tracking device;

(b) "Intercept" means the aural or other acquisition of the contents by wire, electronic or oral communication through the use of any electronic, mechanical or other device;

(c) "oral communication" means any oral communication uttered by a person exhibiting an expectation that such communication is not subject to interception under circumstances justifying such expectation but such term does not include any electronic communication;

(d) "wire communication" means any aural transmission made in whole or part through the use of facilities for the transmission of communications by the aid of wire, cable or other like connection between the point of origin and the point of connection, between the point of origin and the point of reception (including the use of such connection in switching station) and such term includes any electronic storage of such communication.

37. Appointment of Competent Authority

The Central Government or the State Government, as the case may be, may appoint an officer not below the rank of Secretary to the Government in the case of State Government and not below the rank of Joint Secretary to the Government in the case of Central Government, to be the Competent Authority for the purposes of this Chapter.

38. Application for authorization of interception of wire, electronic or oral communication

(1) A police officer not below the rank of Superintendent of Police supervising the investigation of any terrorist act under this Act may submit an application in writing to the Competent Authority for an order authorizing or approving the interception of wire, electronic or oral communication by the investigating officer when he believes that such interception may provide, or has provided evidence of any offence involving a terrorist act.

(2) Each application shall include the following information: –

(a) The identity of the investigating officer making the application, and the head of the department authorizing the application;

(b) A statement of the facts and circumstances relied upon by the applicant to justify his belief that an order should be issued, including –

(i) Details as to the offence of terrorist act that has been, is being, or is about to be committed;

(ii) A particular description of the nature and location of the facilities from which or the place where the communication is to be intercepted;

(iii) A particular description of the type of communications sought to be intercepted; and

(iv)The identity of the person, if known, committing the terrorist act whose communications are to be intercepted;

(c) A statement of the period of time for which the interception is required to be maintained, if the nature of the enquiry is such that the authorization of interception should not automatically terminate after the described type of communication has been first obtained;

(d) A particular description of facts establishing probable cause to believe that additional communications of the same type will occur thereafter; and

(e) Where the application is for the extension of an order, a statement setting forth the results thus far obtained from the interception, or a reasonable explanation of the failure to obtain such results.

(3) The Competent Authority may require the applicant to furnish additional oral or documentary evidence in support of the application.

39. Decision by Competent Authority on application for interception

(1) Upon such application, the Competent Authority may reject the

application, or issue an order, as requested or as modified, authorizing or approving interception of wire, electronic or oral communications, if the Competent Authority determines on the basis of the facts submitted by the applicant that –

(a) there is a probable cause for belief that an individual is committing, has committed, or is about to commit, a particular offence described and made punishable under sections 3 and 4 of this Act;

(b) There is a probable cause of belief that particular communications concerning that offence may be obtained through such interception;

(c) there is probable cause of belief that the facilities from which, or the place where, the wire, electronic or oral communications are to be intercepted are being used or are about to be used, in connection with the commission of such offence, leased to, or are listed in, the name of or commonly used by such person.

(2) Each order by the Competent Authority authorizing or approving the interception of any wire, electronic or oral communication under this section shall specify –

(a) The identity of the person, if known, whose communications are to be intercepted;

(b) The nature and location of the communication facilities as to which, or the place where, authority to intercept is granted;

(c) A particular description of the type of communication sought to be intercepted, and a statement of the particular offence to which it relates;

(d) The identity of the agency authorized to intercept the communications, and the person authorizing the application; and

(e) The period of time during which such interception is authorized, including a statement as to whether or not the interception shall automatically terminate after the described communication has been first obtained.

40. Submission of order of interception to Review Committee

(1) The Competent Authority shall, immediately after passing the order under sub-section

(1) of section 39, but in any case not later than seven days from the passing of the order, submit a copy of the same to the Review Committee constituted under section 60 alongwith all the relevant underlying papers, record and his own findings, in respect of the said order, for consideration and approval of the order by the Review Committee.

(2) An order authorizing the interception of a wire, electronic or oral communication under this section shall, upon request of the applicant, direct

that a provider of wire or electronic communication service, landlord, custodian or other person shall furnish to the applicant forthwith all information, facilities and technical assistance necessary to accomplish the interception unobtrusively and with a minimum of interference with the services that such service provider, landlord, custodian or person is providing to the person whose communications are to be intercepted.

41. Duration of an order of inception, etc.

(1) No order issued under this section may authorize or approve the interception of any wire, electronic or oral communication for any period longer than is necessary to achieve the objective of the authorization, nor in any event longer than sixty days and such sixty days period shall begin on the day immediately preceding the day on which the investigating officer first begins to conduct an interception under the order or ten days after order is issued whichever is earlier.

(2) The extension of an order may be granted, but only upon an application for an extension made in accordance with sub-section (1) of section 38 and the Competent Authority making the findings required by sub-section (1) of section 39, and the period of such extension shall be no longer than the Competent Authority deems necessary to achieve the purposes for which it was granted and in no event for longer than sixty days at a time.

(3) Every order and extension thereof shall contain a provision that the authorization to intercept shall be executed as soon as practicable and shall be conducted in such manner as to minimize the interception of communications not otherwise subject to interception under this section and shall terminate upon attainment of the authorized objective, or in any event on the expiry of the period of said order or extension thereof.

42. Authority competent to carry out interception

(1) An interception under this Chapter may be conducted in whole or in part by a public servant, acting under the supervision of the investigating officer authorized to conduct the interception.

(2) Whenever an order authorizing an interception is issued pursuant to this section, the order may require reports to be made to the Competent Authority who issued the order showing that progress has been made towards achievement of the authorized objective and the need for continued interception and such report shall be made at such intervals as the Competent Authority may require.

43. Interception of communication in emergency

(1) Notwithstanding anything contained in any other provision of this Chapter, an officer not below the rank of Additional Director General of Police or a police officer of equivalent rank who reasonably determines that –

(a) An emergency situation exists that involves –

(i) Immediate danger of death or serious physical injury to any person; or

(ii) Conspiratorial activities threatening the security or interest of the State; or

(iii) conspiratorial activities, characteristic of a terrorist act, that requires a wire, electronic or oral communication to be intercepted before an order from the Competent Authority authorizing such interception can, with due diligence, be obtained; and

(b) There are grounds on which an order should be issued under this section to authorize such interception,

May authorize, in writing, the investigating officer to intercept such wire, electronic or oral communication, if an application for an order approving the interception is made in accordance with the provisions of sub-sections (1) and (2) of section 38 within forty-eight hours after the interception has occurred, or begins to occur.

(2) In the absence of an order approving the interception made under sub-section (1), such interception shall immediately terminate when the communication sought is obtained or when the application for the order is rejected, whichever is earlier; and in the event of an application for permitting interception being rejected under sub-section (1) of section 39 or an application under sub-section (1) of this section for approval being rejected, or in any other case where the interception is terminated without an order having been issued, the contents of any wire, electronic or oral communication intercepted shall be treated as having been obtained in violation of this section.

44. Protection of information collected

(1) The contents of any wire, electronic or oral communication intercepted by any means authorized by this Chapter shall, as far as possible, be recorded on tape or wire or other comparable device and shall be done in such manner as to protect the recording from editing or other alterations.

(2) Immediately upon the expiration of the period of order, or extension thereof, such recording shall be made available to the Competent Authority issuing such order and shall be sealed under his directions and kept in the custody of such person or authority as the Competent Authority orders, and such recordings shall not be destroyed except upon an order of the Competent Authority and in any event shall be kept for ten years.

(3) Applications made and orders issued under this Chapter shall be sealed by the Competent Authority and custody of the applications and orders shall be kept in such manner as the Competent Authority directs, and shall not be

destroyed except on an order of the Competent Authority, and in any event shall be kept for ten years.

45. Admissibility of evidence collected through the interception of communications

Notwithstanding anything in the Code or in any other law for the time being in force, the evidence collected through the interception of wire, electronic or oral communication under this Chapter shall be admissible as evidence against the accused in the Court during the trial of a case:

Provided that, the contents of any wire, electronic or oral communication intercepted pursuant to this Chapter or evidence derived therefrom shall not be received in evidence or otherwise disclosed in any trial, hearing or other proceeding in any court unless each accused has been furnished with a copy of the order of the Competent Authority, and accompanying application, under which the interception was authorized or approved not less than ten days before trial, hearing or proceeding:

Provided further that, the period of ten days may be waived by the judge trying the matter, if he comes to the conclusion that it was not possible to furnish the accused with the above information ten days before the trial, hearing or proceeding and that the accused will not be prejudiced by the delay in receiving such information.

46. Review of authorization order

(1) The Review Committee constituted by the Central Government or the State Government, as the case may be, shall review every order passed by the Competent Authority under section 39.

(2) Every order passed by the Competent Authority under section 39, or disapproved by the officer under section 43, shall be placed before the Review Committee, which shall be considered by the Review Committee within ten days after its receipt, to decide whether the order was necessary, reasonable and justified.

(3) The Review Committee after examining the entire record and holding such enquiry, if any, deemed necessary may, by order in writing, either approve the order passed by the Competent Authority or may issue order disapproving the same.

(4) On issue of an order of disapproval by the Review Committee, the interception, if any, already commenced shall be forthwith discontinued and the intercepted communication, if any, in the form of tape, wire or other device shall, thereupon, not be admissible as evidence in any case and shall be directed to be destroyed.

47. Interception and disclosure of wire, electronic or oral communications prohibited

Except as otherwise specifically provided in section 39, any police officer who—

(a) Intentionally intercepts, endeavours to intercept, or procures any other person to intercept or endeavour to intercept any wire, electronic or oral communication;

(b) intentionally uses, endeavours to use, or procures any other person to use or endeavours to use any electronic, mechanical or other device to intercept any oral communication when -

(i) Such device is affixed to, or otherwise transmits a signal through a wire, cable, or other like connection used in wire communication; or

(ii) Such device transmits communications by radio, or interferes with the transmission of such communication;

(c) intentionally discloses, or endeavours to disclose, to any other person the contents of any wire, electronic or oral communication, knowing or having reason to know that the information was obtained through the interception of a wire, electronic or oral communication in violation of this Chapter;

(d) intentionally uses, or endeavours to use, the contents of any wire, electronic or oral communication, knowing or having reason to know that the information was obtained through the interception of a wire, electronic or oral communication in violation of this Chapter;

(e) Intentionally discloses, or endeavours to disclose, to any other unauthorized person the contents of any wire, electronic or oral communication, intercepted by means authorized by section 39;

(f) Intentionally continues the interception of wire, electronic or oral communication after the issue of an order of rejection by the Competent Authority under this Chapter;

(g) Intentionally continues the interception of wire, electronic or oral communication after the issue of an order of disapproval by the Review Committee under sub-section (3) of section 46,

Shall for such violation be punishable with imprisonment for a term which may extend to one year and with fine up to rupees fifty thousand.

48. Annual report of interceptions

(1) The Central Government and the State Government, as the case may be, shall cause an annual report to be prepared giving a full account of -

(a) the number of applications for authorization of interceptions received by the Competent Authority from the Police Department in which prosecutions have been launched;

(b) The number of such applications permitted or rejected;

(c) The number of interceptions carried out in emergency situations and the number of approvals granted or rejected in such matters;

(d) The number of prosecutions launched based on such interceptions and convictions resulting from such interceptions, along with an explanatory memorandum giving general assessment of the utility and importance of the interceptions authorized.

(2) An annual report shall be laid by the State Government before the State Legislature within three months of the completion of every calendar year:

Provided that, if the State Government is of the opinion that the inclusion of any matter in the annual report would be prejudicial to the security of the State or to the prevention or detection of any terrorist act, the State Government may exclude such matter from being included in such annual report.

(3) An annual report shall be laid by the Central Government before each House of Parliament within three months of the completion of every calendar year:

Provided that, if the Central Government is of the opinion that the inclusion of any matter in the annual report would be prejudicial to the security of the country or to the prevention or detection of any terrorist act, the Central Government may exclude such matter from being included in such annual report.

CHAPTER VI

Miscellaneous

49. Modified application of certain provisions of the Code

(1) Notwithstanding anything contained in the Code or any other law, every offence punishable under this Act shall be deemed to be a cognizable offence within the meaning of clause (c) of section 2 of the Code, and "cognizable case" as defined in that clause shall be construed accordingly.

(2) Section 167 of the Code shall apply in relation to a case involving an offence punishable under this Act subject to the modification that in sub-section (2), –

(a) the references to "fifteen days", "ninety days" and "sixty days", wherever they occur, shall be construed as references to "thirty days", "ninety days" and "ninety days", respectively; and

(b) After the proviso, the following provisos shall be inserted, namely: –

"Provided further that if it is not possible to complete the investigation within the said period of ninety days, the Special Court shall extend the said period up to one hundred and eighty days, on the report of the Public Prosecutor indicating the progress of the investigation and the specific reasons for the detention of the accused beyond the said period of ninety days:

Provided also that if the police officer making the investigation under this Act, requests, for the purposes of investigation, for police custody from judicial custody of any person from judicial custody, he shall file an affidavit stating the reasons for doing so and shall also explain the delay, if any, for requesting such police custody".

(3) Section 268 of the Code shall apply in relation to a case involving an offence punishable under this Act subject to the modification that –

(a) The reference in sub-section (1) thereof –

(i) To "the State Government" shall be construed as a reference to "the Central Government or the State Government",

(ii) To "order of the State Government" shall be construed as a reference to "order of the Central Government or the State Government, as the case may be"; and

(b) The reference in sub-section (2) thereof, to "the State Government" shall be construed as a reference to "the Central Government or the State Government, as the case may be".

(4) Sections 366, 367 and 371 of the Code shall apply in relation to a case involving an offence triable by a Special Court subject to the modification that the reference to "Court of Session", wherever occurring therein, shall be construed as the reference to "Special Court".

(5) Nothing in section 438 of the Code shall apply in relation to any case involving the arrest of any person accused of having committed an offence punishable under this Act.

(6) Notwithstanding anything contained in the Code, no person accused of an offence punishable under this Act shall, if in custody, be released on bail or on his own bond unless the Court gives the Public Prosecutor an opportunity of being heard.

(7) Where the Public Prosecutor opposes the application of the accused to release on bail, no person accused of an offence punishable under this Act or any rule made thereunder shall be released on bail until the Court is satisfied

that there are grounds for believing that he is not guilty of committing such offence:

Provided that after the expiry of a period of one year from the date of detention of the accused for an offence under this Act, the provisions of sub-section (6) of this section shall apply.

(8) The restrictions on granting of bail specified in sub-sections (6) and (7) are in addition to the restrictions under the Code or any other law for the time being in force on granting of bail.

(9) Notwithstanding anything contained in sub-sections (6), (7) and (8), no bail shall be granted to a person accused of an offence punishable under this Act, if he is not an Indian citizen and has entered the country unauthorized or illegally except in very exceptional circumstances and for reasons to be recorded in writing.

50. Cognizance of offences

No court shall take cognizance of any offence under this Act without the previous sanction of the Central Government or, as the case may be, the State Government.

51. Officers competent to investigate offences under this Act

Notwithstanding anything contained in the Code, no police officer, –

(a) in the case of the Delhi Special Police Establishment, below the rank of a Deputy Superintendent of Police or a police officer of equivalent rank;

(b) in the metropolitan areas of Mumbai, Kolkata, Chennai and Ahmedabad and any other metropolitan area notified as such under sub-section (1) of section 8 of the Code, below the rank of an Assistant Commissioner of Police;

(c) in any other case not relatable to clause (a) or clause (b), below the rank of a Deputy Superintendent of Police or a police officer of an equivalent rank,

shall investigate any offence punishable under this Act.

52. Arrest

(1) Where a police officer arrests a person, he shall prepare a custody memo of the person arrested.

(2) The person arrested shall be informed of his right to consult a legal practitioner as soon as he is brought to the police station.

(3) Whenever any person is arrested, information of his arrest shall be immediately communicated by the police officer to a family member or in his absence to a relative of such person by telegram, telephone or by any other means and this fact shall be recorded by the police officer under the signature

of the person arrested.

(4) The person arrested shall be permitted to meet the legal practitioner representing him during the course of interrogation of the accused person:

Provided that nothing in this sub-section shall entitle the legal practitioner to remain present throughout the period of interrogation.

53. Presumption as to offences under section 3

(1) In a prosecution for an offence under sub-section (1) of section 3, if it is proved –

(a) that the arms or explosives or any other substances specified in section 4 were recovered from the possession of the accused and there is reason to believe that such arms or explosives or other substances of a similar nature, were used in the commission of such offence; or

(b) That the finger-prints of the accused were found at the site of the offence or on anything including arms and vehicles used in connection with the commission of such offence,

The Special Court shall draw adverse inference against the accused.

(2) In a prosecution for an offence under sub-section (3) of section 3, if it is proved that the accused rendered any financial assistance to a person, having knowledge that such person is accused of, or reasonably suspected of, an offence under that section, the Special Court shall draw adverse inference against the accused.

54. Bar of jurisdiction of courts, etc.

No civil court or other authority shall have or, be entitled to, exercise any jurisdiction, powers or authority in relation to the matters referred to in sections 19 and 40 of the Act.

55. Saving

(1) Nothing in this Act shall affect the jurisdiction exercisable by, or the procedure applicable to, any court or other authority under any law relating to the naval, military or air forces or other armed forces of the Union.

(2) For the removal of doubts, it is hereby declared that for the purposes of any such law as is referred to in sub-section (1), a Special Court shall be deemed to be a court of ordinary criminal justice.

56. Overriding effect

The provisions of this Act shall have effect notwithstanding anything inconsistent therewith contained in any enactment other than this Act or in any instrument having effect by virtue of any enactment other than this Act.

57. Protection of action taken in good faith

No suit, prosecution or other legal proceeding shall lie against the Central Government or a State Government or any officer or authority of the Central Government or State Government or any other authority on whom powers have been conferred under this Act, for anything which is in good faith done or purported to be done in pursuance of this Act:

Provided that no suit, prosecution or other legal proceedings shall lie against any serving member or retired member of the armed forces or other para-military forces in respect of any action taken or purported to be taken by him in good faith, in the course of any operation directed towards combating terrorism.

58. Punishment and compensation for malicious action

(1) Any police officer who exercises powers corruptly or maliciously, knowing that there are no reasonable grounds for proceeding under this Act, shall be punishable with imprisonment which may extend to two years, or with fine, or with both.

(2) If the Special Court is of the opinion that any person has been corruptly or maliciously proceeded against under this Act, the Court may award such compensation as it deems fit to the person, so proceeded against and it shall be paid by the officer, person, authority or Government, as may be specified in the order.

59. Impounding passport and arms licence of person chargesheeted under the Act

Notwithstanding anything contained in any other law for the time being in force, the passport and the arms licence of a person, who is charge-sheeted for having committed any offence under this Act, shall be deemed to have been impounded for such period as the Special Court may deem fit.

60. Review Committees

(1) The Central Government and each State Government shall, whenever necessary, constitute one or more Review Committees for the purposes of this Act.

(2) Every such Committee shall consist of a Chairperson and such other members not exceeding three and possessing such qualifications as may be prescribed.

(3) A Chairperson of the Committee shall be a person who is, or has been, a Judge of a High Court, who shall be appointed by the Central Government, or as the case may be, the State Government, so however, that the concurrence

of the Chief Justice of the High Court shall be obtained in the case of a sitting Judge:

Provided that in the case of a Union territory, the appointment of a person who is a Judge of the High Court of a State shall be made as a Chairperson with the concurrence of the Chief Justice of the concerned High Court.

61. Power of High Courts to make rules

The High Court may, by notification in the Official Gazette, make such rules, if any, as they may deem necessary for carrying out the provisions of this Act relating to Special Courts within their territories.

62. Power to make rules

(1) Without prejudice to the powers of the High Courts to make rules under section 61, the Central Government may, by notification in the Official Gazette, make rules for carrying out the provisions of this Act.

(2) In particular, and without prejudice to the generality of the foregoing powers, such rules may provide for all or any of the following matters, namely: -

(a) Regulating the conduct of persons in respect of areas the control of which is considered necessary or expedient and the removal of such persons from such areas;

(b) The entry into, and search of -

(i) Any vehicle, vessel or aircraft; or

(ii) Any place, whatsoever,

Reasonably suspected of being used for committing the offences referred to in section 3 or section 4 or for manufacturing or storing anything for the commission of any such offence;

(c) Conferring powers upon -

(i) The Central Government;

(ii) A State Government;

(iii) An Administrator of a Union territory under article 239 of the Constitution;

(iv) An officer of the Central Government not lower in rank than that of a Joint Secretary; or

(v) An officer of a State Government not lower in rank than that of a District Magistrate, to make general or special orders to prevent or deal with terrorist acts;

(d) The arrest and trial of persons contravening any of the rules or any order made thereunder;

(e) the punishment of any person who contravenes or attempts to contravene or abets or attempts to abet the contravention of any rule or order made thereunder with imprisonment for a term which may extend to one year or fine or both;

(f) providing for the seizure and detention of any property in respect of which such contravention, attempt or abetment as is referred to in clause (e) has been committed and for the adjudication of such seizure and detention, whether by any court or by any other authority;

(g) Determination of the price of the forfeited property under sub-section (2) of section 10;

(h) The procedure of making application under sub-section (3) of section 19; and

(i) The qualifications of the members of the Review Committee under sub-section (2) of section 60.

63. Orders and rules to be laid before Houses of Parliament

Every order and every rule made by the Central Government under this Act shall be laid, as soon as may be after it is made, before each House of Parliament, while it is in session, for a total period of thirty days which may be comprised in one session or in two or more successive sessions, and if, before the expiry of the session immediately following the session or the successive sessions aforesaid, both Houses agree in making any modification in the order or rule or both Houses agree that the order or rule should not be made, the order or rule shall thereafter have effect only in such modified form or be of no effect, as the case may be; so, however, that any such modification or annulment shall be without prejudice to the validity of anything previously done under that order or rule.

64. Repeal and saving

(1) The Prevention of Terrorism (Second) Ordinance, 2001 is hereby repealed.

(2) Notwithstanding the repeal of the said Ordinance, anything done or any action taken under the said Ordinance shall be deemed to have been done or taken under the corresponding provisions of this Act.

THE SCHEDULE

(See section 18)

Terrorist organizations

1. **Babbar Khalsa International**

2. Khalistan Commando Force
3. Khalistan Zindabad Force
4. International Sikh Youth Federation
5. Lashkar-e-Taiba/Pasban-e-Ahle Hadis
6. Jaish-e-Mohammed/Tahrik-e-Furqan
7. Harkat-ul-Mujahideen/Harkat-ul-Ansar/Harkat-ul-Jehad-e-Islami
8. Hizb-ul-Mujahideen/Hizb-ul-Mujahideen Pir Panjal Regiment
9. Al-Umar-Mujahideen
10. Jammu and Kashmir Islamic Front
11. United Liberation Front of Assam (ULFA)
12. National Democratic Front of Bodoland (NDFB)
13. People's Liberation Army (PLA)
14. United National Liberation Front (UNLF)
15. People's Revolutionary Party of Kangleipak (PREPAK)
16. Kangleipak Communist Party (KCP)
17. Kanglei Yaol Kanba Lup (KYKL)
18. Manipur People's Liberation Front (MPLF)
19. All Tripura Tiger Force
20. National Liberation Front of Tripura
21. Liberation Tigers of Tamil Eelam (LTTE)
22. Students Islamic Movement of India
23. Deendar Anjuman
24. Communist Party of India (Marxist-Leninist) – People's War, all its formations and front organisations
25. Maoist Communist Centre (MCC), All its formations and front organisations
26. Al Badr
27. Jamiat-Ul-Mujahidden
28. Al-Qaida.
29. Dukhtaran-e-Millat (DEM)

30. **Tamil Nadu Liberation Army (TNLA)**

31. **Tamil National Retrieval Troops (TNRT)**

32. **Akhil Bharat Nepali Ekta Samaj (ABNES)**

Explanation — For the purposes of this Schedule, serial numbers 24 and 25 shall be deemed to have been included with effect from the date of publication of S.O. No. 1194(E), dated the 5th December, 2001.

K.N. CHATURVEDI,

Addl. Secy. to the Govt. of India

APPENDIX N

The SAARC Convention (Suppression of Terrorism) Act, 1993
Enactment Date: [26th April 1993]

1. Act Objective: An Act to give effect to the South Asian Association for Regional Cooperation Convention on Suppression of Terrorism and for matters connected therewith or incidental thereto. WHEREAS a Convention on the Suppression of Terrorism was signed on behalf of the Government of India at Kathmandu on the 4th day of November, 1987; AND WHEREAS India, having ratified the said Convention, should make provisions for giving effect thereto and for matters connected therewith or incidental thereto; BE it enacted by Parliament in the Forty-fourth Year of the Republic of India as follows: -

2. Definitions: In this Act, unless the context otherwise requires: -

(a) "Convention" means the South Asian Association for Regional Cooperation Convention on Suppression of Terrorism signed at Kathmandu on the 4th day of November 1987 as set out in the Schedule;

(b) "Convention country" means a country in which the Convention is for the time being in force.

3. Application of the Convention: Notwithstanding anything to the contrary contained in any other law, the provisions of Articles I to VIII of the Convention shall have the force of law in India.

4. Hostage-taking: (1) Whoever, by force or threat of force or by any other form of intimation, seizes or detains any person and threatens to kill or injure that person with intent to cause a Convention country to do or abstain from doing any act as the means of avoiding the execution of such threat, commits the offence of hostage-taking. (2) Whoever commits the offence of hostage-taking shall be punished with imprisonment for a term which may extend to ten years, and shall also be liable to fine.

5. Provisions as to Extradition Act: For the purposes of the Extradition Act, 1962 (34 of 1962), in relation to a Convention country, an offence under sub-section (1) of section 4 or any other offence specified in Article I of the Convention, shall not be considered to be an offence of a political character.

6. Offences committed outside India: (1) When an offence under sub-section (1) of section 4 or any other offence specified in Article I of the Convention is committed outside India, - (a) by a citizen of India, whether on the high seas or elsewhere; (b) by a person, not being such citizen, on any ship or aircraft, registered in India; or (c) by a person, not being such citizen, in a Convention country, he may be dealt with in respect of such offence as if it had been committed at any place within India at which he may be found. (2) Notwithstanding anything contained in sub-section (1), the Central Government may, by general or special order published in the Official Gazette, direct that the offence under sub-section (1) of section 4 or any other offence specified in Article I of the Convention may be inquired into or tried at any place within India.

7. Previous sanction necessary for prosecution: No prosecution for an offence under this Act shall be instituted except with the previous sanction of the Central Government and the sanction granted under this section shall be deemed to be a sanction granted under section 188 of the Code of Criminal Procedure, 1973 (2 of 1974).

8. Protection of action taken in good faith: (1) No suit, prosecution or other legal proceeding shall lie against any person for anything which is in good faith done or intended to be done in pursuance of the provisions of this Act. (2) No suit or other legal proceeding shall lie against the Central Government for any damage caused or likely to be caused for anything which is in good faith done or intended to be done in pursuance of the provisions of this Act.

THE SCHEDULE

SAARC REGIONAL CONVENTION ON SUPPRESSION OF TERRORISM

APPENDIX O

Additional Protocol to The SAARC Regional Convention on Suppression of Terrorism. The Member States of The South Asian Association For Regional Co-Operation (SAARC)

MINDFUL of the purposes and the principles of co-operation enshrined in the SAARC Charter and the Charter of the United Nations;

RECALLING the Declaration of the Eleventh SAARC Summit adopted at Kathmandu on 6th January 2002;

FURTHER RECALLING that, at the Eleventh SAARC Summit, the Heads of State or Government, reiterated their support to the United Nations Security Council Resolution 1373 of September 28, 2001 and affirmed their determination to re-double efforts collectively as well as individually, to prevent and suppress terrorism in all its forms and manifestations, including, by increased co-operation and full implementation of the relevant international conventions relating to terrorism to which they are parties and called on all Member States, inter-alia, to prevent and suppress the financing of terrorist acts by criminalizing the provision, acquisition and collection of funds for such acts;

BEARING IN MIND the decision of the SAARC Council of Ministers at its Twenty Third Session in Kathmandu on 22nd August, 2002, wherein the Council mandated the preparation of an Additional Protocol to the SAARC Regional Convention on Suppression of Terrorism, recognizing the importance of updating the Convention, in order to meet the obligations devolving in terms of Security Council Resolution 1373 (2001);

HAVE AGREED as follows:

Article 1

Objectives and Purposes

The purpose of this Additional Protocol is to strengthen the SAARC Regional

Convention on Suppression of Terrorism, particularly by criminalizing the provision, collection or acquisition of funds for the purpose of committing terrorist acts and taking further measures to prevent and suppress financing of such acts. Towards this end, State Parties agree to adopt necessary measures to strengthen co-operation among them, in accordance with the terms of this Additional Protocol.

Article 2
Relationship to SAARC Convention

This Additional Protocol supplements the SAARC Regional Convention on Suppression of Terrorism, done at Kathmandu on 4th November, 1987 (hereinafter referred to as the "1987 SAARC Convention"). The 1987 SAARC Convention and this Additional Protocol shall be read and interpreted together as a single instrument.

Article 3
Definitions

1. "Funds" mean assets of every kind, whether tangible or intangible, movable or immovable, however acquired, and legal documents or instruments in any form, including electronic or digital, evidencing title to, or interest in, such assets, including, but not limited to, bank credits, travelers cheques, bank cheques, money orders, shares, securities, bonds, drafts and letters of credit.

2. "Proceeds" mean any funds derived from or obtained, directly or indirectly, through the commission of an offence set forth in Article 4.

Article 4
Offences

1. Any person commits an offence within the meaning of this Additional Protocol if that person by any means, directly or indirectly, unlawfully and willfully, provides or collects funds with the intention that they should be used or in the knowledge that they are to be used, in full or in part, in order to carry out :

(a) An act which constitutes an offence within the scope of and as defined in one of the treaties listed in the Annex to this Protocol; or

(b) Any other act intended to cause death or serious bodily injury to a civilian, when the purpose of such act, by its nature or context, is to intimidate a population, or to compel a Government or an international organization to do or to abstain from doing any act; or

(c) An offence within the scope of any Convention to which SAARC Member States concerned are parties and which obliges the parties to prosecute or grant extradition.

2. (a) On depositing its instrument of ratification, acceptance, approval or accession, a State Party which is not a party to a treaty listed in the annex may declare that, in the application of this Convention to the State Party, the treaty shall be deemed not to be included in the annex referred to in paragraph 1, subparagraph (a). The declaration shall cease to have effect as soon as the treaty enters into force for the State Party, which shall notify the depositary of this fact;

   (b) When a State Party ceases to be a party to a treaty listed in the annex, it may make a declaration as provided for in this article, with respect to that treaty.

3. For an act to constitute an offence set forth in paragraph 1, it shall not be necessary that the funds were actually used to carry out an offence referred to in paragraph 1, subparagraph (a) or (b).
4. Any person also commits an offence if that person attempts to commit an offence as set forth in paragraph 1 of this article.

5. Any person also commits an offence if that person:

(a) Participates as an accomplice in an offence as set forth in paragraph 1 or 4 of this article;

(b) Organizes or directs others to commit an offence as set forth in paragraph 1 or 4 of this article;

(c) Contributes to the commission of one or more offences as set forth in paragraph 1 or 4 of this article by a group of persons acting with a common purpose. Such contribution shall be intentional and shall either:

   i. Be made with the aim of furthering the criminal activity or criminal purpose of the group, where such activity or purpose involves the commission of an offence as set forth in paragraph 1 of this article; or

   ii. Be made in the knowledge of the intention of the group to commit an offence as set forth in paragraph 1 of this article.

Article 5
Domestic Measures

State Parties, in accordance with the provisions of their respective Constitutions, shall endeavour to become Parties to the international instruments listed in the Annex to which they are not yet a Party.

Article 6
Liability of legal entities

1. Each State Party, in accordance with its domestic legal principles, shall take the necessary measures to enable a legal entity located in its territory or organized under its laws to be held liable when a person responsible for the management or control of that legal entity has, in that capacity, committed an offence as set forth in Article 4. Such liability may be criminal, civil or administrative.

2. Such liability is incurred without prejudice to the criminal liability of an individual or individuals who have committed the offences.

3. Each State Party shall ensure, in particular, that legal entities liable in accordance with paragraph 1 above are subject to effective, proportionate and dissuasive criminal, civil or administrative sanctions. Such sanctions may include monetary sanctions.

Article 7
Measures to prevent, suppress and eradicate the financing of terrorism

1. State Parties shall consider and take all practical measures at the national level, inter-alia by adapting their domestic legislation to prevent, suppress and eradicate the financing of terrorism, and for effective international cooperation with respect thereto including:

a) A comprehensive domestic regulatory and supervisory regime for banks, other financial institutions and other entities deemed particularly susceptible to being used for the financing of terrorist activities. This regime shall require banks and other financial institutions and other entities to utilize effective measures for the identification of customers, paying special attention to unusual or suspicious transactions and to report promptly to the Competent Authorities, all complex, unusual large transactions and unusual patterns of transactions, which have no apparent economic or obviously lawful purpose;

b) Measures to detect and monitor movements across national borders, of cash, bearer negotiable instruments and other appropriate movements of value. These measures shall be subject to safeguards to ensure proper use of information and should not impede legitimate capital movements;

c) Measures of assistance in connection with criminal investigations or criminal proceedings relating to the financing or support of any act constituting an offencee within the scope of the international instruments listed in Article 4 of this Additional Protocol, including assistance in obtaining evidence in their possession, necessary for the proceedings; and
d) Establishing and monitoring channels of communication between their competent agencies and services to facilitate the secure and rapid exchange of information concerning all aspects of offences set forth in Article 4, within the conditions prescribed by domestic law.

2. Towards facilitating the above, each State Party shall consider measures to establish and maintain a financial intelligence unit to serve as a national center for the collection, analysis and dissemination of pertinent money laundering and terrorist financing information.

Article 8
Seizure and confiscation of funds or other assets

1. Each State Party shall take appropriate measures, in accordance with its domestic legal principles, for the identification, detection and freezing or seizure of any funds used or allocated for the purpose of committing the offences set forth in Article 4 as well as the proceeds derived from such offences, for purposes of possible forfeiture.

2. Each State Party shall take appropriate measures, in accordance with its domestic legal principles, for the forfeiture of funds used or allocated for the purpose of committing the offences set forth in Article 4 and the proceeds derived from such offences.

3. Each State Party concerned may give consideration to concluding agreements on the sharing with other State Parties, on a regular or case-by-case basis, of the funds derived from the forfeiture referred to in this Article.

4. The provisions of this Article shall be implemented without prejudice to the rights of third parties acting in good faith.

5. The measures referred to in paragraph 1 shall apply with respect to offences committed both within and outside the jurisdiction of a State Party.

Article 9
Predicate offences to money laundering

1. State Parties shall take the necessary measures to ensure that its domestic money laundering legislation also includes as predicate offences those offences set forth in Article 4 of this Additional Protocol.

2. Money laundering predicate offences referred to in paragraph 1, shall include those committed both within and outside the jurisdiction of a State Party.

Article 10
Co-operation on immigration and customs controls

1. States Parties, consistent with their respective domestic legal and administrative regimes, shall promote co-operation and the exchange of information in order to improve immigration and customs control measures to detect and prevent the international movement of terrorists and their accomplices and trafficking in arms, narcotics and psychotropic substances or other materials intended to support terrorist activities.

2. To this end, they shall promote co-operation and the exchange of information to improve their controls on the issuance of travel and identify documents and to prevent their counterfeiting, forgery, or fraudulent use.

3. Such co-operation shall be carried out without prejudice to applicable international commitments in relation to the free movement of people and the facilitation of commerce.

Article 11
Co-operation among law enforcement authorities

States Parties shall work closely with one another, consistent with the respective domestic legal and administrative systems, to enhance the effectiveness of law enforcement action for the prevention, suppression and prosecution of the offences set forth in Article 4.

Article 12
Mutual legal assistance

The provisions of Article VIII of the 1987 SAARC Convention relating to Mutual Legal Assistance shall apply, mutatis mutandis, in respect of the offences set forth in Article 4 of this Additional Protocol.

Article 13
Extradition

1. The provisions of Article III of the 1987 SAARC Convention shall apply, mutatis mutandis, in respect of the offences set forth in Article 4 of this Additional Protocol.

2. The provisions of Article IV of the 1987 SAARC Convention relating to the duty to extradite or prosecute shall apply, mutatis mutandis, in respect of the offences set forth in Article 4 of this Additional Protocol.

Article 14
Exclusion of Fiscal Offence exception

None of the offences set forth in Article 4 shall be regarded, for the purpose of extradition or mutual legal assistance, as a fiscal offence. Accordingly, State Parties may not refuse a request for extradition or for mutual legal assistance on the sole ground that it concerns a fiscal offence.

Article 15
Exclusion of political offence exception

For the purpose of extradition or mutual legal assistance, none of the offences established in the international instruments set forth in Article 4, shall be regarded as a political offence or an offence connected with a political offence or an offence inspired by political motives. Accordingly, a request for extradition or mutual assistance may not be refused on the sole ground that it concerns a political offence or an offence connected with a political offence or an offence inspired by political motives.

Article 16
Denial of refugee status

Each State Party shall take appropriate measures, consistent with the relevant provisions of national and international law, for the purpose of ensuring that refugee status is not granted to any person in respect of whom there are serious reasons for considering that he or she has committed an offence set forth in Article 4 of this Additional Protocol.

Article 17
Non-discrimination

None of the provisions of this Additional Protocol shall be interpreted as imposing an obligation to extradite or to provide mutual legal assistance, if the requested State Party has substantial grounds to believe that the request to extradite or to provide mutual legal assistance, has been made for the purpose of prosecuting or punishing a person on account of that person's race, religion, nationality, ethnic origin or political opinion, or that compliance with the request would cause prejudice to that person's position for any of these reasons.

Article 18
Principles of Sovereign Equality and Territorial Integrity

1. State Parties shall carry out their obligations under this Additional Protocol in a manner consistent with the principles of sovereign equality and territorial integrity of states and that of non-intervention in the domestic affairs of other states.

2. Nothing in this Additional Protocol entitles a State Party to undertake in the territory of another State Party exercise of jurisdiction or performance of functions that are exclusively reserved for the authorities of that other State Party by its domestic law.

Article 19
Rights and Obligations under International Law

Nothing in this Additional Protocol shall be interpreted as affecting other rights and obligations and responsibilities of States and individuals under international law, in particular, the purposes and principles of the Charter of the United Nations, international humanitarian law, and international human rights law.

Article 20
Technical Co-operation

State Parties shall promote, where appropriate, technical co-operation and training programmes with other regional and international organizations conducting activities related to the objectives and purposes of this Additional Protocol.

Article 21
Consultations

State Parties shall hold periodic consultations, as appropriate, with a view to facilitating:
(a) The effective implementation of this Additional Protocol; and
(b) The exchange of information and experiences on effective means and

methods to prevent, detect, investigate and punish offences within the scope of the Additional Protocol.

Article 22
Signature and Ratification

This Additional Protocol is open for signature by all Member States of SAARC at the SAARC Secretariat in Kathmandu. It shall be subject to ratification. Instruments of Ratification shall be deposited with the Secretary General of SAARC.

Article 23
Entry into Force

The Additional Protocol shall enter into force on the thirtieth day following the date of deposit of the seventh Instrument of Ratification with the Secretary-General of SAARC.

Article 24
Depositary

The Secretary-General of SAARC shall be the depositary of this Additional Protocol and shall notify Member States of signatures to this Additional Protocol and all deposits of Instruments of Ratification. The SecretaryGeneral shall transmit certified copies of such instruments to each Member State. The Secretary-General shall also inform Member States of the date on which this Additional Protocol will have entered into force in accordance with Article 23.

IN WITNESS WHERE OF the undersigned, being duly authorized thereto by their respective Governments have signed this Additional Protocol.

DONE in ISLAMABAD, PAKISTAN, On This The Sixth Day of January Of the Year Two Thousand Four, In Nine Originals, In The English Language, All Texts Being Equally Authentic.

M. MORSHED KHAN
Minister for Foreign Affairs
People's Republic of Bangladesh

NADO RINCHHEN
Officiating Minister for Foreign Affairs, Kingdom of Bhutan

YASHWANT SINHA
Minister of External Affairs
Republic of India

FATHULLA JAMEEL
Minister of Foreign Affairs
Republic of Maldives

DR. BHEKH B. THAPA
Ambassador-at-large
for Foreign Affairs
His Majesty's Government of Nepal

KHURSHID M. KASURI
Minister of Foreign Affairs
Islamic Republic of Pakistan

TYRONNE FERNANDO
Minister of Foreign Affairs
Democratic Socialist Republic of Sri Lanka

ANNEX

a) Convention for the Suppression of Unlawful Seizure of Aircraft, signed at the Hague on 16 December 1970.

b) Convention for the Suppression of Unlawful Acts against the Safety of Civil Aviation, signed at Montreal on 23 September 1971.

c) Convention on the Prevention and Punishment of Crimes against Internationally Protected Persons, including Diplomatic Agents, approved by the General Assembly of the United Nations on 14 December 1973.

d) International Convention against the Taking of Hostages, adopted by the General Assembly of the United Nations on 17 December 1979.

e) Convention on the Physical Protection of Nuclear Material, signed at Vienna on 3 March 1980.

f) Protocol for the Suppression of Unlawful Acts of Violence at Airports Serving International Civil Aviation, supplementary to the Convention for the Suppression of Unlawful Acts against the Safety of Civil Aviation, signed at Montreal on 24 February 1988.

g) Convention for the Suppression of Unlawful Acts against the Safety of Maritime Navigation, done at Rome on 10 March 1988.

h) Protocol for the Suppression of Unlawful Acts against the Safety of Fixed Platforms located on the Continental Shelf, done at Rome on 10 March 1988.

i) International Convention for the Suppression of Terrorist Bombings, approved by the General Assembly of the United Nations on 15 December 1997.

j) International Convention for the Suppression of the Financing of Terrorism, approved by the General Assembly of the United Nations on 9 December 1999.

NOTES

Part I

1 Wilkinson, Paul, 'Three Questions on Terrorism' *Government and Opposition* VIII (1973), pp.290-312 as cited in J. Nef, 'Some Thoughts on Contemporary Terrorism: Domestic and International Perspectives' in John Carson (ed), *Terrorism in Theory and Practice* (Toronto, 1978)

2 Laqueur, Walter, *The New Terrorism: Fanaticism and the Arms of Mass Destruction* (New York, 1999), p.72

3 Franck, Thomas M. and Bert B. Lockwood, Jr, 'Preliminary Thoughts Towards an International Convention on Terrorism', *American Journal of International Law* LXVIII (1974), pp.69-90

4 Bell, Bowyer in Michael Walzer, Bowyer Bell, and Roger Morris, 'Terrorism: A Debate', *New Republic* (1975), p.13 as cited in John Carson: *Terrorism in Theory and Practice*

5 Morris, Roger in *ibid*, p.13

6 Whitbeck, John V., *The Daily Star* 7 December 2001

7 *Ibid*

8 O' Brien, Donal Cruise, 'Modernization, Order, and the Erosion of a Democratic Ideal: American Political Science 1960-1970' *Journal of Development Studies* VIII (1972), pp.351-78

9 For details see, Lakos, Amos, *International Terrorism: A Bibliography* (Boulder, 1986); Schmid, Alex P. and Albert J. Jongman at al., *Political Terrorism: A New Guide to Actors, Authors, Concepts, Data Bases, Theories, and Literature* (New Brunswick, NJ, 1988); Mickolus, Edward F., and Peter Flemming, *Terrorism, 1980-1987: A Selectively Annotated Bibliography* (Westport, Conn., 1988)

10 Crenshaw, Martha, (ed), *Terrorism in Context* (Pennsylvania, 1995), p.7

11 *Ibid*, pp.7-8

12 Whittaker, J. David, (ed), *The Terrorism Reader* (New York, 2001), p.1

13 Office for the Protection of the Constitution, *Ibid*

14 *Ibid*

15 Terrorist Research and Analytical Centre, National Security Division, Federal Bureau of Investigation, *Terrorism in the United States 1995* (Washington DC, 1996), p.2

16 U.S. Department of the Army and the Air Force, *Military Operations in Low Intensity Conflict. Field Manual 100-201 Air Force Pamphlet 3-20* (Washington DC, 1990)

17 Office of the Coordinator for Counter-terrorism, *Patterns of Global Terrorism 1996*, US Department of State Publication 10433 (Washington DC, 1997), p.6

18 See, Poland, James, *Understanding Terrorism: Groups, Strategies, and Responses* (New Jersey, 1988)

19 Hoffman, Bruce, *Inside Terrorism* (New York, 1998), p.43

20 Gurr, Robert Ted, 'Political Terrorism: Historical Antecedents', in Robert Ted Gurr (ed), *Violence in America: Protest, Rebellion, Reform*, Vol. II (Newbury Park, CA, 1989)

21 Gibbs, J.P., 'Conceptualization of Terrorism' *American Sociological Review* LIV (1998), p.329

22 Whittaker: *The Terrorism Reader*, p.8

23 See, Tilly, Charles, 'Contentious Repertoires in Great Britain, 1758-1834', in Mark Traugott (ed), *Repertoires and Cycles of Collective Action* (Durham, 1995), pp.15-42

24 See, Turk, Austin T., 'Social Dynamics of Terrorism' *Annals of the American Academy of Political and Social Science* CCCCXXXVI/1 (1982), pp.119-28

25 Quoted by Crenshaw, Martha, in 'The Subjective Reality of the Terrorist: Ideological and Psychological Factors in Terrorism', in Robert O. Slater and Michael Stohl (eds), *Current Perspective on International Terrorism* (London, 1988), p.3

26 Combs, Cindy C., *Terrorism in the Twenty-first Century* (New Jersey, 1997), p.8

27 Taber, Robert, *The War of the Flea* (London, 1969), pp.90-1

28 *Ibid*

29 Clutterbuck, Richard, *Terrorism and Guerrilla Warfare* (London, 1990)

30 Whittaker: *The Terrorism Reader*, p.8

31 Wilkinson, Paul, *Terrorism and the Liberal State* (London, 1986), p.49

32 Linn, Ruth, 'Terrorism, Mortality and Soldiers' Motivation to Fight – an example from the Israeli Experience in Lebanon' *Terrorism* XI/2 (1988), pp.139-49

33 *Ibid*

34 Silke, Andrew, 'Terrorism and the Blind Men's Elephant' *Terrorism and Political Violence* VIII/3 (1996), pp.16-18

35 See, Schmid, Alex P., 'The Response Problem as a Definition Problem', in A.P. Schmid and R.D. Crelinsten (eds), *Western Responses to Terrorism* (London, 1993)

36 Wheeler, Everett L., 'Terrorism and Military Theory: A Historical Perspective' *Terrorism and Political Violence* III/1 (1991), pp.6-33

37 Wilkinson, Paul, 'Pathways out of Terrorism for Democratic Societies', in Paul Wilkinson and Alasdair Stewart (eds), *Contemporary Research on Terrorism* (Aberdeen, 1987), p.455

38 See, Schmid, and Albert Jongman: *Political Terrorism*

39 See, Herman, Edward and Gerry O'Sullivan, *"Terrorism" Industry: The Experts and Institutions That Shape Our View of Terror* (New York, 1989); Pape, Robert A., *Dying to Win: The Strategic Logic of Suicide Terrorism* (London, 2005); Goodwin, Jeff, *No Other Way Out: States and Revolutionary Movements, 1945-1991* (Cambridge, 2001)

40 Newman, G.R., and M.J. Lynch, 'From Feuding to Terrorism: The Ideology of Vengeance' *Contemporary Crises* XI/3 (1987), pp.223-42

41 Martin, Gus, *Understanding Terrorism: Challenges, Perspectives and Issues* (Thousand Oaks, CA, 2003), pp.9-11

42 Wilkinson: 'Terrorism: An International Research Agenda?', p.455

43 Goodwin, Jeff, 'A Theory of Categorical Terrorism' *Social Forces* LXXXIV/4 (2006), p.2028

44 *Ibid*, p.2030

45 *Ibid*, p.2031

46 *Ibid*, p.2037

47 Johnson, Chalmers, *Revolutionary Change* (Stanford, 1966), pp.8-11

48 Crozier, Michel, *The Bureaucratic Phenomenon* (Chicago, 1964), pp.156-62

49 Fromkin, David, 'The Strategy of Terrorism' *Foreign Affairs* LIII (1975), p.686

50 Slater, Robert O., and Michael Stohl (eds.), *Current Perspective on International Terrorism* (London, 1988), p.3

51 Wilkinson: *Terrorism and the Liberal State*, p.56

52 Schelling, Thomas C., 'Compellence', in Mark E.Smith and Claude J. Johns. Jr (eds), *American Defense Policy* (Baltimore, 1968), pp.211-22

53 Wilkinson: 'Three Questions on Terrorism', pp.290- 312

54 Kahn, Herman, 'Some Possible Sizes and Shapes of Thermonuclear Wars', in Mark E.Smith and Claude J. Johns. Jr (eds), *American Defence Policy*, pp.92-96

55 Wilkinson: 'Three Questions on Terrorism', p.310

56 Paust, Jordan, 'Terrorism and International Law of War' *Military Law Review* (1971), quoted by Robert G. Bell in 'The US Response to Terrorism Against International Civil Aviation' *Orbis* XIX (1976), p.1326

57 Kydd, Andrew H., and Barbara F. Walter, 'The Strategies of Terrorism' *International Security* XXXI/1 (2006), p.51

58 Crenshaw: *Terrorism in Context*, p.13

59 Stern, Jessica, *Terror in the Name of God: Why Religious Militants Kill* (Ecco, 2003). Also see, Robison, Kristopher K., Edward M. Crenshaw and J.Craig Jenkins, 'Ideologies of Violence: The Social Origins of Islamist and Leftist Transnational Terrorism' *Social Forces* LXXXIV/4, (2006), pp.2009-2026

60 Schock, Kurt, 'A Conjunctural Model of Political Conflict: The Impact of Political Opportunities on the Relationship between Economic Inequality and Violent Political Conflict' *Journal of Conflict Resolution* XL/1 (1996), pp.98-133. Also see Marshall, Monty G., and Ted Robert Gurr, *Peace and Conflict* (College Park, Md, 2003)

61 Midlarsky, Manus I., Martha Crenshaw and Fumihiko Yoshida, 'Why Violence Spreads: The Contagion of International Terrorism' *International Studies Quarterly* XXIV (1980), pp.262-98

62 See, Crenshaw, Martha, 'The Causes of Terrorism' *Comparative Politics* XIII (1981), p.387. Also see, Bloom, Mia, *Dying to Kill: The Allure of Suicide Terror* (New York, 2005); Rubenstein, Richard E., *Alchemists of Revolution: Terrorism in the Modern World* (New York, 1987)

63 See Tilly, Charles, Louise Tilly, and Richard Tilly, *The Rebellious Century 1830-1930* (Cambridge, 1975); Tilly, Charles, *From Mobilization to Revolution* (Reading Mass, 1978)

64 Turk: 'Social Dynamics of Terrorism', p.122

65 DeNardo, James, *Power in Numbers: The Political Strategy of Protest and Rebellion* (Princeton, NJ, 1985) p.207

66 Crenshaw, Martha, 'The Logic of Terrorism: Terrorist Behaviour as a Product of Strategic Choice', in Walter Reich (ed), *Origins of Terrorism Psychologies, Theologies, State of Mind* (New York, 1990), pp.13-15

67 *Ibid*, pp.16-17

68 *Ibid*, pp.17-19

69 Wieviorka, Michel, 'Terrorism in the Context of Academic Research', in Crenshaw: *Terrorism in Context*, p.600

70 For details see Post, Jerrold M., 'Terrorist Psycho-logic: Terrorist Behaviour as a

Product of Psychological Forces', in Walter Reich (ed), *Origins of Terrorism: Psychologies, Ideologies, Theologies, States of Mind*, pp.25-40. Also see, Domarus, E. von, 'The Specific Laws in Schizophrenia', in J.S. Kasanin (ed), *Language and Thought in Schizophrenia: Collected Papers* (Berkeley, 1944)

71 Crenshaw, Martha, 'The Subjective reality of the Terrorist: ldeological and Psychological Factors in Terrorism', in Slater and Stohl : *Current Perspective on International Terrorism,* p.12

72 For details see, Laqueur, Walter, *The Age of Terrorism* (Boston, 1987); Kernberg, O., *Borderline Conditions and Pathological Narcissism* (New York, 1975)

73 See Kohut, H., *The Analysis of the Self* (New York, 1983)

74 Goldstone, Jack A., 'Population Growth and Revolutionary Crises', in John Foran (ed), *In Theorizing Revolutions* (London, 1997). Also see, Hudson, V., and A. den Boer, *Bare Branches: The Security Implications of Asia's Surplus Male Population* (Cambridge, MA, 2004)

75 For details see, Fromm, Erich, *Fear of Freedom* (London, 1960)

76 See Bion, W., *Experiences in Groups* (London, 1961)

77 *Ibid*

78 Crenshaw, Martha, 'An Organizational Approach to the Analysis of Political Terrorism' *Orbis* XXIX (1985), pp.465-89

79 For details see Post: 'Terrorist Psycho-logic: Terrorist Behaviour as a Product of Psychological Forces', pp.33

80 See, Janis, I., *Victims of Group Think* (Boston, 1972)

81 Ferracuti, Franco, 'A Sociopsychiatric Interpretation of Terrorism' *Annals of the American Academy of Political and Social Science* CCCCLXIII (1982), pp.129-140

82 Pierre, Andrew, 'The Politics of International Terrorism' *Orbis* XIX (1976), pp.1252

83 Haynes, Jeffrey, *Comparative Politics in a Globalizing World* (Cambridge, 2005), p.231

84 Kaldor, Mary, 'Terrorism as Regressive Globalization', see http:/ www.opendemocracy.net/debates/article-3-77-101.jsp

85 *Ibid*

86 Herz, John, *International Politics in the Atomic Age* (New York, 1963), pp.3-48

87 Buzan, Barry, 'Implications for the study of International Relations', in Mary Buckleya and Rick Fawn (eds), *Responses to Terrorism: 9/11, Afghanistan and Beyond* (London, New York, 2003), pp.296-318

88 See, Waltz, Kenneth N., *Theory of International Politics* (MA: Addison-Wesley, Reading, 1979)

89 Buzan: 'Implications for the study of International Relations', p.302

90 For details see, Huntington, Samuel P., *The Clash of Civilizations and the Remaking of World Order* (New York, 1996)

91 Buzan: 'Implications for the study of International Relations', p.302

92 Held, Davis, Anthony McGrew, David Goldblatt and Jonathan Perraton, *Global Transformation: Politics, Economics and Culture* (Cambridge, 1999), pp.3-5

93 Barry Buzan, Ole Waever and Jaap de Wilde, *Security: A New Framework for Analysis* (Boulder Co, 1998), ch.5

94 Ahmed, Imtiaz, 'Contemporary Terrorism and the State, Non-State, and the Interstate: Newer Drinks, Newer Bottles', in Sridhar K. Khatri and Gert W. Kueck (eds), *Terrorism in South Asia* (New Delhi, 2003), pp.353-387

95 Buzan, Bary and Gerald Segal, 'The Rise of the 'Lite' Powers: A Strategy for Postmodern States' *World Policy Journal* XIII/3 (1996), pp.1-10. Also see, Stein, Arthur A. and Steven E. Lobell, 'The End of the Cold War and the Regionalization of International Security', in David A. Lake and Patrick M. Morgan (eds), *Regional Orders: Building Security in a New World* (Pennsylvania, 1997), pp.119-20

96 Buzan, Waever and de Wilde: *Security: A New Framework for Analysis*, ch.5

97 See, Yong, Oran R., 'Political Discontinuities in the International System' *World Politics* XX/3, (1986), pp.369-92

98 Bozeman, Adda B., *Conflict in Africa, Concepts and Realities* (Princeton, 1976), p.18

99 Buzan, Barry, *People, States and Fear: The National Security Problem in International Relations* (Brighton, 1983), pp.105-15

100 *The Oxford English Dictionary* Volume V (Oxford, 1978), p.364

101 *Ibid*, Volume XI, p.216

102 See Sarkesian, Sam C., 'Revolutionary Guerrilla Warfare: An Introduction', in Sam C.Sarkesian (ed), *Revolutionary Guerrilla Warfare* (Chicago, 1975), p.4. Also see, Andrain, Charles F., *Political Life and Social Change* (Belmont, 1974), pp.150-159; and Easton, David, *A System Analysis of Political Life* (New York, 1965), pp.171-219

103 Neill, Bard E.O', *Insurgency and Terrorism: Inside Modern Revolutionary Warfare* (Brassey's, 1990), p.14

104 See Laqueur, Walter, 'Foreword' to Robert Kupperman and Daniel Trent, *Terrorism: Threat, Reality, Response* (Stanford, 1979), p.13-14

105 Laqueur: *The Age of Terrorism*, p.72; Also see, Slater and Stohl: *Current Perspective on International Terrorism*, p.3

106 *Yearbook of the United Nations* (New York, 1971), pp.7790-91

107 United Nations General Assembly, Official Records, 28th Session *Report of the Ad-hoc Committee on International Terrorism*, Suppl. 28 (A/9028), 1973, p.21

108 Cited in Ferencz, Benjamin B., *Defining International Aggression: The Search for World Peace* Volume II (New York, 1975), p.17

109 Cited in Rene'beres, Louis, *Terrorism and Global Security: The Nuclear Threat* (Boulder, 1987), p.125

110 http://www.unodc.org/unodc/terrorism_definitions.html

111 Neill: *Insurgency and Terrorism*, p.3

112 Sahadevan, P, 'Negotiating Peace in Ethnic Wars' *International Studies* XLIII/3, (2006), p.242

113 Huntington, Samuel P., 'Guerrilla Warfare in Theory and Policy', in Franklin Mark Osanka, *Modern Guerrilla Warfare* (New York, 1962), p.16; Also see, Campbell, Arthur, *Guerrillas* (New York, 1968), p.3

114 Neill: *Insurgency and Terrorism*, p.24-25

115 See, Jenkins, Brain, 'International Terrorism: A Balance Sheet' *Survival* July/August (1975), pp.158-160; Crozier, Brain, *A Theory of Conflict* (New York, 1974), pp.27-128

116 Laqueur: *The Age of Terrorism*, p.49

117 Hutchinson, M.C., 'The Concept of Revolutionary Terrorism' *Journal of Conflict Resolution*, VI (1973), p.388

118 Thoronton, T.P., 'Terror as a Weapon of Political Agitation', in H. Eckstein (ed.), *Internal War* (London, 1964), p.74

119 See, King, Charles, 'Ending Civil wars' *Adelphi Paper* 308 (London, 1997), pp.40-50; Mitchell, C.R., *The Structure of International Conflict* (London, 1981), pp.23-38

120 See, Shollom, A.H., 'Nowhere Yet Everywhere', in Franklin Mark Osanka (ed), *Modern Guerrilla Warfare* (New York, 1962), p.19. Also see, Trinquier, Roger, *Modern Warfare* (New York, 1964), pp.16-17; Heilbrunn, Otto, *Partisan Warfare* (New York, 1962), pp.39, 160

121 See, Gurr: *Why Men Rebel* and 'Psychological Factors in Civil Violence' *World Politics* XX/2 (1968), pp.252-3; Davies, James C., 'Towards a Theory of Revolution' *American Sociological Review* XXVII (1962), pp.5-19; Runciman, W.G., *Relative Deprivation and Social Justice* (London, 1966); Huntington, Samuel P., 'Civil Violence and the Process of Development' *Adelphi Paper* 83 (London, 1971), pp.1-15, and *Political Order in Changing Societies* (New Haven, 1968); Also see, Gross, Feliks, *The Seizure of Political Power* (New York, 1958)

122 Wilkinson: *Terrorism and the Liberal State*, p.35

123 Gurr: *Why Men Rebel*, p.119

124 *Ibid*, p.208

125 Cited in Heilbrunn: *Partisan Warfare*, p.87

126 Rothschild, Joseph, *Ethnopolitics: A Conceptual Framework* (New York, 1981), pp.184-87

127 Fall, Bernard B., *Street Without Joy* (Harrisburg, Pa, 1963), p.294

128 Wilkinson, Paul, *Terrorism Versus Democracy: The Liberal State Response* (London, 2001), p.51

129 *Ibid*, p.6

130 *Ibid*, p.5

131 Singh, Manvendra, 'NDC Papers: Low Intensity Conflict' *Indian Defence Review* IX/4, (1994), p.110

132 Kaldor, Mary, *From New and Old Wars* (Stanford, 1999), pp.2-6

133 According to the British Department for International Development, 'a country at $250 GDP per capita has an average 15 per cent risk of experiencing a civil war in the next five years. At $1000 GDP per capita, there is a dramatic drop in the risk of conflict. And at $ 5,000, the risk of civil war is less than 1 per cent. See, *Fighting Poverty to Build a Safer World: A Strategy for Security and Development* (United Kingdom, 2005)

134 Scruton, Roger, *A Dictionary of Political Thought* (New York, 1982), p.164

Part II

1 North East India is located between 21.57°N and 29.30°N Latitude and between 89.46°E and 97.30°E Longitude.

2 Scholars believe that the region acquired a distinct geographical identity only after its occupation by the British and became what it is today – a remote strategic frontier – after the partition of the subcontinent in 1947. See, Bhaumik, Subir, 'North-East India: The Evolution of Post-Colonial Region', in Partha Chatterjee (ed), *Wages of Freedom* (Delhi, 1998), p.301; Nari,Rustomji, *Imperilled Frontiers: India's North-Eastern Borderlands* (Delhi, 1983), pp.15-21

3 Burma was renamed 'Myanmar' by the Military regime in 1989. Acceptance of the changed name has been slow, with many people and nations still using the old name Burma to refer to the country. For the purpose of the present study, the name Myanmar will be used to refer to the current regime, while for other purposes (geographical and cultural) the name Burma will be in usage.

4 The Siliguri Corridor's dimensions extends length wise approximately 200 kms with a width varying between 20 and 60 kms. Unlike most other parts of India, North East India is not joined integrally to the mainland. Rather, it hangs on a narrow stretch of land between Nepal and Bangladesh, touching the two ends of a 2500-mile long international boundary, intersected by swift flowing rivers from the Himalayas into Bangladesh.

5 A number of states in the region have been carved out from the state of Assam and the princely states of Manipur and Tripura were union territories during the 1950s and the 1960s. Through acts passed by the Indian Parliament, notably the North Eastern Areas (Reorganization) Act of 1971, new political units were created as well as the status of the existing ones redefined. Of late, Sikkim has been clubbed as a part of North East India, mainly for developmental purposes. See, Sachdeva, G., *Economy of the North East: Policy, Present Conditions and Future Possibilities* (New Delhi, 2000), pp.60-1

6 Assam shares international borders with Bhutan and Bangladesh, Arunachal Pradesh with China and Burma, Nagaland with Burma, Manipur with Burma, Mizoram with Burma and Bangladesh, Tripura with Bangladesh and Meghalaya with Bangladesh.

7 The 1962 Indo-Chinese war erupted over border claims in the North Eastern Frontier (NEFA). The 1965 war with Pakistan saw mobilization of forces both in the north-western and north-eastern sectors. The 1971 war with Pakistan led to the break-up of East Pakistan and the creation of Bangladesh – a sovereign state.

8 At no point in history was the region mono-lingual, nor was it inhabited by a single nationality. The population is a broad inter-mixture of Mongolian, Indo-Burmese, Indo-Iranian and Aryan races. This diversity gets powerfully reflected in the religious persuasion that extends to all the major world religions – Hinduism, Buddhism, Islam and Christianity. See, Verghese, B.G., *India's Northeast Resurgent – Ethnicity, Insurgency, Governance, Development* (New Delhi, 1997), p.2; Chaube, S.K., *Hill Politics in North East India* (Hyderabad, 1999), pp.1-3; Das, B.M., *The People of Assam* (New Delhi, 1987), pp.60-63

9 Between 1822 to 1826, the whole of Assam was virtually under Burmese occupation. On the invitation of the local ruler, the British intervened in the name of restoring authority, defeated the Burmese invaders and concluded the Yandaboo Treaty. For details see, Aitchison C. U., *A Collection of Treaties, Engagements and Sanads Relating to India and the Neighbouring Countries*, Vol.1, 1892 (3rd ed), Calcutta, pp.198, 291, cited in Chaube: *Hill Politics in North East India*; Also see, Blackburn, Terence R., *The British Humiliation of Burma* (Bangkok, 2000)

10 Chaube: *Hill Politics in North East*, pp.6-7

11 The British zeal for well defined boundaries was fuelled by the intense rivalry among Britain, China and Russia over supremacy in the Himalayas and Central Asia. Consequently, the Durand Line (1893) and the McMahon Line (1914) were proposed. The first divided Afghanistan and British India, while the second, demarcated India and Tibet. For details see, Chakravarty, P.C., *The Evolution of India's Northern Borders* (London, 1971)

12 Chaube: *Hill Politics in North East*, pp.26-27

13 Bezbaruah, Madan.P., 'Cultural Sub-Nationalism in India's North East: An Overview', in Subrata K. Mitra & Alison R. Lewis (eds), *Subnational Movements in South Asia* (Oxford, 1996), pp.178-79

14 Baruah, Sanjib, *Durable Disorder: Understanding the Politics of Northeast India* (New Delhi, 2005), p.7

15 See, Biswas, Prasanjit, 'Nations from Below and Rebel Consciousness: The 'New Subaltern' Emergence in North East India', in R.R. Dhamala and Sukalpa Bhattacharjee (eds), *Human Rights and Insurgency: The North-East India* (New Delhi, 2002), p.140

16 The perception of 'internal colonization' can be traced to the colonial era when consequent to foreign rule, indigenous communities lost their customary rights over land and forests. Post-independence, the replacement of customary laws with constitutional laws created complications that got compounded with the increasing strategic importance of the region. Observers point out that the region's unique location between the Himalayas (China, Bhutan and Nepal), the Indian Ocean (Bangladesh) and the fluvial corridors of the Brahmaputra, Chindwin and Irrawaddy rivers, make it a potential flashpoint for instability in South Asia.

17 Post-independence, in almost every ethnic community, there has emerged an ambitious, educated, parochially conscious urban based neo-class. On the question of distribution of resources, the constituents of the region nurse a strong grudge against the Central Government, for unfair treatment. See, Roy, Sanjay K., 'Conflicting Nations in North-East India' *Economic and Political Weekly* XL/21 (2005)

18 The states of Meghalaya, Mizoram and Nagaland have been carved out from the larger state of Assam.

19 Autonomous district councils have been created in Mizoram, Tripura and Assam. All these political and administrative arrangements have been made by the Indian State, following the provisions of the Indian Constitution. The Sixth Schedule of the Indian Constitution [Article 244 (2) &Article 275 (1)] provides small tribal communities, disadvantaged by lack of opportunity - educational, political and numerical - extensive powers through the creation of autonomous district councils to protect their tradition and their lands. See, Chaube: *Hill Politics in North East India*, pp.100-16

20 As a part of an elaborate system of protective discrimination, Article 342 of the Constitution of India, provides for the President of India by public notification to specify the 'tribes'or tribal communities or parts of or groups within tribes or tribal communities, which shall for the purpose of the Constitution be deemed to be 'Scheduled Tribes'. In favour of groups that fall in this category, there is near total reservation of seats in the legislature in the tribal states of Arunachal Pradesh, Meghalaya, Mizoram, and Nagaland.

21 Article 16 of the Indian Constitution asserts 'There shall be equality of opportunity for all citizens in matters relating to employment or opportunity to any office under the state. No citizen shall, on ground only of religion, race, caste, sex, descent, place of birth, residence or any of them, be ineligible for or discriminated against in respect of any employment or office under the state'. In view of the preferential policies pursued, the concept of single citizenship stands eroded.

22 The Sixth Schedule makes provisions for autonomous districts and autonomous regions within those districts with elected councils authorized to levy some taxes, to constitute courts for the administration of justice involving tribals, and law making powers on subjects including land allotment, occupation or use of land, regulation of shifting cultivation, formation and administration of village and town committees, appointments of chief, inheritance of property, marriage, and social customs.

23 The Bodos, Misings and Tiwas communities of Assam describe themselves as Plains Tribes. Even the Tea Tribes of Assam, whose forefathers were brought as indentured labour to work in the tea plantations of Assam, have been denied 'Scheduled Tribe' status, a status enjoyed by their original kin in their original habitats in Jharkhand, Chhatishgarh, Madhya Pradesh, Bihar and Orissa states of the Indian Union.

24 For details on conflicts in peripheral societies see Brown, Michael E., 'The Causes of Internal Conflict', in Michael Brown (ed), *Nationalism and Ethnic Conflict* (Cambridge, MA, 1997), p.5

25 Bajpai, Kanti P., *Roots of Terrorism* (New Delhi, 2000), p.62

26 The insurgency in Nagaland, Manipur and the rebellion spearheaded by the Mizo National Front in Mizoram in 1966 would safely fall in this category.

27 Internecine in nature, these conflicts have afflicted several states in the region notably Manipur, Nagaland and Assam.

28 These conflicts are evenly spread across the region in all the seven states.

29 Byman, Daniel, 'The Logic of Ethnic Terrorism' *Studies in Conflict and Terrorism* XXI/2 (1998), p.151

30 Hoover, J.,'Do the Politics of Difference Need to be Freed of Liberalism?' *Constellations* VIII (2001), p.201

31 McCord, Arline and William McCord, 'Ethnic Autonomy: A Socio-historical Synthesis', in Raymond Hall (ed), *Ethnic Autonomy: Comparative Dynamics* (New York, 1972), p.427

32 Byman: 'The logic of Ethnic Terrorism', p.151,154

33 Bohman, J., 'Public Reason and Cultural Pluralism: Political Liberalism and the Problem of Moral Conflict' *Political Theory* XXIII (1995), p.253

34 Byman. 'The Logic of Ethnic Terrorism', p.150, 158

35 For further details see, Anderson, Bendict, *Imagined Communities: Reflections on the Origin and Spread of Nationalism* (London, 1983); Hobsbawm, Eric and Terence Ranger, *The Invention of Tradition* (Cambridge, 1983)

36 Wilkinson, Paul, *Terrorism Versus Democracy: The Liberal State Response* (London, 2001), p.46

37 For details see, Hoover, J., 'Do the Politics of Difference Need to be Freed of Liberalism?' *Constellations* VIII (2001), pp.201-18; Purvis, T., and A. Hunt, 'Identity versus Citizenship: Transformations in the Discourses and Practices of Citizenship' *Social and Legal Studies* VIII (1999), pp.457-82

38 Tambiah, Stanley J., *Levelling Crowds: Ethnonationalist Conflicts and Collective Violence in South Asia* (New Delhi, 1997), p.292

39 Kaldor, Mary, *Organized Violence in a Global Era* (Cambridge, 1999), p.78

40 For details see, Brass, Paul R., *Ethnic Groups and the State* (Beckenham, Kent, 1985)

41 Posen, Barry, 'The Security Dilemma and Ethnic Conflict' *Survival* XXXI/1 (1993), pp.17-47; Also see, Milton J. Esman, *Ethnic Politics* Ithaca, (N.Y, 1994), pp.244-245

42 Baruah: *Durable Disorder*, pp.10-11

43 For details on the number and strength of the armed outfits in the states of the region see, *South Asia Terrorism Portal*, http:// www.satp.org

44 While separatist outfits like the United Liberation Front of Assam or the National Socialist Council of Nagaland want to liberate territories still located on the contemporary map of the region, groups like Kamatapur Liberation Army (of the Koch Rajbongshis) and the Hynniewtrep National Liberation Council (of the Khasis tribe in Meghalaya) name places that no longer exist. The People's Revolutionary Party of Kangleipak, a Manipuri outfit, refers to Manipur's historical name Kangleipak. See, Baruah: *Durable Disorder*, p.6

45 The North East Students' Organization (NESO) is an umbrella organization of the leading students associations of the region. It coordinates the activities of the diverse student bodies and acts as a powerful pressure group.

46 The category Naga is an amalgamation of various tribes and the generic term Naga encompasses within its ambit 32 tribes of Indo-Mongoloid origin, spread over a number of Indian states. Of these, sixteen reside in Nagaland, seven in Manipur, three in the Tirap district of Arunachal Pradesh and in the North Cachar and Karbi Anglong districts of Assam. Five tribes reside in Burma as well. Scattered across the Indian-Burmese border, the Nagas are believed to number around 5 million. Nagas speak as many as thirty different languages that linguists classify into two completely distinct branches of Tibeto-Burman. See, Verghese: *India's Northeast Resurgent*, p.83; Mehta, Mandavi, 'India's Turbulent Northeast' *South Asia Monitor*, Washington, No. 35, July 5, 2001; Burling, Robbins, 'The Tibeto-Burman Languages of Northeastern India', in Grahman Thurgood and Randy LaPolla (eds), *The Sino-Tibetan Languages* (London, 2003), p.172

47 Official NSCN-IM Website at http:// www.nscnonline.org/nscn/index-2.html

48 Gundevia, Y.D., *War and Peace in Nagaland* (Dehradun, 1975), p.47

49 The Simon Commission was constituted in November 1927 to prepare a new draft constitution for British India aimed at reviewing the 1919 Government of India Act that was in place.

50 Organized Naga representation commenced for the first time in 1918 with the formation of the Naga Club. The Club brought about a convergence of the different strands of thought among the Nagas in regard to their future after India gained Independence. For details see, *Simon Memorandum*, 'Memorandum of the Naga Hills to the Statutory Commission on Constitutional Reforms (Simon Commission)', 10 January 1929.

51 *Inner Line Regulation Act, 1873*

52 Gundevia: *War and Peace in Nagaland*, p.48

53 Eaton, Richard M., 'Comparative History as World History: Religious Conversion in Modern India' *Journal of World History* VIII/2 (1997), p.245

54 See Verghese: *India's Northeast Resurgent*

55 The present religious mix of the state is around 88 per cent Christian, 10 per cent Hindus and 2 per cent Muslims (Census of India, 2001). The massive Naga conversion to Christianity, second only to the Filipinos, remains a critical factor in the politics of the state and often manifests in slogans such as 'Nagaland for Christ'. See, Annual Report of 1992-1993, *Nagaland for Christ*, Oking: Council of Nagaland Churches, 30 June 1993

56 Nibedon, Nirmal, *Nagaland: The Night of the Guerrillas* (New Delhi, 2000), p.28

57 Aram, M, *Peace in Nagaland: Eight Years Story, 1964-1972* (New Delhi, 1974), p.120, cited in Goswami, Namrata, 'The Naga Rebel Groups' Narratives of Dissent', in Pushpita Das and Namrata Goswami (eds), India's *North East: New Vistas for Peace* (New Delhi, 2008)

58 See, *Selected Works of Jawaharlal Nehru - Second Series,* Vol. I (New Delhi, 1984), pp.604-5

59 The Nine-point Accord was signed between the then Governor of Assam, Akbar Hydari and the representatives of the Naga National Council at Kohima after three days of deliberation. See, Appendix A

60 Nibedon: Nagaland: The Night of the Guerrillas, p.63

61 By the terms of the agreement, the Naga Hills would become the State of Nagaland with a Legislative Assembly and elected members in the Indian Parliament. It was agreed that without the consent of the Nagaland Assembly, no Act of the Indian Parliament in regard to Naga social and religious practice, customary law and procedures relating to civil and criminal justice as well as land ownership would come into effect. Special financial packages as well as the continuation of the Inner Line Regulation were part of the agreement. A Naga regiment for the army was to be raised - a commitment that eventually took shape in 1970.

62 The State of Nagaland was for a population of not more than 500,000. Along with full statehood, came a legislature, cabinet and the offices of the chief minister and governor. See, Sinha, S.K., 'Violence and Hope in India's North East', in K.P.S. Gill and Ajai Sahni (eds), *Faultlines* (New Delhi, 2002), p.8

63 In accordance to the terms of the Accord, the Central Government agreed to release all political prisoners besides stopping all security operations against the militants. The Naga militants on their part decided to accept the Indian Constitution and to give up violence. See, Appendix B

64 Since 1995, serious high-level talks have been held with the Naga leaders. The Indian Prime Minister Narasimha Rao (1991-96) met Swu and Muivah for the first time in Paris in June 1995. Rao's successor Dewe Gowda (1996-97) met the Naga leaders in Zurich in February 1997. Dewe Gowda's successor I.K Gujral (1997-98) signed the first ceasefire agreement with the NSCN (IM) in July 1997. Ever since, the one year ceasefire continues to be extended every year on almost the same conditions. Talks between the GOI's representative Mr Padmanabhaiah and the NSCN (IM) have progressed through a number of rounds outside India, with a significant one held between 9-11 July 2002, at Amsterdam. The next round of talks were held in New Delhi in January 2003. These talks were historic in that both Issac Szu and Muivah came to Delhi and held talks with all the major leaders of the Government including the Prime Minister, Deputy Prime Minister, Home Minister and Defence Minister. The leaders accepted a vital decision to 'neither participate nor interfere' in the state elections in Nagaland that were scheduled for 26 February 2003. They also held consultations with a number of representatives of Naga civil society groups, such as the Naga People's Movement

for Human Rights, Naga Mothers' Association, Naga Students' Federation and Naga Hoho – the state's apex tribal council. There clearly is a political consensus among New Delhi's political establishment on the Naga talks. Prime Ministers A.B. Vajpayee (1998-2004) and Manmohan Singh (2004–09) have continued the dialogue process with both NSCN factions

65 Article 13 of the 16-Point Agreement of 1960 is cited for the demand of a common Unified Naga homeland or Greater Nagaland, five times larger than the current Nagaland. The controversial Article talks about 'facilitating the Nagas inhabiting the contiguous areas in Manipur, Assam and Arunachal Pradesh to come under a single administrative umbrella should they desire'. See, *Frontline*, 'Protests and Threats' XVIII/15 (2001)

66 The NSCN (U) is an outcome of a inter-factional 'truce meeting' between senior cadres of the NSCN(IM) and NSCN (K) factions, aimed at what was described as the 'unification of both the warring factions'. The 'Niuland Declaration' of 3 November 2007, which resulted in the birth of this faction, has been rejected by the NSCN (IM). The developments clearly are a reflection of the increasing social divisiveness of the Naga society along tribal lines: NSCN (IM) dominated by the Thangkhul tribe, NSCN (U) by the Semas and the NSCN (K) by Konyaks. The NNC mainly comprises of the Angamis. Other tribes are known to oscillate between these main factions.

67 Available online, *South Asia Terrorism Portal* <http://www.satp.org

68 Four days prior to India's independence on 15 August 1947, the King of Manipur signed the instrument of accession entrusting defence, communication and foreign affairs to the GOI. Thereafter a new state constitution, applicable to both hill and plain regions of Manipur was adopted. The elections that followed, the first in independent India for any region, gave Manipur a democratically elected state government. However, by virtue of the 15 October 1949 Manipur Merger Agreement, signed between the GOI and the King of Manipur, Manipur lost its autonomy and an Indian official was appointed to run the state. The merger was never ratified by a popular vote and the widely held perception remains that the King was intimidated to sign the instrument of merger. A number of separatist groups regard the merger as illegal and unconstitutional. See, Appendix C

69 With the adoption of the Indian Constitution in 1950, different categories of states were created: Part A, B and C. The nine Part A states, the former provinces, were administered by an elected governor and state legislature. The eight Part B states, former princely states or groups of princely states, were governed by appointed governors. The ten Part C states included both former chief commissioners' provinces and former princely states. They were governed by a chief commissioner. Manipur, five times bigger than the current state of Nagaland, was incorporated into India as a 'Part C state'.

70 In its Eighth Schedule (Articles 344 and 351), the Constitution of India has specified 18 modern Indian languages. The states have the freedom to choose one or more languages of the Eighth Schedule or languages spoken in the region as their official language.

71 The Manipuris are divided into four major groups. The four groups are the Meiteis, the Bishnupriya, the Pangal (Manipuri Muslim) and the Hill tribes (which include the Nagas). The Hill tribes can further be divided into two main tribal groups: the 'Naga Group' and the 'Chin-Mizo-Kuki' group. Besides there are also some sub-tribes and intermediary tribes. See Thomas, Joshua. C., 'Insurgency in Manipur', in B. Pakem, (ed), *Insurgency in North East India* (New Delhi, 1997), pp.299-300

72 The ethnic term Meiteis distinguishes Manipur's lowlanders from the people of the hills. Meiteis, who mainly inhabit the Imphal valley, constitute 57 per cent of the state's population. The hill people, among whom are the Nagas, have lived in uneasy coexistence with culturally different Meiteis of the lowlands.

73 The five hill districts are inhabited by 29 recognized STs and other tribal groups still awaiting official recognition. The recognized ST groups are constitutionally entitled to certain privileges, such as reservations in government jobs, protection of their land from settlement and ownership by non-STs including Meiteis.

74 Manipur's tribal population is about 32 per cent of the state's population, though the hills comprise about 90 per cent of the state's territory.

75 The 1994 call by the Nagaland Assembly seeking unification of all Naga areas, led the Manipur Assembly to unanimously adopt a resolution upholding the territorial integrity of Manipur. The ceasefire between the GOI and the Naga rebel group NSCN (IM) that came into effect on 1 August 1997, was greeted with violent street protests throughout Manipur. Similar protests were also witnessed after the June 2001 announcement of the GOI, extending the Naga ceasefire with 'no territorial limits'. The protests manifested in the form of general strikes, boycott of political parties, burning of the Indian national flag and the effigies of Indian political leaders. The mayhem resulted in police firings, death and injuries, besides significant destruction of public property

76 AMCTA (All Manipur College Teachers Association), *Manipur Fact File* (Imphal, Manipur, 2001)

77 'The Manipur Land Revenue and Land Reform Act, 1960', in Kangujam, Sanatomba, 'An Analytical Perspective of Manipur's Territorial Question', *The Sangai Express*, 13 May 2003

78 The Manipuri Pangals (Muslims) set-up a socio-cultural organization, the Islamic Revolutionary Front (IRF) in 1989. Soon this organization acquired a fundamentalist character. The Islamic National Front (IRF), North East Minority Front (NEMF), United Islamic Liberation Army (UILA) and United Islamic Revolutionary Army (UIRA) are the other Islamic outfits in Manipur. See, Narahari, S.N., *Security Threats to North-East India* (New Delhi, 2002), p.164. Also see, Upadhyay, R., 'Manipur – In a Strange Whirlpool of Cross-current Insurgency', *South Asia Analysis Group*, Paper No. 1210, 3 January 2005

79 Available online, *South Asia Terrorism Portal* <http::// www.satp.org

80 Groups like All Bodo Students' Union (ABSU), which came into existence on 15 August 1967, demand greater autonomy and statehood. The agitation against illegal migrants was spearheaded by the All Assam Students' Union (AASU) and the All Assam Gana Sangram Parishad (AAGSP).

81 In response to widespread violence in several parts of the state, on 12 December 1979 President's rule was imposed in Assam. The Assam Disturbed Area Act and the Armed Forces (Special Power) Act was invoked on 6 April 1980. It was only in 1983, that a popular government was sworn into office. The election to the state legislature took place amidst a boycott call by the leaders of the movement. With only a small percentage (17.16 per cent) of the state's eligible voters exercising their franchise, the legitimacy of the government came under a scanner. See, Marwah, Ved, *Uncivil Wars: Pathology of Terrorism in India* (New Delhi, 1995), p.303

82 Hazarika Sanjoy, *Rites of Passage, Border Crossings, Imagined Homelands, India's East and Bangladesh* (New Delhi, 2000), p.55, 66; For details on the Assam Accord, see Appendix D

83 In the early years, the ULFA's crusade against all pervading corruption in the society and the government fired the popular imagination. The theme of alleged exploitation of Assam by the Indian State and the 'outsiders' residing in the state, fell on receptive ears and added to it's support base. Bengalis, Nepalis, the Hindi-speakers, government officials, civil servants, businessmen and the security forces became targets for abduction and killing. Destruction of vital installations, mainly gas and oil pipelines, railway tracks, and telephone exchanges, figured highly in their destructive agenda. See, *Frontline*, 'Outrage in Assam and Targeting outsiders' XX/25 (2003); Baruah, Sanjib, *India Against Itself: Assam and the Politics of Nationality*, (New Delhi, 1999)

84 The Bodos, believed to have migrated to Assam from China, Mangolia, Tibet and Siberia, are the oldest inhabitants of the region. Over a period of time, depending on the areas they settled, they acquired new and distinct names such as the Boro-Kacharis, Rabha, Sonowal, Lalung, Deori, Dimasa, Barman, Garo, Hajong and Hojai Kachari. Political awareness among the Bodos was evident by the time the Simon Commission had arrived in India, in 1929. The Bodos submitted a memorandum to the Commission, on behalf of the Plains Tribe seeking autonomy and distinct treatment. In 1933, they formed the Tribal League. Post-partition, unabated influx of refugees into the Bodo dominated areas of Kokrajhar and Goalpara districts of Assam from Bangladesh and the Indian state of Bengal, altered the demography of the area to the disadvantage of the Bodos. The establishment of the Bodo Sahitya Sabha, the apex literary body of the Bodos, in 1952 crystallized the demand for the introduction of Bodo as an optional language in the schools of the state. The linguistic assertion impacted the process of political consolidation in a very profound way.

85 Distinct phases, characterize the evolution of Bodo nationalism. The phase of political awakening, between 1933 to 1966, manifested in yearnings for concrete political representation for the Bodos as a distinct tribe. This was followed by a more assertive phase (1967-86), that witnessed growing demands for autonomy. The third phase, between 1987-92, was characterized by aggressive demands for autonomy, with the ABSU emerging in the forefront of the movement. Thereafter the fourth phase began and was characterized by largescale violence including ethnic cleansing targeting the Santhals (a normadic Dravidian tribe) and the Muslims. The conflict soon acquired the character of a low intensity conflict. The principle political demands of the ABSU were: creation of a separate state of Bodoland; creation of two District Councils on the southern bank of the Brahmaputra; and the inclusion of the Bodo-Kacharis of the Karbi Anglong district in Assam into the Scheduled Tribes (Hills) list. Radical outfits like the NDFB and its military wing, the Bodoland Army, demand a sovereign state outside of the Indian Union. See, ABSU booklet titled *Why Separate State of Bodoland?*

86 The Bodoland Liberation Tigers Front (BLTF) is the militant outfit representing the Bodo State Movement Council (BSMC), which is an amalgamation of different Bodo political parties. The Accord, signed between the Government of India, the Government of Assam and the BLTF, paved the way for the formation of the Bodo Territorial Council (BTC) and proposed the scrapping of the BAC immediately after the formation of the new BTC. See, Appendix E

87 It is noteworthy that in April 2005, the US Government added the ULFA to its international 'terror list'. See, *The Hindustan Times*, 'The US names Al-Mansoorian, ULFA, CPI-Maoist as terrorist outfits', 28 April 2005; *The Indian Express,* 'ULFA, CPI-Maoist in US terror list', 28 April 2005

88 Available online, South *Asia Terrorism Portal* <http://www.satp.org

89 The partition of the country in 1947, deprived the state of its traditional trade routes and markets. The trade links, connecting Tripura with the outside world was lost with the creation of East Pakistan. The loss of Chittagong, as a trade centre proved to be a major economic set-back. In the absence of alternative livelihood sources, land became the only means of sustenance. The monopolization of white-collar jobs by better educated immigrants added to the feeling of deprivation among the tribals. The Tripuri-Bengali ethnic divide runs through the society, with the 'aboriginal' inhabitants viewing large-scale migrations as colonization of their homeland.

90 Although the TUJS did not officially take a militant posture, its association with the Tripura Sena (Tribal Army) under the leadership of a Christian Tribal leader Bijoy Hrangkhawal is noteworthy.

91 Hazarika: *Rites of Passage*, pp.174-75; For details on the peace accord between TNV and GOI, see Appendix F

92 Available online, *South Asia Terrorism Portal* < http://www.satp.org

93 Located between Burma and India, the Mizo region is mostly inhabitated by the Tibeto-Burman tribal groups. The generic term 'Mizo' includes sub-tribal groups such as the Kukis, Lushais, Reangs, the Lakher, the Hmars, the Pawi and the Panei. More than two thirds of the population of Mizoram, is mainly Christian and represented by the Mizo-Lusai community. Creation of a Greater Mizoram independent from the Indian State, was the declared aim of the Mizo separatist movement led by the 1961 established MNF. Active support from the Burmese insurgent groups, such as the Chin Independence Army and the Kachin Independence Organization and also Pakistan's ISI and later from Bangladesh sustained this movement for about two decades.

94 Southern Mizoram has a population of about 85,000 Brus. Between 1997 and 2001, about 40,000 displaced Brus were living in makeshift camps in the adjacent state of Tripura. For details see, Dutta, Subrata Kumar , *Uprooted Reang: Strangers in Their Motherland* (New Delhi, 2005); *Frontline*, 'The Reang Refugees' XV/15 (1998)

95 *North East News Agency*, 'Will Terrorism Surface in Mizoram Again?' I/44 (1999)

96 Carved out of the state of Assam, Meghalaya became a full-fledged state in 1972. Three ethnic groups dominate the ethnic profile: the Garos who represent nearly 33 per cent of Meghalaya's population mainly inhabit the western hills, the Khasis who account for around 40 per cent of the population, live in central Meghalaya, and the Jaintias who form nearly 10 per cent of the population mainly reside in eastern Meghalaya. Over the years, a significant non-tribal population engaged in economic activities have also settled in the state.

97 With active support from NSCN (IM) and other militant groups in neighbouring Assam, these outfits preside over a huge extortion empire targeting businessmen, members of rival tribes, government and army officials as well as immigrant workers. In July 2004, a new outfit by the name of Hynniewtrep National Special Red Army (HNSRA) declared that it would militarily oppose the mining plans of the Uranium Corporation of India Ltd in the state. See, *The Assam Tribune*, 'NSCN (I-M) still helping Black Widow, other groups', 12 June 2008; *Frontline*, 'Once more in Meghalaya' XVIII/26 (2001)

98 *The Assam Tribune*, 'NSCN creates panic in Tirap, Changlang', 8 February 2008; *The Assam Tribune* 'Insurgency on the Rise in Arunachal Pradesh', 3 April 2002; *The Hindu*, 'Crime and Punishment in Arunachal Pradesh', 12 October 2002

99 The Buddhist Chakma community, a mongoloid tribe had to flee from their place of origin in the Chittagong Hill Tracts in Southeast Bangladesh to escape discrimination and religious persecution. Out of the 100,000 displaced Chakmas (between 1964-65), about 35,000 found shelter in Arunachal Pradesh. Presently, there are about 65,000 Chakmas in the State. The Hajongs, a Hindu tribe of Bangladesh were also displaced in the 1960s. See, 'Chakmas and Hajongs denied their rightful place in Arunachal Pradesh,' *South Asia Human Rights Documentation Centre*, HRF/42/01 (New Delhi, 2001)

100 The Naga and Kuki tribes in Manipur are engaged in a vicious cycle of violence and counter-violence and often locate their brutalities within a historical context. Other communities in Manipur, strongly contest the presumed support of the Indian State for carving Naga dominated areas from Manipur to create Greater Nagaland. The Bodo assertion in Assam emerges through multiple contestations: against the Indian State, against the subjugation of the dominant Assamese community within Assam and a clash with other ethnic identities such as Adivasi, Bengali, and Koch. The Nellie massacre in Assam in February 1983, resulted in the annihilation of about 2,000 Bengali Muslims in a single night. Over the years, in Tripura underground militants, have engineered mass killings and mass exodus of the non-tribal population.

101 See, Taylor, Charles, 'The Politics of Recognition', in Amy Gutman (ed), *Multiculturalism: Examining the Politics of Recognition* (Princeton, NJ, 1994), pp.25-73

102 See, Shafer, Boyd, *Faces of Nationalism* (New York, 1990), pp.313-342

103 The conflict between the Karbis and the Dimasa tribes revolve around the Dhansiri forests. The Dima Halam Daogarh (DHD), the Dimasa militant outfit, has a designated camp in the forest following a ceasefire with the Centre. It has now sought to make Dhansiri a contagious corridor to link their base in North Cachar Hills (in Assam) to Dimapur in Nagaland, the historical capital of the Dimasa kingdom. Their demand for a separate state encompasses the Dhansiri forest and Dimapur, which is now under NSCN (IM) control. As Dhansiri forest is located inside Karbi Anglong (in Assam), the Karbi outfit, the United People's Democratic Solidarity (UPDS) is determined to check the DHD's expansion. The overlapping of the areas claimed by both outfits has led to bloody confrontations. In 2003, the Dimasas fought a bloody battle with the Hmars, while the Karbis fought with the Kukis. In 1996 and 1998, the Bodos and the Adivasis (Santhals) were caught in a violent conflict in Kokrajhar and Bongaigaon districts of western Assam. Fratricidal violence among ethnic groups has been common in Karbi Anglong district, spread over 10,434 sq. kms. There have been clashes between Karbis and Khasis, Karbis and Kukis, and also other ethnic confrontations. Reports suggest that the inaccessible hill-tops in Karbi Anglong, located close to Nagaland's Dimapur area have become sanctuaries for small armed gangs that operate like mercenaries willing to offer services to interested parties. Established rebel groups seek such services mainly for their extortion operations or for settling scores. See, *The Assam Tribune*, 'NSCN (IM) still helping Black Widow, other groups', 12 June 2008; *The Times of India* 'Enemy Within in Ethnic Bloodbath', 27 October 2005; Hussain, Wasbir, 'Assam: Turf War in a Time of Truce', *South Asian Intelligence Review* IV/14 (2005)

104 The Nagas and Kukis in Manipur are caught in the trap of violence and counter-violence. Similarly the exclusion of Hmars, Brus, and the Chakmas from Mizoram and the exclusion of Muslims and some smaller tribal communities such as the Tea Tribes in Assam, have triggered violent retaliations. The resistance and

assertions of the subordinate communities like the Adivasis, Bengalis and Kochs against the Bodos and the expatriation of Brus from Mizoram and Paites from Manipur are examples of increasingly hostile inter-ethnic coexistence. The ongoing ethnic clashes between the Karbis and Dimasas in the Karbi Anglong district of Assam, is another example of inter-ethnic conflict. A striking development in recent times is the formation of a string of small militant outfits styled as self-defence groups, to resist the ethnic cleansing perpetuated by dominant xenophobic outfits. Some examples of such self-defence outfits are: the Bengali Tiger Force (Bengalis have been primarily targeted in Assam, Meghalaya and Tripura), the Gurkha Tiger Force (for securing the interest of the Nepali community scattered all over North East India), the Adivasi Security Force (for the protection of aboriginals of the region).

105 The region does not enjoy significant political clout in the national decision-making process. The representation of North East India in the 524 member Lower House of the Parliament is: Assam-14, Arunachal Pradesh- 2, Meghalaya-2, Nagaland-1, Mizoram-1, Manipur-2 and Tripura-2.

106 Hazarika: *Rites of Passage*, p.176

107 The Sino-Indian borders remain unsettled. While India sticks to the British demarcation of the 1896 Durand Line in the Western sector and the 1914 McMahon Line in the Eastern Sector, China has not accepted it. China claims substantial portions of the territory of Arunchal Pradesh and till very recently questioned Sikkim's accession to India. For details see, Maxwell, Neville, *India's China War* (London, 2000). Also see, 'India's Turbulent Northeast' *South Asia Monitor*, Centre for Strategic and International Studies (Washington DC), No. 35, 5 July 2001

108 Through Burma, China has expanded its naval influence in the Indian Ocean where it has sought strategic outposts on Burmese islands close to India's Andaman and Nicobar Islands. Chinese Naval facilities at Hianggyi Island, Sittwe, Mergui and the surveillance station at Coco Islands have been upgraded. Strategic road links between Chinese border towns to railheads and sea ports in Burma have been constructed. China has formalized border trade with Burma in 1988 and is also its largest arms supplier. See, Satish, M., 'Bid to woo Myanmar away from China', *The Economic Times*, 10 April 1995

109 It was in the Yunan province of China that the leader of the NNC, Issac Muivah and his band of 300 men, were imparted training in arms and guerrilla tactics. See, Sarin, V.I.K., *India's North East in Flames* (New Delhi, 1980), pp 105-22. Also see, *Northeast Sun*, (New Delhi) 'Unwanted force' III/19 (1998), p.8; The *Times of India*, 'Nasty Neighbourhood', 21 August 2005; *The Times of India*, 'Rebels get foreign help: PM', 30 October 2005

110 See, *The Pioneer*, 'NSCN Ultras negotiate arms deal in China', 31October 2003

111 The arms shipment seized in Chittagong in April 2004 included 1790 assault rifles, 25,000 hand grenades, 1.1 million ammunition and it is believed to have originated from Hong Kong and was meant for the North East India insurgents. See, Davis, Anthony, 'New Details Emerge on Bangladesh Arms' Haul', *Jane's Intelligence Review* September 2004

112 Both India and China are committed to a powerful programme of economic reforms and have made serious efforts to work on areas of disagreement such as the border dispute, the issue of Tibet and also the issue of Chinese support to Indian rebel groups. However, ties between the two countries continue to be under strain. India's decision to reopen the 4,960 metre Daulatbeg Oldi airbase in Ladakh after 43 years, has not gone down well with Beijing. The base will give

India coverge over Aksai Chin as well as the Karakoram highway which connects China with Pakistan. The Chinese have reacted by staking a claim to a small area on the Sikkim border, an issue which according to India was no longer contentious after China's official recognition of Sikkim as Indian territory in 2004. In India, there is increasing concern about China building up road and rail capabilities that connect it with Nepal, as well as the proposed rail routes that would bring it closer to Nathu La in Sikkim, the Arunachal Pradesh border and the Myanmar border junction. Over the past few years, there has been an increase in construction activity close to the Line of Actual Control (LAC), across Arunachal Pradesh. Much to India's discomfort, the Indian army has reported a series of Chinese incursions. In 2007 alone, over 140 intrusions were reported in all three sectors of the 4,000 km border between the two countries – western (Ladakh), middle (Uttarkhand, Himachal Pradesh) and eastern (Sikkim, Arunachal Pradesh). Till June 2008, around 65 incursions had been reported on the 206 km Sikkim-Tibet border. The 90,000 sq. kms claimed by China as its territory, fall in the far eastern state of Arunachal Pradesh. See, *The Times of India,* 'Ladakh base fresh crimp in ties with China', 4 June 2008; *The Times of India,* 'India to raise Sikkim incursion with China', 20 June 2008; *Mail Today,* 'Chinese incursion into Sikkim a regular feature', 20 June 2008

113 India registered a strong protest against China taking exception to Prime Minister Manmohan Singh's visit to Arunachal Pradesh in early February 2008, on the ground that major parts of the territory of the state did not belong to India. The outbust is an indication that the disputed borders between the two countries continue to be a source of security concern for India, a sentiment strongly voiced by the Defence Minister A.K. Antony. See, *The Assam tribune,* 'China Protests PM's visit to Arunachal', 9 February 2008; *The Assam Tribune,* 'Chinese threat real: Antony', 7 April 2008

114 Bhutto, Z.A., *The Myth Of Independence* (London, 1969), p.163

115 Bajpai: *Roots of Terrorism,* p.103-4

116 It is noteworthy that Pakistan's support came to a predominantly Christian outfit. Chinese and Burmese assistance to the Nagas came in much later. In 1956, the Naga National Council leader A.Z. Phizo escaped to Dhaka from where he was flown to London on a false passport arranged by Pakistan. The Naga ultras, enroute to the training camps in the Chittagong Hill Tracts used the Burmese corridor made available to them by the Burmese rebel outfit, the Chin Independence Army. For details see, Nibedon, Nirmal, *Night of the Guerrillas* (New Delhi, 1985)

117 Bhaumik, Subir, *Insurgent Crossfire* (New Delhi, 1996), p.42

118 In 1963, the Mizo leader Laldenga along with his volunteers reached Pakistan for arms and training. The trained rebels are believed to have returned to Mizo Hills from East Pakistan in 1966. After the outlawing of the MNF by the GOI following its declaration of independence in February 1968, Laldenga and his followers escaped to the Chittagong Hill Tracts in East Pakistan, from where they continued their war against the Indian State. See, Verghese: *India's Northeast: Resurgent,* p.40; Sarin: *India's North-East in Flames,* p.154; Raman, B., 'Pakistan and Terrorism: The Evidence', *South Asia Analysis Group,* Paper No. 390, 8 January 2002

119 Verghese: *India's Northeast: Resurgent,* p.143

120 Bhaumik: *Insurgent Crossfire,* p.44

121 For an analysis of the ISI structure and activities see, B. Raman, 'Pakistan's Inter-Services Intelligence (ISI)' *India Intelligence Review* XVI/3 (2001). Also see

Federation of American Scientists, *Intelligence Resource Program*, < http://www.fas.org/irp/world/pakistan/isi. >

122 See, Saikia, Jaideep, 'The ISI Reaches East: Anatomy of a Conspiracy', *Faultlines: Writings on Conflict &Resolution* VI (New Delhi, 2002), pp.61-78; *The Times of India*, 'ISI invites leader for rebel meet in Karachi', 25 August 2005; *The Asian Age*, 'Bodo militants link to ISI unearthed', 15 January 2003; *The Assam Tribune*, 'Sarkar concerned over ISI abetted Tripura militancy', 26 March 2003

123 A 'Volcano Unit' of the ULFA, specialized in the use of Programmable Time Devices was formed and trained by the ISI in the Afghanistan-Pakistan border areas. An ULFA cache busted by the Police in Meghalaya in 2003, led to the discovery of Taliban rockets. See, *The Assam Tribune*, 'ULFA Trained in Pak to Handle PTD', 31 January 2005; *The Times of India*, 'Nabbed militant spills ULFA chief's Pak jaunt', 28 September 2005; *Press Trust of India*, 'Police Seize Taliban Arms from ULFA', 12 April 2003

124 The Siliguri Corridor – the gateway to North East India – has emerged as a hub of ISI's subversive activities. In January 2000, the NSCN leader Muivah on arrival from Pakistan was arrested at the Bangkok International Airport for traveling on a fake South Korean passport. For details on ISI activities see, Saikia: 'The ISI Reaches East'; *The Sentinel*, 'The ISI factor', 2 January 2003

125 See, Kumar, Vinay, 'ISI Trained ULFA in use of Explosives', *The Hindu*, 25 December 2003; *The Sentinel*, 'ULFA Leaders have become puppets of ISI', 14 August 2000; Datta, Sreeradha, *The Northeast Complexities and its Determinants* (New Delhi, 2004), p.104

126 *The Assam Tribune*, 'Islamic Ultras trained in Pak, Bangla: Govt', 1 April 2008; *The Assam Tribune*, 'ISI behind NE terrorism: Fernandes', 8 June 2007; Shahin, Sultan, 'Pakistan Shifts Proxy War to India's East', *Asia Times* (Hong Kong), 6 February, 2002

127 Insurgent groups operating under Pakistani intelligence cover within East Pakistan, suffered a setback with the creation of Bangladesh. The situation altered after the assassination of President Mujibur Rehaman in 1975, after which the new regime once again allowed the Indian insurgents to establish their bases in the Chittagong Hill Tracts. See, *The Assam Tribune*, 'NE Militant Camps exist in Bangla', 2 April 2004. Also see, *The Assam Tribune*, 'NE Ultras in Bangla – BSF to submit fresh list of over 150 camps', 6 January 2004

128 Dixit, J.N., *My South Block Years: Memoirs of a Foreign Secretary* (New Delhi, 1997), p.159

129 http://www.pinr.comreport.php?ac=view_report&report_id=562&language-*id*-110/5/2006 cited in Ahmed, Abu Nasar Saied, *Fundamentalism in Bangladesh: Its Impact on India* (New Delhi, 2008), pp.201-202

130 Former Border Security Force (BSF) Director General Ajai Raj Sharma, at a press conference in Kolkata airport on 14 April 2004, stated that the BSF had evidence of at least 195 Indian rebel camps in Bangladesh. Border Security Forces say that Naga insurgents have their base camps at Salopi near the Mizoram-Bangladesh-Myanmar borders in the Cox's Bazaar area, as well as in Bandarban in the Chittagong Hill Tracts of Bangladesh. Manipuri rebels too are known to be running camps at Nagar and Chitalhiya, both within the Bangladesh border in villages under Sylhet, Commilla, and Moulobi Bazar districts. See, *The Times of India*, 'ISI, Bangla helping north-east insurgents, says US think-tank', 25 April 2007; *Times of India*, 'Whose Sonar Bangla?', 12 December 2004; Also see, *Assam Tribune*,

'India seeks closure of 155 ultra camps in Bangladesh', 12 May, 2003; *Sentinel*, (Guwahati) 'Does ULFA have camps in CHT?', 29 June 2002

131 The DGFI, a prototype of the ISI, was set-up in 1978 to sustain the predominance of the armed forces in the governance of the country. In the initial planning and crafting of the DGFI, Pakistan played a vital role and the relationship between the two agencies has continued ever since. See, Nandy, Bibhuti Bhusan, 'DGFI: State within a State', in Jaideep Saikia (ed), *Bangladesh Treading The Taliban Trail* (New Delhi, 2006), p.173-187; Bhaumik, Subir, 'Politics of Sanctuary, Indian Rebel Bases in Bangladesh', in Saikia: *Bangladesh Treading The Taliban Trail,* p.189

132 Extraditions of known militant leaders are at the core of India's diplomatic row with Bangladesh. Bangladesh has consistently refused to sign an extradition agreement with India. *The Assam Tribune,* 'Bangla rules out Chetia's extradition', 3 April 2004; *The Hindu,* 'Delhi, Dhaka to fight Terrorism', 22 March 2006

133 India and Burma jointly conducted Operation Golden Bird against the North East militants in 1995, to destroy camps on Burmese soil. In case of Bhutan, under pressure from India, Bhutan launched 'Operation All Clear' against the North Eastern insurgents, notably the ULFA, NDFB and KLO. While the ULFA and NDFB's declared objective is the creation of a sovereign state through an armed struggle, the Kamtapur Liberation Organization (KLO) formed on 28 December 1995, aims to carve out a separate Kamtapur State for the Rajbongshi tribe from the states of West Bengal and Assam. See, *The Times of India*, 'Bhutan Launches Operations Against ULFA', 10 March 2004; Also see, Kumar, Praveen, 'External Linkages and Internal Security: Assessing Bhutan's Operation All Clear' *Strategic Analysis* XXVIII/3 (New Delhi, 2004)

134 India shares, 1670 kms long land border and a maritime border of 200 kms with Burma. The India states of Arunachal Pradesh (520 kms), Nagaland (215 kms), Manipur (398 kms) and Mizoram (510 kms), share borders with the Chin and Kachin states and the Sagaing Division of Burma.

135 Tucker, Shelly, *Among Insurgents, Walking Through Burma* (Delhi, 2000), pp.82-82; Hussain, Wasbir, 'We picked up our Aks and fled', *Sentinel*, 24 December 2003

136 The INCB report ranks Burma second to Afghanistan in opium production. See, *INCB Annual Report 2003*, cited in Larry Jagan, 'Southeast Asia remains drugs hotspot', BBC Online, 26 February 2003

137 Reportedly, the NSCN (both Khaplang and Issac-Muivah factions) as well as the ULFA are involved in drug trafficking, the proceeds of which are used for procuring arms and ammunitions. See, *The Assam Tribune*, 'ULFA still has bases in Myanmar', 21 January 2005

138 *Mizzima News Report*, 'India-Burma – Drug Cultivation, Consumption and Trafficking', January 2004; *Mizzima News*, 'No government can dismantle the camps, said surrendered militant' 18 July 2002; *Mizzima News,* 'Militant group of Indo-Burma border get together', 6 October 2002

139 Significant presence of Indian rebels in Burma has been reported. It is believed that the NSCN (Khaplang faction), the ULFA and the Manipur rebel groups maintain camps in Burmese territory, mainly in the Sagaing region. The Sagaing region has some Naga-inhabited areas and the Eastern Naga Regional Council (ENRC), is active here. The ENRC joined the NNC in propounding the concept of a 'Greater Naga Nation', inclusive of the Nagas of India and Burma. The ENRC is known to have provided the NNC its first links to the KIA. It was in the mid-

1966, that NNC established contact with the KIA in the Kachin Hill tracts of Burma. The ENRC also helped the Naga rebels reach China. The Manipur Peoples Liberation Front (MPLF), a coalition of leading Meitei rebel groups, has a number of bases around the town of Tamu in Burma. It is noteworthy, that some Burmese ultras belonging to the Kuki Chin group are known to be fighting for merger of lands inhabited by them with India and the underground Zomi Liberation Front of Myanmar is known to recruit cadres for guerilla warfare against the Burmese State. After the crackdown on pro-democracy supporters, many of these cadres have been in hiding in Manipur and Mizoram. See Tarapot, Phanjouban, *Insurgency Movement in North-Eastern India* (New Delhi, 1993); Datta: *The Northeast Complexities*, pp.83-85; Bhaumik, Subir, 'Guns, drugs and rebels' *Seminar* 550 (2005), pp.40-41

140 Subir Bhaumik: *Ibid*

141 In April 1995, the armies of India and Burma launched a 44 day cooperative anti-insurgency offensive codenamed 'Operation Golden Bird', along the border of Mizoram. Around 60 ULFA rebels and other North Eastern ultras were ambushed. See, Hussain, Wasbir, 'Golden Bird: Army morale soars high', *The Asian Age*, 18 May, 1995

142 Dutta: *The Northeast Complexities*, pp.85-86

143 Given the porous nature of the borders with Bhutan, militant groups from Assam took refuge in Bhutan. It is reported that at one time around 4,000 cadres of the outlawed ULFA and more than a thousand Bodo militants were based in camps in southern Bhutan. The ULFA is reported to have established training camps and sanctuaries in the Manas Reserve and the densely forested areas of South Bhutan.

144 Wasbir, Hussain, 'Bhutan – King Size Problem' *South Asia Intelligence Review* II/10 (2003)

145 *Frontline*, 'Crackdown in Bhutan', XXI/1 (2004); Also see, *The Assam Tribune*, 'Bhutan launches more combing operations against NE ultras', 16 March 2004

146 Rediff.com, 'ULFA trying to reestablish camps in Bhutan', 24 March 2005

147 *The Assam Tribune*, 'Nepal Maoists, ULFA forging links', 11 November 2004

148 Indian leaders have met Naga leaders abroad. Prime Ministers Narasimha Rao and A.B. Vajpayee met Naga representatives in Paris in 1997 and 1998. In May 2002, the Mizoram Chief Minister on behalf of the Central Government, met NSCN (IM) representatives in Thailand. Representatives of the present Congress-led United Progressive Alliance government have also met Naga representatives abroad. The peace process currently in motion is an outcome of such meetings. See, Bajpai: *Roots of Terrorism*, p.100; *Hindustan Times*, 'Mizo CM to facilitate Naga talks', 4 May 2002

149 Groups like the ULFA have negotiated with experienced rebel groups like the NSCN (IM) in Nagaland, KIA in Burma and the LTTE in Sri Lanka. Bodo militants are also known to have received support from the ULFA, the NSCN (IM), the ISI and Bangladesh intelligence agencies. The linkages between these outfits are in the fields of training, intelligence sharing and the use of each other's sanctuaries. Initial training to any new outfit is provided by the larger and older groups like NSCN (IM), NSCN (K) and ULFA and subsequently these outfits set-up their own training camps. Training is also provided by Burma based Kachin Independence Army, Shan State Army, Kachin National Army as well as umbrella organizations like SDUFSEHR. Till 1998, the fee for arms training by Burma

based outfits was believed to be IR 50,000 per insurgent, which has since been enhanced. See, Ramana, P.V., 2002, 'Networking' the Northeast Partners in Terror', Available online at the South Asia Terrorism Portal, *Faultlines*, http://www.satp.org/satporgtp/publication/faultlines/vol11/article6.htm. Also see, Sharma, A.K., 'Insurgency Defies Solution', *Communication*, April-June (1998), pp.38-40

150 Adidi, S.N.M., 'India, Burma Rebels work on Breakaway Plan, *Illustrated Weekly of India*, Supplement to Magazine, 15 December 1990, p.1

151 Pillai, S.K., 'Insurgencies in Northeast India', *Aakrosh* (Asian Journal on Terrorism and Internal Conflicts) V/17 (2002), pp.31-52

152 John Sisline et al, argues that 'Light Weapons' such as AK-47 rifle, mortars and grenade launchers are the mainstay of ethnic conflicts. See, Sisline, John, et al, 'Pattern of Arm Acquisitions by Ethnic Group in conflict' *Security Dialogue* (London) XXIV/4 (1988), pp.393-408. Also see, *The Times of India*, 'N-E terror flows through small arms', 31 May 2006

153 Some of the fiercest battles of the Second World War, between the Allied and Axis forces were fought in the North Eastern frontiers – in and around Kohima (Nagaland) and Imphal (Manipur).

154 Most of the militant-ethno-nationalist groups in North East India have been actively assisted by the KIA, a rebel outfit in Burma.

155 The LTTE procured the services of the 'Karikal Muslims' who hailed from the Tamil speaking French dependency of Karikal and settled down in Indo-China. See Bhaumik: 'Guns, drugs and rebels', p.44

156 The LTTE is believed to have been granted permission by the Burmese authorities to establish a base in the Island of Twante, from where they coordinate their arms trafficking operations. Peiris, G.H., 'Liberation Tigers of Tamil Eelam and the Global Drug Trade: An Overview', paper presented to the First Symposium on Governance and Corruption in Sri Lanka and South Asia, ICES (Kandy), Colombo, 9-10 January 1999, pp.12-13, cited in P.S. Ghosh, *Unwanted and Uprooted* (New Delhi, 2004), pp.129-130

157 During the course of the counter insurgency operation named 'Operation Rhino' against the ULFA in 1991, documentary evidence of ties between the KIA of Burma, the NSCN and the LTTE came to light. The ULFA-LTTE links came out in the open during 1991-1992 Jain Commission inquiry into the Rajiv Gandhi assassination. See, Jain Commission Report, 1992 available online at: http://www.india-today.com/jain/vol7/chap10.html; Also see, Verghese: *India's Northeast Resurgent*, p.123

158 The 27,000 population of Moreh, comprises of ten communities, namely, Kukis, Tamils, Meiteis, Punjabis, Nepalis, Marwaris, Nagas, Bengalis, Assamese and Maliyalees. Since 1995, border trade between India and Burma (in 22 items) has been legalized through Moreh. From the point of view of militancy, it is the drug connection that makes Moreh a strategic point. See, Ghosh: *Unwanted and Uprooted*, p.130

159 Driven by profit motive, State run ordinance factories have been selling large quantity of weapons even to mafia groups. For details see, Bhaumik: 'Gun, Drugs and Rebels', p.44

160 In April 2004, huge quantities of weapons meant for ULFA were seized in Bongura and Chittagong in Bangladesh as well as Calcutta in West Bengal. See, *Ibid*

161 Operation Leech mounted by the Indian armed forces, off the Andaman coast in

1998 is proof of such shipments. For details on the transfer of weapons see, Gunaratna, Rohan, 'Illicit Transfer of Conventional Weapons; Role of State and Non-State Actors in South Asia', in Jayanatha Dhanapala et.el, *Small Arms Control: Old Weapons, New Issues* (Vermont, 1999), p.251-278

162 Some of the outfits in the region are believed to be armed by the Indian security agencies such as RAW. See, Kartha, Tara, *Tools of Terror: Light Weapon and India's Security* (New Delhi, 1999), p.262. Also see, Nephram, Binalaxmi, 'Society under siege – the proliferation of small arms and narcotics in India's North East region', paper presented at a workshop organized by Oxfam-VMAP on the conflict situation in North East held at Shillong, 4-6 June 2001; Mentschel Nepram, Binalakshmi, 'Armed Conflict, Small Arms Proliferation and Women's Responses to Armed Violence in India's Northeast' *Heidelberg Papers in South Asian and Comparative Politics*, Working Paper No 33, December 2007

163 International Institute of Strategic Studies, *Armed Conflict Data Base* available online, <http://acd.iiss.org/armedconflict/mainpages/dsp_conflictsummary 1D+171,172,173,174&180> accessed on 23 March 2006

164 'Long March' is the technical term that describes the arms procurement routes of North East militants and other related processes in terms of planning and logistics. There are at least four routes used by gunrunners in the region. The Manipur gun runner's route originates in Tamu bazaar, at the Burma-Manipur border. The Garo Hills in Meghalaya, bordering Bangladesh, is another notable arms route for the insurgents. The Naga gun route, runs through the porous Indo-Burma border, notably from Yairipok (Burma Border) and Ukhrul. The Nagas also have another route starting from CHT in Bangladesh to Jantaia Hills and from there to Karbi Anglong and North Cachar in Assam and then to Nagaland. The Mizo small arms route is another important route, facilitated by the fact that Mizoram shares international borders with both Bangladesh and Burma. The border town Champhai has emerged as the major arms route from where arms are pushed into places like Silchar in Assam, Shillong in Meghalaya and Churachandpur in Manipur. It is believed that most of the arms come from Bangladesh's Cox's Bazaar. Over the years, Bangladesh has emerged as an important centre of gun running in South and South East Asia. Seizure of enormous hoard of arms in 2003 and 2004, meant to be routed to North East India, are pointers to this reality. For details see, Nepram, Binalakshmi, 'Gun wars and Drug Deaths in South Asia: A Narrative of Armed Ethnic Conflict, Narcotics and Small arms trafficking in India's North East', Paper presented at a meeting organized by the South Asia Partnership Canada and CPCC Small Arms Working group, Canada on 22 March 2004, Ottawa; Karlekar, Hiranmay, *Bangladesh The Next Afghanistan?* (New Delhi, 2005), pp.275-276; Dasgupta, Anindita, 'Small Arms Proliferation in India's North-East: A Case Study of Assam' *Economic and Political Weekly* XXXVI/1 (2001), pp.59-64; *The Times of India,* 'Intelligence Worried Over Arms Haul', 18 April 2004

165 The average retail price for a gram of heroin in 1999, in India was $ 5.2, while that in Netherlands was $ 42.5, in Canada $ 187.3 and in the USA $ 475. See, *UNDCP, World Drug Report 2000* (Oxford, 2000)

166 Wedged between Northern Burma, Thailand, Western Laos and Southern China, the Golden Triangle is one of the major producer of opium poppies, the raw material for morphine and heroin. The inhospitable terrain of the region, makes any kind of effective governmental control a difficult task. Consequently, the writ of non-state actors such as insurgents, outlawed communist groups and drug-trafficking agglomerations runs at large. According to the World Drug Report 2007, Burma alone accounts for 65 per cent of estimated total world opium poppy

cultivation and 60 per cent of the total potential opium gum production. According to the US Drug Enforcement Administration, Burma is responsible for 60 per cent of the world supply of heroin. Over the years, the routes used to transport opium and heroin out of the Golden Triangle have changed – first through Thailand in the nineteenth century, then via Yunan in the first half of the twentieth century, and presently via Laos and India. See, World Drug Report, 2007; Kumar, Sunita, 'Drug Trafficking in the Golden Triangle', in Singh, J., (ed), *Asian Strategic Review* (New Delhi, 1998); Lintner, Bertil, *Cross Border Drug Trade in the Golden Triangle* (Durhman, N.C, 1991)

167 The ethnic rebel army, the United Wa State Army (UWSA), the core fighting force of the Burmese Communist Party till the late 1980s, has taken to drugs in a big way by eclipsing the traditional druglords. The UWSA monopolizes the amphetamine output, the production of which has risen more than eight times since 1993. The ongoing wars between the druglords have forced the smaller cartels to relocate their drug refineries, away from the traditional heroin export routes. Many of these refineries have been located in areas bordering India's North East and the Yunan province of China. See, *Burma Prospect – Focus on Burma Issues*, Bangkok, February 2002

168 Mizoram with its 704 kms international border with Bangladesh and Burma, has emerged as an important centre for drug smuggling. Opium poppy cultivation in the state, mainly confined to some pockets in the hilly terrain of the Indo-Burmese borders, have come to light. Most of the key cities in the region – Imphal, Aizal, Kohima, Dimapur, Silchar – fall on the trafficking route. It is believed, around 39 trafficking routes connect Burma to North East India. See, Mentschel Nepram: 'Armed Conflict, Small Arms Proliferation and Women's Responses to Armed Violence in India's Northeast'.

169 In the traditional conflicts between the Paite tribes' Zomi Revolutionary Army (ZRA) and the Kuki tribes' Kuki National Front (KNF) in the Churachandpur district of Manipur, heroin is used knowingly to weaken the rivals. See, *World Geopolitics of Drug*, Annual Report 1998-99, p.56

170 Outfits such as the UNLF, PLA and even NSCN (IM) have not only campaigned against drug trafficking and abuse but also taken stern action against drug peddlers.

171 The disastrous consequences of drug trafficking in the region are too obvious to be ignored. The UNDCP estimates about 40,000 addicts each in Manipur and Mizoram, 30,000 in Nagaland and 1,50,000 in Assam. The city of Guwahati in Assam has emerged as the main transit route for drugs to Nepal, which perhaps explains the high number of addicts in the city. Shillong, the capital of Meghalaya is also witnessing a rise in addiction. Besides, illegally diverted pharmaceuticals mostly synthetic drugs like Proxyvon and Spasmo-Proxyvon are also having similar effects as opiates. See, *World Geopolitics of Drugs*, p.56

172 *The Hindu*, 'Truck loads of ephedrine seized', 1 February 2003

173 Bhaumik: 'Gun, Drugs and Rebels', p.43. Also see, *Times of India*, 'Drug use takes epidemic form', 2 June 2006; Jagan, Larry, 'Poppy Barons on the speedboat', *Outlook India*, 16 February 2004; *Jane's Intelligence Review*, 'New drug trafficking routes in Southeast Asia', 1 July 2002; *The Telegraph*, 'Crackdown on Cannabis Racket', 28 November 2002

174 Enormous funds are a requirement for the maintenance of organizational structures of the outfits. Salaries to cadre, arms procurement and training (both inside and outside the region), travel and propaganda entail huge expenditure. See Sahni, Ajai, and J. George, 'Security and Development in India's NorthEast: An

Alternative Perspective', in K.P.S Gill (ed), *Terror and Containment Perspectives of India's Internal Security* (New Delhi, 2001), p.295-318; Saikia, Jaideep, 'Finances of War', *The Sentinel*, 6 April 2000; Saikia, Jaideep, 'Revolutionaries or Warlords: ULFA's Organizational Profile' *Faultlines* IX (2001), pp.105-129

175 The economy of the region is less developed than the rest of India. The share of the secondary sector in the GDP at 15 per cent is much lower than the national average of 23.7 per cent (1999-2000). As per 2000-01 figures, states in the North Eastern region have much higher levels of population living below poverty line (35.13 per cent) as compared to the national average (26.1 per cent). The share of urban population to total in the region at 14.6 per cent is also lower than the national average, although states like Mizoram have a higher urban population. More significantly, the region represents one of the highest rates of unemployment in the country, with an unemployment rate close to 12 per cent against the national average of 7.7 per cent (1999-00). Sahni, Ajai, 'The Terrorist Economy in India's North East' available online in <http://www.satp.org/satporgtp/publication/faultlines/volume 8/article 5.htm>4

176 Army operations are mainly at the initiative of the Central Government. The search-and-arrest operations, have often resulted in human rights violations such as custody deaths, rapes and torture. The alienated local population are disinclined to extend cooperation, at times due to suspicion and at times fearing a backlash from the militants.

177 In this connection it needs to be noted that the states of North East India are categorized as special category states, which means that 90 per cent of the plan assistance is grant and only 10 per cent loan. For the other states in India, it is 30 per cent grant and 70 per cent loan. The Finance Commission, due to the continued 'backwardness' of the region recommends special favourable allocations. The central devolution to the states in the North East, accounts for over 80 per cent revenue receipts in the region. Also, the development expenditure as a percentage of revenue expenditure is higher than the national average by at least 10 percentage points. The per capita income in the region is IR 5070 per annum as compared to the national average of IR 4, 485. Much of the development package, however, ends up financing militancy. See, Sahni: 'The Terrorist Economy in India's North East'

178 A well knitted network of militants, contractors, bureaucrats and members of the political class successfully divert nearly 70 per cent of the allocated funds meant for rural development. During 1992-99, out of a total of IR 11.65 million, only less than 4 million went to the assigned sectors. These revenues are compounded manifold by the massive racquet of extortion and 'taxation' that these terrorist groupings administer in their zones of influence. It is noteworthy that on 14 June 2001, the Union Rural Development Minister Venkiah Naidu, in a meeting of the Rural Development Ministers of North Eastern states, warned that the Centre would stop distributing rural development funds to those states, where the bulk of these funds were getting diverted to the coffers of the militants. See *Ibid; The Sentinel*, 'Centre's Money is Not for the Militants – Venkiah Naidu', 15 June 2001

179 Totaling 965 kms, three National Highways: NH-39, NH-53 and NH-150 connect Manipur to the rest of India and to Burma. Blockade of these highways have been the most common and effective method for militants and agitators to exert pressure on the state government. Extortion is rampant on these highways. See, Singh, Amarjeet 'Highways of Extortions' *South Asia Intelligence Review* IV/47 (2006)

180 According to the joint *United Nations Programme on HIV/AIDS 2006 Report on the Global AIDS Epidemic,* 5.7 million people are carrying the AIDS virus in India. India has overtaken South Africa (which has a HIV/AIDS population of 5.3 million) as the country with the largest number of infected people. Among the states, Andhra Pradesh and Tamil Nadu in the south, Maharashtra in the west and Manipur in the north-east are the worst affected. While in Maharashtra and Tamil Nadu, the infections are mostly due to heterosexual contract, injecting drug use is the main problem in Manipur, where 55 per cent of drug users are HIV-infected and 1 per cent of women attending antenatal clinics are infected with HIV. Although the estimates of AIDS infected persons vary widely and there is a dearth of reliable statistics on the issue, the fact remains that AIDS has become a major scourge in North East India, particularly in Manipur, Nagaland, and Mizoram. See, *The Assam Tribune*, 'NE facing multiple crises', 10 April 2008; *The Times of India*, 'Drug users transmitting virus to women in N-E', 1 December 2007; Editorial 'HIV/AIDS Spreading Scourge' *Economic and Political Weekly* LXI/29 (2006); *Times of India,* 'AIDS bomb ticks away in Mizoram', 25 February 2005; Talukdar, Sushanta, 'Fighting AIDS in Manipur', *The Hindu,* 16 August 2005; Also see, Singh, Pr. Brajachand, 'Drug Abuse and AIDS Menace in Manipur', in Gopalkrishna & al. (eds), *Constraints in Development of Manipur* (New Delhi, 2001); Hazarika, Sanjoy, *Strangers of the Mist* (New Delhi, 1994), p. 322

181 *North East Sun*, 14 November 1998, p.18; *Mail Today*, 'Assam's poachers now carry AK-47s', 1 May 2007

182 The NDFB's safe haven in Bhutan received a set-back when the Royal Bhutan Army launched operations against the ULFA, NDFB and KLO camps on 15 December 2003, destroying 30 camps.

183 On 23 April 2006, the Manipur Chief Minister confessed in a public meeting that all development projects had been stalled due to interventions by militants, demanding a certain percentage of the development funds. The construction of the Assembly complex as well as the Imphal flyover (capital of Manipur) had come to a halt on account of such pressures. See, Routray, Bibhu Prasad, 'Manipur: The State Abdicates' *South Asian Intelligence Review* IV/42 (2006); Rammohan, E.N., 'Manipur: A Degenerated Insurgency', in K.P.S.Gill and Ajai Sahni (eds), *Faultlines,* XI (New Delhi, 2002) pp.1-15

184 Nag, Sajal, 'Funding the Struggle: Political Economy of Insurgency', in Pushpita Das and Namrata Goswami (eds), *India's North East: New Vistas for Peace* (New Delhi, 2008), pp.37-55

185 *Ibid*

186 Five Manipuri outfits – the KCP, the PLA, the PREPAK, the UNLF-M and the KYKL – have fallen under the Prevention of Terrorism Act and have been declared terrorist organizations. On 13 December 2004, KYKL militants kidnapped the Vice-Chancellor and Registrar of Manipur University as a 'punishment' for violating appointment rules. Five days later, they were released with bullet injuries in the left leg. On 16 April 2005, the Kangleipak Communist Party (KCP) took six editors of Imphal based media organizations, as hostage for allegedly writing against the banned outfit. See, *The Deccan Herald*, 'Manipur Ultras 'punish' Varsity VC, Registrar', 19 December 2004; *The Times of India*, 'Imphal Scribe hostage row rages', 20 April 2006; *The Sangai Express*, 'KYKL to Embark on a New Tax Policy', 25 April 2005. For more details on the Manipur situation see, Tarabot, Phanjoubam, *Bleeding Manipur* (New Delhi, 2003)

187 Around 600 tea gardens of Assam and those in the Dooars in West Bengal, have

been at the receiving end of the extortion drive of the ULFA, NDFB, NSCN (IM), DHD and several other outfits. Documentary evidence cited by the Indian Army reveal, that the ULFA demanded and possibly got huge sums from major tea corporations – IR 10 million from MacNeil and Magor, IR 9 million from Assam Company, IR 6.5 million from Warren Company, IR 2 million from Stewart Hall, and IR 4 million from Doom Dooma Tea. Such payments at regular intervals are no secret and are in the official knowledge of the government. Depending upon the size of the tea company, extortion rates are worked out. Despite the exorbitant sums paid to the ultras, there have been instances of high profile kidnappings and murders of top ranking tea officials. In July 1991, ULFA kidnapped and killed an official of the Oil and Natural Gas Commission (ONGC), a public sector enterprise and a Soviet citizen who was in Assam as consultant to Coal India Limited, another public sector enterprise. More recently in January 2006, the ULFA served an extortion notice to ONGC demanding Indian rupees worth hundreds of million. See, *The Telegraph* 'ULFA calls up ONGC on Rs 500-cr. Demand', 20 January 2006; *The Assam Tribune*, 'Special forces to guard oil, industrial units', 5 February 2008; Gokhale, Nitin, *The Hot Brew: The Assam Tea Industry's Most Turbulent Decade 1987-97* (Guwahati, 1998); Baruah: *Durable Disorder*, p.154

188 So widespread is the problem that the Nagaland Chief Minister N Rio is known to have suggested to the Centre to provide 'fixed grants' to both factions, of the NSCN, in the hope that it would contain their extortion drive. See, *The Telegraph*, North East Edition, 11 June 2005; Sashinungla, 'Nagaland: The Dynamics of Extortion' *South Asia Intelligence Review* II/22 (2003)

189 The *Assam Tribune*, 'Insurgency on the rise in Arunachal Pradesh', 12 October 2002

190 For details see, Sashinungla, 'Meghalaya: Extortion Dynamics' *South Asia Intelligence Review* II/40 (2004). Also see, *Outlook India*, 'Pay Up or Else... New Delhi, 19 April 2004

191 The HNSRA deserves special mention as it has announced to militarily oppose the uranium mining plans of the Uranium Corporation of India Limited – a public sector enterprise. Objections have also been raised at some other quarters within the state. See, *The Times of India*, 'Challenge, counter-attack spice up uranium row', 26 May 2006

192 Mizoram is sandwiched between Myanmar and Bangladesh and shares 722 kms porous border with these countries.

193 All kind of weapons, from small handguns to rocket launchers, from Russian Kalashnikov to Chinese version of Ak-47, and from American M-16 to German HK-33 and Chinese SKS rifles, are freely available in the thriving underground arms market of Mizoram. See, *The Times of India*, 'Narco-terrorist endanger Mizoram's "most peaceful" tag', 17 December 2005

194 *The Times of India*, 'Web exposes Tripura rebels' sexcapades', 25 August 2005; *BBC News*, 'Indian rebels making porn films', 27 August 2005; *The Hindustan Times*, 'Militants mint money by making porn films', 10 September 2005; *The Times of India*, 'Ultras snare tribal girls into sex racket', 30 September 2005

195 In December 2005, the Army Chief J.J. Singh accused the Manipur chief minister Ibobi Singh of contributing a sum of IR 15 million to two ultra outfits KYKL and PLA. See, Routray, Bibhu Prashad, 'Manipur: The State Abdicates' *South Asia Intelligence Review* IV/42 (2006); Bertil Litner, *Land of Jade: A Journey from India through Northern Burma to China* (Bangkok, 1996), p.56

196 In the seven states of the region, electioneering and militancy have become synonymous, though degrees may differ. This is particularly evident in Assam, Nagaland, Manipur and Tripura. The spillover effects of this phenomenon have afflicted even peaceful states like Mizoram and Arunachal Pradesh. See, *The Times of India,* 'Militants leave imprint on North-East poll track', 27 August 2005

197 In case of Assam, it has resulted in the phenomenon of the SULFA or Surrendered ULFA. The rehabilitation policy announced by the Assam Chief Minister in 1991 included a cash incentive of IR 50,000 and a soft loan of IR 200,000. Training in some trade or vocation was to be given to the surrendered militant in a rehabilitation camp, on a monthly stipend not exceeding IR 2000. Finance for business projects were to be provided on easy terms, including a guaranteed IR 690 million of loans by various banks. The SULFA soon evolved as an independent player in the conflict dynamics of the state and acquired both political and economic clout. It also played a role in the counter-insurgency operations against the ULFA, by collaborating with the security forces. See, *Government of India, 2000,* Press Information Bureau Archives, 'Scheme of Margin Money to Surrendered Militants', statement by I.D. Swami, Minister of Home Affairs. Available online: http:// pib.nic.in/ archieve/Ireleng/lyr2000/rdec2000/ r13122000.html. Also see, Appendix L

198 Normal conventions have often been compromised to accommodate 'fake militants' who are provided with financial assistance, vocational training and a monthly stipend. Militants involved in murder and heinous crimes have been given amnesty. See, *The Times of India*, 'Rebels take "surrender" route to riches', 9 September 2005

199 Pillai, S.K., 'Three Matryoshkas: Ethnicity, Autonomy& Governance', paper presented at a seminar on '*Addressing Conflicts in India's North East*', organized by the Institute for Conflict Management, India International Centre, New Delhi, on 25-27 June 2001.

200 Gill, K.P.S., 'State must fight terrorism Industry', *The Pioneer*, 31 March 2001

201 The accords have resulted in political arrangements that have helped consolidate the economic, political and social positions of the neo-class. There are several examples of complete transformation of the leaders of the separatist movements, from a position of rebellion to law-abiding integrative agents. Laldenga in Mizoram (spearheaded the Mizo freedom movement between 1966-86), Bijoy Hrankhwal in Tripura (spearheaded the freedom movement in Tripura) and the leaders of the now disbanded Bodo Liberation Tigers, to name a few. The leaders of the BLT have accepted positions such as the chief executive member and deputy chief executive member of the interim council of the Bodoland Territorial Council. See, Das, Samir Kumar, 'Nobody's Communiqué: Ethnic Accords in North-eastern India', in Ranabir Samaddar and Helmut Reifeld (ed), *Peace as Process, Reconciliation and Conflict Resolution in South Asia* (New Delhi, 2001), pp.231- 252

202 *The Assam Tribune*, 'North East surpasses J&K in violence', 23 April 2008; *The Assam Tribune*, 'NE insurgency threat to Security: Centre', 24 April 2008

203 *Annual Report of the Home Ministry, 2000-2001*, New Delhi, Government of India, Publication Division, 2001

204 It is estimated that in 1869, there were 22,800 imported and 11,633 local labourers on tea plantations. In 1884-85, 44.7 per cent of the labourers were from Chotanagpur, 27.6 per cent from Uttar Pradesh and Bihar, 5.5 per cent local and

0.9 per cent from Bombay and Madras. In 1901, the non-indigenous population of the Assam valley was estimated at 0.5-0.6 million in the total of 2.2 million. See, Guha, Amalendu, *Planter-Raj to Swaraj: Freedom Struggle and Electoral Politics in Assam 1826-1947* (New Delhi, 1977). According to another estimate, the migrant population, which was around 4,25,000 in 1891 had exceeded to 1.3 million by 1911. See, Verghese: *India's Northeast Resurgent*

205 Das, S.K., 'Immigration and Demographic Transformation of Assam, 1891-1981' *Economic and Political Weekly* XVIII/18 (1983), pp.850-59

206 See, Hussain, Monirul, *The Assam Movement: Class, Ideology and Identity* (New Delhi, 1993)

207 In 1920 the British introduced the 'Line System' to restrict outsiders from settling beyond a certain limit in migration rampant areas. Restrictions were also placed on the purchase of land within specified areas. Such steps forced the migrants into riverine areas and thus segregated them from the indigenous people.

208 Mullen, C.S., *Census of Assam*, 1931

209 Hazarika: *Rites of Passage*, p.73

210 Government of India, *Census of India*, 1941

211 Choukri, Nazli, 'The Pervasiveness of Politics' *Populi* V/3 (1978), pp.30-31. Also see the Chapter 'The Causes and Consequences of Migration', in J. Beaujeu-Garnier, *Geography of Population* (London, 1978)

212 Weiner, Myron, *Sons of the Soil: Migration and Ethnic Conflict in India* (New Delhi, 1978); Also see, Murayama, Mayumi, 'Borders, Migration and Sub-Regional Cooperation in Eastern South Asia' *Economic and Political Weekly* XLI/14 (2006), pp.1351- 59

213 Bona-fide Indian citizens have often been at the receiving end of xenophobic outbursts. Mistrust and fear is the obvious fallout of inter-community clashes.

214 The Chakma Tribes fled from their homeland in the CHT in Bangladesh to escape state repression and religious persecution. The construction of the Kaptai hydroelectric project in 1962, submerged their traditional lands making them homeless. Further, the state-sponsored schemes meant to settle people from the plains in their traditional habitat resulted in ethnic strife. All this led to the flight of the Chakmas to neighbouring India. By 1987, there were about 30,000 such refugees spread over several camps in North East India. See, Ghosh: *Unwanted and Uprooted*, p.37

215 Hazarika: *Strangers of the Mist*, p.10

216 Available online at http://www.unicef.org/infobycountry bangladesh_ bangladesh_ statistics.html

217 For detail on environmental migrants see, Maddock, Rowland T., 'Environmental Security', in M. Jane Davis (ed), *Security Issues in the Post-Cold War World* (UK, 1996)

218 See, Wriggins, W. Howard and James F. Guyot, 'Demographic Change and Politics: An Introduction', in W. Howard Wriggins and James F. Guyot (eds), *Population, Politics and the Future of Southern Asia* (New York, 1973), pp.1-29

219 The Task Force on Border Management puts the figure to 15 million with 300,000 Bangladeshi's illegally crossing over to India every month. See, 'Task Force to Consider Measures for Improving Border Management', No.C-182/1/2000,available at http://mod.nic.in/new additions/annexe.pdf. Also see, Bhuyan, J.C., 'Illegal Migration from Bangladesh and the Demographic Change in the

N.E. Region' *Dialogue Quarterly* III/3 (2002), pp.71-82; Saikia, Anil, Homeswar Goswami and Atul Goswami, *Population Growth in Assam 1951-1991: With Focus on Migration* (New Delhi, 2003); *The Times of India*, 'Bangladesh influx posing threat to security', 19 April, 2008; *The Times of India*, 'Bangladesh will eat up N-E, warns Neso', 18 September 2004

220 Bhuyan: 'Illegal Migration from Bangladesh and the Demographic Change in the N.E. Region', pp.71-82; Also see, *The Times of India*, 'Census report rattles Assam: influx blamed for high growth', 9 September 2004

221 *Ibid*

222 Between 1971 and 1991, there was 77.42 per cent growth in Muslim population in Assam. The proportion of Muslims in the total population of the state grew from 28.43 in 1991 to 30.91 per cent in 2001. The 2001 GOI census reveals that six districts in Assam have a Muslim majority population. The language data also presents an alarming picture. The percentage of Assamese speakers in the state declined to 48.80 in 2001, down from 57.81 in 1991. See, Talukdar, Sushanta, 'On the boil' *Frontline* XXV/1 (2008), pp.36-38

223 *The Arunachal Times* (Itanagar) 'Abnormal Rise in Assam Population Draws UN Attention', 21 May 2005

224 See, Kotwal, Dinesh, 'Instability Parameters in Northeast India' *Strategic Analysis* XXIV/1 (2000), pp.137-149

225 Although Nagaland does not share borders with Bangladesh, illegal migrants are infiltrating into the state from Assam, with which Nagaland shares nearly 500 kms long land border. Accurate estimates of the numbers of illegal migrants staying in Nagaland are not easy to come by. Available estimates vary between 75,000 and 300,000. In a state of barely 2 million population, the number is significant. See, Singh, M. Amarjeet, 'Nagaland: Another Bangladeshi Destination' *South Asia Intelligence Review* V/4 (2006). Also see, Das, Amiya Kumar, *Assam's Agony* (New Delhi, 1992)

226 For details see, Weiner, Myron, (1985) 'On International Migration and International Relation' *Population and Development Review* XI/3 (1985), pp.441-455; Weiner, Myron, (1993) 'Rejected Peoples and Unwanted Migrants in South Asia' *Economic and Political Weekly* XXVIII/35, (1993), pp.1745-46

227 It is extremely difficult to establish the numbers of illegal migrants as they are not counted in official statistics. It is an undocumented phenomenon.

228 See, Governor's Report to the President of India on Illegal Migration from Bangladesh, 8 November 1998. Available online, *South Asia Terrorism Portal* <http://www.satp.org>

229 According to the White Paper published by the Government of Arunachal Pradesh in 1996, the settlement of the Chakma and Hajong refugees by the GOI in the vacant lands of certain districts of the state was a strategic decision to help 'strengthen our frontiers and their defence'. The 1981 census recorded the Chakma population as 24,083 and that of the Hajongs as 1,433. The numbers rose to 30,062 and 2,134 respectively in 1991 and as of now the combined figures are believed to be around 65,000. See, Talukdar, Ratna Bharali, 'State of Denial', *Frontline* XXV/17 (2008)

230 *The Arunachal Times,* 'Arunachal Revolutionary Forces unite under NLFA', 18 June 2004

231 Hazarika: *Rites of Passage*, p.121; Also see, *The Times of India*, 'Eastern Disturbance', 27 May 2007; *The Times of India*, 'Battle Ground N-E', 27 May 2007; *The Times of*

India, 'ISI, Bangla helping north-east insurgents, says US think-tank', 25 April 2007; *The Times of India*, 'Immigrants from Bangla: Threat within', 14 July 2006

232 See, Perry, Alex, 'Deadly Cargo', *Time Asia*, 21 October 2002

233 *The Times of India*, 'ISI, Al-Qaeda assisting Assam Militants', 27 May 2004; *The Times of India*, 'Whose Sonar Bangla?', 12 *December* 2004. Also see, Perry, Alex, 'Deadly Cargo', *Time Asia*, 21 October 2002

234 Several transnational Islamic terrorist groups including Al-Qaeda, are known to have a presence in Bangladesh. The international linkages between the Jaish-e-Mohammed (JeM), Lashkar-e-Toiba (LeT) and the Harkat-ul-Jihad-Islami (HUJI) branches of Pakistan and Bangladesh came out into the open in the aftermath of the 2 January 2002 attack on the US Consulate in Kolkata. Despite repeated official denials, Bangladesh's active support to the ultra groups in India's North East is an open secret. Bangladesh's involvement in case of the Rohingya Muslims, the non-Burmese ethnic group of Burma is far more telling. The Rohingyas share religious affinity with the Bangladeshis and hence receive large-scale political and logistic support. The Rohingyas have emerged as the prime recruits for the Al-Qaeda operations in Bangladesh and elsewhere.

235 Char lands are the mid-channel sand bars that emerge in riverine border areas as the rivers change their course due to floods. For statistical data on the 'Chars', see, Government of Assam, *Socio-Economic Survey Report 2002-2003 of Char Areas of Assam*, Guwahati, Directorate of Char Areas Development Assam.

236 Cited in Jamwal, N.S., 'Border Management: Dilemma of Guarding the India-Bangladesh Border' *Strategic Analysis* XXVIII/1 (2004), p.6

237 While 'Enclaves' are the independent exclaves of a neighbouring country that perforate the host country, 'Adverse' possessions are the areas belonging to one country under the control of another. These territories have emerged as convenient points for illegal activities such as smuggling, import of contraband and entry point for infiltrators. See, Jamwal, N.S., 'Management of Land Borders' *Strategic Analysis* XXVI/3 (2002), p.47. Also see, Banerjee, Sumanta, 'Indo-Bangladesh Border: Radcliffe's Ghost' *Economic and Political Weekly* XXXVI/18 (2001)

238 India and Bangladesh share 4,095.7 kms long, topographically diverse, extremely porous border. The share of West Bengal is 2,216.7 kms, Tripura 856 kms, Meghalaya 443 kms, Mizoram 318 kms and Assam, 263 kms. See, *The Times of India*, 'CMs seek more security along border', 16 April 2005

239 The Director General of the Border Security Force (BSF) in a candid disclosure stated that cattle smugglers are involved in 90 per cent of the firing incidents on the Indo-Bangladesh border. According to him, the 300 odd cattle seized every day by the BSF get re-smuggled to Bangladesh. It is noteworthy that Bangladesh has emerged as one of the largest beef exporters in the world and also has a flourishing leather industry. See, 'BSF Fights Hustlers on Bangladesh Border' *Mail Today*, 28 August 2008; Hazarika: *Rites of Passage*, pp.204-238. Also see, Pramanik, Bimal 'Cattle Smuggling across the Indo-Bangladesh Border – An Analysis' *Dialogue* Quarterly VI/1 (2004), pp.66-73

240 The political arithmetic of the coalition that was voted to power in 2001, gave a fillip to the conservative ascendancy in Bangladesh. The coalition led by the Bangladesh National Party of Khaleda Zia was a four party alliance together with the Jamaat-e-Islami, Islamic Oikyo Jote and the Jatiyo Party. See, Parry, Alex, 'Deadly Cargo', *Time Asia*, 21 October 2002. Also see, *The Times of India*, 'Bangla terrorists thriving under state support', 27 February 2006

241 The leaders and the rank and file of most extremist organizations are drawn from the private madrassas that are spread across Bangladesh. A majority of these madrassas provide religious instructions according to the Deobandi school of Islam, the teachings of which has become synonymous with the radical variant of Islam, the origins traced to Maulana Abul Ala Maudidi (a Muslim intellectual in India) who in the 1950s defined Muslim politics in opposition to Indian nationalism. Lack of educational reforms is primarily responsible for the communalization of education in Bangladesh. A majority of the students in the Madrassas come from poor families and eventually end up as foot soldiers of the extremist organizations. Within Bangladesh, more than 3.34 million students are enrolled in the Madrassas spread across the country. It is believed that the number is nearly five times more than in Pakistan. See, Grisworld, Eliza, 'The Next Islamist Revolution?', *The New York Times*, 23 January 2005. Also see, Karlekar: *Bangladesh The Next Afghanistan?* ; Habib, Haroon, '17 August 2005: Milestone of Terror', in Jaideep Saikia (ed), *Bangladesh Treading The Taliban Trail*, pp.251-258

242 Barkat, Abul, 'Bangladesh Moulabader Arthaniti' (The Economics of Fundamentalism in Bangladesh), Dhaka: Jatiya Sahitya Prakashani, 2005, p.19, cited in Karlekar: *Bangladesh The Next Afghanistan?*

243 The author's conversations with BSF officials during a visit to the Indo-Bangladesh border in Tripura on 5 October 2007

244 Bhat, Anil, 'Pakistan and ISI's Eastward Operations', *The Sangai Express*, 26 January 2003. Also see, *The Northeast Sun*, 'Exposing the ISI-ULFA nexus', V/18 (2001)

245 Talukdar, Surajit, and Swapan Kumar Paul, 'High Security on Indo-Bangla Border: Assam Districts Fear Entry of Bangladesh-trained Militants', *The Pioneer*, 6 November 2003. Also see, Saikia, Jaideep, *Terror sans Frontiers: Islamic Militancy in North East India* (New Delhi, 2004); Pandey, Onkareshvar, 'ISI and New Wave of Islamic Militancy in the N.E.' *Dialogue Quarterly* III/3 (2002)

246 Litner, Bertil, 'Islamist Fundamentalism in Bangladesh', in Jaideep Saikia (ed), *Bangladesh: Treading the Taliban Trail* (New Delhi, 2006), p.57

247 The Ahmadiyyas have been living in Bangladesh since 1912. The Islamists demand that they be declared as non-muslims. See, Karlekar: *Bangladesh, The Next Afghanistan*, pp.59-60, pp.259- 264. Also see, Ghosh, Partha S., 'Conservative Ascendancy in Bangladesh' *South Asian Survey* XII/2 (2005)

248 Litner, Bertil, 'A Cocoon of Terror', *Far Eastern Economic Review*, 4 April 2002, p.14

249 See, US Department of State website, www.state.gov/it/rts/pgtrpt/2993, Appendix C, posted on 29 April 2004. Also see, Routray, Bibhu Prasad, 'India-Bangladesh: HUJI: Lengthening Shadow of Terror', *South Asia Intelligence Review* V/3 (2006)

250 Gunaratna, Rohan, *Inside Al Qaeda: Global Network of Terror* (New Delhi, 2002), p.219

251 The 23 February 1998 fatwa of Osama bin Laden, urging Jihad against the United States was co-signed by two Egyptian clerics, another one from Pakistan and Fazlul Rahman, the leader of the Jihad Movement in Bangladesh. See Bodansky, Yossef, *Bin Laden: The Man Who Declared War on America* (Rocklin, CA, 1999), pp.225-26

252 One such blast on 21 May 2004, at the shrine of Hazrat Shahjalal in the Sylhet district wounded the British High Commissioner to Bangladesh, Anwar Choudhury. Another blast on 21 August 2004, aimed at wiping the entire top

most leadership of the opposition Awami League resulted in the killing of several top leaders of the opposition. Again on 17 August 2005, Islamist terrorists triggered off as many as 459 timed explosive devices in 63 of Bangladesh's 64 districts within a span of thirty minutes. See, *The Daily Star*, 'It was an Attempt to Kill our Democracy', 24 August 2004; The *Daily Star*, 'Human Rights and the Assassination Attempt', 29 August 2004; *The Times of India*, 'Bangla gets taste of enemy within', 19 August 2005

253 Religious extremism in Bangladesh is not a new phenomenon. Hidden training camps, some inside mosques, madrassas and even orphanages are known to provide expertise in the art of assemblage and weapon use. Confessional statements of arrested militants reveal that they had been funded by Saudi Arabia and Pakistan. Fundings from the Revival of Islamic Heritage Society (RIHS), a Kuwait based organization has also been diverted for extremist cause. In 2002 the US State Department blacklisted some RIHS fronts, citing their support for Al-Qaeda. See, Habib, Haroon, '17 August 2005: Milestone of Terror', in Saikia: *Bangladesh: Treading the Taliban Trail*, pp.251-258

254 *The Assam Tribune*, 'Bangla influx posing threat to security', 19 April, 2008; *The Assam Tribune*, 'MPs concerned over unabated Bangla influx', 22 April, 2008; *The Times of India*, 'B'desh migrants pose security threat: house Panel', 19 April, 2008

255 For details on the proceedings of the conference see, *The Sentinel*, 2 November 2006; *The Assam Tribune*, 3 November 2006

256 Karlekar: *Bangladesh The Next Afghanistan*, pp.78-79

257 Talukdar, Sushant, 'On the boil', *Frontline* XXV/18 (2008), pp.36-38

258 According to Indian intelligence reports, in recent years there has been an unprecedented proliferation of madrassas, close to about 100,000, some of which are funded by the Jeddah based Islamic Development Bank. Saudi Wahabism and pro-Pakistanism are the dominant sentiments in many of these institutions. See, Shourie, Arun, 'Silent Demographic Invasion: Another Conference, Another Warning', *Indian Express*, 12 October 2004; *The Hindu*, 'Madarasas Along Bangla Border Have Increased: BSF', 4 May 2007

259 'ISI Activities in Assam', Statement laid on the table of the House of Assam Legislative Assembly, under item No. 12, dated 6.4.2000, by Shri Prafulla Kumar Mahanta, Chief Minister of Assam. Also see, *The Times of India*, 'Neso tells Centre: Curb ISI menace', 20 December 2005

260 Mukherjee, Krittivas, 'Madrassas are being used to provide shelter to ultras: Muslim clerics opposed action against unauthorized seminaries', *The Pioneer*, 25 January 2002

261 According to an estimate provided by the Assam Governor in his report, 5000-6000 Bangladeshi's illegally enter India on a daily basis. Also see, *The Assam Tribune*, 'MPs concerned over unabated Bangla influx', 22 April, 2008

262 See, Kumar, Anand, 'Bangladesh emerges as Biggest Clandestine Arms Supplier in South Asia', *South Asia Tribune*, 11-17 April 2004

263 Routray, Bibhu Prasad, 'Beyond the Bandarban Recoveries' *South Asia Intelligence Review* IV/18 (2005)

264 *Ibid*

265 The author's interview with a senior BSF official in New Delhi on 3 May 2008

266 Saikia, Jaideep, 'Terror sans Frontiers: Islamic Militancy in North East India', *Occasional Paper*, Program in Arms Control, Disarmament and International

Security, University of Illinois, Urbana-Champaign, 2003. Also see, Routray, Bibhu Prasad, 'India: Northeast: Long Shadows of Subversion' *South Asia Intelligence Review* V/2 (2006)

267 The author's conversations with BSF officials revealed that at least 176 insurgent camps are actively operating in Bangladesh under the patronage of DGFI and ISI. See, *The Hindu*, 'Madrasas along Bangla Border have increased: BSF', 4 May 2007; *Assam Tribune*, 'India seeks closure of 155 Ultra Camps in Bangladesh', 12 May 2003; *Assam Tribune*, 'Ultra camps in Bangladesh', 14 May 2003

268 Terrorist strikes on Hindi-speaking population – mainly migrant labourers – have hit the headlines in November-December 2003. There has been repetition of similar strikes in the following years with major strikes in January 2007 and in August 2007. According to the Indian intelligence reports, Bangladesh based fundamentalist outfits actively helped the ULFA in targeting Hindi speaking people as well as in executing a series of terrorist strikes. Between 2007 and 2008, the ULFA killed nearly 70 Hindi speaking people across several districts of Assam. The violence against the migrants also engulfed the hill district of Karbi Anglong where about 40 Hindi speaking people lost their lives during 2007-2008. See, *The Times of India* 'Centre sleeps as Ulfa Strikes again', 12 August, 2007

269 Sanjukta Mukti Bahini, Asom, Prachar Patra, July 1992, cited in Udyon Misra, *The Periphery Strikes Back*, pp.141-142

270 For details on predicaments of migrants see, Basch, Linda, Nina Glick Schiller and Cristina Szanton Blanc, *Nations Unbound: Transnational Projects, Postcolonial Predicaments and De-territorialized Nation-States* (Langhorne, Pa.: Gordon and Breach, 1994); Sheffer, Gabriel, *Diaspora Politics: At Home Abroad* (Cambridge, 2003)

271 Das: *Assam's Agony*, p.58, as cited in Vivek Chadha, *Low Intensity Conflicts in India – An Analysis* (New Delhi, 2005), p.235

272 Fernandes, Walter, 'IMDT Act and Immigration in North-Eastern India' *Economic and Political Weekly* XL/30 (2005), pp.3237-3240

273 The Illegal Migrants (Determination by Tribunals) Act, 1983. Available online, *South Asia Terrorism Portal* http://www.satp.org/satporgtp/countries/india/states/assam/documents/actsand ordinances/the_illegal_ migrants_act.htm

274 Editorial, *The Sentinel*, 16 December 2004

275 Governor of Assam's Report to the President of India on Illegal Migration from Bangladesh.

276 Hussain, Wasbir 'Assam: New Turn to Citizenship Politics' *South Asia, Intelligence Review* IV/1 (2005). Also see, Prabhakara, M.S., 'Understanding a Controversial Legislation', *The Hindu*, 23 July 2005

277 The Congress Party, during whose tenure in New Delhi the Act was introduced in 1983, has all along backed the Act. The Party, as head of the United Progressive Alliance (UPA) coalition government in Delhi, promised to enact a new exclusive law to deal with the foreigners issue in Assam – a law that would take into consideration the grievances of the minorities. In a meeting chaired by the Prime Minister on 14 July 2005 in Delhi, it was decided to form a Group of Ministers to hear different points of view on the IMDT Act and come up with appropriate response. Subsequently the Union Government passed an amendment to the Foreigners Order of 2006 (Tribunals of Assam), where once again the onus of proving the nationality was put on the complainant. This Order was challenged in the Supreme Court and a bench of Justices S.P. Sinha and P.K. Balasubramanian,

declared the 2006 Government Order as illegal and unconstitutional. See, *The Hindu*, 'Centre to amend Foreigners Act', 11 February 2006

278 *The Times of India*, 'SC blames Act for surge in migrants', 16 July 2005. Also see, *The Times of India*, 'Court caution on Bangla influx', 27 April 2006; *The Times of India*, 'Politics behind Bangla influx: BSF', 31 January 2006

279 Talukdar, Sushant, 'On the boil' *Frontline* XXV/18 (2008), pp.36-38

280 *The Daily Star* (Internet edition), News Report, 'Morshed Comments: India Summons Envoy, Expresses Dismay', 11 September 2004

281 See, Krasner, Stephen D., *Sovereignty: Organized Hypocrisy* (Princeton, NJ, 1999)

282 The Kargil war was an armed conflict between India and Pakistan that took place between May and July 1999 in the Kargil district of Kashmir. Infiltration of Pakistani soldiers and Kashmiri militants into positions on the Indian side of the Line of Control (the *de facto* border), triggered the conflict. The GOI constituted a four-member committee on 29 July 1999, to recommend measures to strengthen the security of the nation. The committee presented its report to the Parliament on 23 February 2000.

283 See Subrahmanyam, K., *Kargil Review Committee*, Government of India, Para 14.16

284 The GoM was headed by the Home Minister and included the Defence Minister, External Affairs Minister and the Finance Minister. *Recommendations of the Group of Ministers*, 'Reforming the National Security System', Government of India, February 2001; 'Task Force to Consider Measures for Improving Border Management', No.C-182/1/2000-NSCS (CS), Cabinet Secretariat, (National Security Council Secretariat), 16 May 2000, available at http://mod.nic.in/newadditions/annexe. pdf

285 See, Singh, Prakash, 'Border Management', *BSF Journal*, Border Security Force (BSF) Academy Tekanpur (Gwalior), July 2001, p.11

286 There is about 6.5 kms of area with Bangladesh that still remain undemarcated. About 1.5 kms in the Daikhata (Berubari sector in West Bengal), about 2.5 kms in Muhuri River (Belonia sector of Tripura), and about 2.5 kms in Lalthitilla (Dumabari area of Assam). See, Jamwal: 'Border Management: Dilemma of Guarding the India-Bangladesh Border', pp.18-20

287 *Ibid.*, p.21-22; *The Times of India*, 'Fencing on Indo-Bangla border in full swing in Assam', 6 February 2008

288 *The Assam Tribune*, 'Land Acquisition Delaying Border Fencing: CM', 26 April 2007

289 *Times of India*, 'Bangladeshi smugglers thrive on child couriers', 16 April 2006

290 Datta, Sreeradha, 'Indo-Bangladesh Relations: An Overview of Limitations and Constraints' *Strategic Analysis* XXVI/3 (2002), p.433

291 *The Telegraph*, 'BDR Objects to fence range', 14 March, 2008

292 The Agreement, subject to ratification by the two countries was ratified by Bangladesh in November 1974. Ratification by India is still awaited on the ground that in the absence of complete demarcation of the border, parliamentary approval cannot be obtained. See, Jamwal: 'Border Management: Dilemma of Guarding the India-Bangladesh Border', p.30

293 Besides the BSF, there are other agencies active on the borders for the purpose of intelligence gathering, law enforcement and implementation of development programmes.

294 The author interviewed a senior BSF official in New Delhi on 10 April 2008

295 Bangladesh is one of the poorest country in the world, characterized by continued low level of socio-economic development, low literacy and high infant mortality, low status of women and a predominantly agrarian economy. Considering its economic standing, illegal migration is likely to intensify in the years to come. The fallout of global warming will also have significant implications on population displacement. A metre rise in sea level, according to a study by the Bangladesh Centre for Advanced Studies, will result in about 17.5 per cent of the total land area being inundated and 11 per cent of the population being displaced. Consequently, the displaced population will have little option but to look for living space in the sparsely populated neighbourhood. See, Amin, J.R. Chowdhury, A.U. Ahmed, R. B. Hill and M. Kabir, 'Reproductive Change in Bangladesh: Evidence from Recent Data', *Asia-pacific Population Journal* VIII/4 (1993), pp.39-58; Saha, Bimal Kumar, 'Changing Pattern of Agrarian Structure in Bangladesh: 1984-1996', in Abu Abdullah (ed), *Bangladesh Economy 2000, Selected Issues* (Dhaka, 2001), pp.73-85

296 For details on the 'self-perpetuating dynamism' of illegal migration see, Hugo, Grame, 'Illegal International Migration in Asia', in Robin Cohen (ed), *The Cambridge Survey of World Migration* (Cambridge, 1995), pp.397-402

Part III

1 Sonderland, Walter C., 'An Analysis of Guerrilla Insurgency and Coup d' Etat as Techniques of Indirect Aggression' *International Studies Quarterly* (1970), p.345

2 Crenshaw, Martha, 'Questions to be answered, research to be done, knowledge to be applied', in Walter Reich (ed), *Origins of Terrorism: Psychologies, Ideologies, Theologies, State of Mind* (New York, 1990), p.258

3 Crenshaw: 'Questions to be answered', p.256

4 Bealey, F., *The Blackwell Dictionary of Political Science* (Oxford, 1999), p.319

5 Bajpai, Kanti P., *Roots of Terrorism* (New Delhi, 2000), p.104

6 Nieburg, H.L., *Political Violence: The Behavioral Process* (New York, 1969), p.13

7 Huntington, Samuel P., *Political Order in Changing Societies* (New Haven, 1968), pp.4-5

8 Tilly, Charles, *From Mobilization to Revolution* (New York, 1978), pp.69-70

9 Gurr, Ted, Robert, *Minorities at Risk: A Global View of Ethnopolitical Conflicts* (Washington, 1993), pp.123-124

10 Kanti: *Roots of Terrorism*, p.118

11 For details see, Sharma, Arvind K., 'District Councils in the North-East', in T.N. Chaturvedi (ed), *Fifty Years of Indian Administration: Retrospect and Prospect* (New Delhi, 1998)

12 Relatively large scale military operations by units of at least a company strength have been conducted in the region. There are also instances of even larger operations. See, Rajgopalan, Rajesh, 'Restoring Normalcy: The Evolution of the Indian Army's Counter-insurgency Doctrine' *Small Wars & Insurgencies* XI/1 (2000), pp.44-68

13 Among the paramilitary forces, the Assam Rifles is the oldest and the largest. Although its home territory is Assam, it has an all India representation and is led

by Indian Army officers on secondment and also by officers appointed from its own ranks.

14 The 'Unified Command' was formed in January 1997.

15 Several incumbents to the office of the Governor have been individuals from the security establishment, ranging from retired military personnels, retired police officers to the head of the Research and Analysis Wing (RAW) – the intelligence agency engaged in operations abroad and at home. Continuing with this trend, an Ex-Army Chief was appointed the Governor of Arunachal Pradesh and the former Border Security Force Director was made the Governor of Meghalaya. See, Baruah, Sanjib, *Durable Disorder, Understanding the Politics of Northeast India* (New Delhi, 2005), pp.59-80; *Mail Today*, 'Ex-Army Chief J.J. Singh new Arunachal Guv', 25 January 2008; *Mail Today*, 'Generals who are Centre's eyes & ears', 27 January 2008

16 See, Appendix I

17 These courts were established in 1984, after the launching of 'Operation Bluestar' by the security forces to flush out Sikh militants from the Golden Temple Complex in Amritsar (Punjab). This Act was especially meant to deal with terrorist offences.

18 Section 2 (1)h, Terrorist Affected Areas (Special Powers) Act. See, Appendix J

19 Section 2 (f) Terrorist and Disruptive Activities Prevention Bill 1985. See, Appendix K

20 POTA was to be a diluted version of TADA. While an accused could be kept in police custody for 60 days under TADA, under POTA, the confinement in police custody could not go beyond 30 days. Besides, while TADA permitted an accused to be kept in judicial custody for one year, POTA allowed that for 180 days. The minimum punishment under TADA was five years while under POTA it was three years. For the full text of POTA see, Appendix M

21 173rd Report of the Law Commission, p.10.

22 For the full text of the Ordinance see, http:// www.satp.org/satporgtp/countries/india/document/actandordinances/the_unlawful_activities__amendord2004.htm.

23 Pillai, S.K., 'Preparing for the Future', in Pushpita Das and Namrata Goswami (eds), *India's North East: New Vistas for Peace* (New Delhi, 2008), p.193

24 Bhaumik, Subir, 'Insurgencies in India's Northeast: Conflict Co-option & Change' *East West Center* Working Paper No.10 (Washington, 2007), p.12

25 Indian Army Training Command, Doctrine for Sub-Conventional Operations (Shimla, Headquarters Army Training Command, 2007)

26 Indian Army Doctrine, October 2004, p.54. Available online at http:// indianarmy.nic.in/indianarmydoctrine.htm.

27 Government of India, 'Armed Forces (Assam and Manipur) Special Powers (Amendment) Act-1972'. No. 7 of 1972 (April 5). Reprinted in *Where 'Peacekeepers' Have Declared War*, New Delhi: National Campaign Committee Against Militarization and Repeal of the Armed Forces (Special Powers) Act, 1997. For the full text of the Act see Appendix G

28 Baruah: *Durable Disorder, Understanding the Politics of Northeast India*, p.70-72

29 The 2006 State Assembly elections in Assam, brought in new actors who till very recently, were described as terrorists and had relentlessly waged war against the State. The Hagrama Mohilary faction of the Bodo People's Progressive Front (BBPF-H), with its leadership comprising principally of surrendered militants of the Bodo Liberation Tigers, secured an overwhelming victory in the Bodo

Territorial Council (BTC) areas, capturing 12 out of the 18 seats it contested in the 126-member Assam Assembly. They became a part of the ruling coalition, occupying three ministerial berths. See, Singh, Amarjeet, 'Assam: Bodos' Troubled Politics' *South Asian Intelligence Review* IV/44 (2006)

30 Hampshire, Stuart, *Innocence and Experience* (Cambridge, 1989), p.72-78

31 For further details see, Murphy, Jeffrie G., and Jean Hampton, *Forgiveness and Mercy* (Cambridge, 1990)

32 Bhargava, Rajiv, 'Between Revenge and Reconciliation', in Ranabir Samaddar (ed), *Peace Studies* (New Delhi, 2004), pp.390-412

33 Ramesh, Jairam, 'Northeast India in a new Asia' *Seminar* 550 (2005), pp.17- 21

34 The GOI contributes heavily towards the total expenditure of the North Eastern States. In case of Arunachal Pradesh it is 85 per cent of the total expenditure; in Assam 51 per cent; in Meghlaya 70 per cent; in Manipur 80 per cent; in Nagaland 80 per cent; in Tripura 70 per cent and in Mizoram 72 per cent. Out of the IR 30,0000 million that is spent in the region annually, close to IR 20,0000 million directly comes from the Central Government. *Ibid*, p.19

35 Sachdeva, Gulshan, 'Demystifying Northeast' *Dialogue Quarterly* VII/3 (2006), pp.74-84

36 Boulding, Kenneth, 'Peace and the Evolutionary Process', in Raimo Vayrynem, Dieter Senghaas and Christian Schmidt (eds), *The Quest for Peace: Transcending Collective Violence and War Among Societies, Cultures, and States,* (Beverly Hills, CA, 1987), pp.48-59

37 Deutsch, Karl, et al., 'Political Community and the North Atlantic Area', pp.5-9 as cited in Kanti P. Bajpai, 'Peace Audit on South Asia', in Ranabir Samaddar: pp.38-71

38 Bajpai: 'Peace Audit on South Asia', *Ibid*, pp.62- 63

39 For a detailed understanding of the concept of 'Social Capital' see, Putnam, Robert, *Making Democracy Work* (Princeton, 1993), pp.48-59

40 See, Dreze, Jean & Amartya Sen, (eds) *Indian Development: Selected Regional Perspectives* (New Delhi, 1997)

41 Smith, Antony, 'Culture, Community and Territory: The Politics of Ethnicity and Nationalism' *International Affairs* LXXII/3 (1996), p.454

42 Ray, Animash, *Mizoram Dynamics of Change* (Calcutta, 1982), p.57

43 Established in 1917, the Assam Sahitya Sabha is a premier literary organization of Assam. The Bodo Sahitya Sabha was established in 1952, as the vanguard of Bodo language and literature. These bodies not only provide cultural anchorage but also serve as a forum for public action.

44 Saikia, Yasmin, 'The Tai-Ahom connection' *Seminar* 550 (2005), pp.59-64

45 See, Baruah, Sanjib, *India Against Itself, Assam the Politics of Nationality* (New Delhi, 1999); Nag, Sajal, *Roots of Ethnic Conflict: Nationality Question in North East India* (New Delhi, 1990); Verghese, B.G., *India's Northeast Resurgent, Insurgency, Governance, Development* (New Delhi, 1996)

46 The NSCN (IM) demand for 'Greater Nagaland', Mizo National Front's demand for 'Greater Mizoram', during the hey days of the Mizo insurgency and the Kuki National Army's demand for 'Kukiland', cut across the political boundaries of India, Bangladesh, Burma and China. The Imperial policy of leaving the borders loosely unadministered in the erstwhile NEFA (present day Arunachal Pradesh)

is the source of contentious territorial claims between India and China. See, Hazarika, Joyshankar, *Geopolitics of North East India* (New Delhi, 1996), pp.108-39

47 See, Ingam, Attracta, *A Political Theory of Rights* (Oxford, 1994), pp.118-9

48 *Agradoot*, 25 February 1990. Cited in Das, Samir Kumar, *Ethnicity, Nation And Security* (New Delhi, 2003), p.68

49 Some important bilateral agreements between India and the countries in her eastern neighbourhood are: the December 1968 Agreement of Trade between the Government of the Republic of India and the Government of Thailand (December 1968); Agreement of Trade between the Government of the Republic of India and the Government of the Union of Burma (May 27, 1970); Trade Agreement between the Government of the Republic of India and the Government of the Republic of the Philippines (May 29, 1979); Indo-Nepal treaties of trade, of transit, and agreement for co-operation to control unauthorized trade (December 3, 1996); and Trade Agreement between the Government of the Republic of India and the Government of Malaysia (October 11, 2000).

50 On his India visit in September 2004, the Director General of the Bangladesh Rifles, Major Gen. Mohammad Jahangir Alam Khan Chowdhury, blatantly denied any cross-border movements of population from Bangladesh to India. He also categorically denied about the existence of a 'single insurgent camp in Bangladesh'. See, Vij-Aurora, Bhavana, 'No Infiltration from Bangla, Says BDR DG', *The Indian Express*, 29 September 2004; Rana, Ajit, 'Indian Economy no better than ours', *The Pioneer*, 29 September 2004

51 There is historical evidence to suggest that North East India had extensive economic and social links with the neighbouring region of Tibet, Bhutan, Burma and Indo-China. It formed the southern trail of the silk route that connected Western China with Central and South Asia. See, Khanna, Sushil, 'Economic opportunities or continuing stagnation', *Seminar* 550 (2005), pp.22-27; Baruah, Sanjib, 'Between South and Southeast Asia: Northeast India and the Look East Policy', *CENISEAS PAPERS – 4* (Guwahati, 2004); Sarma, Atul, 'Northeast as Gateway to Southeast Asia: Big Dreams and Home Truths', in S. Borbora and J.K. Gogoi (eds), *Development Issues in the Northeast in the Turn of the Century* (Guwahati, 2007), pp.11-27.

52 Mohan, C. Raja, 'A Foreign Policy for the East', *The Hindu*, 27 August 2004

53 Ramesh: 'Northeast India in a new Asia', pp.17-21

54 Although India has formally stated its support for democratization and political reconciliation in Myanmar/Burma, it has also taken cognizance to the dictates of realpolitik that demands constructive engagement with the military junta. This becomes necessary mainly due to Bangladesh's policy of denial and non-cooperation in regard to the existence of sanctuaries for Indian ultras in its territory. Accordingly in 1993, there was a reversal in India's policy towards Burma. Both the countries conducted a joint operation – 'Golden Bird' – in April-May 1995, against the North East ultras. However, Myanmar abandoned the operation mid-way after India awarded the Nehru Peace Prize to Aung Sang Suu, the leader of the Restoration of Democracy Movement. In 1998, India obliged Myanmar through the controversial 'Operation Leech' operations in the high seas, by cracking down on Burmese rebel groups. In October 2004, India and Myanmar signed a memorandum of understanding on 'cooperation in non-traditional security issues'. The MOU covers terrorism, arms smuggling, money laundering, drug smuggling and so forth. Myanmar's Senior General Tah Shwe

assured India that terrorist groups would not be allowed to operate from Myanmar. There is also an economic imperative behind India's attempt to improve ties with Myanmar. These include, stronger transport links and exploitation of energy resources. Haider, Salman, 'The General's visit: uneasy questions', *The Statesman*, 2 November 2004; The *Times of India*, 'Myanmar begins 'crackdown' on ULFA', 11 June 2006

55 Proposals for a multi-modal transport corridor liking Burma to North East India was formally approved during this visit. The project on completion will provide North East India an outlet to the sea. See, *Times of India*, 'Transport corridor tops Myanmar gen's agenda', 31 March 2008

56 For further details see, Grare, Frederic & Amitabh Mattoo, (eds) *India and ASEAN* (New Delhi, 2001)

57 Sarma: 'Northeast as Gateway to Southeast Asia: Big Dreams and Home Truths' pp.11-27

58 Samarasinghe, Stanley W., and Dushyantha Mendis, 'The Concept of Gateways in a Globalizing World', Paper presented in a Seminar on *Towards Greater Cooperation Between South and South East Asia: The Importance of India's North East Playing Bridge and Buffer Role,* organized by O.K.D. Institute of Social Change and Development, Guwahati (Assam), 16-19 November 2004

59 The South Asian Association for Regional Co-operation or SAARC, proposed by Ziaur Rahman, the then president of Bangladesh, was established on 8 December 1985. SAARC is an association of 8 countries of South Asia, namely Afganistan, Bangladesh, Bhutan, India, Maldives, Nepal, Pakistan and Sri Lanka. These countries comprise about a fifth of the population of the world. SAARC was conceptualized as an organization that would accelerate economic growth, create conducive conditions for the formation of unified market, promote a regional transportation network and bring about social development in the region.

60 Haider, Salman, 'Sub-regional initiatives', *The Statesman*, 10 August 2004

61 *The Times of India*, 'Singh ushers in more Indo-Asean trade, says an Asian community can create an 'Arc of Advantage' against EU, Nafta', 20 October 2004

62 Pandey, Nishchal N., *India's North-Eastern Region: Insurgency, Economic Development and Linkages with South-East Asia* (New Delhi, 2008), pp.105

63 It was an exercise in Track-II diplomacy, initiated by Yunan, the southwest province of China with full support from Beijing. It was a conference on regional cooperation and development with participation from China, India, Burma and Bangladesh. The thrust of the conference was to prompt the respective governments to improve connectivity and interactions between the south-western region of China and the north-eastern Indian states with road, waterway, air and rail links.

64 *The Hindu*, 'Centre Approves Agreement on Asian Highways', 26 August 2004.

65 See, Sarma: 'Northeast as Gateway to Southeast Asia: Big Dreams and Home Truths', pp.11-27; Choudhury, Saswati, 'North-East India and the Look East Policy: A Contextual Analysis' *Dialogue Quarterly* VII/3; Nath. D., (ed), *Reopening of The Stilwell Road, Prospects And Problems* (New Delhi, 2004)

66 Hilly terrain accounts for 70 per cent of the region.

67 At present, all commerce to North East India, skirts along the long border with Bangladesh and travels through the narrow Siliguri corridor in northern West

Bengal. This is due to the reluctance on the part of Bangladesh to allow the movement of Indian goods across its territory.

68 See, Sharma, Ashok B., 'India, Myanmar expects Kaladan project to increase border trade' *The Financial Express*, 4 April 2008; Mohan, C. Raja, 'To the North East through Myanmar' *The Hindu*, 28 November 2002

69 Keynote address of External Affairs Minister at the Institute for Security and International Studies (ISIS), Chulalongkorn University, on 'India's Look East Policy: Implications for Thailand and South East Asia'.

70 *The Assam Tribune*, 'Move to improve NE-Bangla links', 15 February, 2008

71 See, Egreteau, Renaud, *Wooing the Generals, India's new Burma Policy* (New Delhi, 2003)

72 Bajpai: *Roots of Terrorism*, p.139-141

73 The initiative began in October 1997 and took shape a year later in November 1998.

74 See, Sobhan, R., 'Regional Cooperation in South Asia: A Quest for Identity' *South Asian Survey* V/1 (1990), pp.3-26

75 Das, Samir Kumar, 'The ethnic dimension' *Seminar* 550 (2005), pp.65-69

76 See, 'PM releases North Eastern Region Vision 2020 Document, 2 July 2008, available online at http://www.pmindia.nic.in/speech/content4print.asp?id=693; *The Times of India*, 'In a first, MEA to be involved in N-E growth', 5 November 2007; *The Times of India*, 'Aiyar: Liberate N-E states from geopolitical trap', 25 September 2007

77 Das: *Ethnicity, Nation and Security*, pp.174-178

78 *Ibid*

79 For details see, Gundevia, Y.D., *War and Peace in Nagaland* (Dehradun, 1975)

80 For details on the role of the Naga Mothers' Association towards conflict resolution see, Patra, Soumyajit and Samita Manna, 'Integrative Reconciliation: Mothers in the Naga Movement' *Economic and Political Weekly* XLIII/10 (2008), pp.21-23

81 On 23 November 2007, armed cadres and some senior functionaries of the warring NSCN (IM) and NSCN (K) factions met at Hovishe under the Niuland sub-division of Dimapur district, to work out a inter-factional truce aimed at unifying the two warring factions. The agreement led to the emergence of the NSCN (U) and triggered a fresh wave of interceneine violence that has claimed many lives. The alignment of Naga groups along tribal lines has accentuated the schism among them. It is noteworthy that the NSCN is mostly made of the Thangkhuls, the NSCN (U) of Semas, the NSCN (K) of Konyaks, while the Naga National Council (NNC) comprises mainly of Angamis. The other major tribe is the Ao, having cadres in all the three factions but mainly NSCN (IM).

82 Presidents Rule was declared in the State on 3 January 2008, two months prior to the completion of the five year tenure of the coalition government led by Democratic Alliance of Nagaland. In retaliation, the NSCN (IM) declared a 'state of emergency' in Nagaland, protesting against the imposition of the President's Rule. See, Routray, Prasad Bibhu, 'Confusion Compounded' *South Asia Intelligence Review* VI/28 (2008); *The Times of India*, 'NSCN-K slaps quit notice on Muivah's tribe', 18 August 2006

83 Mukhim, Patricia, 'Of Ambiguous Peace Dialogues' *Dialogue Quarterly* VII/4 (2006), pp.13-16

84 The Thirteenth Amendment of the Constitution of India (1962), which led to the creation of the State of Nagaland, inserted Clause 371A that enjoined some special provisions to preserve the Naga 'way of life'. This clause stated in unambiguous terms that notwithstanding anything in the Constitution, no act of parliament would apply to the State of Nagaland in regard to religious and social practices of Nagas; Naga customary law and procedure; administration of civil and criminal justice; and ownership and transfer of land and its resources, unless the Nagaland legislative assembly resolves to opt for it. See, Misra,Udayon, 'Naga Peace Talks, High Hopes and Hard Realities' *Economic and Political Weekly* XXXVIII/7 (2003)

85 Quoted in Misra : *Ibid*

86 In the 2003 Nagaland Assembly elections, the Democratic Alliance of Nagaland – a coalition of Naga regional parties and the Bharatiya Janata Party formed the government.

87 Over the past ten years, little progress has been made in resolving the conflict, except extending the ceasefire agreement. The National Security Advisor M.K. Narayanan, on a visit to Nagaland in February 2008, admitted that the Naga peace process had slowed down and the process could only move forward if the NSCN (IM) agreed to a solution within the parameters of the Constitution. *The Hindu*, 'Naga peace process has slowed down', 18 February 2008; *The Assam Tribune*, 'Centre tells NSCN(IM) to study statute', 14 May 2008; Talukdar, Sushanta, 'Rebel Rule' *Frontline* XXIV/17 (2007)

88 *The Times of India*, 'Truce snap may spill blood', 19 May 2006. Also see, *The Times of India*, 'Back to war if talks fail: Naga Hoho', 29 May 2006

89 On 22 January 2006, upto ten bombings and grenade attacks engineered by the outlawed ULFA across Assam disrupted operations in the gas, oil and power sectors. See, Hussain, Wasbir, 'ULFA Talks Tough With Bombings' *South Asia Intelligence Review* IV/24 (2006)

90 Between 8 and 10 June 2006, Assam was rocked by twenty explosions, leaving six civilians dead and more than 70 wounded, several of them security force personnel. The attacks carried out by Improvised Explosive Device (IED) and hand grenades targeted the capital city Guwahati, the police and the paramilitary, railway tracks and crude oil and natural gas pipelines. As recently as 30 October 2008, nearly a dozen serial blasts went off almost simultaneously in Guwahati and the adjoining districts of Barpeta, Bongaigaon and Kokrajhar, killing at least 80 people and injuring around 300. RDX based explosives were used in some of these blasts and it is believed to be the handiwork of the local militants in collaboration with HUJI. See, *The Indian Express,* 'Terror wave across Assam', 31 October 2008; *The Hindu*, 'Assam blasts death toll 75', 1 November 2008; *The Times of India*, 'Car bombs were used in Guwahati blasts', 1 November 2008

91 The PCG threatened to pull out of the peace talks, on the eve of the second round of talks, in protest against what it called 'atrocious actions by men in uniform'. This reaction was in protest to the killing of a person in Upper Assam on 6 February 2006. The person was earlier apprehended by the Army on charges of being an ULFA linkman and died while in custody. See, Routrary, Bibhu Prasad, 'Terror, Migrants and Politics' *South Asia Intelligence Review* IV/32 (2006)

92 The 28th battalion of the ULFA is believed to be its strongest wing with more than 250 trained cadres and training facilities in Burma. *The Hindu,* 'Two companies of ULFA battalion declare ceasefire', 25 June 2008; *The Times of India*, 'Rift in ULFA camp as 'rebels' want leaders to hold talks', 1 September 2008

93 In Mizoram, several rounds of talks have been held between the Mizo Government and the leadership of the Bru National Liberation Front over the repatriation of 35,000 Bru refugees. In November 2003, the Government of Assam announced a general amnesty for the Bodo Liberation Tigers (BLT), which resulted in the surrender of a big number of BLT cadres, including its chairman, Hagrama Basumatary. Since 1 July 2005, ceasefire has been in place between the GOI and the NDFB. In April 2004, two factions of the NLFT signed a ceasefire agreement with the Tripura government. In July 2004, the Achik National Volunteer Council (ANVC) signed a tripartite agreement with the GOI, and the Meghalaya government for an immediate six-month ceasefire to be followed by the initiation of a peace process. A Joint Monitoring Group, with representatives from the Meghalaya government, ANVC, Army and the Central Reserve Police Force was assigned the task of monitoring the ceasefire.

94 *The Times of India*, 'Seven Sisters, One Resolution: Peace', 1 January 2006

95 Muni, S.D., 'Terrorism and Interstate Relations in South Asia', in Sridhar K. Khatri & Gert W. Kueck (eds), *Terrorism In South Asia* (New Delhi, 2003), pp.330

96 Chari, P. R., 'Combating Terrorism: Devising Cooperative Countermeasures', in *Ibid*, p. 438

97 See, Lewis, William. H., 'The War on Terror: A Retrospective' *Mediterranean Quarterly* XIII/4 (2002), pp.21-37

98 Kumar, Rupesinghe, 'Developing a Cooperative Framework for Dealing with Terrorism', in Sridhar K. Khatri & Gert W. Kueck (eds), *Terrorism In South Asia*, p.411

99 *Ibid*, p.415-416

100 Preamble of the SAARC Convention. Text in *From SARC to SAARC*, Volume I, 1980-1988, (Katmandu, 1998), p.294

101 Pattanaik, Smruti S., 'Making Sense of Regional Cooperation: SAARC at Twenty' *Strategic Analysis* XXX/1(2006)

102 *The Hindu*, 'Terrorism single biggest threat to S.Asia: Manmohan', 3 August 2008

103 Declaration of the Fifteenth SAARC Summit, 2-3 August, 2008

104 *The Hindu*, 'Legal assistance treaty gets SAARC approval', 3 August 2008

REFERENCES

Abdullah, Abu, (2001). (ed) *Bangladesh Economy 2000, Selected Issues* (Dhaka: Bangladesh Institute of Development Studies).

Acharya, Amitav, (2003). 'Southeast Asia: Imagining the Region' *Himal South Asian* XVI/1 (January).

Adamson, Fiona B., (2006). 'Crossing Borders: International Migration and National Security' *International Security* XXXI/1.

Adidi, S.N.M., (1990). 'India, Burma Rebels work on Breakaway Plan' *Illustrated Weekly of India* Supplement to Magazine. December 15-16.

Aitchison, C. U., (1892). *A Collection of Treaties, Engagements and Sanads Relating to India and the Neighbouring Countries*, Volume1, (3rd edition), Calcutta.

Ahmed, Imtiaz, (2003). 'Contemporary Terrorism and the State, Non-State, and the Interstate: Newer Drinks, Newer Bottles', in Sridhar K. Khatri and Gert W. Kueck (eds), *Terrorism in South Asia* (New Delhi: Shipra Publications).

Ahmed, Saied Nasar Abu, (2008). *Fundamentalism in Bangladesh: Its Impact on India* (New Delhi: Akansha).

Akoijam, A. Bimol and T. Tarunkumar, (2005). 'Armed forces (special powers) Act 1958: Disguised War and its Subversions' *Eastern Quarterly* III/1.

Alagappa, M., (2003). (ed) *Asian Security Order: Instrumental and Normative Features* (Stanford: Stanford University Press).

Alexander, Y., and S.M. Finger, (1977). (eds) *Terrorism: Interdisciplinary Perspective* (New York: The John Jay Press).

Amin, J.R. Chowdhury, A.U. Ahmed, R.B. Hill and M. Kabir, (1993). 'Reproductive Change in Bangladesh: Evidence from Recent Data' *Asia- pacific Population Journal* VIII/4.

Anderson, Bendict, (1983). *Imagined Communities: Reflections on the Origin and Spread of Nationalism* (London: Verso).

Andrain, Charles, (1974). *Political Life and Social Change* (Belmont, Calif: Duxbury Press).

Ao, Lanunungsang A., (2002). *From Phizo to Muivah: The Naga National Question in North-east India* (New Delhi: Mittal Publications).

Apter, David E., (1997). (ed) *The Legitimization of Violence* (Basingstoke: Macmillan).

Aron, Raymond, (1966). *Peace and War* (London: Weidenfeld & Nicolson).

Asher, Mukul G. and Rahul Sen, (2005). 'India-East Asia Integration: A Win-Win for Asia' *Economic and Political Weekly* XL/36.

Asia Watch, (1993). 'No End in Sight: Human Rights Violation in Assam' (New York: Asia Watch).

Ayoob, M., (1990). *India and Southeast Asia: Indian Perceptions and Policies* (London and New York: Routeldge).

Bajpai, Kanti P., (2002). *Roots of Terrorism* (New Delhi: Penguin).

_____, (2004). 'Peace Audit on South Asia', in Ranabir Samaddar (ed), *Peace Studies* (New Delhi: Sage Publications).

Banerjee, Sumanta, (2001). 'Indo-Bangladesh Border: Radcliffe's Ghost' *Economic and Political Weekly* XXXVI/18.

Barbora, Sanjay, (2002). 'Ethnic Politics and Land Use: Genesis of Conflicts in India's Northeast' *Economic and Political Weekly* XXXVII/13.

Barpujari, H.K., (1998). *India's Northeast: Problems, Policies and Prospects* (New Delhi: Spectrum Publications).

Barth, Fredik, (1969). (ed) *Ethnic Groups and Boundaries: The Social organization of Cultural Difference* (London: Allen & Unwin).

Baruah, Sanjib, (1999). *India Against Itself: Politics of Nationality in Assam* (New Delhi: Oxford University Press).

_____, (2004). 'Between South and Southeast Asia: Northeast India and the Look East Policy' *CENISEAS PAPERS – 4* (Guwahati: Centre for Northeast India, South and Southeast Asian Studies and OKD Institute for Social Change and Development).

_____, (2005). *Durable Disorder: Understanding the Politics of Northeast India* (New Delhi: Oxford University Press).

Basch, Linda, Glick Schiller and Cristina Szanton Blanc, (1994). *Nations Unbound: Transnational Projects, Post Colonial Predicaments, and De-territorialized Nation-States* (Langhorne, Pa.: Gordon and Breach).

Batayal, A., (2004). 'ASEAN's Quest for Security: A Theoretical Explanation' *International Studies* XLI/4.

Bealey, F., (1999). *The Blackwell Dictionary of Political Science* (Oxford: Blackwell).

Beaujeu-Garnier, J., (1978). *Geography of Population* (London: Longman).

Bell, Robert G., (1976). 'The US Response to Terrorism against International Civil Aviation' *Orbis* XIX(Winter).

Bezbaruah, Madan P., (1996). 'Cultural Sub-Nationalism in India's North East: An Overview' in Subrata K. Mitra & Alison R. Lewis (eds), *Subnational Movements in South Asia* (Oxford: Westview Press).

Bezbaruah, Madan P. and M.K. Dutta, (2001). 'Economic Transition in the North-Eastern Region before and after Liberalization' *Assam Economic Journal* XIV/1.

Bhargava, Rajiv, (2004). 'Between Revenge and Reconciliation', in Ranabir Samaddar (ed), *Peace Studies* (New Delhi: Sage Publications).

Bhasin, Avtar Singh, (2007). (ed) *India's Foreign Relation – 2007 Documents, Part II* (New Delhi, Geetika Publishers).

Bhattacharjee, Chandana, (1996). *Ethnicity and Autonomy: Case of Bodo Kacharis of Assam* (New Delhi: Vikas Publications).

Bhaumik, Subir, (1996). *Insurgent Crossfire* (New Delhi: Lancer Publishers).

_____, (2005). 'Guns, drugs and rebels' *Seminar* Volume 550, June.

_____, (2006). 'Politics of Sanctuary, Indian Rebel Bases in Bangladesh', in Jaideep Saikia (ed), *Bangladesh Treading The Taliban Trail* (New Delhi: Vision Books).

_____, (2007). 'Insurgencies in India's Northeast: Conflict, Co-option & Change', *East-West Center*, Working Paper-No.10 (Washington: East-West Center).

Bhutto, Z.A., (1969). *The Myth of Independence* (London: Oxford University Press).

Bhuyan, J.C., (2002). 'Illegal Migration from Bangladesh and the Demographic Change in the N.E. Region' *Dialogue Quarterly* III/3.

Bion, W., (1961). *Experiences in Groups* (London: Tavistock Publications).

Blackburn, Terence R., (2000). *The British Humiliation of Burma* (Bangkok: Orchid Press Books).

Bloom, Mia, (2005). *Dying to Kill: The Allure of Suicide Terror* (New York: Columbia University Press).

Bohman, J., (1995). 'Public Reason and Cultural Pluralism: Political Liberalism and the Problem of Moral Conflict' *Political Theory* XXII.

Bose, Manilal, (1979). (ed) *Historical and Constitutional Documents of Northeast India: 1824: 1973* (Delhi: Concept Publishing Company).

Boulding, Kenneth, (1987). 'Peace and the Evolutionary Process', in Raimo Vayrynem, Dieter Senghaas and Christian Schmidt (eds), *The Quest for Peace: Transcending Collective Violence and War Among Societies, Cultures, and States* (Beverly Hills, CA: Sage Publications).

Bozeman, Adda B., (1976). *Conflict in Africa, Concepts and Realities* (Princeton: Princeton University Press).

Brara, N. Vijaylakshmi, (1998). *Politics, Society and Cosmology in India's, North East* (Delhi: Oxford University Press).

Brass, Paul R., (1991). *Ethnicity and Nationalism: Theory and Comparison* (New Delhi: Sage Publications).

_____, (1995). *Ethnic Groups and the State* (Beckenham, Kent: Croom Helm).

Brown, Michael, (1997). (ed) *Nationalism and Ethnic Conflict* (Cambridge, MA: MIT Press).

Buckleya, Mary and Rick Fawn, (2003). (eds) *Responses to Terrorism: 9/11, Afghanistan and Beyond* (London, New York: Routledge).

Burling, Robbins, (2003). 'The Tibeto-Burman Languages of Northeastern India', in Grahman Thurgood and Randy LaPolla (eds), *The Sino-Tibetan Languages* (London: Curzon Press).

Buzan, Barry, (1983). *People, States and Fear: The National Security Problem in International Relations* (Brighton: Harvest Press/Chapel Hill: North Carolina Press).

_____, (2003). 'Implications for the Study of International Relations', in Mary Buckleya and Rick Fawn (eds), *Responses to Terrorism: 9/11, Afghanistan and Beyond* (London, New York: Routledge).

_____, and Gerald Segal, (1996). 'The Rise of the "Lite" Powers: A Strategy for Postmodern States' *World Policy Journal* XIII/3.

_____, Ole Waever and Jaap de Wilde, (1998). *Security: A New Framework for Analysis* (Lynne Rienner, Boulder Co).

Byman, Daniel, (1998). 'The Logic of Ethnic Terrorism' *Studies in Conflict and Terrorism* XXI/2.

Campbell, Arthur, (1968). *Guerrillas* (New York: The John Dat Company).

Carson, John, (1978). (ed) *Terrorism in Theory and Practice*, Proceedings of a Colloquium, (Toronto: The Atlantic Council of Canada).

Chadha, Vivek. (2005). *Low Intensity Conflicts in India: An Analysis* (New Delhi: Sage Publications).

Chakravarty, P.C., (1971). *The Evolution of India's Northern Borders* (London: Asia Publishing House).

Chari, P. R., (2003). 'Combating Terrorism: Devising Cooperative Countermeasures', in Sridhar K. Khatri & Gert W. Kueck (eds), *Terrorism In South Asia* (New Delhi: Shipra Publications, RCSS).

Charters, David, (1990). (ed) *Democratic Responses to International Terrorism* (New York: Transnational Publishers).

Chaturvedi, N. T., (1998). (ed) *Fifty Years of Indian Administration: Retrospect and Prospect* (New Delhi: Indian Institute of Public Administration).

Chaube, S.K. (1999). *Hill Politics in North East India* (Hyderabad: Orient Longman).

Choudhury, Saswati, (2006). 'North-East India and the Look East Policy: A Contextual Analysis' *Dialogue Quarterly* VII/3.

Choukri, Nazli, (1978). 'The Pervasiveness of Politics' *Populi* V/3 (New York).

Cline, Lawrence E., (2006). 'The Insurgency Environment in Northeast India' *Small Wars and Insurgencies* XVII/2.

Clutterbuck, Richard, (1990). *Terrorism and Guerrilla Warfare* (London: Routledge).

_____, (1993). *International Crises and Conflict* (London: Macmillan).

Cohen, Robin, (1995). (ed) *The Cambridge Survey of World Migration* (Cambridge: Cambridge University Press).

Collier, Paul, (2001). 'Economic Causes of Civil Conflict and their Implications for Policy', in Chester A. Crocker et al. (eds), *Turbulent Peace: The Challenge of Managing International Conflict* (Washington D.C.: United States Institute of Peace).

Combs, Cindy C., (1997). *Terrorism in the Twenty-first Century* (Upper Saddle River, NJ: Prentice Hall).

Crawford, Young M. (1976). *The Politics of Cultural Pluralism* (Madison: University of Wisconsin Press).

Crenshaw, Martha, (1981). 'The Causes of Terrorism' *Comparative Politics* XIII.

_____, (1985).'An Organizational Approach to the Analysis of Political Terrorism' *Orbis* XXIX pp. 465-89.

_____, (1988). 'The Subjective Reality of the Terrorist: Ideological and Psychological Factors in Terrorism', in Robert O. Slater and Michael Stohl (eds.), *Current Perspective on International Terrorism* (London: Macmillan).

_____, (1990). 'Questions to be answered, research to be done, knowledge to be applied', in Walter Reich (ed), *Origins of Terrorism: Psychologies, Ideologies, Theologies, State of Mind* (New York: Cambridge University Press).

_____, (1995). *Terrorism in Context* (Pennsylvania: The Pennsylvania State University Press).

Crozier, Brain, (1974). *A Theory of Conflict* (New York: Charles Scribner's Sons).

Crozier, Michel, (1964). *The Bureaucratic Phenomenon* (Chicago: University of Chicago Press).

Das, Amiya Kumar, (1992). *Assam's Agony* (New Delhi: Lancers).

Das, B.M., (1987). *The People of Assam* (New Delhi: Gian Publishing House).

Das, Pushpita and Namrata Goswami, (2008). (eds) *India's North East: New Vistas for Peace* (New Delhi: Manas).

Das, S.K., (1983). 'Immigration and Demographic Transformation of Assam, 1891-1981' *Economic and Political Weekly* XVIII/18.

Das, Samir Kumar, (2001). 'Nobody's Communiqué: Ethnic Accords in North-eastern India', in Ranabir Samaddar and Helmut Reifeld (ed), *Peace as Process, Reconciliation and Conflict Resolution in South Asia* (New Delhi: Manohar Publications).

_____, (2003). *Ethnicity, Nation and Security* (New Delhi: South Asian Publications).

_____, (2005). 'The ethnic dimension' *Seminar* 550, June.

Dasgupta, Anindita, (2000). 'Political Myth-making in Post-Colonial Assam' *Himal South Asia* XIII/8.

_____, (2001). 'Small Arms Proliferation in India's Northeast: A Case Study of Assam' *Economic and Political Weekly* XXXVI/1.

Dasgupta, J., (1997). 'Community, Authenticity and Autonomy: Insurgency and Institutional Development in India's Northeast' *The Journal of Asian Studies* LVI/2.

Datta, P.S., (1995). (ed) *North East and the Indian State: Paradoxes of a Periphery* (New Delhi: Vikas Publishing House).

Datta, Sreeradha, (2002). 'Indo-Bangladesh Relations: An Overview of Limitations and Constraints' *Strategic Analysis* XXVI/3.

Davidson Smith, G., (1990). *Combating Terrorism* (London: Routledge).

Davies, James C., (1962). 'Towards a Theory of Revolution' *American Sociological Review* XXVII (February).

Davis, M. Jane, (1996). (ed) *Security Issues in the Post- Cold War World* (UK: Edward Elger).

DeNardo, James, (1985). *Power in Numbers: The Political Strategy of Protest and Rebellion* (Princeton, NJ: Princeton University Press).

Dewitt, David, David Hagland and John Kirton, (1991). (eds) *Building a New Global Order: Emerging Trends in International Security* (Toronto: Oxford University Press).

DFID, (2005). *Fighting Poverty to Build a Safer World: A Strategy for Security and Development* (United Kingdom: Department for International Development).

Dhamala, R.R. and Sukalpa Bhattacharjee, (2002). (eds) *Human Rights and Insurgency: The North-East India* (New Delhi: Shipra Publications).

Dhanapala, Jayanatha et.el, (1999). *Small Arms Control: Old Weapons, New Issues* (Vermont: Ashgate Publishing).

Dixit, J.N., (1997). *My South Block Years: Memoirs of a Foreign Secretary* (New Delhi: UBSPD).

Domarus, E. von, (1944). 'The Specific Laws in Schizophrenia', in J.S. Kasanin (ed), *Language and Thought in Schizophrenia: Collected Papers* (Berkeley: University of California Press).

Donald Horowitz, Donald, (1985). *Ethnic Groups in Conflict* (Berkeley: University of California Press).

Dreze, Jean & Amartya Sen, (1977). (eds) *Indian Development: Selected Regional Perspectives* (New Delhi: Oxford University Press).

Dutta, Subrata Kumar, (2005). *Uprooted Reang: Strangers in Their Motherland* (New Delhi: Akansha Publications).

Easton, David, (1965). *A System Analysis of Political Life* (New York: John Wiley and Sons).

Eaton, Richard M., (1997). 'Comparative History as World History: Religious Conversion in Modern India' *Journal of World History* VIII/2.

Eckstein, H., (1964). (ed) *Internal War* (London: Collier-Macmillan).

Editorial, (2006). 'HIV/AIDS Spreading Scourge' *Economic and Political Weekly* XLI/29.

Egreteau, Renaud, (2003). *Wooing the Generals: India's New Burma Policy* (New Delhi: Centre De Sciences Humaines).

_____, (2006). 'Instability at the Gate: India's Troubled Northeast and its external Connections', CSH Occasional Paper-No.16 (New Delhi: Centre de Sciences Humaines).

Esman, Milton J., (1994). *Ethnic Politics* (Ithaca, N.Y: Cornell University Press).

Falk, Richard, (1988). *Revolutionaries and Functionaries: The Dual Face of Terrorism* (New York: Dutton).

Fall, Bernard B., (1963). *Street without Joy* (Harrisburg Pa: Stackpole Books).

Ferenez, Benjamin B., (1975). *Defining International Aggression: The Search for World Peace* Volume: 2 (New York: Oceana).

Fernandes, Walter, (2005). 'IMDT Act and Immigration in North-Eastern India' *Economic and Political Weekly* XL/30.

Franck, Thomas M. and Bert B. Lockwood, Jr. (1974). 'Preliminary Thoughts Towards an International Convention on Terrorism' *American Journal of International Law* LXVIII (January).

Friedberg, Aaron, (1993). 'Ripe for Rivalry: Prospects for Peace in a Multipolar Asia' *International Security* XVIII/3 (Winter).

Fromkin, David, (1975). 'The Strategy of Terrorism' *Foreign Affairs* LIII/July.

Ganguly, R. and MacDuff, Ian, (2003). *Ethnic Conflict and Secessionism in South and South East Asia: Causes, Dynamics, Solutions* (New Delhi: Sage Publications).

Garnier, J. Beaujeu, (1978). *Geography of Population* (London: Longman).

Garver, John, (2001). *Protracted Contest: Sino-Indian Rivalry in the Twentieth Century* (New Delhi: Oxford University Press).

George, Alexander, (1991). (ed) *Western State Terrorism* (Cambridge: Cambridge University Press).

Ghose, Sanjoy, (1998). *Sanjoy's Assam: Diaries and Writings of Sanjoy Ghose* (edited and with an afterword by Sumita Ghose) (New Delhi: Penguin).

Ghosh, Partha S., (2005). 'Conservative Ascendancy in Bangladesh' *South Asian Survey* XII/2.

_____, (2004). *Unwanted and Uprooted* (New Delhi: Samskriti).

Gibbs, J.P, (1989). 'Conceptualization of Terrorism' *American Sociological Review* LVI.

Gill, K.P.S., (2001). (ed) *Terror and Containment Perspectives of India's Internal Security* (New Delhi: Gyan Publishing House).

Gokhale, Nitin, (1998). *The Hot Brew: The Assam Tea Industry's Most Turbulent Decade 1987-97* (Guwahati: Spectrum).

Goldstone, Jack A., (1997). 'Population Growth and Revolutionary Crises', in John Foran (ed), *In Theorizing Revolutions* (London: Routledge).

Goldstone, Jack, Ted Gurr, Monty Marshal and Jay Ulfelder, (2004). 'It's All About State Structure: New Findings on Revolutionary Origins from Global Data' *Homo Oeconomicus* XXI/2.

Goodwin, Jeff, (2001). *No Other Way Out: States and Revolutionary Movements, 1945-1991* (Cambridge: Cambridge University Press).

_____, (2006). 'A Theory of Categorical Terrorism' *Social Forces* LXXXIV/4.

Gordon, Sandy and Stephen Henningham, (1995). (eds) *India Looks East: An Emerging Power and its Asia Pacific Neighbors* (Canberra, Australia: Strategic and Defence Studies, Australian National University).

Goswami, Arnab, (2002). *Combating Terrorism, The Legal Challenge* (New Delhi: Har-Anand Publications).

Grare, Frederic and Amitabh Mattoo, (2001). (eds) *India and ASEAN: The Politics of India's Look East Policy* (New Delhi: Manohar Publications).

Gross, Feliks, (1958). *The Seizure of Political Power* (New York: Philosophical Library).

Guha, Amalendu, (1977). *Planter-Raj to Swaraj: Freedom Struggle and Electoral Politics in Assam 1826–1947* (New Delhi: Indian Council for Historical Research).

Gunaratna, Rohan, (2002). *Inside Al Qaeda: Global Network of Terror* (New Delhi: Roli Books).

Gurr, Ted R., (1968). 'Psychological Factors in Civil Violence' *World Politics* XX/2.

_____, (1970). *Why Men Rebel* (Princeton, NJ: Princeton University Press).

_____, (1989). 'Political Terrorism: Historical Antecedents', in Robert Ted Gurr (ed), *Violence in America: Protest Rebellion, Reform* Volume 2 (Newbury Park. CA: Sage Publications).

_____, (1993). *Minorities at Risk: A Global View of Ethnopolitical Conflicts* (Washington: United States Institute of Peace).

Guru, Dev S., (1996). *Anatomy of Revolt in North East India* (New Delhi: Lancers).

Gutman, Amy, (1994). (ed) *Multiculturalism: Examining the Politics of Recognition* (Princeton, NJ: Princeton University Press).

Habib, Haroon, (2006). '17 August 2005: Milestone of Terror', in Jaideep Saikia (ed), *Bangladesh Treading The Taliban Trail* (New Delhi: Vision Books).

Hall, Raymond, (1972). (ed) *Ethnic Autonomy: Comparative Dynamics* (New York: Pergamon Press).

Hamm, S. Mark, (1994). (ed) *Hate Crime: International Perspectives on Causes and Control* (Highland Hights, KY: Academy of Criminal Justice Sciences and Cincinnati, OH: Anderson).

Hampshire, Stuart, (1989). *Innocence and Experience* (Cambridge: Harvard University Press).

Haynes, Jeffrey, (2005). *Comparative Politics in a Globalizing World* (Cambridge, UK: Polity Press).

Hazarika, Joyshankar, (1996). *Geopolitics of North East India* (New Delhi: Gyan Publications).

Hazarika, Sanjoy, (1995). *Strangers of The Mist: Tales of War and Peace from India's Northeast* (New Delhi: Penguin Books).

_____, (2000). *Rites of Passage: Border Crossings, Imagined Homelands, India's East and Bangladesh* (New Delhi: Penguin Books).

Heilbrunn, Otto, (1962). *Partisan Warfare* (New York: Frederick A. Praeger).

Held, Davis, Anthony McGrew, David Goldblatt and Jonathan Perraton, (1999). *Global Transformation: Politics, Economics and Culture* (Cambridge: Polity Press).

Herman, Edward and Gerry O'Sullivan, (1989). *"Terrorism" Industry: The Experts and Institutions That Shape Our View of Terror* (New York: Pantheon).

Hobsbawm, Eric and Terence Ranger, (1983). *The Invention of Tradition* (Cambridge: Cambridge University Press).

Hoffman, Bruce, (1998). *Inside Terrorism* (New York: Columbia University Press).

Hoover, J., (2001). 'Do the Politics of Difference Need to be Freed of Liberalism?' *Constellations* VIII.

Horowitz, Donald, (1985). *Ethnic Groups in Conflict* (Berkeley: University of California Press).

Howard, Lawrence, (1992). (ed) *Terrorism: Roots, Impact, Responses* (New York: Praeger).

Hudson, V. and A. den Boer, (2004). *Bare Branches: The Security Implications of Asia's Surplus Male Population* (Cambridge MA: MIT Press).

Hugo, Grame, (1995). 'Illegal International Migration in Asia', in Robin Cohen (ed), *The Cambridge Survey of World Migration* (Cambridge: Cambridge University Press).

Human Rights Watch, (1995). 'Playing the "Communal Card": Communal Violence and Human Rights' (New York: Human Rights Watch).

Huntington, Samuel P., (1962). 'Guerrilla Warfare in Theory and Policy', in Franklin Mark Osanka (ed), *Modern Guerrilla Warfare* (New York: The Free Press of Glencoe).

_____, (1968). *Political Order in Changing Societies* (New Haven: Yale University Press).

_____, (1971). 'Civil Violence and the Process of Development' *Adelphi Paper* 83 (London: IISS).

_____, (1996). *The Clash of Civilizations and the Remaking of World Order* (New York: Simon & Schuster).

Hussain, Monirul, (1993). *The Assam Movement: Class, Ideology and Identity* (New Delhi: Manak Publishers).

Hussain, Wasbir, (2002). 'Mizoram: Negotiating with Terror, Yet Again' *South Asia Intelligence Review* I/15.

_____, (2003). 'Bhutan – King Size Problem' *South Asia Intelligence Review* II/10.

_____, (2005). 'Assam: New Turn to Citizenship Politics' *South Asia Intelligence Review* IV/1.

_____, (2005). 'Assam: Turf War in a Time of Truce' *South Asia Intelligence Review* IV/14.

_____, (2005). 'ULFA Talks Tough with Bombings' *South Asia Intelligence Review* IV/24.

_____, (2006). 'Assam: ULFA Bombs its Way to Peace Talks' *South Asia Intelligence Review* V/48

_____, (2006). 'India-Assam: Delhi's I- Day Gambit' *South Asia Intelligence Review* V/5.

Hutchinson, Martha Crenshaw, (1972). 'The Concept of Revolutionary Terrorism' *Journal of Conflict Resolution* VI.

Ingam, Attracta, (1994). *A Political Theory of Rights* (Oxford: Clarendon Press).

Jacobs, Julian, Alan MacFarlane, Sarah Harrison and Anita Herle, (1990). *The Nagas: The Hill People of Northeast India: Society, Culture and the Colonial Encounter* (London: Thames and Hudson).

Jamwal, N.S., (2002). 'Management of Land Borders' *Strategic Analysis* XXVI/3.

_____, (2004). 'Border Management: Dilemma of Guarding the India-Bangladesh Border' *Strategic Analysis* XXVIII/1.

Jaun, L. Linz, (1978). *The Breakdown of Democratic Regimes* (Baltimore: Johns Hopkins University Press).

Jenkins, Brain, (1975). 'International Terrorism: A Balance Sheet' *Survival* (July/ August).

Jerrold, M., (1990). 'Terrorist Psycho-logic: Terrorist Behaviour as a Product of Psychological Forces', in Walter Reich (ed), *Origins of Terrorism: Psychologies, Ideologies, Theologies, States of Mind* (New York: Cambridge University Press).

Johnson, Chalmers, (1983). *Revolutionary Change* (Harlow: Longman).

Jongman, A.J. and A.P.Schmid, (1998). 'Mapping Dimensions of Contemporary Conflicts and Human Rights Violations' *PIOOM- Interdisciplinary Research Programme on Causes of Human Rights Violations* (Leiden: Leiden University PIOOM).

Juergensmeyer, (1993). The *New Cold War*? (Berkeley: University of California Press).

_____, (2000). *Terrorism in the Mind of God* (Berkeley: University of California).

Kahn, Herman, (1968). 'Some Possible Sizes and Shapes of Thermonuclear Wars', in Mark E.Smith and Claude J. Johns. Jr (eds), *American Defence Policy* (2nd ed) (Baltimore: Johns Hopkins University).

Kalam, Abul, (2001). *Subregionalism in Asia: ASEAN and SAARC Experiences* (Dhaka: University Press).

Kaldor, Mary, (1999). *From New and Old Wars* (Stanford: Stanford University Press).

_____, (1999). *Organized Violence in a Global Era* (Cambridge: Polity Press).

Karlekar, Hiranmay, (2005). *Bangladesh, The Next Afghanistan?* (New Delhi: Sage Publications).

Kartha, Tara, (1999). *Tools of Terror: Light Weapon and India's Security* (New Delhi: Knowledge World & IDSA).

Kaufmann, Chaim, (1996). 'Possible and Impossible Solutions to Ethnic Civil Wars' *International Security* XX/4 (Spring).

Kegley Jr, Charles, (1990). (ed) *International Terrorism: Characteristics, Causes, Controls* (New York: St Martin's Press).

Kenny, Michael, (2004). *The Politics of Identity* (Cambridge, UK: Polity Press).

Kernberg, O., (1975). *Borderline Conditions and Pathological Narcissism* (New York: Jacob Aronson).

Khanna, Sushil, (2005). 'Economic Opportunities or Continuing Stagnation' *Seminar* 550, June.

Khatun, Fahmida Akter, (2000). 'Population and Environment in Bangladesh: Designing a Policy Account for Linkages' Paper No 12, (Dhaka: Centre for Policy Dialogue).

Kirkham, James F., Sheldon G. Levy and William J. Crotty, (1969). (eds) *A Report to the National Commission on the Causes and Prevention of Violence* (Washington, DC: US Government Printing Office).

Kohut, H., (1983). *The Analysis of the Self* (New York: International University Press).

Kotwal, Dinesh, (2000). 'Instability Parameters in Northeast India' *Strategic Analysis* XXIV/1.

Krasner, Stephen D., (1999). *Sovereignty: Organised Hypocrisy* (Princeton, NJ: Princeton University Press).

Kumar, Anand, (2004). 'Bangladesh Emerges as Biggest Clandestine Arms Supplier in South Asia' *South Asia Tribune* 11-17 April.

Kumar, Nagesh, (2004). (ed) *Towards An Asian Economic Community: Vision of a New Asia* (New Delhi: RIS for Developing Countries and Singapore; Institute of Southeast Asian Studies).

_____, (2005). 'A Broader Asian Community and a Possible Roadmap' *Economic and Political Weekly* XL/36.

Kumar, Praveen, (2004). 'External Linkages and Internal Security: Assessing Bhutan's Operation All Clear' *Strategic Analysis* XXVIII/3.

Kumar, Rupesinghe, (2003). 'Developing a Cooperative Framework for Dealing with Terrorism', in Sridhar K. Khatri & Gert W. Kueck (eds), *Terrorism In South Asia* (New Delhi: Shipra Publications).

Kupperman, Robert and Daniel Trent, (1979). *Terrorism: Threat Reality, Response* (Stanford, California: Hoover Institution Press).

Kydd, Andrew H., and Barbara F. Walter, (2006). 'The Strategies of Terrorism' *International Security* XXXI/1.

Lake, David A. and Patrick M. Morgan, (1997). (eds) *Regional Orders: Building Security in a New World* (University Park: Pennsylvania State University Press).

Lakos, Amos, (1986). *International Terrorism: A Bibliography* (Boulder: Westview Press).

Lacina, Bethany, (2007). 'Does Counterinsurgency Theory Apply in Northeast India?' *India Review* VI/3.

Laqueur, Walter, (1987). *The Age of Terrorism* (Boston: Little, Brown).

_____, (1999). *The New Terrorism: Fanaticism and the Arms of Mass Destruction* (New York: Oxford University Press).

_____, and Yonah Alexander, (1987). (eds) *The Terrorism Reader* (New York: Meridian)

Levitt, Geoffrey M., (1988). *Democracies against Terror: The Western Democracies' Response to State-supported Terrorism* (New York: Praeger).

Lewis, William. H., (2002). 'The War on Terror: A Retrospective' *Mediterranean Quarterly* XIII/4.

Lim, R., (1998). 'The ASEAN Regional Cooperation: Building on Sand' *Contemporary Southeast Asia* XX/2.

Linn, Ruth, (1998). 'Terrorism, Mortality and Soldiers' Motivation to Fight – an example from the Israeli Experience in Lebanon' *Terrorism* XI/2.

Lintner, Bertil, (1991). *Cross Border Drug Trade in the Golden Triangle* (Durhman, N.C: International Boundaries Research Unit).

_____, (1996). *Land of Jade: A Journey from India Through Northern Burma to China* (Bangkok: White Orchid Press).

_____, (2002). 'A Cocoon of Terror' *Far Eastern Economic Review* April 4.

_____, (2006). 'Islamist Fundamentalism in Bangladesh', in Jaideep Saikia (ed), *Bangladesh: Treading the Taliban Trail* (New Delhi: Vision Books).

Linz, Jaun. L., (1978). *The Breakdown of Democratic Regimes* (Baltimore: Johns Hopkins University Press).

Ludden, David, (2003). 'Where is Assam? History to locate Current Social Realities' *CENISEAS PAPERS – 1* (Guwahati: Centre for Northeast India, South and Southeast Asian Studies and OKD Institute for Social Change and Development).

Mackenzie, Alexander, (2001). *The North-East Frontier of India* (New Delhi: Mittal Publications).

Maddock, Rowland T., (1996). 'Environmental Security', in M. Jane Davis (ed), *Security Issues in the Post- Cold War World* (UK: Edward Elger).

Malik, M., (1994). 'Sino-Indian Rivalry in Myanmar: Implications for Regional Security' *Contemporary South-east Asia* XVI/2.

_____, (1995). 'China-India Relations in Post-Soviet era: The Continuing Rivalry' *The China Quarterly* XLII /June.

Marshall, Monty, (2002). *Global Terrorism: An Overview and Analysis*, (University of Maryland: Integrated Network for Societal Conflict Research and Centre for International Development and Conflict Management).

Martin, Gus, (2003). *Understanding Terrorism: Challenges, Perspective and Issues* (London: Sage Publications).

Marwah, Ved, (1995). *Uncivil Wars: Pathology of Terrorism in India* (New Delhi: Harper Collins).

Maxwell, Neville, (2000). *India's China War* (London: Random House).

Mentschel Nepram, Binalakshmi, (2007). 'Armed Conflict, Small Arms Proliferation and Women's Responses to Armed Violence in India's Northeast', *Heidelberg Papers in South Asian and Comparative Politics*, Working Paper No 33 (Heidelberg: South Asia Institute, University of Heidelberg).

Midlarsky, Manus I., Martha Crenshaw, and Fumihiko Yoshida, (1980). 'Why Violence Spreads: The Contagion of International Terrorism' *International Studies Quarterly* XXIV.

Milton J. Esman, (1994). *Ethnic Politics* (N.Y, Ithaca, 1994).

Misra, Udayon, (2000). *The Periphery Strikes Back: Challenges to Nation State in Assam and Nagaland* (Shimla: Indian Institute of Advanced Study).

_____, (2003). 'Naga Peace Talks, High Hopes and Hard Realities' *Economic and Political Weekly* XXXVIII/7.

Mitra, Subrata K. & Alison R. Lewis, (1996). (eds) *Subnational Movements in South Asia* (Oxford: Westview Press).

Mukhim, Patricia, (2006). 'Of Ambiguous Peace Dialogues' *Dialogue Quarterly* VII/4.

Muni, S., (1997). 'India and Southeast Asia: Challenges and Opportunities' *Contemporary Southeast Asia* XIX/2 September.

_____, (2003). 'Terrorism and Interstate Relations in South Asia', in Sridhar K. Khatri & Gert W. Kueck (eds), *Terrorism In South Asia* (New Delhi: Shipra Publications).

Murayama, Mayumi, (2006). 'Borders, Migration and Sub-Regional Cooperation in Eastern South Asia' *Economic and Political Weekly* XLI/14.

_____, Kyoko Inoue and Sanjoy Hazarika, (2005.) *Sub- regional Relations in the Eastern South Asia: With Special Focus on India's North Eastern Region* (Joint Research Program Series No. 133) (Tokyo: Institute of Developing Economies).

Murphy, Jeffrie G. and Jean Hampton, (1990). *Forgiveness and Mercy* (Cambridge: Cambridge University Press).

Murphy, John F., (1989). *State Support of International Terrorism* (Boulder: Westview Press).

Nag, Sajal, (2002). *Contesting Marginality: Ethnicity, Insurgency and Subnationalism* in *North-East India* (New Delhi: Manohar Publications).

Nandy, Bibhuti Bhusan, (2006). 'DGFI: State Within a State', in Jaideep Saikia (ed), *Bangladesh Treading The Taliban Trail* (New Delhi: Vision Books).

Narahari, S.N., (2002). *Security Threats to North-East India* (New Delhi: Manas Publications).

Nath. D., (2004). (ed) *Reopening of The Stilwell Road, Prospects And Problems* (New Delhi: Anamika).

Nayar, V.K., (2000). *Low Intensity Conflicts in India* (New Delhi: USI).

Nef, J., (1978). 'Some Thoughts on Contemporary Terrorism: Domestic and International Perspectives', in John Carson (ed), *Terrorism in Theory and Practice* Proceedings of a Colloquium (Toronto: The Atlantic Council of Canada).

Neill, Bard E.O', (1990). *Insurgency and Terrorism: Inside Modern Revolutionary Warfare* (Brassey's (US): Inc Maxwell Pergamon Publishing Corporation).

Nepram, Binalakshmi, (2002). *South Asia's Fractured Frontier: Armed Conflict, Narcotics and Small Arms Proliferation in India's North East* (New Delhi: Mittal Publications).

Newman, G.R. and M.J. Lynch, (1987). 'From Feuding to Terrorism: The Ideology of Vengeance' *Contemporary* Crises XI/3.

Nibedon, Nirmal, (1985). *Night of the Guerrillas* (New Delhi: Lancer Books).

Nieburg, H.L, (1969). *Political Violence: The Behavioral Process* (New York: Martin's Press).

O'Brien, Cf Donal Cruise, (1972). 'Modernization, Order, and the Erosion of a Democratic Ideal: American Political Science 1960-1970' *Journal of Development Studies* VIII.

Osanka, Franklin Mark, (1962). (ed) *Modern Guerrilla Warfare* (New York: The Free Press of Glencoe).

Pakem, B., (1990). (ed) *Nationality, Ethnicity and Cultural Identity in North-East India* (New Delhi: Omsons Publications).

_____, (1997). (ed) *Insurgency in North East India* (New Delhi: Omsons Publications).

Pandey, Nishchal N., (2008). *India's North-Eastern Region: Insurgency, Economic Development and Linkages with South-East Asia* (New Delhi: Manohar)

Pandey, Onkareshvar, (2002). 'ISI and New Wave of Islamic Militancy in the N.E' *Dialogue Quarterly* III/3.

Pape, Robert A., (2005). *Dying to win: The Strategic Logic of Suicide Terrorism* (London: Random House).

Pattanaik, Smruti S., (2006). 'Making Sense of Regional Cooperation: SAARC at Twenty' *Strategic Analysis* XXX/1.

Patra, Soumyajit and Samita Manna, (2008). 'Integrative Reconciliation: Mothers in the Naga Movement' *Economic and Political Weekly* XLIII/10.

Paust, Jordan, (1971). 'Terrorism and International Law of War' *Military Law Review* (Spring).

Perdue, William D., (1989). *Terrorism and the State* (New York: Praefer).

Pierre, Andrew, (1976). 'The Politics of International Terrorism' *Orbis* XIX.

Pillai, S.K., (2002). 'Insurgencies in Northeast India' *Aakrosh* (Asian Journal on Terrorism and Internal Conflicts) V/17.

Poland, James, (1998). *Understanding Terrorism: Groups, Strategies, and Responses* (New Jersey: Prentice-Hall).

Posen, Barry, (1993). 'The Security Dilemma and Ethnic Conflict' *Survival* XXXV/1.

Prabhakara, M.S., (2004). 'Is North-east India landlocked?' *Economic and Political Weekly* XXXIX/42.

Pramanik, Bimal, (2004). 'Cattle Smuggling across the Indo-Bangladesh Border – An Analysis' *Dialogue Quarterly* VI/1.

Prasad, R. N., (1997). *Autonomy Movements in Mizoram* (New Delhi: Vikas).

Purvis, T., and A. Hunt, (1999). 'Identity versus Citizenship: Transformations in the Discourses and Practices of Citizenship' *Social and Legal Studies* VIII.

Putnam, Robert, (1993). *Making Democracy Work* (Princeton: Princeton University Press).

Rabasa, Angel M. et al., (2004). *The Muslim World After 9/11* (Washington, DC: RAND Corporation).

Rahman, Fazal-ur, (2000). 'India's Evolving Security Relations with Southeast and East Asia' *Strategic Studies* (Islamabad) XXI/2.

Raman, B., (2001). 'Pakistan's Inter-Services Intelligence (ISI)' *India Intelligence Review* XVI/3.

_____, (2002). 'Pakistan and Terrorism: The Evidence' *South Asia Analysis Group* Paper No. 390, January 8.

Ramana, P.V., (2002). 'Networking the Northeast Partners in Terror'. Available online at the South Asia Terrorism Portal, *Faultlines*, http://www.satp.org/satporgtp/publication/faultlines/vol 11/article6.htm.

Ramesh, Jairam, (2005). 'Northeast India in a new Asia' *Seminar* 550 June.

_____, (2005). *Making Sense of Chindia: Reflections on China and India* (New Delhi: India Research Press).

Rammohan, E.M., (2002). 'Manipur: A Degenerated Insurgency', in K.P.S. Gill and Ajai Sahni (eds), *Faultlines* Volume 11 (New Delhi: Bulwark Books and the Institute of Conflict Management).

_____, (2002). 'Blueprint for Counterinsurgency in Manipur' *USI Journal* April-June.

Rapoport, David C. and Yonah Alexander, (1982). (eds) *The Morality of Terrorism* (New York: Pergamon Press).

Ray, Animesh, (1982). *Mizoram: Dynamics of Change* (Calcutta: Pearl Publishers).

_____, (1993). *India – the Land and the People: Mizoram* (New Delhi: National Book Trust of India).

Ray, Jayant Kumar and Prabir De, (2004). (eds) *Promotion of Trade and Investment in Eastern South Asia Sub-region* (New Delhi: Bookwell).

Reddy, K. Raja, (2005). (ed) *Indian and ASEAN: Foreign Policy Dimensions for the Twenty First Century* (New Delhi: New Century).

Reich, Walter, (1990). *Origins of Terrorism: Psychologies, Ideologies, Theologies, States of Mind* (New York: Cambridge University Press).

Rene'beres, Louis, (1987). *Terrorism and Global Security: The Nuclear Threat* (Boulder: Westview Press).

Robb, Peter, (1997). 'The Colonial State and Constructions of Indian Identity: An Example on the Northeast Frontier in the 1880s' *Modern Asian Studies* XXXI/2.

Robison, Kristopher K., Edward M. Crenshaw and J. Craig Jenkins, (2006). 'Ideologies of Violence: The Social Origins of Islamist and Leftist Transnational Terrorism' *Social Forces* LXXXIV/4.

Roger Trinquier, Roger, (1964). *Modern Warfare* (New York: Frederick A. Praeger).

Roucek, Joseph, (1962). 'Sociological Elements of a Theory of Terror and Violence' *American Journal of Economic and Sociology* XXI/April.

Routray, Bibhu Prasad, (2005). 'Beyond the Bandarban Recoveries' *South Asia Intelligence Review* IV/18.

_____, (2006). 'India: Northeast: Long Shadows of Subversion' *South Asia Intelligence Review* V/2.

_____, (2006). 'India-Bangladesh: HUJI: Lengthening Shadow of Terror' *South Asia Intelligence Review* V/3.

_____, (2006). 'Manipur: The State Abdicates' *South Asia Intelligence Review* IV/42.

_____, (2006). 'Terror, Migrants and Politics' *South Asia Intelligence Review* IV/32.

Roy, Sanjay K., (2005). 'Conflicting Nations in North-East India' *Economic and Political Weekly* XL/21.

Rubenstein, Richard E., (1987). *Alchemists of Revolution: Terrorism in the Modern World* (New York: Basic Books).

Runciman, W. G., (1966). *Relative Deprivation and Social Justice* (London: Routledge and Kegan Paul).

Rustomji, Nari, (1973). *Enchanted Frontiers: Sikkim, Bhutan and India's North-eastern Borderlands* (Calcutta: Oxford University Press).

Sachdeva, Gulshan, (2000). *Economy of the North-East: Policy, Present Conditions and Future Possibilities* (Delhi: Konark Publishers).

_____, (2006). 'Demystifying Northeast', *Dialogue Quarterly* VII/3.

Saha, Bimal Kumar, (2001). 'Changing Pattern of Agrarian Structure in Bangladesh: 1984-1996', in Abu Abdullah (ed), *Bangladesh Economy 2000, Selected Issues* (Dhaka: Bangladesh Institute of Development Studies).

Sahadevan, P, (2006). 'Negotiating Peace in Ethnic Wars' *International Studies* XLIII/3.

Sahani, V., (2004). 'From Security in Asia to Asian Security' *International Studies* XLI/3.

Sahni, Ajai, 'The Terrorist Economy in India's North East' available online in <http://www.satp.org/satporgtp/publication/faultlines/volume8/article5.htm>4

Sahni, Ajai and J. George, (2001). 'Security and Development In India's NorthEast: An Alternative Perspective', in K.P.S Gill (ed), *Terror and Containment Perspectives of India's Internal Security* (New Delhi: Gyan Publishing House).

Saikia, Anil, Homeswar Goswami and Atul Goswami, (2003). *Population Growth in Assam 1951-1991: With Focus on Migration* (New Delhi: Akansha).

Saikia, Jaideep, (2001). 'Revolutionaries or Warlords: ULFA's Organizational Profile' *Faultlines* IX/July.

_____, (2002). 'The ISI Reaches East: Anatomy of a Conspiracy' *Faultlines* VI.

_____, (2003). 'Terror sans Frontiers: Islamic Militancy in North East India' Occasional Paper, Program in Arms Control, Disarmament and International Security (Urbana-Champaign: University of Illinois).

_____, (2004). *Terror sans Frontiers: Islamic Militancy in North East India* (New Delhi: Vision Books).

_____, (2006). (ed) *Bangladesh Treading The Taliban Trail* (New Delhi: Vision Books).

Saikia, Yasmin, (2005). 'The Tai-Ahom connection' *Seminar* 550 June.

Samaddar, Ranabir, (2004). (ed) *Peace Studies* (New Delhi: Sage Publications).

_____, and Helmut Reifeld, (2001). (ed) *Peace as Process, Reconciliation and Conflict Resolution in South Asia* (New Delhi: Manohar Publications).

Sarin, V.I.K., (1980). *India's North East in Flames* (New Delhi: Vikas Publishing House).

Sarkesian, Sam C., (1975). (ed) *Revolutionary Guerrilla Warfare* (Chicago: Precedent Publishing).

Sarma, Atul, (2001). 'Economic Development of the North eastern Region' *Strategic Analysis* XXV/2.

_____, (2007). 'Northeast as Gateway to Southeast Asia: Big Dreams and Home Truths', in S. Borbora and J.K. Gogoi (eds), *Development Issues in the Northeast in the Turn of the Century* (Guwahati: North Eastern Economic Association and Papyrus).

_____, and Pradeep Kumar Mehta, (2002). *Exploring Indo-ASEAN Economic Partnership in a Globalizing World* (New Delhi: Little Brown).

Sashinungla, (2003). 'Nagaland: The Dynamics of Extortion' *South Asia Intelligence Review* II/22.

_____, (2004). 'Meghalaya: Extortion Dynamics' *South Asia Intelligence Review* II/40.

Sawhny, Karan R., (1998). 'Insurgency and Counter-Insurgency: Ending Two Decades of Deadly Conflict in a Fracturing Polity' *Peace Initiative* IV/1&2.

Schelling, Thomas C., (1968). 'Compellence', in Mark E.Smith and Claude J. Johns. Jr (eds), *American Defense Policy* (2nd ed) (Baltimore: John Hopkins University Press).

Schmid, Alex P., Albert J. Jongman at al., (1988). *Political Terrorism; A New Guide to Actors, Authors, Concepts, Data Bases, Theories, and Literature* (New Brunswick, NJ: Transaction Books).

Schmid, Alex P. and Ronald D. Crelinsten, (1993). (eds) *Western Responses to Terrorism* (London: Frank Cass).

Schock, Kurt, (1996). 'A Conjunctural Model of Political Conflict: The Impact of Political Opportunities on the Relationship between Economic Inequality and Violent Political Conflict' *Journal of Conflict Resolution* XL/1.

Scruton, Roger, (1982). *A Dictionary of Political Thought* (New York: Hill and Wang).

Selth, Andrew, (1996). 'Burma and the Strategic Competition Between India and China' *Journal of Strategic Studies* XIX/2.

Sen, Rahul, Mukul Asher and Ramkishen S. Rajan, (2004). 'ASEAN-India Economic Relations: Current Status and Future Prospects' *Economic and Political Weekly* XXXIX/29.

Sheffer, Gabriel, (2003). *Diaspora Politics: At Home Abroad* (Cambridge: Cambridge University Press).

Shafer, Boyd, (1990). *Faces of Nationalism* (New York: Paragon).

Shimray, Ungshungmi, (2001). 'Ethnicity and Socio-political Assertion' *Economic and Political Weekly* XXXVI/39.

_____, (2004). 'Socio-political Unrest in the Region Called North-east India' *Economic and Political Weekly* XXXIX/42.

Shollom, A. H., (1962). 'Nowhere Yet Everywhere', in Franklin Mark Osanka (ed), *Modern Guerrilla Warfare* (New York: The Free Press of Glencoe).

Silke, Andrew, (1996). 'Terrorism and the Blind Men's Elephant' *Terrorism and Political Violence* VIII/3 (Autumn).

Silverman, Jerry M. and Peter M. Jackson, (1970). 'Terror in Insurgency Warfare' *Military Review*, October.

Singh, Amarjeet, (2006). 'Assam: Bodos' Troubled Politics' *South Asia Intelligence Review* IV/44.

_____, (2006). 'Highways of Extortions' *South Asia Intelligence Review* IV/47.

_____, (2006). 'Nagaland: Another Bangladeshi Destination' *South Asia Intelligence Review* V/4.

Singh, Manvendra, (1994). 'NDC Papers: Low Intensity Conflict' *Indian Defence Review* IX/4.

Singh, Pr. Brajachand, (2001). 'Drug Abuse and AIDS Menace in Manipur', in Gopalkrishna &al. (eds), *Constraints in Development of Manipur* (New Delhi: Regency Publications).

Singh, Prakash, (2001). 'Border Management' *BSF Journal* (Gwalior: Border Security Force (BSF) Academy, Tekanpur).

Sinha, S.K., (2002). 'Violence and Hope in India's North East', in K.P.S. Gill and Ajai Sahni (eds), *Faultlines*, Volume.10 (New Delhi: Bulwark Books and the Institute of Conflict Management).

Sisline, John et al, (1988). 'Pattern of Arm Acquisitions by Ethnic Group in conflict' *Security Dialogue* (London) XXIX/4.

Slater, Robert O. and Michael Stohl, (1988). (eds.) *Current Perspective on International Terrorism* (London: Macmillan).

Smith, Antony, (1996). 'Culture, Community and Territory: The Politics of Ethnicity and Nationalism' *International Affairs* LXXII/3.

Smith, Mark E. and Claude J. Johns. Jr ,(1968). (eds) *American Defense Policy* (2nd ed) (Baltimore: John Hopkins University Press).

Sobhan, R., (1998). 'Regional Cooperation in South Asia: A Quest for Identity' *South Asian Survey* V/1.

Sonderland, Walter C., (1970). 'An Analysis of Guerrilla Insurgency and Coup d' Etat as Techniques of Indirect Aggression' *International Studies Quarterly* December.

Sondhi, M.L., (2000). (ed) *Terrorism and Political Violence: A Source Book* (New Delhi: Har-Anand Publications).

South Asia Human Rights Documentation Centre, (2001). 'Chakmas and Hajongs denied their rightful place in Arunachal Pradesh' HRF/42/01, New Delhi, August 6.

South Asia Monitor, (2001). 'India's Turbulent Northeast' Centre for Strategic and International Studies (Washington DC), Number 35, July 5.

Sridharan, K., (1996). *The ASEAN Region in India's Foreign Policy* (Aldershot: Dartmouth Publishing Company).

_____, (2004). 'Wooing the Generals: India's New Burma Policy' *Contemporary Southeast Asia* XXVI/2.

Stein, Arthur A. and Steven E. Lobell, (1997). 'The End of the Cold War and the Regionalization of International Security', in David A. Lake and Patrick M. Morgan (eds), *Regional Orders: Building Security in a New World* (Pennsylvania: Pennsylvania State University Press).

Stern, Jessica, (2003). *Terror in the Name of God: Why Religious Militants Kill* (Ecco: Harper Collins).

Sundarraman, S., (2004). 'Politics and Security in South East Asia: Prospects for India-ASEAN Cooperation' *International Studies* XLI/4.

Taber, Robert, (1969). *The War of the Flea* (London: Paladin).

Tambiah, Stanley J., (1997). *Leveling Crowds: Ethnonationalist Conflicts and Collective Violence in South Asia* (New Delhi: Vistaar Publications).

Tarabot, Phanjoubam, (1996). *Insurgency Movement in North-Eastern India* (New Delhi: Vikas Publishing House).

_____, (2003). *Bleeding Manipur* (New Delhi: Har Anand Publications).

Taylor, Charles, (1994). 'The Politics of Recognition', in Amy Gutman (ed), *Multiculturalism: Examining the Politics of Recognition*, Princeton (NJ: Princeton University Press).

Taylor, Peter, (1993). *States of Terror: Democracy and Political Violence* (London: BBC Books).

Thomas, Joshua. C., (1997). 'Insurgency in Manipur', in B. Pakem (ed), *Insurgency in North East India* (New Delhi: Omsons Publications).

Thornton, T., (1992). 'India Adrift: The Search for Mooring in a New World Order' *Asian Survey* XXXII/12.

Thoronton, T.P., (1964). 'Terror as a Weapon of Political Agitation', in H. Eckstein (ed.), *Internal War* (London: Collier-Macmillan).

Tilly, Charles, (1978). *From Mobilization to Revolution* (New York: Random House).

_____, (1995). 'Contentious Repertoires in Great Britain, 1758-1834', in Mark Traugott (ed), *Repertoires and Cycles of Collective Action* (Durham, NC: Duke University Press).

_____, Louise Tilly and Richard Tilly, (1975). *The Rebellious Century 1830-1930* (Cambridge: Harvard University Press).

Tucker, Shelby, (2002). *Among Insurgents: Walking Through Burma* (New Delhi: Penguin Books).

Turk, Austin T., (1982). 'Social Dynamics of Terrorism' *Annals of the American Academy of Political and Social Science* CCCCXXXVI/1.

UNDCP, *World Drug Report* (2000). (Oxford: Oxford University Press).

Unicef (2006) Statistics available at http://www.unicef.org/infobycountry/bangladesh_ bangladesh_statistics.html.

Upadhyay, R., (2005). 'Manipur – In a Strange Whirlpool of Cross-current Insurgency' *South Asia Analysis Group* Paper No. 1210, January 3.

Van Ham, Peter and Aglaja Stirn, (2001). *The Seven Sisters of India: Tribal Worlds between Tibet and Burma* (Munich: Prestel Publishing and Ahmedabad: Mapin Publishing).

Vashum, R., (2000). *Naga's Right to Self Determination: Anthropological-historical Perspectives* (New Delhi: Mittal Publications).

Vayrynem, Raimo, Dieter Senghaas and Christian Schmidt, (1987). (eds) *The Quest for Peace: Transcending Collective Violence and War among Societies, Cultures, and States* (Beverly Hills, CA: Sage Publications).

Verghese, B. G., (1996). *India's Northeast Resurgent: Ethnicity, Insurgency, Governance, Development* (New Delhi: Konark Publishers).

_____, (2001). *Reorienting India: The New Geo-politics of Asia* (New Delhi: Konark Publishers).

_____, (2004). 'Borders Matter More Than Boundaries: From the North-east Looking Out' *Man and Society: A Journal of North East Studies* I/1 (Spring).

Vertzberger, Y., (1982). 'India's Border Conflict with China: A Perceptual Analysis' *Journal of Contemporary History* XVII/4.

Walker, Connor, (1994). *Ethnonationalism: The Quest for Understanding* (Princeton, NJ.: Princeton University Press).

Walter, Eugene V., (1969). *Terror and Resistance* (New York: Oxford University Press).

Waltz, Kenneth N., (1979). *Theory of International Politics* (MA: Addison-Wesley, Reading).

Walzer, Michael, Bowyer Bell, and Roger Morris, (1975). (ed) 'Terrorism: A Debate' *New Republic*, December.

Wardlaw, Grant, (1982). *Political Terrorism: Theory, Tactics and Countermeasures* (Cambridge: Cambridge University Press).

Weber, Max, (1979). *Economy and Society* (Berkeley: University of California Press).

Weinberg, Leonard B. and Paul B. Davis,(1989). *Introduction to Political Terrorism* (New York: McGraw Hill Publishing Company).

Weiner, Myron, (1985). 'On International Migration and International Relations', *Population and Development Review* XI/3.

_____, (1993). 'Rejected Peoples and Unwanted Migrants in South Asia' *Economic and Political Weekly* XXVIII/34.

_____, (1995). 'Security, Stability, and International Migration', in *The Global Migration Crisis Challenges to States and to Human Rights* (New York: Harper Collins).

Wheeler, Everett L., (1991). 'Terrorism and Military Theory: A Historical Perspective' *Terrorism and Political Violence* III/1 (Spring).

Where "Peacekeepers" Have Declared War, (1977). National Campaign Committee Against Militarization and Repeal of the Armed Forces (Special Powers Act) (New Delhi) April.

Wieviorka, Michel, (1993). *The Making of Terrorism* (Chicago: Chicago University Press).

_____, (1995). 'Terrorism in the Context of Academic Research', in Martha Crenshaw (ed), *Terrorism in Context* (Pennsylvania: The Pennsylvania State University Press).

Wilkinson, Paul, (1974). *Political Terrorism* (London: Macmillan).

_____, (1979). (ed) *Terrorism: Theory and Practice* (Boulder: Westview Press).

_____, (1986). *Terrorism and the Liberal State* (London: Macmillan).

_____, (1993). (ed) *Technology and Terrorism* (London: Frank Cass).

_____, (2001). *Terrorism versus Democracy: The Liberal State Response* (London: Frank Cass).

_____, and Alasdair Stewart, (1988). (eds) *Contemporary Research on Terrorism* (Aberdeen: AUP).

Wolf, John B., (1989). *Antiterrorist Initiatives* (New York: Plenum Press).

Wriggins, W. Howard and James F. Guyot, (1973). (eds) *Population, Politics and the Future of Southern Asia* (New York: Columbia University Press).

Yahya, F., (2003). 'India and Southeast Asia Revisited' *Contemporary Southeast Asia* XXV/1.

Yearbook of the United Nations 1970, (1971). (New York: UN, Office of Public Information).

Yong, Oran R., (1986). 'Political Discontinuities in the International System' *World Politics* XX/3.

Yunuo, Asoso, (1974). *The Rising Nagas: A Historical and Political Study* (Delhi: Vivek Publishing House).

INDEX